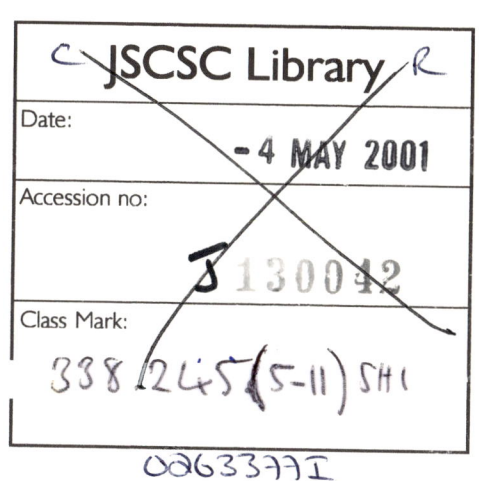

POWER AND PROSPERITY

IGCC Studies Published with Transaction

Power and Prosperity:
Economics and Security Linkages in Asia-Pacific,
edited by Susan L. Shirk and Christopher P. Twomey

Strategic Views from the Second Tier:
The Nuclear Weapons Policies of France, Britain, and China,
edited by John C. Hopkins and Weixing Hu

POWER AND PROSPERITY

Economics and Security Linkages in Asia-Pacific

SUSAN L. SHIRK
AND
CHRISTOPHER P. TWOMEY
EDITORS

TRANSACTION PUBLISHERS
New Brunswick (U.S.A.) and London (U.K.)

This book is printed on acid-free paper that meets the American National Standard for Permanence of Paper for Printed Library Materials.

Library of Congress Catalog Number: 95-44245

ISBN: 1-56000-252-2 (cloth)

Printed in the United States of America

9 8 7 6 5 4 3 2 1

Library of Congress Cataloging-in-Publication Data

Power and prosperity : economics and security linkages in Asia-Pacific / edited by Susan L. Shirk and Christopher P. Twomey.

    p.   cm.

    Includes bibliographical references and index.

    ISBN 1-56000-252-2 (alk. paper)

    1. Asia--Economic conditions. 2. Pacific Area--Economic conditions. 3. National security--Asia. 4. National security--Pacific Area. 5. Asia--Foreign economic relations. 6. Pacific Area--Foreign economic relations. I. Shirk. Susan L. II. Twomey, Christopher P.

HC412.P66 1996

330.95--dc20   95-44245

                                                                          CIP

Contents

Tables and Figures

Preface and Acknowledgments

The chapters in this volume grew from IGCC's project on Pacific security relations after the Cold War, which examined both economic and military security issues and brought together senior scholars, policy officials, and international journalists from the United States, Australia, Canada, China, Indonesia, Japan, Malaysia, North Korea, Russia, Singapore, South Korea, Taiwan, Thailand, and Vietnam. Generously funded by the Ford Foundation, the project included four international research conferences, the most recent in La Jolla, California in May 1993. The papers included in this volume were originally drafted for the third of these, held in Hong Kong in 1992.

We are especially proud of the international scope of the contributors, who hail from eight different Pacific Rim countries. Their varied backgrounds provide diverse perspectives on regional dynamics and domestic intricacies. IGCC and the editors are indebted to all the participants in this project for the high quality of the following chapters.

The editors would also like to thank Michael Stankiewicz for assisting with the final revision, Jenny Lind for initial manuscript preparation, William J. Richardson Associates for thoughtful indexing, Laurence Mintz and Transaction's production department for careful proofreading and invaluable technical assistance, and IGCC Managing Editor Jennifer R. Pournelle for securing publication and seeing this book to press.

Our special thanks go to Mary Curtis and Irving Horowitz of Transaction Publishers, who made publication possible.

Abbreviations

$ U.S. dollars, unless otherwise annotated

AEW	Airborne Early Warning
AFTA	ASEAN Free Trade Area
APCs	Armed Personnel Carriers
APEC	Asia-Pacific Economic Cooperation
ARAT	Association of Relations Across the Taiwan Strait
ARF	ASEAN Regional Forum
ASEAN	Association of Southeast Asian Nations

CBM	Confidence Building Measure
CC	Central Committee
CCP	Chinese Communist Party
CFC	Combined Forces Command
CMC	Central Military Commission
COCOM	Coordinating Committee embargo
CSBMs	Confidence and Security Building Measures
CSCA	Council on Security and Cooperation in Asia
CSCAP	Council for Security and Cooperation in the Asia Pacific
CSCE	Conference on Security and Cooperation in Europe
CSIS	Centre for Strategic and International Studies

DPP	Democratic Progressive Party
DPRK	Democratic People's Republic of Korea
DRAM	Dynamic Random Access Memory

EAEG/C	East Asia Economic Grouping/Caucus
EEC	European Economic Community
EEZ	Exclusive Economic Zone

FDI	Foreign Direct Investment
FBIS	Foreign Broadcast Information Service
FEER	Far Eastern Economic Review
FMS	Foreign Military Sales

G4	Group of Four (Japan, Australia, Singapore, and Hong Kong
G7	Group of Seven (Industrialized Nations)
GATT	General Agreement on Tariffs and Trade
GDP	Gross Domestic Product
GNP	Gross National Product
GSP	Generalized System of Preferences
IGCC	Institute on Global Conflict and Cooperation
IISS	International Institute for Strategic Studies
JMSDF	Japanese Maritime Self-Defense Force
KATUSA	Korean Augmentees to the United States Army
KFP	Korean Fighter Program
KMT	Kuomintang
MFN	Most-Favored Nation
MITI	Ministry of International Trade and Industry
MOU	Memorandum of Understanding
NAFTA	North American Free Trade Agreement
NET	Natural Economic Territory
NGOs	Non-governmental Organizations
NICs	Newly Industrialized Countries
NIEs	Newly Industrialized Economies
NPT	Nuclear Non-Proliferation Treaty
NWFZ	Nuclear Weapons Free Zone
ODA	Official Development Assistance
OECD	Organization for Economic Cooperation and Development
OPTAD	Organization for Pacific Trade and Development
OSCE	Organization for Security and Cooperation in Europe
PACTAD	Pacific Trade and Development
PAFTA	Pacific Asian Free Trade Agreement
PAFTAD	Pacific Free Trade and Development
PBEC	Pacific Basin Economic Council
PECC	Pacific Economic Cooperation Conference
PLA	People's Liberation Army
PMC	Post Ministerial Conference
PRC	People's Republic of China

PSA   Patent Secrecy Agreement

R&D   Research and Development
RMAF   Royal Malaysian Air Force
ROK   Republic of Korea
RTAF   Royal Thai Air Force

SAM   Surface-to-Air Missiles
SCM   Security Consultative Meeting
SEATO   Southeast Asian Treaty Organization
SEF   Strait Exchange Foundation
SEZs   Special Economic Zones
SLOCs   Sea Lines of Communication
SOM   Senior Officials Meeting

TAC   Treaty of Amity and Cooperation

UN   United Nations
UNCLOS   United Nations Conference on the Law of the Sea
USDP   Undersecretary of Defense for Policy

ZOPFAN   Zone of Peace, Freedom, and Neutrality

1 Understanding the Economic-Security Nexus

Christopher Twomey and Susan L. Shirk

INTRODUCTION

Economic growth and interdependence have important implications for regional security patterns, while the uncertainties on the security side have reciprocal effects on economic relations and growth. This book examines the nature of these mutual implications.

The linkages between economics and security in international relations are increasingly relevant in the post-Cold War era. While military issues still abound, perceptions about the relative significance of each of the two sets of issues have shifted. For some governments, this shift was dramatic and led to a nearly exclusive focus on economic issues. This policy shift to economics is particularly conspicuous in the United States, as expressed in the comments of both commentators and politicians:

> Post-Cold War national security is centered on economic security.
> —Rosabeth Moss Kanter, Harvard Business School.[1]

> As U.S. military dominance of the alliance passes into history, we must secure our interests with a post-Cold War policy of economic and political leadership.
> —Robert Hunter, Center for Strategic and International Studies.[2]

> Economic power is the new determinant of international stature.
> —Representative Lee H. Hamilton (D-Indiana).[3]

> ...[T]he world [is] mov[ing] from a half century of obsession with geopolitics to stress instead geo-economics...
> —Representative James A. Leach (R-Iowa).[4]

The signs of this shift are visible both in the perceptions and actions of many foreign policy elites. However, we must be careful not to overstate this shift. Security concerns have not evaporated in the aftermath of the fall of the Soviet Union. Some analysts view "the coming decades [as] a time of heightened, not diminished, threat of war."[5] Examples of continued strife are abundant: Yugoslavia, the Caucusus, the Persian Gulf, Somalia, and Rwanda. Future risks of conflict lie in the possible rise of the so-called middle powers or a decline of the United States that would lead to dangerous and unstable multipolarity.[6] Loss of superpower backing may encourage countries to pursue policies of nuclear self-reliance, which result in new threats of proliferation. Ethnic conflict and civil wars may produce a post-Cold War world much bloodier than its predecessor.

While economic issues are important in the post-Cold War era, ignoring security concerns is perilous. This book contends that policymakers must consider both security and economic implications during the decision-making process. However, those same policymakers must also understand those situations when it is necessary to de-couple economic and security issues during foreign policymaking.

Some of the questions raised by this volume include: How much influence do economic ties have on security preferences, and how much impact do security issues have on economic relations? Is increasing interdependence necessarily beneficial to all concerned? And finally, how is it possible to measure "power" when considering the linkage between economic power and security power?

THE ASIA-PACIFIC REGION

The Asia-Pacific region presents a microcosm of these global changes: economics is an increasingly important arena of international policy, but many security issues still linger unresolved.

The big news in the region is its economic performance. Asian countries have the fastest growing economies in the world. Table 1.1 lists a number of individual plus one group of Asian nations—the Association of Southeast Asian Nations (ASEAN)—and addresses the questions: How fast have they grown? How important to them are their international economic ties? And how important is Asia, in particular, to these ties? The answers are: fast, very important, and increasingly dominant. For each of the Asian countries above (except Japan), the level of gross domestic product has doubled in the last decade alone. Additionally, the role that trade plays in these economies is substantial and attests to the importance of the foreign sector for each of these economies.

However, most striking in the figures above is increasing intra-Asian trade flows. This regionalization is also occurring in the context of a substantial role for both foreign investment generally, and intra-Asian investment in particular. These ties of ownership are illustrated in the following chart which shows the stock of inward foreign direct investment (FDI) that has come from other Asian nations, as a percentage of the stock of all inward FDI.

Figure 1.1 shows the heavy impact of intra-Asian investment on foreign investment stock.[7] Today, investment flows are dominated by intra-Asian investment: for 1989 alone, the flow of investment from Japan and the newly

Table 1.1: General Economic Statistics

Country	Average annual growth rates in real GDP		Two-way trade as a percentage of GDP		Trade within Asia as a percentage of total trade	
	1970s	1980s	1980	1990	1980[a]	1991[b]
Japan	4.3%	4.1%	29%	21%	27%	31%
South Korea	9.0%	9.7%	75%	64%	34%	41%
Taiwan	9.4%	8.2%	107%	90%	33%	43%
China	5.5%	9.9%	15%[c]	32%[c]	55%[e]	65%[e]
ASEAN	5.2%	7.4%	66%[d]	117%[d]	52%	54%
United States	2.8%	2.9%	21%	21%	24%	30%

Source: United Nations, Handbook of International Trade and Development Statistics (New York: United Nations, 1992), Charts 3.4, 3.5, 6.2, and 6.4.

[a] China data from 1984-85.
[b] ASEAN data calculated using 1988-89 for Brunei.
[c] Note that these are based on official Chinese GDP figures, and so may be substantially overstated.
[d] Estimated figures, excluding Brunei.
[e] These figures are overstated because they include exports to Hong Kong that are ultimately destined for outside the region (mostly Europe and North America).

Figure 1.1: Stock of Inward FDI from Asia as a Proportion of all FDI Stock (1988)

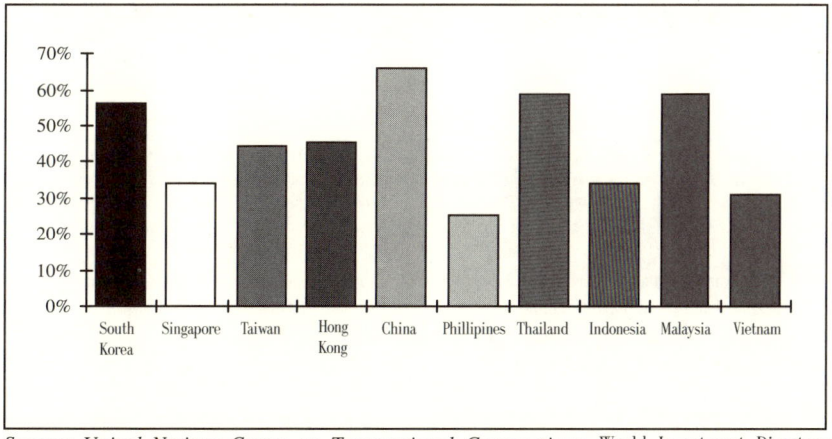

Source: United Nations Center on Transnational Corporations, World Investment Directory 1992, Volume 1 (Asia and the Pacific) (New York: United Nations 1992), Table 9 in each of the county sections. Figures for China and Malaysia are for 1987; figures for Singapore, Hong Kong, Philippines, and Vietnam are for 1989.

industrialized economies (NIEs) (Taiwan, Hong Kong, Singapore, and South Korea) accounted for 75 percent of all FDI in China, 72 percent in Malaysia, 51 percent in the Philippines, and 70 percent in Thailand.[8] In both major strands of foreign economic ties (trade and foreign investment), intra-Asian links are becoming paramount. This economic integration is important to consider when analyzing security-economics interaction in the region.

Another significant characteristic of the Asian economic situation is that the United States remains a major market for the exports of all Asian countries. This reality is reflected in the reluctance of almost all these countries to hive off from the United States in an Asian trade bloc. Dependence on the U.S. market is shown in Figure 1.2. From the U.S. perspective as well, Asia has grown in economic importance, with trans-Pacific flows now accounting for a larger percentage of U.S. trade than those across the Atlantic.[9]

Figure 1.2: Exports to the United States as a Proportion of all Exports (1993)

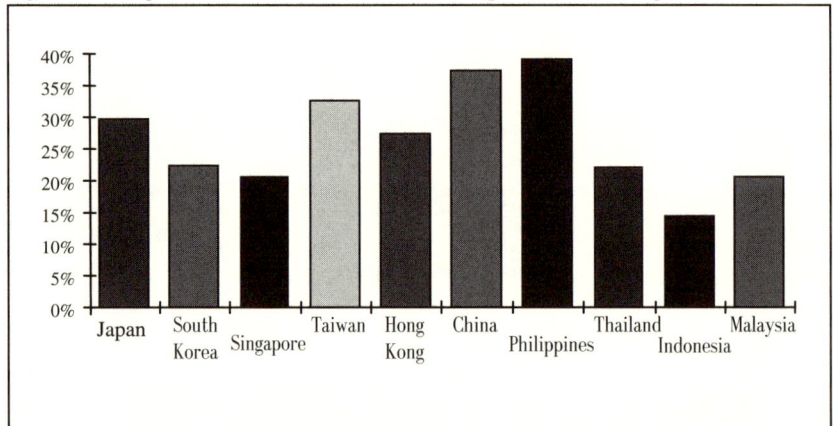

Sources: *International Monetary Fund*, Direction of Trade Statistics Yearbook *(Washington, DC, 1993); Hong Kong, Yun-wing Sung,* Hong Kong and the Economic Integration of the China Circle *(Hong Kong, 1994), Table 4; and Taiwan, Directorate-General of Budget, Accounting and Statistics, Executive Yuan,* Statistical Yearbook of the Republic of China *(Republic of China, 1993), Table 141.*

Note: Hong Kong figures used are Hong Kong domestic exports (according to Sung), which corrects for re-exports from/to China in calculating trade statistics. Also, China export figures were calculated using U.S. import figures from China—although this corrects for the Hong Kong re-export distortion, these figures still will be exaggerated because of the difference in calculating value of exports and imports.

On the security side, the Asia-Pacific is presently peaceful but fraught with future dangers. Many of these dangers arise from systemic factors: the presence of four great powers in the region—Russia, China, Japan, and the United States—and uncertainty about their future relations. For some analysts, this confluence of the majority of the world's leading powers hearkens back to the dilemma of multipolarity in Europe during the early nineteenth century.[10] The breakdown of bipolarity creates uncertainties, and major determinants of the stability of multipolarity in the region will be the amounts and the long-term credibility of the U.S. military commitment. A United States forces withdrawal could destabilize the region and produce competition between China and Japan, the two ascendant powers. Another alarming scenario is a North Korean nuclear threat triggering domino-like proliferation in Japan and South Korea. These systemic factors contribute to instability and uncertainty in the region.

More narrow, country-level analysis suggests alternate sources of danger for the future security of the region: many Asian governments have taken advantage of economic growth to invest in their military defenses. Although as Kusuma Snitswongse's chapter points out, there is no evidence of an actual arms race, national military buildups are underway throughout the region.

Table 1.2: Real Growth in Military Spending, 1985-92

Japan	China	Taiwan	South Korea	North Korea	ASEAN	Vietnam	East Asia Average	U.S.
29%	13%[*]	30%	63%	22%	20%	-27%	22%	-6%

Source: calculated from The Military Balance: 1993-94 (London: The International Institute for Strategic Studies/IISS, 1994), pp. 224–226. Original data used 1985 prices/rates in U.S. dollars. East Asia Average is an average of those East Asian nations listed in the chart only.

[*] Official Chinese statistics are universally assumed to underestimate the actual levels of spending. This figure also does not reflect significant increases between 1992 and 1994.

Table 1.2 shows that with the exception of Vietnam, nearly every country in Asia substantially increased its military spending after 1985. While these spending increases affect each country's capabilities differently, the scale of the growth is dramatic and worrisome.

Furthermore, both the volume of weaponry and its uneven distribution throughout the region contribute to instability and insecurity. Because of the region's geography, many consider air and naval military assets to be the most threatening type of military hardware. Broad figures for these categories, as well as ground troop strength are presented in Table 1.3.[11] The figures for the great powers of the region—China, Russia, the United States, and Japan—clearly stand out.

Although Asian defense officials insist that their new acquisitions are solely for defensive purposes, these acquisitions come in a number of areas—including advanced fighter aircraft and anti-ship missiles—that enhance projection force capabilities.[12] The presence of all this new weaponry in the region creates security dilemmas among neighboring states—the defensive policies of one state may be viewed as threats by another.

Within the context of these security dilemmas, there are a number of territorial disputes that could ignite armed conflict in the region. The potentially oil-rich Spratly Islands in the South China Sea are claimed by some seven different

Table 1.3: Size of Military Forces in the Asian Region

	Ground Forces[a] (1000s of troops)	Combat Aircraft	Major Combat Vessels[b]	Other Combat Vessels
Japan	150	600	79	52
China	2,330	5850	103	1047
Taiwan	342	516	37	139
South Korea	545	512	42	145
North Korea	1,000	730	28	641
ASEAN (6)	650	618	33	268
Vietnam	730	240	7	73
Eastern Russia [c]	NA	1640	115	140
U.S.	78	588	109	NA

Source: The Military Balance, 1993-94, *op. cit.*

[a] Ground forces include both army and naval infantry/marines.

[b] Major Combat Vessels include submarines, aircraft carriers, cruisers, destroyers, and frigates.

[c] Including forces in Siberia, Transbaykal, and Far East Military Districts, as well as the Pacific fleet.

nations.[13] The Diaoydao (Senkaku) Islands in the East China Sea are contested by China and Japan. Russia and Japan, which have never normalized relations after World War II, have also never reconciled their claims over the North Territories islands.

Thus, the Asia-Pacific is experiencing change in both economic and security dimensions. Given the now more-equal footing between economics and security, subtle interactions between them have become more apparent than during the Cold War. The following chapters highlight specific examples of the economics-security interaction throughout the region or in a particular subregional or national context. Before turning to those examples, we will examine various ways that the interaction between economics and security can affect regional relations.

HOW TO THINK ABOUT THE ECONOMICS-SECURITY NEXUS

While understanding that "real world" examples combine elements from more than one archetypal formulation, we separately consider three categories of economic-security interaction in order to better understand their impact: the *national strength* of a country, which depends upon both its economy and its military; *national preferences*; (for example, choice of military allies or trade partners), formed from both economic and security interests; and economic or military actions that can be used as *policy tools* to affect one another. Within these three categories, (strengths, preferences, and tools) influence can run either from economics to security or vice-versa. Table 1.4 delineates the possible six combinations across these three categories and two directions.

Table 1.4: Forms of Interaction

	National Strengths	National Preferences	Policy Tools
Economics affects Security	A strong economy creates the foundation necessary for the equipping and sustaining of a strong military.	The structure of a nation's economic ties creates a set of politico-military interests (choice of enemies and allies, relative cost of war).	International economic policy can serve as a tool for politico-military policies and goals (e. g. sanctions, embargoes, aid)
Security affects Economics	Military spending may limit economic growth (opportunity costs) or military mobilization may lead to economic progress.	Security goals and commitments structure or limit a nation's preferred foreign economic partners.	Security alliances, military threats, and direct military action can all be used to secure economic benefits.

National Strengths

A relatively large economic surplus allows for diversion of resources toward achieving security goals. Economic surplus can be spent directly on increasing the prowess of a nation's military, either quantitatively or qualitatively. In specific terms, factors such as high growth rates (of GDP, personal income, etc.), increases in technology level, and expansion of the industrial base are relevant to the potential military power of a nation. A nation's technology level enhances and is enhanced by its military might: see the recent attention paid to the "spin-on" concept of military applications of civilian technologies.[14]

The importance of national wealth for a nation's security and its place in the international structure is a core tenet of the realist school of international relations. To quote Kenneth Waltz, "great power status cannot be maintained without a certain economic capacity" or "without a considerable economic capability no state can hope to sustain a world role."[15]

Several authors in this volume consider this line of reasoning. Snitwongse discusses it most directly and thoroughly by asking the question: Does "ability to pay" account for growth in military spending in the region? Although she finds that there is much more variation than can be explained through this simple available bucks-and-bullets relationship, economic resources remain a necessary but not sufficient cause for military buildup.

Japan is an extreme case of the importance of economics to a nation's security. By virtue of its wealth and technological capabilities, developed under the U.S. security umbrella, Japan has achieved world power status and a virtual nuclear deterrence without engaging in overseas military activities or building bombs.[16] Eiichi Katahara's chapter analyzes the Japanese policy of comprehensive security. Here, the role of economic strength in paving the way for security is fundamental to Katahara's conclusion that "Japan's concept of comprehensive security..remains viable and effective in the post-Cold War world."

China's neighbors assume that economic wealth translates into military power when they look at the PRC's double-digit economic growth rates and see a China threat. Tai Ming Cheung's chapter argues that, in the early 1990s, although economic growth allowed a 50 percent nominal increase in the People's Liberation Army budget, much of the new spending was for long-deferred technological upgrading. Cheung stresses that since the Chinese military modernization program started from a deficient foundation, while it may create perceptions of a China growing in power, it does not alter the current military balance in the region.

Russia illustrates that too much security, or at least an exaggerated concern with security, can warp a domestic economy and thereby threaten the viability of the state. One of the main factors that destroyed the U.S.S.R and left Russia in its present weakened position was the economic problems caused by the Soviet Union's excessively large investment in military hardware. The chapters by James Clay Moltz and Tsuneo Akaha both highlight the profound negative impacts of Russia's economic decline upon its military capabilities and international influence.

National Preferences

The central premise here is that foreign policy preferences within a nation depend to a certain extent on its economic structure (including both domestic policies and international trade and investment relationships). There are several ways in which this relationship might play out. High levels of foreign trade and investment might increase the costs of war to a country and thus motivate it to maintain peaceful foreign relations. Or the structure of a nation's trading relationships could lead to a set of preferences regarding its allies and enemies. These arguments are commonly identified with the liberal version of the international relations literature on interdependence. According to Keohane and Nye, "Transnational relations..affect interstate politics by altering the choices open to statesmen and the costs that must be born for adopting various courses of action."[17]

Thus, economic interdependence can create a set of domestic interests that are translated into policy through the domestic political process. These ties may, for instance, limit the "freedom of action" for political leaders on issues of national security; or the absence of such economic interdependence may decrease the likelihood of a given alliance.[18] In either case a nation's preferences about alliance partners are affected by its economic structure. Finally, such increased economic interaction might also affect the security preferences of nations through the creation of a sense of "regionhood" that eases feelings of insecurity.[19]

This interaction works the other way as well. For a nation with "exogenous" security preferences regarding a particular neighbor, we expect its economic policies and relationships to be structured accordingly. The economic impact of security concerns is evident in domestic economic development strategies (as with China's dispersal of its industrial complex to its interior in the 1960s and 1970s to protect against the Soviet threat) and can be seen in the structure of international economic relations. Examples of the latter are Cold War attempts by the West to limit trade with the East through the use of COCOM (the Coordinating Committee embargo)[20] and the formation of the European Union during the Cold War by the governments of Western Europe.

K.S. Nathan provides us with an example of security concerns shaping economic patterns in his chapter looking at the international institutions in Southeast Asia. He finds that many of the institutionalized economic relationships in the region can trace their origins to strong politico-military relationships. The example of ASEAN is convincingly argued.

Nathan notwithstanding, most of the authors in the volume focus upon the economic influences on security preferences. Akaha's chapter on Russo-Japanese relations points to the benefits to Asian security of integrating the Russian Far East into the broader regional economy. Wang Jisi argues that economic trends within the PRC—the economic opening to the outside world and decentralization of the domestic economy—produced a broad shift in Chinese foreign economic ties toward the Asian region and a foreign policy that emphasizes stable and secure relations with Asian neighbors. Tai Ming Cheung's chapter makes the same observation about China's newfound foreign economic interests generating changes in security policies. He also notes evidence that the Beijing leadership for the first time recognizes the overlapping effects of its economic and political foreign policies. Nathan notes many Asian nations are strengthening economic ties with the United States to guarantee continuing U.S. military presence in the region. Finally, dramatic increases in economic flows among China, Taiwan, and Hong Kong offer the promise of political rapprochement or even the peaceful political integration of the three, as the chapters by He Di and by Jia Qingguo and Susan Shirk suggest.

However, skepticism about some of the optimistic predictions of the interdependence literature has begun. In this volume, authors such as Shirk and Jia (looking at China and Taiwan) and Zysman and Borrus (looking at Asia more generally) begin to revise this thinking. Their chapters point to an uncertain impact of economic interdependence, noting in some cases an increased likelihood of conflict because of the creation of new "lines of fracture" and the problem of asymmetric interdependence. In the first case, there is a danger that various nations' developmental strategies will come into competition or even conflict in the region. The crux of this problem, note Zysman and Borrus, is based on the question of relative gains versus absolute gains. If economic issues are perceived in a "relative gains" framework, then there will likely be severe conflict over dividing up the available gains; in this case increased economic interdependence simply creates more areas in which relative gains can be contested.

In the second case, Shirk and Jia note that there is an inherent instability in a relationship characterized by asymmetric interdependence even though powerful incentives to cooperate may exist. They find several examples of this in the Taiwanese-PRC relationship that may have profoundly negative implications for the future of both sides of the Taiwan Strait.

Finally, one might view the economics-security linkage in cognitive terms, as is done by Desmond Ball's chapter. The chapter asks the question "can habits developed in one arena (i.e., the economic association of APEC) shape preferences in another (a hypothetical, multilateral security grouping)?" Ball concludes that habits and knowledge collected can spill across issue-areas.

Policy Tools

A final view of the economics-security connection acknowledges that both can be used as tools by one nation in order to change the behavior of another nation.[21] This is essentially a "fungibility of power" argument, which asserts that threats on the economic front can achieve security aims, and vice versa.[22] Real world examples are substantial, including on the economic side sanctions, embargoes, the placing of conditions on U.S. most favored nation trading status, and nationalizations; and on the military side forced port openings and bombing of industrial targets. All of these policies create a credible link between action in one arena and a goal in the other.[23]

Chung In Moon's chapter most powerfully captures this linkage. His examination of the United States-South Korea relationship provides numerous examples of U.S. techno-nationalism—an American attempt to maintain tight control of shared military technologies in order to preserve U.S. economic competitiveness. The U.S. uses its military strength and Korea's security dependence to limit threats to its own economic base. The example of burden sharing, as cited in his chapter, can also be viewed as a form of military and economic policy linkage.

According to the Zysman and Borrus analysis, Japan exhibits similar techno-nationalism in its relations with other Asian countries. Japan's dominance of the countries where it invests capital and produces goods derives from its monopolistic control over key technologies, not from any security guarantees.

In his chapter on Russo-Japanese relations, Tsuneo Akaha presents a different perspective. He argues that there is an important imbalance along the following lines: Japanese power is economic and Russian power is military. Akaha refutes the notion of a "fungibility" across these two disparate international policy arenas and claims that this disjunction will cause significant problems for the region. Making a similar argument, Moltz notes that Russia's poor international economic position limits its policy options in the international arena to military power.

COMMON LESSONS

It is in and of itself a hopeful pointer that, while the chapters that follow neither come from a single perspective nor arrive at a single set of conclusions, deriving as they do from common questions they teach surprisingly common lessons.

Beginning with more academic concerns, there are several areas that would benefit from further research. First, most apparent from our study of the Asia-Pacific is the influence of economic ties on national security preferences and the persistent effects of security ties on economic relations. While political science literature historically focused on the contribution of economic resources to "national strength,"[24] our authors found the mutual effects on "national preferences" to be extremely important in this economically interdependent region. Furthermore, several of our authors (Shirk and Jia, and Zysman and Borrus, in particular) question the frequent presumption of a benevolent impact of economic interdependence. The creation of new sources of friction and the role of asymmetric interdependence may worsen tensions in the Asian region (or indeed in any region). Additional work is necessary at both the theoretical and applied levels addressing the impact of these hypotheses and integrating them into a policy framework.

Second, the question of how to measure power is clearly more problematic than is traditionally conceived. Nearly every element of international relations theory makes use of the concept of power, and yet the definition of power has never been clear, either in the neorealist world or in any subsequent revisionism.[25] Its meaning—in particular the variables that it includes—has profound implications for applying these theories in the Asia-Pacific or other regions. For instance, when we hope for a balance of power to emerge in Asia, what sort of power are we talking about? As noted, Asian nations' power bases are very diverse. How would we know when China, with its huge population and army, is in balance with the smaller, but wealthier Japan? Theories about international institutions and the role of hegemony similarly are dependent on their conception of power. There is more involvement of economics in the concept of power than simply the creation of "national strength." The ability to manipulate other countries through trading relations is a separate conception of power from the power of a large economy with the capacity to produce a tremendous amount of tanks and other military hardware. Our authors provide several examples of these alternatives. However, developing a rigorous definition of national power that makes explicit such links has yet to be done and is essential for a more useful understanding of international relations.

The policy implication of this basic conclusion is obvious: security policy cannot be considered in isolation from economics, and vice versa. While in an extreme sense this linkage already occurs in the minds of policymakers, our chapters highlight a degree of connectedness that is not commonly recognized in policymaking arenas. It will be necessary to go beyond merely recognizing this linkage; policymakers must learn to manage, or even exploit, it. In the anarchic and conflict prone world described by realists, a nation must take advantage of every form of "power" at its disposal to survive. Economic-security interaction provides many nations with a new source, or at least a newly recognized source, of such power. Particularly for the Asia-Pacific region in the post-Cold War era, foreign policymakers must consider a wider range of possible inputs and outputs.

The test for the future will be: Can policymakers in the Asia-Pacific meet the challenge of building on the positive dimensions of regional economic ties, thus increasing trust and limiting the development of security dilemmas? Given the extraordinarily high levels of economic growth in Asia, all countries benefit substantially from a stable security situation. The costs of the alternative also are substantial: a backlash against mercantilist policies by Asian nations could lead to hostile trade wars. Since an open economic system and a peaceful neighborhood in Asia can be viewed as public goods, multilateral means for preserving both economic and security stability are appropriate. Whatever the method, however, careful policy-making that considers and makes use of the complexities of the security-economic interaction are imperative for the future of Asia.

NOTES

1. Rosabeth Moss Kanter, "Foreign Policy Comes Out of Its Box," *Los Angeles Times*, Thursday, 3 September 1992, p. B7.
2. Robert Hunter, "A Farewell to Arms, Not Influence," *Los Angeles Times*, Friday, 2 February 1990, p. B7.
3. Lee H. Hamilton, "A Democrat Looks at Foreign Policy," *Foreign Affairs*, 71:3 (Summer 1992), p. 34.
4. James A. Leach, "A Republican Looks at Foreign Policy," *Foreign Affairs*, 71:3 (Summer

1992), p. 25.

5. Charles Krauthammer, "The Unipolar Moment," *Foreign Affairs* 70:1, p. 23.

6. For a discussion of how this might play out in Europe, see John Mearsheimer, "Back to the Future: Instability in Europe After the Cold War," *International Security* 15:1 (Summer 1990).

7. Note, however, that these figures are ratios of total FDI, and are not scaled by either gross domestic capital formation nor by GDP. Since countries vary in their dependence on both FDI (versus domestic savings) and on capital intensive sectors, these figures do not directly show the importance of Asian FDI to the economic well-being of these nations. What the figures do show is the increasing regionalization of the capital market in Asia.

8. Data computed from the internal database of the Institute of Developing Economies (in Tokyo), cited in Mitsuhiro Kagami, "Lessons from Trade and Investment in East Asia," Inter-American Development Bank and United Nations Economic Commission for Latin America and the Caribbean Working Papers on Trade in the Western Hemisphere, no. 53 (August 1993), Table 5.

9. James A. Baker, III, "America in Asia," *Foreign Affairs 70:5* (Winter 1991-92), p. 5.

10. For several interesting discussions of the possibilities for great power conflict or accommodation see Aaron L. Friedberg, "Ripe for Rivalry: Prospects for Peace in a Multipolar Asia" and Richard K. Betts, "Wealth, Power, and Instability: East Asia and the United States after the Cold War" both in *International Security* 18:3 (Winter 1993/94), and Susan L. Shirk, "Asia-Pacific Security: Balance of Power or Concert of Powers?" in David A. Lake and Patrick Morgan, eds., *Regional Orders: Building Security in a New World*, forthcoming c1996. Friedberg makes the comparison to Europe explicitly and is decidedly pessimistic about the future in Asia.

11. Of course, simple spending figures and broad quantities of military assets carry little explanatory power, as Professor Snitwongse notes in her chapter. We present these figures here to simply provide a sense of scale to the rapidity of the changes taking place in the region.

12. Desmond Ball notes that the recent acquisitions have come primarily in the following areas: command, control, and communications; technical intelligence; multirole fighter aircraft; maritime reconnaissance; modern surface combatants; antiship missiles; submarines; electronic warfare capabilities; and rapid deployment forces. Many of these areas have clear offensive implications. See Ball's, "Arms and Affluence: Military Acquisitions in the Asia-Pacific Region," *International Security* 18:3 (Winter 1993/94), pp. 95-103.

13. See, for instance, John W. Garver, "China's Push Through the South China Sea: The Interaction of Bureaucratic and National Interest," *The China Quarterly*, no. 132 (December 1992), pp. 999-1028.

14. See for instance, Ashton Carter, et al., *Beyond Spinoff: Military and Commercial Technologies in a Changing World* (Boston, MA: Harvard Business School Press, 1992). Chapters 8 and 12 are particularly relevant.

15. Kenneth Waltz, "The Emerging Structure of International Politics," *International Security* 18:2 (Fall 1993), pp. 50 and 63. This line of reasoning is also implicit in chapter 8

"Structural Causes and Military Effects" of Waltz's *Theory of International Politics* (New York: McGraw-Hill, 1979).

16. It has been suggested that due to its high technological level, Japan possesses a "virtual nuclear deterrent" since some believe that it could rapidly develop and deploy nuclear weapons. This is a deterrent value that exists independent of the American umbrella.

17. While Keohane and Nye define "transnational relations" fairly broadly in the abstract, most of their empirical focus remains on economics. See Robert O. Keohane and Joseph S. Nye, Jr., *Transnational Relations and World Politics* (Cambridge, MA: Harvard University Press, 1972), pp. 374-75. Other classic works in the interdependence vein were authored by Ernst Haas and Karl Deutsch.

18. For a study that discusses these possibilities and considers their implications for credibility in alliances and the strength of balancing, see Paul A. Papayoanou, "Economic Interdependence and the Balance of Power: The Strategy of Commitment and Great Power Politics," unpublished dissertation, University of California, Los Angeles, 1992.

19. This sense of regionhood is clearly apparent in the creation of the ASEAN Regional Forum; however, it should be noted that this sense has not removed all threats to peace or stability in the Asia-Pacific.

20. For a discussion of the West's varying goals in COCOM, as well as an argument regarding the feasibility of such sanctions for these goals, see Michael Mastanduno, "Strategies of Economic Containment: U.S. Trade Relations with the Soviet Union," *World Politics* 37:4 (July 1985), pp. 503-531.

21. The classic work here is Albert Hirshmann's *National Power and the Structure of Foreign Trade* (Berkeley, CA: University of California Press, 1945). Hirshmann writes of the supply and influence effects of trade. The latter is quite similar to our conception of use as a policy tool.

22. Keohane notes that fungible power resources are those that "can be used to achieve results on any of a variety of issues without significant loss of efficacy." He also notes that this fungibility frequently seems to be an assumption in Structural Realism, at least in its strong form. For both, see comments by Robert Keohane in "Theory of World Politics: Structural Realism and Beyond," in Keohane, ed., *Neorealism and its Critics* (New York: Columbia University Press, 1986).

23. It should be noted that this third source of interaction *is* analytically distinct from the other two. The interaction depends on the artificial linking of two issue-areas that each have inherent, independent value to a nation: because economics is independently valuable to nations, nation A can secure concessions on the security front by threatening to punish nation B by hurting its economic welfare, or vice versa.

24. This remains the constant strain in the dominant realist paradigm ranging from Thucydides through Carr to Waltz. See for example Thucydides, *History of the Peloponnesian War* (New York: Penguin Books, 1972), Book I, para. 83; Carr, E. H., *The Twenty Years' Crisis, 1919–39* (New York: Harper Torchbooks, 1964), chapter 8; and Waltz, Kenneth, *Man, the State, and War* (New York: Columbia University Press, 1959), chapter 7.

25. Waltz has relied on the following "kitchen sink" list of criterion for years: "size of population and territory, resource endowment, economic capability, military strength,

political stability and competence." See his "The Emerging Structure of International Politics," 1993, *op. cit.*, p. 50 or *Theory of International Politics*, 1979, *op. cit.*, p. 131.

Part I

The Security-Economic Linkage:
Regional Settings

2 Economic Development and Military Modernization in Southeast Asia

Kusuma Snitwongse

ECONOMIC DEVELOPMENT AND MILITARY MODERNIZATION: THE "ABILITY" ASPECT[1]

Previous studies of the linkages between military spending and economic growth of the Association of Southeast Asian Nations (ASEAN) countries show positive correlations.[2] Geoffrey Harris' study covering the period from the early 1960s to the early 1980s, concludes that domestic economic conditions, especially government current revenue, appear to exert at least a moderate influence on annual changes in defense expenditure in ASEAN."[3] David B.H. Denoon's study, which covers the period from 1973 to 1983, concludes that the "availability of resources" largely explains the increases in military spending.[4] Andrew L. Ross' study, which covers the period from 1980 to 1987, demonstrates that regional economic growth and increased military spending are not mutually exclusive.[5]

Evidence to support conclusions about states' ability to pay for defense spending abound. In Malaysia, in the context of high economic growth, the allocation for defense increased substantially between 1966-85 under the second through fourth Malaysia Plans. In the fifth Malaysia Plan, which was formulated in the context of an expectation of lower growth, the allocation for defense was drastically reduced despite the fact that there was no radical change in the country's strategic environment.[6]

A linkage between oil revenue and military spending was established by Ross in the case of Indonesia. Indonesia's sharp rise in military expenditure in 1979-81 coincided with the oil export boom which substantially increased its GNP growth rate. When earnings from oil began to fall in 1982, military spending also declined. Ross sees oil revenues, external indebtedness, and military spending in Indonesia as closely related. For all ASEAN countries, he believes that countries with relatively high levels of external indebtedness will adjust by cutting military spending.[7]

For ASEAN, Denoon finds it clear that military spending was highly and positively correlated with GNP growth. Singapore and Malaysia, the two countries with the highest GNP growth, were the second and third highest in defense increases whereas Indonesia and the Philippines with the slowest GNP growth were the slowest in raising defense spending.[8]

Ross' findings in his study of the ASEAN countries (except Brunei) between 1980-87 support the views of Harris and Denoon. He finds coexistence of GNP and military expenditure growth to be clearly in evidence. He also finds a tendency for GNP growth rates to be greater than military expenditure growth rates. All six ASEAN countries also appropriated smaller shares of central government expenditures to the armed forces during 1982-87 than during the earlier period 1977-82. Military spending growth rates have also tended to be lower than central government expenditure growth rates.

While Denoon believes that "availability of resources" determines the rise in defense spending, Harris makes a useful distinction between the ability and the willingness to spend. Ability is the equivalent of Denoon's "resources available," that is, the country's GNP that the government controls. Denoon also suggests that a significant indicator of "availability of resources" is to be found not in military expenditure per capita but rather in the country's high level of income that made the expenditure possible. The country's balance of payment position also appears critical to Denoon for explaining increases in arms imports. The surge in Malaysia's import during the periods of high oil prices was one case in point.

Recent developments broadly support these contentions. ASEAN countries enjoyed economic growth that expanded especially after 1986 (see Figure 2.1). Brunei is not included because of lack of current data). These economic statistics are indicators of "availability of resources," which translate into ability to spend.

When ability is compared with defense expenditure, their positive relations can be seen in Figure 2.2. As the economies started to perform better, their defense expenditures climbed in absolute terms. This effect is particularly notable after 1989, when several countries enjoyed spectacular growth rates.

If defense expenditure is looked at as a percentage of GDP, a number of countries show declines in spending. However, as there is absolute growth in GDP, Indonesia and Thailand in particular still register growth in defense expenditure in absolute terms. The lower percentages (Figure 2.3) merely mean that because of the higher GDP growth rate, there are decreases in military burden in those countries.

The recent defense buildup in ASEAN countries was dominated by increasing arms acquisitions. However, since data on defense expenditure often do not disaggregate buildup (namely acquisition of new equipment) from the cost of personnel, operation, and maintenance, correlation of economic development with arms acquisition specifically becomes difficult.

Figure 2.1: Index of GDP
(Base year 1983 = 1, measured in local currency)

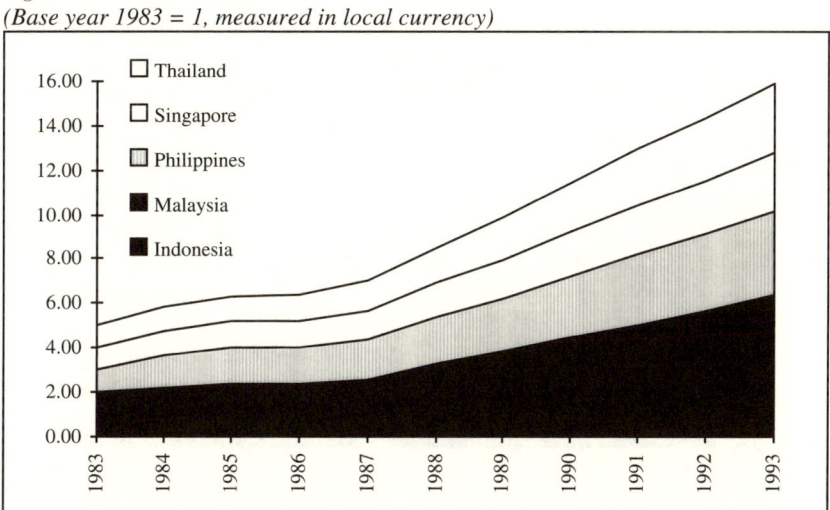

Source: Military Balance *(London: International Institute for Strategic Studies, 1985–95).*

Figure 2.2: Index of Real Defense Spending
(Base year 1983 = 100, measured in constant U.S.$)

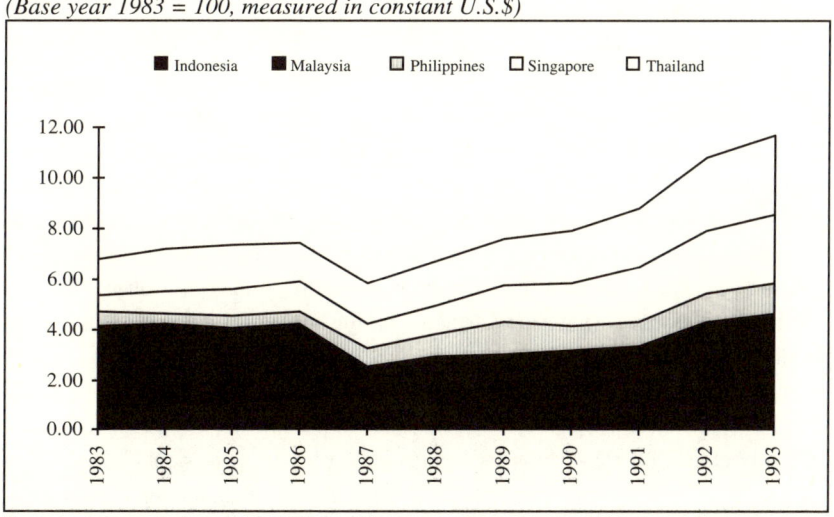

Source: Defense Budget Brief 1993-94 *(Canberra: Department of Defense Resources and Financial Division, August 1993);* Asia-Pacific Defense Reporter, *December 1994 and January 1995;* Military Balance, *op. cit.*

ASEAN military spending in recent years confirms the previous contentions of Denoon, Harris, and Ross. The ability to spend frequently results in more military spending and more acquisition of military equipment.

Figure 2.3: Defense Expenditure as a Percentage of GDP

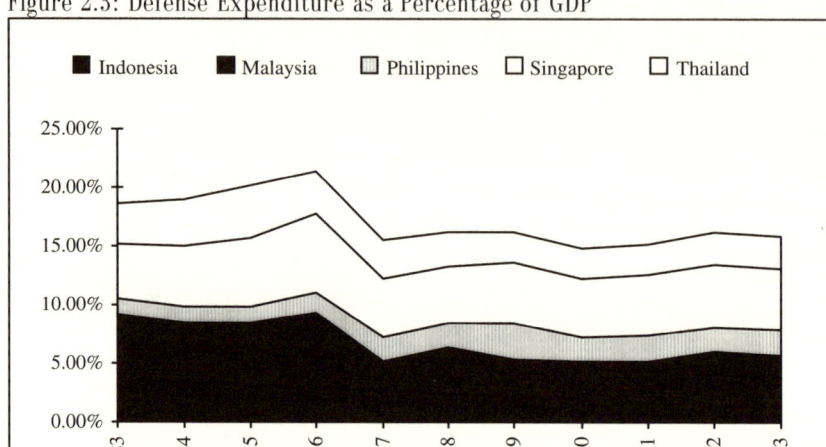

Source: Defense Budget Brief 1993-94, *op. cit.;* Military Balance, *op. cit.*

Another recent development that enhanced the ability of countries to acquire arms is the arms market. The end of the Cold War further reinforced the buyers' advantage in the market, and commercialization of the market increased because of the removal of ideological constraints.[9] The end of the Cold War caused a decline in defense spending in the major arms exporting countries, the United States and Russia. As demand at home declines, there is a need to increase exports for the continued viability of the industry. Competition also became more intense partly because of the greater number of arms suppliers. In need of hard currency, many former communist countries are offering bargain prices. Buyers are thus in a position to make demands that suppliers are more willing to oblige than was previously the case. One such demand is for state-of-the-art weapons which suppliers like the United States previously had been reluctant to sell. Because of intense competition, buyers also were able to demand compensatory trade arrangements (or offset agreements) such as co-production, licensed production, subcontractor production, counter-trade, and even the provision of investment capital, as attractive long-term financing arrangements that border on subsidies. Some suppliers also resort to corrupt business practices to win contracts from powerful persons.

ABILITY AND RECENT ARMS ACQUISITIONS

Defense expenditures by all ASEAN states, with the exception of the Philippines, have increased steadily since 1973. Even more significant is the increase in the quality of arms acquired. Since the mid-1980s, Southeast Asian governments consistently purchased near state-of-the-art major weaponry, in contrast to downgraded or lightweight types bought in the past.[10] This reflects (in addition to the new availability of advanced weaponry on the international market) the shift within ASEAN nations from counterinsurgency to conventional warfare doctrine (with special emphasis on air and small, fast, missile-equipped naval forces), and their growing capability to pay higher prices.

The sequential orders of F-16s by Singapore in 1984, Thailand in 1985, and Indonesia in 1986 demonstrate dramatically the trend towards air forces modernization. Singapore leads with the acquisition of airborne early warning (AEW) E-2 C Hawkeyes, and possibly eleven upgraded F-16s on top of its original eight.[11] With more than 218 aircraft deployed as of early 1994, Singapore's air force is the biggest among ASEAN countries. Besides the 12 F-16As acquired in the 1980s, Indonesia has purchased at least 68 aircraft,[12] and may eventually seek to acquire a force of 48 F-16s.[13] Thailand's force structure includes 14 F-16As and four F-16Bs.[14]

In 1988, Malaysia signed a memorandum of understanding (MOU) with the British government to purchase weapons systems. However, the Royal Malaysian Air Force (RMAF) recognized the need to acquire high performance combat aircraft to supplement its existing F-5s and achieve equivalency with F-16s operating in neighboring countries. Malaysia finally settled on the Russian MIG-29, among the most advanced front-line combat aircraft in the world, and may eventually acquire up to 40 of these.[15] Malaysia also signed an MOU with India to provide training, maintenance and engine overhaul facilities, as well as a joint venture in production of spare parts.

The same modernizing trend is evident in ASEAN navies, improving their range of operation and strike capability. Most striking was Thailand's decision in 1992 to acquire a helicopter carrier, now under construction in Spain, featuring a "ski-jump" to allow the operation of short-take-off-and-landing jets. Thailand also purchased four frigates from China and three P-3B Orian aircraft from the United States. Future force structure requirements call for a replenishment tanker, which will allow the Royal Thai Navy to form a task group around the carrier. The long-term intention is to develop the capability to deploy two carrier-based task forces.[16] Indonesia bought six Van Speijk-class frigates and plans to acquire as many as 20 FG-90 class frigates starting in the mid-1990s. In 1992, it announced plans to purchase 39 former East German vessels.[17] Malaysia ordered two sophisticated frigates from Britain.

Despite economic difficulties, President Cory Aquino of the Philippines initiated a 10-year $1 billion naval modernization plan and signed a contract to acquire from Spain three Exocet missile-carrying offshore patrol boats.[18] She also called for a credible air defense system. The air force pushed for the purchase of F-16s and a radar system for the island of Palawan, but for lack of economic resources had to settle for 18 Czech Albatross light combat aircraft.

Wealthy Brunei is primarily constrained by limited human resources. Nevertheless, Brunei reconstituted its forces, creating for the first time an army, navy and air force, and can be expected to make new acquisitions. Three missile-carrying offshore patrol boats from the U.K. are under consideration.[19]

An equally important modernizing trend is the acquisition of anti-ship missiles and submarines. All ASEAN navies are acquiring, or have already acquired, Harpoon and/or Exocet anti-ship missiles.[20] While Indonesia is the only ASEAN country that operates submarines (two type 209/1300) and has ordered an additional three boats,[21] Malaysia, Singapore, and Thailand are reported to be considering submarine acquisition,[22] although Malaysia may have shelved the plan for the time being in favor of two more new corvettes.

While modernization of the air forces and navies was given the highest priority, the armies have not been neglected. New or planned acquisitions point to increasing emphasis on rapid deployment forces and on armor and artillery. There are indications that the Malaysian army's modernization program is strengthening. The Malaysians are looking for up to 60 tanks and up to 68 armoured personnel carrier (APC)/mechanized infantry combat vehicles (MICV).[23] Thailand, which bought a large number of Chinese tanks and armored personnel carriers in 1989, recently acquired 50 M-60 tanks. Indonesia recently acquired 160 APCs and took delivery of 25 more Rapier surface-to-air missile fire units.

Development of the defense industry in ASEAN countries should also be considered. Singapore's industry is the most advanced, as evidenced by the locally manufactured technological upgrade of the A-4 Skyhawk. Singapore's defense sector is a highly integrated, high technology, diversified industrial complex.[24] Along with Singapore, Indonesia has one of the most developed local defense industries in the region.[25]

ASEAN countries' defense industries, however, still rely heavily on foreign technology despite the fact that the buyers can demand greater access to technology through co-production and co-development of military hardware. All except one of the aircraft programs in Indonesia, the Philippines, Singapore, and Thailand involved assembly, licensed production, or modification of foreign aircraft.[26] Naval construction programs are less dependent on foreign technology. Nevertheless, all the countries except Brunei invested substantial resources in defense industrialization programs that "provided ASEAN's military establishment with an increasingly diverse array of small arms, ammunition, ordnance, light aircraft and small naval vessels."[27]

MILITARY SPENDING AND "WILLINGNESS"

It was argued that the single best predictor of increased defense expenditure is not, as conventional wisdom would suggest, an increase in perceived external threats, but rather the rate of increase in GDP.[28] But why does Indonesia spend less on defense in absolute terms today than it did 20 years ago, devoting an increasingly smaller percentage of GDP to defense? The answer can be found in the idea of willingness to spend, which Harris suggests is distinct from ability to spend.[29]

Threat Perceptions

One factor that might influence willingness to spend on defense is threat perception, although Denoon's findings dismiss this. Denoon found that, except for Thailand, which faced a direct external threat from Vietnam's occupation of Cambodia, none of the ASEAN countries faced an "actual threat" that justified at least a 70 percent increase in its defense spending. Harris, on the other hand, does not deny the significance of the more diffuse geo-political situation for threat perceptions. Chin Kin Wah concludes that even though conventional wisdom assumes that threat perception is the major determinant of military spending, a mix of other variables influences military spending in Southeast Asia.[30] These include the geopolitical environment, the domestic political-security-economic environment, the sense of threat and vulnerability, the decision-making structure, and external affiliations.

Yet threat perception and sense of vulnerability, both from external and domestic sources, do appear to have some bearing on defense spending, as seen in the sharp rise in spending in most ASEAN countries after Vietnam's invasion of Cambodia, and the high level of military expenditure during high insurgency periods.

The loss of external affiliation is also a factor that helps to explain the willingness to sharply increase defense spending. The withdrawal of the Commonwealth forces from Malaysia and Singapore, climaxing in the ending of the Anglo-Malaysian Defense Arrangement in 1971 and, similarly, the United States' withdrawal from mainland Southeast Asia in 1975 both coincided with an increase in Malaysian, Singapore and Thai military budgets. The Philippines' decision not to renew the base agreement with the United States meant a loss to the Philippines' external defense, previously provided by the Unites States' umbrella. Such reliance plus a poor economy left the Philippine armed forces with obsolete equipment.

Philippine leaders, therefore, believe they must acquire more arms under a 10-year modernization program. In this case, however, considering the state of the country's economy, willingness will be constrained by the lack of ability.

Denoon's dismissal of any direct-threat justification for ASEAN's 70 percent increase in defense spending neglects the fact that threat perceptions are intangible. Additionally, it is difficult to judge what level of defense is suitable for any particular threat. Nevertheless, national leaders' estimates of security risks influence their willingness to spend on defense. These estimates also provide the basis for the formulation of strategies and doctrines, among other things, which in turn determine the types and quantity of arms to be procured. For countries in high-threat environments, threat perception influences defense expenditures to a high degree. Thus, the fall of Indochina to communist rule in 1975 and the subsequent invasion of Cambodia by Vietnam in 1978 marked the shift from counterinsurgency to conventional warfare doctrine.

The end of the Cold War brought a new strategic environment to the nations of Southeast Asia as bipolarity gave way to an uncertain multipolar system. With the withdrawal of the Soviet Union, and with the United States considering cutting its forward military deployment in the region, there are two major powers looming on the horizon: Japan and China. Either one could become a new hegemon and create regional instability.

These evolving and uncertain strategic scenarios will produce new security threats. In the face of such an uncertain security situation, ASEAN countries are turning more towards security self-reliance, best pursued through modernization of armed forces and the adoption of a deterrence strategy. This explains the quantity and quality of arms presently being acquired.

Nevertheless, the linkage between threat perception and willingness to spend is not uniform among ASEAN countries because a country's threat perception is a function of factors that include geographic location and historical experience. The changing strategic environment in Southeast Asia mentioned above, therefore, produces different threat perceptions as to the source and degree of threat and leads to different allocations of resources.

Military Factors

Studies by Harris and Denoon find changes in defense expenditure in ASEAN countries to be gradual. According to Harris, a government's ability to alter defense expenditure from year to year, especially downward, is limited by the high personnel, maintenance, and operating cost component in defense expenditures. As it is more difficult to defer maintenance and reduce personnel in the short run, Harris argues that an equipment purchase is more likely to be postponed or canceled. Malaysia's cancellation of the deal to purchase the Tornado aircraft is one example. According to Denoon's finding, even when a government changed the percentage allocation to the military, the changes were almost never more than one percent per year. It is his conclusion that organizational momentum and political restraints make quick changes in military spending unlikely.

The importance of a particular geo-political environment on a country's willingness to spend on defense is illustrated by Singapore. Both its size, in terms of territory and population, and location make it particularly vulnerable and motivate its strategy of deterrence. Its small size makes for a lack of strategic depth, while its small population also limits the size of its standing army. As a country with important maritime stakes, it is particularly conscious of its location at the juncture of important sea lanes between the Indian Ocean and the South China Sea. Its recent experiences with neighboring countries with different ethnic make-up (Indonesia and Malaysia) add to its sense of vulnerability. Its arsenal, replete with technologically sophisticated weaponry and heavy volume of fire power, bespeaks a strategy emphasizing mobility and forward defense to compensate for the lack of defense in depth. In pursuit of this strategy, Singapore spent on defense at an almost constant average of 5.2 percent of GDP from 1981-92. This is the highest percentage among ASEAN countries. On the other hand, Indonesia's geographical environment, as the world's largest archipelagic nation, reduced its willingness to spend. Its defense spending in terms of percentage of GDP ranks it next to the Philippines, the country that spends the least.

Willingness to spend on defense is also influenced by the timing of the need to replace aged hardware, that is, modernization. As Karp argues, in the late 1990s, ASEAN countries need to retire much of their aging and vulnerable hardware acquired over the past 30 years.[31] Indonesia's purchase of various high performance weapons systems in the 1980s was required to replace aging equipment purchased secondhand in the 1970s.[32] The same is true for Malaysia, when it acquired Hawks to replace aging A-4s.

External Economic Interests

The willingness to acquire arms that extend both the capability and range of operations beyond one's territory is also explained by the expansion of maritime territory which was produced by the extension of territorial waters and the Exclusive Economic Zone (EEZ) provisions of the Third United Nations Conference on the Law of Sea (UNCLOS III). The resulting overlapping claims from such extensions and the growing importance of offshore resources for the countries' economic development provide added rationale for more arms acquisition, especially in view of potential territorial conflict in the South China Sea. Particularly worrisome is China's extensive claims of sovereignty over the Spratly and Parcel Islands, which are also claimed by Vietnam, the Philippines, Brunei, Taiwan, and Malaysia. China has promulgated a maritime law that calls for the use of force to protect its claims and has expanded its growing naval and air capabilities in the area.[33]

Competing Social Demands

When threat is lacking or unclear, the question of affordability plays a more important role in defense policy decision making. Defense expenditures have to compete with other uses for funds. In the 1993 Thai budget, there was a cutback in defense and national security in favor of agriculture, education, and public health to improve income distribution. In 1979-81, when the Malaysian economy was strong, the sharp increase in defense spending responding to the perceived threat from Vietnam's invasion of Cambodia was not seen to be at the expense of development. Yet there was a revision downward in 1984 because of economic recession. When security is defined comprehensively, as it is in most ASEAN countries, there is a reluctance to put substantial money into defense spending at the expense of domestic programs considered crucial to the maintenance of other dimensions of security. Malaysian Prime Minister Mahathir Mohamad emphasized that "national security is inseparable from political stability, economic success and social harmony" and that "the first line of defense lies in [a country's] national resilience."[34]

A different example is the impact of Indonesia's historical experience on its military stance. The birth pangs of the Republic of Indonesia, including external intervention, caused the Indonesian ruling elite of the Old Order and the New Order alike to define the core security issue in terms of territorial integrity and political unity of the centralized state. National security and economic development have a symbiotic relationship. How to achieve capabilities for the maintenance of security is the doctrine of "national resilience"—the capability of the nation to confront crisis situations, both domestic and external. Such capacity is understood not to mean military strength alone. The concept of "national resilience" recognizes the linkages between security, political stability, economic development, and social welfare. This perspective explains the dual function of the military. While not neglecting the external security environment, Indonesian leaders tend to view it as benign. Domestic security concerns, therefore, take priority over external ones. This is reflected in military spending patterns.[35]

Prestige

Prestige as a factor in the willingness to acquire advanced weapons system is hard to ascertain. There are indications that the competition for international prestige influenced the previously discussed sequential ordering of F-16s. The arming of Singapore's fast attack craft with Gabriel and Harpoon missiles during the 1980s may have encouraged other ASEAN navies to develop interest in anti-ship missiles.

Thailand's recent spectacular economic growth engendered self-confidence and a self-image as a center of influence on mainland Southeast Asia as expressed in the word *Suwannaphume* (Golden Peninsula). In this connection, a senior Thai army officer argued that Thailand must have military capabilities commensurate with its perceived regional influence.[36]

Domestic Political Role of the Military

The domestic decision-making structure also influences a country's willingness for arms acquisition. Thailand and Indonesia represent contrasting examples. Thailand's decision to purchase a squadron of F-16A in 1984 was made following the adoption of the Fifth Plan (1982-86). For the first time, there was an effort to coordinate economic and security development plans so that military expenditure and financial capability are considered simultaneously. Nevertheless, the government complied with the military's demand for more spending even in the face of dangerous levels of external debt and opposition from the media, the minister of finance, and the Parliament. Thai military and civilian technocrats involved in defense policy planning were described as "highly rational, meticulous and even sophisticated in their approach to this task."[37] However, it was observed that the military obtained more in defense spending than justified by the threat perceptions and the well-formulated planning guidelines.

This divergence between arms purchases and threat perceptions could be seen in the mid-to-late 1970s, even before Vietnam invaded Cambodia.[38] Thereafter, Thailand's mid-1980s purchase of F-16A fighter aircraft and air-defense system were at odds with the "actual" threat of land-based border incursions from Vietnam. Indeed, while equipment was acquired, doctrine, logistics, and joint training were largely ignored. The consequence was evident when the Thai military performed poorly in a border conflict with Laos in mid-1987.

Arms procurement by the Thai military also was characterized by an uncoordinated procurement cycle that often resulted from the three services not communicating with one another.[39] From 1975-86, annual defense budgets make up about 20 percent of the total government budget, except in 1975 and 1976 when the military's power and prestige were at their nadir and democratically elected governments were in power. Internal power equations, rather than threat perceptions or ability to spend, were the most influential determinants of defense spending, at least in the Thai case.

Thai military officers played three concurrent roles: those of professional soldier, bureaucrat, and central political actor, and the balance among these roles shifts over time.[40] After a May 1992 incident—in which the military's image was badly tarnished after unarmed demonstrators calling for democracy were fired on, resulting in a large number of casualties, the officer corps lost political influence, and shifted toward its professional soldier status. However, by 1993 it was still unclear whether this would reduce or increase the military's influence over defense spending.

Indonesia provides an interesting contrast to Thailand with regard to the link between decision-making structure and defense spending, mainly because its military also enjoys a dominant role in politics. But military spending in that country shows greater restraint and sensitivity to the country's economic state. For example, Indonesia's defense expenditure pattern follows its level of external indebtedness because, in contrast to Thailand, the Indonesian military had little voice in budgetary decisions.[41] Spending priorities are shaped by economists in the Ministry of Finance and the Economic Planning Agency and a larger share was allotted to serve developmental objectives.

IMPLICATIONS FOR THE FUTURE

The recent trend in arms acquisition/military modernization in Southeast Asia supports previous studies that positively linked economic development with defense expenditure. It can be expected that present trends will continue. The ability of ASEAN countries to increase their acquisitions of military hardware stems in part from vibrant economic growth in most countries, particularly during the past several years. Economic growth means not only that the government can spend more on the military, but also that an increase in military spending is not perceived to be a social burden. Denoon's observation that "for the past 15 years (1973-87), military spending has not been a critical burden for the ASEAN countries" is still valid today. ASEAN countries, with the exception of the Philippines, demonstrated that military spending does not to adversely effect economic development.

Considering this association in the converse case, there are instances when spending was cut as ability declined. Malaysia's cancellation of the plan to purchase Tornado aircraft reflected an unwillingness to commit an inordinate amount of resources, which finally led to the decision to acquire the much cheaper MIG-29. A number of countries also opted for a larger number of cheap light fighters to complement the more sophisticated platforms, as the acquisition and planned acquisition of Hawk aircraft seems to indicate.

It appears that when security is defined comprehensively to include dimensions other than military, concerns with economic and social well-being constrain military spending, except in the face of imminent threats. The overall decline in military expenditures as a percentage of GDP in ASEAN countries indicates a general sense of restraint. Any conclusion must recognize that both ability and willingness influence military expenditures. Willingness is much less, if at all, amenable to quantitative analysis. It is reasonable that military expenditure is a function of a combination of factors, and their respective weight of influence depends on a particular situation.

The present trend in Southeast Asia is a result of a combination of both ability and willingness. However, the implications of this trend are disturbing. While the present trend cannot be called an arms race, there was at least one clear instance of "keeping up with the neighbors"—the sequential purchases of F-16A, mentioned above. Malaysia's signing of a memorandum of understanding indicating an intention to buy Tornado aircraft was followed by the RTAF's consideration to acquire Tornados. After Malaysia decided to acquire MIG-29s, the commander-in-chief of the RTAF remarked that this would give Malaysia air superiority. It is not yet evident what impact the two-carrier task force of the RTN, should it be realized, will have on other ASEAN navies. Such growing military capability can be potentially destabilizing. It could put in doubt ASEAN's status as a "security community." What is disconcerting is that while ASEAN was successful in "crisis avoidance," existing conflicts among the member states were not resolved. These conflicts include territorial disputes, disputes over offshore resources, ethnicity, and emerging conflict over migration. Suspicions still linger among the members and are enhanced by the growing military capabilities in the region.

There is concern about this new security environment and arms buildup. One indication of this was the pledge made at the ASEAN Summit in Singapore in 1992 that "ASEAN shall seek avenues to engage member states in new areas of cooperation in security matters." Then, in 1994, ASEAN established its first official dialogue devoted to security issues (the ASEAN Regional Forum, or ARF), to begin the process of developing security dialogue and cooperation among all the Pacific rim states (including the United States and Russia). Accordingly, the ASEAN Ministerial meeting will have on its agenda security matters, and moves have been made to promote exchanges of military personnel, even at the general staff level. Efforts need to be made to promote greater transparency in military matters, including arms procurement, and defense policies. With a tradition of military secrecy, a move towards transparency will be difficult. However, this is the best alternative in promoting stability.

NOTES

1. The author wishes to acknowledge the valuable assistance received from Dr. Panitan Wattanayagorn in the form of suggestions and data for revising her original paper.
2. Analysts trying to study military expenditure data are often a frustrated lot. The best data of such known sources frequently differ from one another in computing methods. There are also inconsistencies between one year to the next. Difficulties arise when one turns to official statistics as these may not represent the actual amount being spent. See Nicole Ball, *Security and Economy in the Third World* (Princeton, NJ: Princeton University Press, 1988),pp. 84-122. To deal with some of these problems, this article will use the

term defense spending instead of defense modernization because data that disaggregate the cost of personnel, operation, and maintenance from development (i.e., acquisition of new equipment) often are not readily available.

3. Geoffrey Harris, "The Determinants of Defense Expenditure in the ASEAN Region," *Journal of Peace Research* 23 (1986), p. 46.

4. David B. Denoon, "Defense Spending in ASEAN : An Overview" in Chin Kin Wah, ed. *Defense Spending in Southeast Asia* (Singapore: Institute of Southeast Asian Studies, 1987), p. 50.

5. Andrew L. Ross, "Growth, Debt and Military Spending in Southeast Asia" *Contemporary Southeast Asia* 11 (1990), p. 259.

6. Muthiah Alaqappa, "Malaysia : From Commonwealth Umbrella to Self-reliance," in Chin Kin Wah, op. cit., pp. 190-191.

7. Ross, "Growth, Debt and Military Spending in Southeast Asia," p. 257.

8. Denoon, "Defense Spending in ASEAN: An Overview," p. 50.

9. Andrew L. Ross, "The International Arms Trade Arms Import, and Local Defense Production in ASEAN," in Chandran Jeshurun, ed. *Arms and Defense in Southeast Asia* (Singapore: Institute of Southeast Asian Studies, 1989), pp. 10-13.

10. Aaron Karp, "Military Procurement and Regional Security in Southeast Asia," *Contemporary Southeast Asia* 23 (March 1990), p. 336.

11. The entry into service of three fully operational A-4 Super Skyhawk squadrons equipped with 62 aircraft also was impressive. Weapons systems used by the A-4su include the (air-to-ground missile) AGM-65 MAVERICK, (air intercept missile) AIM-9P SIDEWINDER, Mk82 bombs, CRV-7 rocket pods, and PAVEWAY III laser-guided bombs. David Saw, "Politics and Defense Modernization in Southeast Asia," *Military Technology* (April 1992), pp. 19-20 and *Asia–Pacific Defense Reporter,* December 1994 and January 1995.

12. Including 14 Hawk jet fighters, 28 A-4 Skyhwks, 14 F-5 Tigers, and 12 OV-10 Broncos. *Asia–Pacific Defense Reporter,* op. cit.

13. David Saw, "Defense Spending in Southeast Asia," *Military Technology,* (February 1992), p. 20.

14. There were talks of a possible acquisition of attack aircraft, including the Tornado, the A-7, the AMX and the Hawk 200. However, this will be difficult to implement since the Royal Thai Air Force (RTAF) already has other expenditures planned for its budget through 1998. With air defense being a priority item, the RTAF purchased five air defense radars and SAM systems, with 20 launchers and 320 missiles. David Saw, op. cit., p. 24.

15. Malaysia went on to buy ten Hawk 100s and six Hawk 200s, as well as two GEC Marconi Martello S-743D surveillance radars and a comprehensive command, control, and communications (C3I) system, but canceled its option to acquire Tornados. Ibid., p. 15. In mid-1992, the MIG Study team was reported to highly recommend the purchase, subject to certain modifications to the fighter. Bilveer Singh, "The Russians Are Coming," *Business Times,* 10 February 1993.

16. *Asian Military Review* 1 (August/September 1993), p. 59.

17. Comprising nine Kondor minesweepers, 16 Parchim corvettes and 14 Forsch landing craft David Saw, op. cit., p. 20.

18. Andrew Mack and Desmond Ball, "The Military Build-up in the Asia-Pacific Region: Scope, Causes and Implications for Security," Working Paper no. 254 (Canberra: Strategic and Defense Studies Centre, Australian National University, 1992), pp. 5-6.

19. Ibid.

20. Mack and Ball, "The Military Build-up in the Asia-Pacific Region," p. 5.

21. Ibid., p. 6.

22. Ibid.

23. Saw, op. cit., p. 16.

24. Bilveer Singh and Kwa Chong Guan, "The Singapore Defense Industries: Motivations, Organizations, and Impact," in Jeshurun, op. cit., p. 100

25. Indeed, Indonesia is now making its bid as a global civil aviation contender as well, with the launch of an agressive marketing campaign for its domestically-developed turboprop aircraft. National Public Radio, *All Things Considered*, 10 August 1995. See also A. Hasnan Habib, "Indonesia Defense Industry: Its Role, Mission, and Set-up," in Jeshurun, op. cit.

26. Ross, op. cit., p. 29.

27. Ibid., pp. 29-35.

28. Daniel P. Hewitt, "What Determines Military Expenditure," *Finance and Development* (December 1991), p. 22.

29. Harris, op. cit.

30. Chin Kin Wah, "Conclusion" in Chin Kin Wah, op. cit., p. 308.

31. Karp, op. cit., p. 354.

32. MacIntrye, "Arms and Defense Planning in Indonesia," a paper presented at the Workshop on Arms and Defense Planning, Institute of Southeast Asian Studies, Singapore, 5-7 December 1991, p. 13.

33. See *Far Easter Economic Review*, 12 March 1992, p. 8.

34. Richard Stubbs, "Malaysian Defense Policy: Strategy versus Structure," *Contemporary Southeast Asia* 3 (June 1991), p. 51.

35. Indonesia's recent purchase of weapons of the type suited to conventional warfare such as the F-16 may seem to be incompatible with the emphasis on internal threat. A number of factors may explain this anomaly: a weapons modernization cycle, geography, technological competence, and prestige. As the world's largest archipelagic nation, Indonesia's geography requires it even for domestic reasons to develop its maritime capabilities, in order to link its scattered territory together and protect the marine-based resources within its Exclusive Economic Zone. The small numbers of the advanced weaponry it has purchased would not be of operational significance against an external threat and may be surmised to demonstrate only a motivation to keep abreast of the latest technology. See MacIntrye, "Arms and Defense Planning in Indonesia," p. 13.

36. Robert Karniol, "The Thai Armed Forces on Transition: The Shift from Counter-Insurgency to Conventional Warfare," a paper presented at the workshop on Arms and Defense Planning, Institute of Southeast Asian Studies, Singapore, 5-7 December 1991, p. 26.

37. Sukhumbhand Paribatra, "Thailand Defense Spending and Threat Perceptions," in Chin Kin Wah, op. cit., p. 95.

38. In the 1970s, Thailand acquired F-5E fighter aircraft, SIDEWINDER and EXOCET missiles, and Scorpion and M-48 tanks—all utterly unsuited to coping with insurgency, at the time considered to be serious.

39. Karniol, op. cit., p. 19.

40. Sukhumbhand Paribatra, "Thailand Defense Spending and Threat Perceptions," in Chin Kin Wah, op. cit., p. 103.

41. MacIntyre op. cit., p. 13.

3 The Benefits of APEC for Security Cooperation in the Asia-Pacific Region

Desmond Ball

INTRODUCTION

The relationship between economics and security is pervasive, profound, and extremely complex. Although there is no single theory or conceptual framework which explains this relationship, it is possible to adumbrate a plethora of connections, from the most profound (for example, the role of economic factors in determining the basic structure of geostrategic systems) to particular issues (for example, the economic aspects of competing claims to offshore islands and exclusive economic zones). These connections can most fruitfully be addressed in terms of two analytic categories, *systemic* or *instrumental*.

At the most fundamental level, as recognized by Sun Tzu around 400 BC, it is economic resources which determine the relative abilities of states to maintain large military forces and power projection capabilities. As Sun Tzu wrote:

> To raise an army of a hundred thousand soldiers and march them a thousand *li*
> to battle entails a heavy burden on both the people and the State's treasury, as
> expenses can amount to a thousand pieces of gold a day.[1]

It is the relative economic strength of the principal states in a system which ultimately defines that system as hegemonic, bipolar, or some form of multipolarity. Economic strength became the single most important index of national power, eclipsing over the long haul the possession of significant quantities of advanced military capabilities. It is the ability of national economies to sustain high levels of growth, to generate and capitalize on advanced technological products and processes, and to engage competitively and energetically in the international marketplace that will determine rankings in international power lists at the turn of the century.

The determinate role of economic factors in shaping the structure of security in the Asia-Pacific region was recognized by regional defense planners. For example, U.S. Undersecretary of Defense for Policy (USDP) Paul Wolfowitz testified to the Senate Armed Services Committee in April 1990:

> You've got to recognize the name of the game in the Pacific is economics. I don't think we should be under any illusions that 10 years from now the U.S. role is going to be determined by our military posture. It's going to be determined most of all by our economic competitiveness and by the kinds of trading and economic relationships we have out there.[2]

The structural features comprise only one dimension of the *systemic* category. The other dimension, which most concerned students of international political economy, addresses the dynamics of the economic-security relationships within geostrategic structures—that is, the implications of the prevailing patterns of economic development for systemic tendencies toward conflict or peace.

It is frequently asserted that a liberal economic order substantially discourages the use of force among states and sustains an international security system which avoids major conflict and war, whereas a mercantilist economic order stimulates conflict and the use of force.[3] Liberal economic systems are characterized by relatively high degrees of economic interdependence. It was argued that the collapse of the liberal economic order and the retreat into protectionism in the 1930s "led not only to economic disaster, but also to international war."[4]

According to the *functionalist* perspective, the security implications of increasing economic interdependence are strongly positive. Interdependence breeds familiarity, an appreciation of each others' interests and perceptions, and a recognition that, since "we swim or sink together," efforts will be directed at common purposes. Moreover, the confidence engendered in this common endeavor will, according to *neofunctionalist* theory, "spill-over" from the economic to the political realm.[5] Hence, as Sir John Crawford argued:

> It is probable that improved cooperative effort in the economic field which promotes economic growth in the Pacific is likely on the one hand to lessen political friction and political misunderstanding and, on the other, to strengthen the economic base required for effective strategic and defense policies for member countries.[6]

Growing economic ties between former adversaries (such as Russia and South Korea) affect threat perceptions and shift national security interest calculations.

However, the relationship between economic interdependence and security is more complex. It depends on numerous factors, including the extent and nature of interdependence and the actors' definition of security. Interdependence is and will remain far from absolute. Even if some two-thirds of the trade conducted by Asia-

Pacific countries is intraregional, there remains a significant proportion—in the cases of particular countries involving critical sectors of economic activity—outside the region. The nature of interdependence in commodity trade, particularly where resource-based exports and/or major bilateral imbalances are involved, is very different from interdependence in production activities. Perceptions also are important, since all parties in an interdependent relationship do not always see things the same way. In some circumstances, interdependence is as likely to cause resentment and tension as to promote mutual trust and confidence. Much depends on the maintenance of economic growth. If growth falters, then interdependence is unlikely to be a constraint on disputes, but leads to mutual recriminations and a tense strategic environment.

While the structural and functionalist dimensions constitute the systemic category, another two dimensions, the *utilitarian* and *cognitive*, make up the *instrumental* category. The utilitarian dimension is concerned with the use of the myriad of networks, consultations, study groups, and dialogue forums dependent upon high degrees of economic interdependence for the discussion, negotiation, and resolution of common security issues. The distinction between the utilitarian activity and the functionalist dimension of the previous category is not always clear-cut. Whereas the functionalist processes are more or less autonomous, with interdependence breeding familiarity, generating common perspectives and mutual confidence, spilling over into common political and security endeavors, the utilitarian dimension is more dependent on the deliberate creation of dialogues and arrangements by government policy or nongovernmental efforts directed at adapting or broadening economic cooperation.

The cognitive dimension is different. Analogies are designed to structure and focus information about policy issues to permit systematic comparison and inform policymaking.[7] They are empirically based cognitive devices that assist policymakers and analysts to confront new situations through diagnosis and assessment of comparable and familiar situations, providing warning of pitfalls that lie in particular paths and suggesting benefits that accrue from alternative routes.[8]

Most of the current academic discussion and analysis of the relationship between economics and security is concerned with the systemic category of the relationship. This chapter, however, addresses the instrumental category, and, most particularly, the cognitive dimension, through a case study of the experience with the institutionalization of economic cooperation in the Asia-Pacific region. Although not usually diagnosed in this way, the analogy of Asia-Pacific economic cooperation is familiar in that it is both well documented and part of the "cognitive map" of many of the policymakers and analysts currently involved in security cooperation in the Asia-Pacific region. It should prove to be a very fruitful exercise in the institutionalization of security cooperation in this region.

APEC CASE STUDY

The relevance of the Asia-Pacific Economic Cooperation (APEC) process to the promotion of regional confidence and security is threefold: first, APEC is increasingly important to the maintenance of economic growth in the Asia-Pacific region and to the liberalization of the global economy (hence to the promotion of regional stability and security, as the functionalists would argue); second, APEC provides a forum for the discussion and resolution of economic issues which have significant security aspects (and thus exemplifies the utilitarian dimension of the economic security relationship); and, third, an examination of the APEC process provides numerous "lessons" which are relevant to the design and political acceptance of confidence and security building measures (CSBMs) in the Asia-Pacific region (that is, the cognitive dimension of the relationship between economics and security).

APEC AND LIBERALIZATION OF THE GLOBAL ECONOMY

The Asia-Pacific region experienced extraordinary growth over the last few decades. The East Asian economies grew more rapidly and for a longer period of time than any other economies in world history. East Asia's production has grown from less than 10 percent of world GNP in the early 1960s (at which time North America accounted for around 40 percent) to almost one-quarter of world GNP (or about the same proportion as North America) by the end of the 1980s. During the same period, the share of the Asia-Pacific region (here including North America and Australasia as well as East Asia) in world trade grew from around 30 percent to some 37 percent, with most of the increase coming from East Asia. East Asia also became the most important source of world savings and overwhelmingly the largest source of surplus savings for international investment. Much of this increased economic activity was intraregional, making the Asia-Pacific economies highly interdependent by the end of the 1980s.[9] The maintenance of this economic dynamism and strengthening of interdependence are the most critical factors for stability and security in the Asia-Pacific through the rest of this century.

APEC is very important in this exercise. It provides the most important means for securing benefits of economic interdependence and ensuring that accompanying frictions and tensions are manageable.

APEC also contributes to the liberalization of the global economy. The concept of "open regionalism," fundamental to APEC, is radically different from the discriminatory nature of the European Community.[10] Rather than forming a trade bloc, cooperation among Asia-Pacific economies is designed to strengthen an open, multilateral trading system fully consistent with GATT principles.

APEC AND DISCUSSION OF SECURITY RELATED ISSUES: THE UTILITARIAN DIMENSION

It is suggested that APEC might become a forum for region-wide security dialogue. In part, this reflects an appreciation of the increasing importance of the economic dimensions of security. It also reflects an appreciation, as expressed by the former Secretary of the Australian Department of Foreign Affairs and Trade, Mr. Richard Woolcott, that APEC "is now the core forum for ministerial exchange in the Asia-Pacific region."[11] In the case of some countries—such as Australia, where the Foreign Affairs and Trade responsibilities are incorporated into a single ministerial portfolio—foreign ministers are the principals at the APEC meetings. Rather than create new and separate arrangements for regional security dialogue, it is possible to expand the purview of APEC to include political and security issues as well. Former Chair of the East Asian and Pacific Affairs Subcommittee of the U.S. Senate Alan Cranston agreed in October 1991.[12] He specifically proposed that the problem of nuclear proliferation in the region is an appropriate issue for inclusion in a broadened APEC agenda.[13]

However, it would be a mistake to broaden the APEC process in this way. It is unacceptable to most APEC members, especially in ASEAN countries. Notwithstanding its remarkable development over the past five years, APEC is still a fledgling institution. To encomber it with a security agenda would risk disrupting the regional consensus and retarding momentum generated over the past several years. And there is no longer a need for such a broadened APEC agenda, because ASEAN held its first official security dialogue meeting in July 1994. Named the ASEAN Regional Forum (ARF), the dialogue of 18 Asia Pacific countries and the European Union established the following agenda items for future ARF discussions: "preventive diplomacy," increased transparency, confidence and security building measures (CSBMs), nuclear nonproliferation, regional peacekeeping, exchange of military information, maritime security, and preemptive prevention of conflict.

On the other hand, there are many important economic issues which fall within the accepted purview of APEC that also have significant security dimensions. Although issues such as nuclear proliferation would be excluded, APEC could serve as a forum for discussion of security-related economic issues, such as:

* the implications of economic interdependence for regional security;
* the future of the United States-Japan economic relationship, including the implications of possible developments in this relationship for regional security;
* the relationship between economic growth and political stability;
* the relationship between economic growth and defense expenditures;

- the relationship between defense expenditures, economic growth, and technological development;
- issues such as trade diversion, dumping, subsidies, tariffs and other forms of protection, and violations of international trade agreements which could lead to disputation and conflict;
- regional rationalization of defense industrial infrastructures for production and maintenance of defense equipment;
- the dependence of Asia-Pacific economies on overseas trade and the vulnerability of sea lines of communication (SLOCs);
- the possibilities for joint development zones in areas of disputation and potential conflict (for example the South China Sea);
- the use of official development assistance (ODA) and foreign investment for promoting regional stability;
- environmental issues which can cause conflict;
- the problems of piracy, smuggling, and other illegal activities in Asian waters.

The adumbration of these issues is illustrative of the range of security-related economic issues that lie within the utilitarian dimension of the economics-security relationship. It is not meant to be comprehensive. An agenda for utilitarian activity can be constructed that extends well beyond the dozen issues listed above. However, this discussion shows that the range and character of economic issues falling within the accepted purview of APEC covers many of the most critical security issues confronting the region.

LESSONS FOR THE CSBM PROCESS: THE COGNITIVE DIMENSION

The emergence of APEC is relevant to the process of establishing viable and meaningful CSBMs in the Asia-Pacific region. Concerns that drove the APEC process are conceptually very similar to those currently at the top of the regional security agenda. Successive rounds of multilateral trade negotiations under GATT auspices lowered worldwide tariffs, but other less transparent forms of protection became more common. The end of the Cold War removed the threat of superpower war, but regional conflicts are likely to increase. Both APEC and CSBMs are responses to increasing regional interdependence. Economists anticipated in the 1960s that "growing interdependence would require progressively closer coordination of policy-making to identify new economic opportunities and to resolve potential frictions and bottlenecks in the way of mutually beneficial trade."[14] Security analysts similarly are concerned with frictions that lead to regional conflict and with instability that is a "bottleneck" to regional stability.

Regional reactions to the initial APEC proposal in January 1989 were mixed, although there was less enthusiasm than suspicion and derision. One press account, for example, described the proposal as "divorced from reality."[15] Some countries, such as Malaysia and Indonesia, initially were reluctant to participate in APEC, while others, such as the Philippines, were simply not interested. The initial proposal was considered too vague with respect to both the objectives and the membership of APEC to be taken seriously. As a Malaysian commentator noted:

> The form is vague: many questions are unanswered: Should China be invited? The United States has its reservations. The Soviet Union? Ditto Japan. What does it aim to achieve? Who would be members? And there are many more.[16]

There was widespread reluctance to create any new regional structure, as well as a particular hesitancy about institutionalized, multilateral, inter-governmental arrangements. There was a fear, particularly in ASEAN, that APEC would be dominated by the more powerful countries (Japan and the United States). There also was a fear that the establishment of APEC would aggravate or create trade hostilities with the European Community and other excluded countries or groups.[17] There was suspicion concerning the motivations and interests of the sponsors, Australia in particular. And there was concern that in citing the "model" of the Paris-based Organization for Economic Cooperation and Development (OECD) in Prime Minister Hawke's initial proposal, the region was being presented with another Western structure unsuitable for the Asia-Pacific.[18]

Some of the arguments raised in response to the APEC proposal in 1989 are similar to those put against some current proposals for CSBMs in the region. How, then, did APEC start?

The features of APEC relevant to the process of constructing CSBMs include both the substantive features of arrangements (for example, the terms of reference and mode of operation) as well as aspects of the development of APEC which pertain to the design and acceptance of CSBMs.

Managing Reality

For APEC to succeed, it had to reflect regional economic realities. For the Asia-Pacific region in the 1970s and 1980s, the dominant economic reality was extraordinary growth and growing intraregional economic activity. For many commentators, it is the "reality...of economic interdependence" which has driven the evolution of regional economic cooperation.[19]

Through the 1970s and 1980s, dramatic restructuring of many of the Asia-Pacific economies and development of new industries and services occasioned by extraordinary economic growth and rapid technological changes produced much greater economic complementarity, as evidenced in the introduction to this volume. This increasing regional economic interdependence extends beyond trade in merchandise to also include services, especially tourism. As important as the interdependence in trade is the fact that most of the region's capital exports flow to other parts of the region.[20]

Transforming and Aligning Regional Perceptions

Regional cooperation is dependent upon the development of a common perception that cooperation is in everyone's interest. The realities of economic dynamism and increasing interdependence, and the opportunities and challenges they present do not autonomously generate cooperative mechanisms. Regional leaders must perceive this "reality" and be persuaded that multilateralism is the most appropriate approach to managing this economic dynamism and increasing interdependence.

Perceptions differ. For example, U.S. Secretary of State James Baker argued that the scale of intra-Asian trade involves a degree of interdependence which necessitates the institutionalization of regional economic cooperation:

> Last year [1988] intra-Asian trade approached $200 billion, reflecting the rapid pace of Pacific rim integration. Yet unlike Europe, there are inadequate regional mechanisms to deal with the effects of interdependence....Clearly, the need for a new mechanism for multilateral cooperation among the nations of the Pacific rim is an idea whose time has come.[21]

To others in the region, however, extensive trade did not mean interdependence, and the need for new multilateral institutions was not evident. As Mahathir bin Mohamad, Deputy Prime Minister of Malaysia stated in January 1980:

> Interdependence is still very much an economic concept that has no reality for a lot of poor nations. True interdependence must mean not just being mutually dependent on each other but some degree of equality of strength to support each other.[22]

Supporting each other, moreover, requires efforts to identify "the basic interests" of each country in the region.[23] It is the perception of these interests, combined with the feasibility and practical promise of a particular proposal for cooperation that determines its political acceptability.

The Importance of Form and Process

The evolution of Asia-Pacific economic cooperation was more about processes than about institutional structures or decisional outcomes—processes of dialogue and confidence building, gradual refinement of regionally acceptable agendas, consultation and consensus, and increasing governmental interest in the exercise. In the 1960s and 1970s, governments began to accept involvement in regional economic cooperation.[24]

Process and outcomes are inseparable. Pursuit of a particular outcome requires mapping and traversing the routes to it. The means of implementation define the character and scope of the product. Especially in Asian culture, form and substance are fungible. As one commentator reported on the reaction of the ASEAN foreign ministers (meeting in Brunei in July 1989) to Prime Minister Hawke's APEC proposal of January 1989:

> The public support in Brunei for the form but not the substance of Mr. Hawke's proposal is balanced by a private acceptance of substance but not the form.[25]

The connections between process and substance are just as inseparable in the case of security building. As the Australian Minister for Foreign Affairs and Trade, Gareth Evans, argued with respect to regional security dialogue: "[It] is both process and outcome, facilitating progress and at the same time cementing it."[26]

The Virtues of Patience and Modesty

The institutionalization of some form of inter-governmental Asia-Pacific economic cooperation took a long time. Although only six years since Prime Minister Hawke suggested the formation of APEC, the concept has direct historical linkage to other proposals dating back to the 1960s. ASEAN was established in August 1967 and developed into an extremely successful regional cooperative arrangement during this period.

But what was really accomplished during this period? The institutionalization of the process of regular intergovernmental meetings on regional economic issues is a significant development. This alone exceeded the expectations of many observers and even, perhaps, its founders.[27] But it is difficult to point to anything tangible or concrete that APEC has achieved.

Doing Business "the Asian Way"

Many of the proposals for regional economic cooperation put forward in the 1960s and 1970s, including those advanced by Asian economists such as Kiyoshi Kojima, foundered because they were similar to Western models—European Economic Community (EEC) and the Organization for Economic Cooperation and Development (OECD). By 1980, it generally was accepted that "EEC-style discriminatory trading arrangements were inappropriate in the Pacific"[28] and that the purposes of regional economic cooperation, as well as the processes of its implementation, must be grounded in Asian ways. At a major conference on economic cooperation organized by the Centre for Strategic and International Studies (CSIS) in Jakarta and held in Bali in January 1980, the following conclusion was reached:

> [N]ations should "follow the Oriental approach by talking things over slowly and patiently" rather than trying to solve problems quickly the way some Western countries try to.[29]

As Mahathir bin Mohamad argued at that conference, the Asian way involves dialogue and confidence-building rather than the development of formal plans or "clear-cut formula."[30] A report of that conference in the *Far Eastern Economic Review* noted that this approach "is foreign to Westerners who are intent on setting up organizations, deciding modalities and delineating responsibilities."[31]

This approach is not that difficult to comprehend. Its essential features are patience; informality and attention to processes rather than structures; emphasis on dialogue, consultation and consensus; and pragmatism. Implicit in these is an appreciation of regional diversity and political sensitivities.

Appreciation of Regional Diversity

A characteristic of the Asia-Pacific region recognized immediately was the extraordinary heterogeneity of the region in political, cultural, social, institutional and economic terms.[32] Although Asia-Pacific countries share a common interest in regional economic cooperation, their speciYfic interests vary. For example, ASEAN countries are more interested in arrangements for commodity trade, while South Korea and ASEAN countries are concerned about access for manufactured goods to the more developed countries in the region. Others are more interested in foreign investment and official development assistance (ODA) issues.

Appreciation of regional diversity was one of the "guiding principles" in structuring the APEC process. As Andrew Elek reported:

> It was recognized that some regional economies were much larger than others, but relative weights were changing rapidly and continuously. A workable process of cooperation would need to recognize diversity, but avoid domination of the process by any single participant or sub-group of economies. To ensure that due weight was given to the views of all participants, the process would need to be based on consultations aimed at building consensus on a gradually broader range of economic issues. Conversely, the process should not develop into a formal negotiating process in which some sought to force their views on others.[33]

Appreciation of Regional Sensitivities

Asians are interested in the motivations behind particular proposals for regional cooperation. Most proposals for regional economic cooperation originated in Japan and Australia. While there is general Yacceptance that regional economic cooperation is meaningless without the active involvement of Japan and the United States, there is concern that these countries not dominate the process and suspicion that many proposals implicitly reflect Japanese economic interests. There is puzzlement concerning the prominent role of Australian academics and officials in the advancement of many of these proposals. Why is Australia, by some accounts not even part of Asia, so active? Is Australia willing to engage in a more radical restructuring of its economy and to further liberalize its own trade policies? Is it serving as a "stalking horse" for U.S. or Japanese interests?[34]

It is extremely important that, mindful of these regional suspicions and sensitivities, proposals for regional cooperation be advanced carefully, with full explication of their motivations and practical purposes. Some countries (for example, Indonesia) had reservations about the meeting in Canberra in September 1980 and the PECC process which it initiated because "of the way they feel to have been approached" and a suspicion that the Japanese and Australian governments were orchestrating the process.[35] According to Indonesian Foreign Minister Mochtar Kusumaatmadja, the PECC idea was presented to Indonesia in a "clumsy" way.[36] A "continuing search for hidden motives" was generated which confused, distracted, and politicized subsequent discussions.[37]

Living with the Dragons

While many countries in the Asia-Pacific region are apprehensive about the economic power of Japan and a reforming China, they nonetheless accept that they have to live with them. Cooperative arrangements provide a mechanism for both attuning major regional powers to the interests and sensitivities of the smaller and weaker countries, as well as enabling these countries to offset the weight of the major powers. This rationale for regional economic cooperation was recognized in the late 1960s, as reported by Bernard Gordon:

> These apprehensions—especially concerning Japan's great economic might—and latent resentments growing from the wartime experiences cannot be erased altogether, but a greater degree of collaboration among Southeast Asian states is expected to better enable these small states to stand up to Japan. Lacking some degree of cohesion, the developing states of Southeast Asia must otherwise remain too easily susceptible to Japan's sheer weight in Asian affairs. Southeast Asian leaders are indeed the first to stress this, and their recognition acts as an additional incentive towards regional cooperation. For they [believe] that the objective factors of location and Japan's economic interest will lead her inexorably to more involvement in Southeast Asia; regionalism among the weaker and smaller Southeast Asian nations appears to them as one more way by which to be better able to deal with the Japanese.[38]

More recently, Wendy Dobson made the point in functionalist terms that APEC was a structural response to increasing U.S.-Japanese economic tensions and the emergence of China as "an economic powerhouse" by providing a means for the smaller economies in the region "to offset dominance by the three giants."[39]

It is a means which is as applicable in political and security affairs as in the economic arena and offers the region the possibility of developing a combined counterweight to the regional security "dragons": Japan, China and India.

The "Building Block" Approach

During the 25 years in which Asia-Pacific economic cooperation was actively considered, numerous proposals for institutional cooperative arrangements have fallen by the wayside. They have been too much inspired by Western experience and practice, without sufficient empathy for Asia-Pacific circumstances. They were too ambitious, particularly those which posited profound actions such as the elimination of tariffs in the region rather than the establishment of consultative processes. And they were premature, as with proposals for intergovernmental arrangements prior to the late 1980s. It took 25 years for the countries to finally agree to the declaration of free trade principles which followed the APEC ministerial meeting in Indonesia in November 1994. The Bogor Declaration that emerged from this meeting committed APEC to free trade within the Asia Pacific region by 2020. It also opposed an inward-looking trading bloc of the European Community type.

Kiyoshi Kojima, who inspired much of the thinking about Asia-Pacific economic cooperation,[40] acknowledged that his original proposal for a Pacific Asia Free Trade Area (PAFTA) was too ambitious and argued that strengthening the "functional integration" of the Asia-Pacific economies through regionally-agreed "codes of international behavior" was a more practical alternative to "institutional integration."[41] Peter Drysdale, another inspirator of the APEC process, also acknowledged that some of his earlier proposals, such as an Organization for Pacific Trade and Development (OPTAD), were too closely associated with OECD/European Community mechanisms, and in 1983, he acknowledged that "a strictly inter-governmental mechanism for consultation among Pacific countries on foreign economic issues is a premature idea" and nonofficial forums involving official participation was a more promising alternative mechanism.[42]

Other proposals were explicitly based on the "building block" approach. For example, the Pacific Basin Cooperation Study Group established by Japanese Prime Minister Masayoshi Ohira in March 1979 recommended that the region adopt a "step-by-step approach," and that a quasi-formal structure of committees and conferences be institutionalized as a "first step in building machinery for Pacific Basin cooperation."[43] The first important product of this was a seminar in Canberra in September 1980, involving businessmen, academics, and government officials, which initiated the innovative and influential Pacific Economic Cooperation Conference (PECC).[44]

The founders of APEC were concerned about having as little new formal machinery as possible; wished to take care that any new structures did not cut across extant arrangements (for example, weaken ASEAN cohesion); and that APEC "build constructively on the foundations for regional dialogue established by ASEAN, as well as by the PECC, rather than compete with existing structures."[45] As Indonesian Foreign Minister Ali Alatas stated in July 1989, APEC's eventual structure needed to "start with and fully utilize the existing mechanisms rather than create new ones, and to improve, expand and adapt them to the agreed requirements and objectives."[46]

The first step in any regional cooperative process is the creation of a dialogue process. As Mahathir bin Mohamad stated in January 1980:

> The first move towards a Pacific [economic] Community should not be a comprehensive economic plan or some such clear-cut formula for cooperation but the tedious one of getting to know each other.[47]

Institutionalizing Dialogue

By 1980, it was recognized among those concerned with the development of Asia-Pacific economic cooperation that the most important initial step in the process was to institutionalize regional dialogue rather than construct new economic and trading arrangements. Not only is dialogue necessary to develop consensus on regional policy priorities, it is also necessary to develop mutual trust and understanding required for meaningful political action.

The basic "building blocks" of the Asia-Pacific economic dialogue process have been the innumerable workshops, seminars, and conferences organized throughout the region since the late 1960s. The most important of the early steps were the initiation in 1968 of the series of Pacific Trade and Development (PAFTAD) conferences of regional academics, and the establishment in 1967 of the Pacific Basin Economic Council (PBEC) for regionwide consultations and exchanges of information by businessmen.

The initiation of PECC in 1980 was particularly innovative in that it instituted the involvement of government officials from throughout the region (albeit in their "private capacity") in a "tripartite structure" which also includes academics, researchers, and businessmen. This ensured both that the official community would be aware of the thinking, studies, and analyses from within the business and academic/research sectors, and that researchers and businessmen would be aware of the practical policy interests and concerns of government officials.

Even the agendas of these conferences are suggestive. Some were designed to address issues with significant regional, security dimensions such as "Towards a Pacific Community," "Organizations for Pacific Trade, Aid and Development," "A Pacific Economic Community and Asian Developing Countries," and "The Pacific Economy: Growth and External Stability." In other instances, concepts and methodologies developed in discussion of "Obstacles to Trade in the Pacific Area" and "Structural Adjustment in Asia-Pacific Trade" are applicable to obstacles to greater regional security cooperation and defense modernization. The practical, action-oriented nature of these agendas is also instructive.

APEC represents an advanced form of institutionalized intergovernmental dialogue and consultation in the region. The basic principles of APEC include "a commitment to open dialogue" and cooperation "based on non-formal consultative exchanges of views."[48]

Practicality and Pragmatism

APEC is founded on the premise that dialogue can produce substantive benefits beyond merely the appropriate first step towards regional cooperation. It was a "guiding principle" of the APEC process that the dialogue should be "action-oriented" and concerned with practical issues.[49] As Prime Minister Hawke stated in January 1989:

> What we are seeking to develop is a capacity for analysis and consultation on economic and social issues, not as an academic exercise but to help inform policy development by our respective governments.[50]

The APEC process already generated a wide range of practical suggestions to further enhance and strengthen gains from regional economic interdependence. These cover further liberalization measures and facilitate other aspects of interdependence, such as industrial cooperation, technology transfers, and flows of direct investment. Some of these measures could be implemented unilaterally, but others require harmonization of national policies or reciprocal policy adjustments, and they can be pursued most effectively through multilateral processes.

Membership of APEC

The trade-oriented market economies of East Asia, Southeast Asia, and Australasia comprised the core group in successive proposals for Asia-Pacific economic cooperation. It is now accepted that the United States should also be included because maintaining the U.S. economic presence and active policy interest in the region is vital.

Prime Minister Hawke's initial APEC proposal was limited to Pacific Asia and excluded the United States and Canada. It soon became apparent, however, that most of the countries in the region favored the inclusion of the United States and Canada—if only "to avoid the perception that this was the beginning of a closed bloc."[51]

Although Washington was unhappy because it was not consulted before the Hawke initiative was announced in Seoul and, although it remained opposed to the formation of any regional trade bloc or economic community, it quickly supported the APEC concept.[52] In November 1991, James Baker described APEC as "the hallmark of American engagement in the region," and stated that the success of

APEC meant that the United States "should be attentive to the possibilities for such multilateral action" in the security field.[53]

A more awkward issue concerned involvement of China, Hong Kong, and Taiwan. The initial round of regional consultations in early 1989 suggested that they should be included because of their significant and growing economic status. However, China is not yet transformed into a free trading market economy and there were sensitive issues of sovereignty. Consultations with China went into abeyance after the 1989 Tiananmen Square massacre, but as a result of especially adroit diplomacy in 1991, China, Taiwan, and Hong Kong were simultaneously admitted to APEC at the Third APEC Ministerial Meeting in Seoul. The sovereignty issue between China and Taiwan was bypassed with a compromise in which Taiwan is called "Chinese Taipei" for APEC purposes.[54]

Remarkable pragmatism was evinced by all parties—by China seeking membership in an arrangement dedicated to capitalism, by the acceptance by the market economies of China's involvement, by the side-stepping of the sovereignty issues, and by China's sending a foreign minister to South Korea (which it does not recognize and which would have risked offense to its traditional ally, North Korea).[55] But the inclusion of Taiwan and Hong Kong in APEC makes it more difficult to use APEC as a forum for comprehensive discussion of security-related issues because Beijing refuses to discuss international security issues with any Taiwanese representative in the room.

This is another example of how multilateral dialogues in Asia have little opportunity to address existing disputes, such as Taiwanese independence, the Spratly Islands dispute in the South China Sea, the China-Japan dispute over the Senkaku Islands, and the Russia-Japan dispute over the Kurile Islands. This is the biggest frustration for participants in ARF discussions.

The Role of Nongovernmental Organizations (NGOs)

The activities of nongovernmental organizations (NGOs) concerned with Pacific Basin economic issues were critical to the APEC process. The most important of these NGOs was the Pacific Basin Economic Council (PBEC), established in 1967 to provide a dialogue forum for businessmen concerned with "the creation and maintenance of a public policy climate favorable to the orderly and profitable conduct of commercial transactions";[56] the Pacific Trade and Development Conference (PAFTAD), initiated in 1968 and described as "the intellectual driving force of the cooperation movement";[57] and the Pacific Economic Cooperation Conference (PECC). In addition to these three principal organizations, there were a myriad others of lesser endurance or profile which supported and complemented them. As Lawrence Woods argued, the activities of these NGOs with respect to the initiation of the APEC process "demonstrate the virtues and shortcomings of a non-governmental approach to regional diplomacy."[58]

These NGOs contributed to the APEC process in several critical ways. They developed and disseminated ideas and stimulated the discussion that engendered the process. They conducted technical economic studies and analyses, showing the benefits of liberalization of trade in the region, either through formal free trade arrangements or "open regionalism." They demonstrated to government officials that meaningful and productive dialogue on complex policy matters is possible notwithstanding the extraordinary disparity in the sizes and interests of the numerous parties involved. Some of them (especially the PECC) explicitly structured themselves to involve government officials in this dialogue, even in unofficial capacities. PECC even engaged in negotiations to resolve differences between states that arose during the dialogue process.[59] By providing forums for unofficial dialogue, the NGOs contributed to greater official interaction and enhanced mutual confidence, as well as providing a sound "building block" for supporting cooperative arrangements at the official level.

The contribution which NGOs can make to the processes of regional cooperation is limited by the amount of respect and official confidence NGOs command. Individuals such as Saburo Okita and Kiyoshi Kojima in Japan and Sir John Crawford in Australia, who were at the forefront of greater Asia-Pacific economic cooperation, enjoyed high public stature. It is unclear whether there are comparable individuals or organizations committed to regional security cooperation.

The appropriate relationship between NGOs and government agencies is a complex and difficult matter. As Lawrence Woods noted, in order to contribute to the processes of regional cooperation, NGOs "need to attract and maintain state interest, state support and state involvement," but they must also preserve their independence and avoid state control.[60]

CONCLUSIONS

The systemic category of the relationship between economics and security determines the basic structure of a regional security system. The functionalist dimension of the systemic category describes the behavioral dynamics of the system, and in particular the systemic tendencies towards the use of force as opposed to cooperative mechanisms for conflict resolution. On the other hand, international political and security processes and outcomes cannot be fully explained in economic terms. Policymakers are not economic automatons. Policies are made and decisions are taken on the basis of a multitude of beliefs, values, perceptions, and interests which cannot be reduced to economic terms. Cultural factors and power-political considerations (which run the whole gamut from leadership struggles through regime maintenance to calculations of national interests) are just as important.

Structures and processes for political and security cooperation are not autonomous functions of economic variables. They are, at least as much, the product of policies and decisions made on other grounds. In the creation of new security discourses and constructs, however, the instrumental category of the economics-security relationship has much to offer. On the one hand, the utilitarian dimension of the instrumental category provides an opportunity to use the myriad networks, consultations, study groups, and dialogue forums which are attendant upon high degrees of economic interdependence for the discussion, negotiation and resolution of common and important security-related economic issues. And, on the other hand, the cognitive dimension of the instrumental category can provide prescriptions for new policy formation and implementation based on diagnosis of experience with regional economic cooperation. It is likely that the instrumental devices can be just as potent and profound as the systemic forces in shaping the mechanisms and processes for regional security cooperation.

The analogical lessons or "cognitive map" drawn from the experience with Asia-Pacific economic cooperation are fairly clear. There must be a sufficient degree of functional interaction, whether occasioned by economic interdependence or common security concerns, to demand cooperative modalities. Moreover, objective conditions must be commonly perceived and appreciated by the relevant policymakers. There are evident virtues in patience, pragmatism, modesty, and doing business "the Asian way." Extraordinary regional diversity and the existence of deep sensitivities must be appreciated at the outset. Informal arrangements and processes are likely to be more productive than formal plans or organizational structures. The institutionalization of dialogue—or, in Mahathir bin Mohamad's words, "the tedious [process] of getting to know each other"—is a fundamental building block.[61] Nongovernmental activities and institutional linkages, now generally referred to as the "second track" process, provide critical support to the official mechanisms of dialogue and cooperation.[62]

An important recent initiative in regional security cooperation, which takes explicit direction from this "cognitive map," is the establishment of the Council for Security Cooperation in the Asia Pacific (CSCAP).[63] Conceived at a meeting of representatives of key regional strategic studies institutes in November 1992 and formally announced at the *Seventh Asia–Pacific Roundtable on Confidence Building and Conflict Reduction in the Pacific* in Kuala Lumpur on 9 June 1993, CSCAP is designed to provide "a more structured regional process of a non-governmental nature...to contribute to the efforts towards regional confidence building and enhancing regional security through dialogues, consultations and cooperation."[64]

Three essential themes permeated the establishment of CSCAP. The first was that the Council should be a nongovernmental institution that involves government officials, albeit in their private capacities. The second was acceptance of the need to build on extant arrangements in the region wherever possible rather than construct new structures and processes. The third theme derived directly from the experience of NGOs such as the Pacific Trade and Development Conference (PAFTAD) and the Pacific Economic Cooperation Council (PECC). Many of the institutions involved in the establishment of CSCAP also are actively involved in the PAFTAD and PECC processes. Several of the institutions serve as coordinators of their national PECC committees. CSCAP is intended to support official forums concerned with regional security dialogue and cooperation, such as the ASEAN Post-Ministerial conferences (PMC), the ASEAN Regional Forum (ARF) and the Senior Officials Meetings (SOMs), in much the same way that PECC supports the APEC process. The establishment of CSCAP national committees and working groups closely reflects those established in the PECC process in terms of their operational activities.

Expectations concerning the prospects for CSCAP must be modest. It has taken three years of discussion of regional security cooperation to get this far, and difficult issues remain, such as the incorporation of China (and Taiwan) into the CSCAP process. However, the second track process now has acquired considerable momentum and security concerns in the region are likely to intensify rather than enervate. More conscious exploitation of the instrumental category of the economics-security relationship only serves to enhance its prospects. For example, consideration might be given to the establishment of a joint CSCAP-PECC Working Group on economics and security. This not only provides a mechanism for institutionalizing the utilitarian dimension of the economics-security relationship, but it also enshrines the cognitive dimension into the processes of security cooperation. Ultimately, it ensures that the emerging security architecture of the Asia-Pacific region is one of enduring cooperative and comprehensive security.

NOTES

1. Khoo Kheng-Hor, ed., and Hwang Chung-Mee, trans. *Sun Tzu's Art of War* (Petaling Jaya, Malaysia: Pelanduk Publications, 1992), p. 51.
2. Wolfowitz, Paul. Testimony to the Senate Armed Services Committee, April 1990.
3. These postulates have been challenged by Barry Buzan, who has argued that liberal structures can also stimulate the use of force while mercantilist structures can be benign; and that, in any case, economic factors are relatively unimportant in determining the broader issues of war and peace. See Barry Buzan, "Economic Structure and International Security: The Limits of the Liberal Case," *International Organization*, 38:4 (Autumn 1984), p. 597. Moreover, the Cold War international economic order differed significantly from any previous order in that it featured "bloc actors sufficiently large to contain most of the resources and markets needed by their industrial cores,"

and hence it should be able to effectively suppress the more malevolent tendencies of mercantilism. Ibid., p. 613.

4. Joan Edelman Spero, *The Politics of International Economic Relations*, second edition (New York: St. Martin's Press, 1981), p. 75. See also Robert Gilpin, "Economic Interdependence and National Security in Historical Perspective," in Klaus Knorr and Frank Trager, eds., *Economic Issues and National Security*, (Lawrence, KS: University of Kansas Press, 1977), p. 55; and L.B. Krause and J.S. Nye, "Reflections on the Economics and Politics of International Economic Organizations," in C.F. Bergsten and L.B. Krause, eds., *World Politics and International Economics* (Washington, DC: The Brookings Institution, 1975), p. 324.

5. See Ernst B. Haas, *Beyond the Nation State. Functionalism and International Organization* (Stanford, CA: Stanford University Press, 1964), p. 48; and Ernst B. Haas, "International Integration: The European and the Universal Process," *International Organization* 15:3 (Summer 1961), 366-392. For a discussion of the *neofunctionalist* approach and the "spill-over" phenomenon in the context of proposals for Asia-Pacific economic cooperation, see Han Sung-po, "Political Conditions of Pacific Regional Cooperation: Theoretical and Practical Considerations," in Hadi Soesastro and Han Sungjoo, eds., *Pacific Economic Cooperation: The Next Phase* (Jakarta: Centre for Strategic and International Studies, 1983), pp. 63-64.

6. Sir John Crawford, "The Pacific Basin Co-operative Concept," in Sir John Crawford and Greg Seow, eds., *Pacific Economic Cooperation: Suggestions for Action* (Singapore: Heinemann Educational Books (Asia) Ltd., 1981), p. 38.

7. See Dwain Mefford, "Analogical Reasoning and the Definition of the Situation: Back to Snyder for Concepts and Forward to Artificial Intelligence for Method," in Charles F. Hermann, Charles W. Kegley, Jr., and James N. Rosenau, eds., *New Directions in the Study of Foreign Policy* (Boston: Allen & Unwin, 1987), pp. 225-230.

8. See Yuen Foon Khong, *Analogies at War: Korea, Munich, Dien Bien Phu, and the Vietnam Decisions of 1965* (Princeton, NJ: Princeton University Press, 1992), Chapters 1 and 2; and Charles A. Powell, Helen E. Purkitt and James W. Dyson, "Opening the Black Box: Cognitive Processing and Optimal Choice in Foreign Policy Decision Making," in Charles F. Hermann, Charles W. Kegley, Jr., and James N. Rosenau, eds., *New Directions in the Study of Foreign Policy*, Chapter 11.

9. See Ross Garnaut, *Australia and the Northeast Asian Ascendancy*, (Canberra: Australian Government Publishing Service, 1989), pp. 3-5; and Peter Drysdale, "Australia's Asia-Pacific Economic Diplomacy," *Current Affairs Bulletin* 66:10 (March 1990), p. 14-15.

10. See Andrew Elek, "Asia Pacific Economic Co-operation (APEC)," *Southeast Asian Affairs 1991* (Singapore: Institute of Southeast Asian Studies, 1991), p. 38; and Peter Drysdale, "Open Regionalism: A Key to East Asia's Economic Future," *Pacific Economic Papers no.197* (Canberra: Australia-Japan Research Centre, Australian National University, July 1991).

11. Cited in "APEC Now Region's Top Forum," *The Canberra Times*, 30 November 1991, p. 14.

12. Cited in Peter Stephens, "U.S. Proposal to Expand APEC," *The Age*, 1 November 1991, p.

8.

13. Ibid.

14. Andrew Elek, "Asia Pacific Economic Co-operation (APEC)," *Southeast Asian Affairs 1991*, (Singapore: Institute of Southeast Asian Studies, 1991), p. 34.

15. Gregory Clark, "A Trade Bloc Divorced From Reality," *The Australian*, 1 November 1989, p. 11.

16. M.G.G. Pillai, "ASEAN Won't Be Rushed Into a Pacific Rim League," *The Canberra Times*, 28 July,1989, p. 9.

17. See Sarah Sargent, "Canberra's Courtship of ASEAN Put to Test," *Australian Financial Review*, 3 November 1989, p. 17.

18. See "Australia: An Asia-Pacific Approach to Freer World Trade," *Australian Financial Review*, 25 May 1989, p. 14.

19. See, for example, Hadi Soesastro, "Institutional Aspects of Pacific Economic Cooperation," in Hadi Soesastro and Han Sung-joo, eds., *Pacific Economic Cooperation: The Next Phase* (Jakarta: Centre for Strategic and International Studies, October 1983), p. 12; and Russell H. Fifield, "ASEAN and the Pacific Community," *Asia Pacific Community*, no.11 (Winter 1981), pp. 14-15.

20. Mohamed Ariff, "Introduction," in Mohamed Ariff, *The Pacific Economy: Growth and External Stability* (Sydney: Allen & Unwin, 1991), p. 1; William E. James, "Basic Directions and Areas for Cooperation: Structural Issues of the Asia-Pacific Economies," in Jang-Won Suh and Jae-Bong Ro, eds., *Asia–Pacific Economic Cooperation: The Way Ahead* (Seoul: Korea Institute for International economic Policy, 1990), pp. 61-65; and Fu-chen Lo, "Comment," in Jang-Won Suh and Jae-Bong Ro, op.cit., p. 47.

21. Secretary of State James Baker, "A New Pacific Partnership: Framework for the Future," (Address to the Asia Society, New York, 26 June 1989), in *Department of State Bulletin* 89:2149 (August 1989), p. 65.

22. Mahathir bin Mohamad, "Tak Kenal Maka Tak Cinta," in *Asia–Pacific in the 1980s: Towards Greater Symmetry in Economic Interdependence* (Jakarta: Centre for Strategic and International Studies, May 1980), p. 22.

23. See Lawrence B. Krause, "Highlights of the Korea University Workshop on the Pacific Community," *Pacific Community Newsletter* 1:2 (Summer 1981), cited in Hadi Soesastro, "Institutional Aspects of Pacific Economic Cooperation," in Hadi Soesastro and Han Sung-joo, op. cit., p. 11.

24. See Hadi Soesastro, "Institutional Aspects of Pacific Economic Cooperation," in Hadi Soesastro and Han Sung-joo, op. cit., p. 7.

25. M.G.G. Pillai, "ASEAN Won't Be Rushed Into a Pacific Rim League," *The Canberra Times*, 28 July 1989, p. 9.

26. Gareth Evans, "Security in the Asia Pacific Region," *International Defense Review* (1992), p. 44.

27. See Tom Ormonde, "APEC's Search for Achievement," *Sydney Morning Herald*, 11 November 1991, p. 16.

28. See "Summary Report of Proceedings and Main Recommendations," in Sir John Crawford and Greg Seow, op. cit., p. 29.

29. *Asia–Pacific in the 1980s: Toward Greater Symmetry in Economic Interdependence A Report* (Jakarta: Centre for Strategic and International Studies, 1980), p. 27.

30. Mahathir bin Mohamad, op. cit., p. 18.

31. Derek Davies, "The Pacific Community: Hands Across the Sea," *Far Eastern Economic Review*, 29 February 1980, p. 35.

32. See Peter Drysdale, "Prospects for Economic Cooperation Among Pacific Basin Countries," in Hadi Soesastro and Han Sung-joo, op. cit., p. 86.

33. Andrew Elek, "Asia Pacific Economic Co-operation (APEC)," *Southeast Asian Affairs 1991* (Singapore: Institute of Southeast Asian Studies, 1991), p. 38.

34. See, for example, Hadi Soesastro, "Institutional Aspects of Pacific Economic Cooperation," in Hadi Soesastro and Han Sung-joo, op. cit., pp. 44-45; Derek Davies, "The Pacific Community: Hands Across The Sea," *Far Eastern Economic Review*, 29 February 1980, pp. 34-35; and Helen Elster, "Slow Start in the Pacific," *Far Eastern Economic Review*, 26 September 1980, pp. 90-91.

   For a critique of Australia's leadership role in the APEC process, see Richard A. Higgot, Andrew Fenton Cooper and Jenelle Bonnor, "Asia-Pacific Economic Cooperation: An Evolving Case Study in Leadership and Cooperation Building," *International Journal* 45:4 (Autumn 1990), especially pp. 845-851.

35. See Hadi Soesastro, "Institutional Aspects of Pacific Economic Cooperation," in Hadi Soesastro and Han Sungjoo, op. cit., p. 10.

36. Ibid.

37. Ibid.

38. Bernard K. Gordon, *Toward Disengagement in Asia: A Strategy for American Foreign Policy* (Englewood Cliffs, NJ: Prentice-Hall, Inc., 1969), pp. 66-67.

39. Wendy Dobson, "APEC: Redefining the Region?" (Paper prepared for an international conference on *Southeast Asia. Challenges of the 21st Century* (Singapore: Institute of Southeast Asian Studies, 29 August-1 September 1993), pp. 2, 12. See also Derwin Pereira and Martin Soong, "APEC Can 'Help Counter Major Economic Players'," *The Straits Times*, 2 September 1993, p. 12.

40. See Kiyoshi Kojima, "A Pacific Economic Community and Asian Developing Countries," *Hitotsubashi Journal of Economics* 7:1 (June 1966), pp. 17-37; Kiyoshi Kojima, ed., *Pacific Trade and Development* (Tokyo: The Japan Economic Research Center, Center Paper no.9, February 1968); Kiyoshi Kojima, *Japan and a Pacific Free Trade Area*, (Berkeley, CA: University of California Press, 1971); and Kiyoshi Kojima, *Japan and a New World Economic Order*, (Boulder, CO: Westview Press, 1977), especially Chapter 8.

41. Kiyoshi Kojima, *Japan and a New World Economic Order*, pp. 173-174. See also Hadi Soesastro, "Institutional Aspects of Pacific Economic Cooperation," in Hadi Soesastro and Han Sung-joo, op. cit., p. 30.

42. Peter Drysdale, "Prospects for Economic Cooperation Among Pacific Basin Countries," in Hadi Soesastro and Han Sung-Joo, op. cit., p. 88.

43. Cited in Hadi Soesastro, "Institutional Aspects of Pacific Economic Cooperation", in Hadi Soesastro and Han Sung-joo, op. cit., pp. 6, 34.

44. See Sir John Crawford and Greg Seow, op. cit.

45. Andrew Elek, "Asia Pacific Economic Co-operation (APEC)," *Southeast Asian Affairs 1991*, (Singapore: Institute of Southeast Asian Studies, 1991), p. 38.

46. Cited in Sarah Sargent, "Canberra's Courtship of ASEAN Put to Test," *Australian Financial Review*, 3 November 1989, p. 17.

47. Mahathir bin Mohamad, op. cit., p. 18.

48. "Chairman's Summary of APEC II Meeting," Singapore, November 1989, cited in Andrew Elek, op. cit., p. 45.

49. Andrew Elek, op. cit., p. 38.

50. Cited in Michelle Grattan and Carmel McCauley, "Hawke Pushes for Regional Economic Body," *The Age*, 1 February 1989, p. 5.

51. Daniel Sneider, "Pacific Rim Nations Strengthen Economic Ties," *Christian Science Monitor*, 6 November 1989, pp. 10-11.

52. See John Edwards, "U.S. Set to Join New Trading Group," *Sydney Morning Herald*, 18 March 1989, p. 3.

53. James A. Baker, "America in Asia: Emerging Architecture for a Pacific Community," *Foreign Affairs* 70:5 (Winter 1991/92), pp. 5, 6.

54. See Tom Ormonde, "APEC's Search for Achievement," *Sydney Morning Herald*, 11 November 1991, p. 16.

55. Ibid.

56. Lawrence T. Woods, "Non-governmental Organizations and Pacific Cooperation: Back to the Future?," *The Pacific Review* 4:4 (1991), p. 315.

57. Ibid., p. 313.

58. Ibid., p. 312.

59. Ibid., p. 317.

60. Ibid., p. 319.

61. Mahathir bin Mohamad, op. cit., p. 18.

62. See Desmond Ball, "Tasks for Security Cooperation in Asia," in Desmond Ball, Richard L. Grant and Jusuf Wanandi, *Security Cooperation in the Asia–Pacific Region* (Washington, DC: The Center for Strategic and International Studies, 1993), pp. 31-32.

63. See Desmond Ball, "The Council for Security Cooperation in the Asia Pacific," *Asia–Pacific Defense Reporter*, 20:6/7 (December 1993/January 1994), pp. 20-23.

64. "Seoul Statement on Security Cooperation in the Asia-Pacific," in Desmond Ball, Richard L. Grant and Jusuf Wanandi, op. cit., pp. 36-38.

4 Linkages between Asia-Pacific Regional Economic and Security Relations: Emerging Trends in the Post-Cold War Era

K.S. Nathan

Introduction: Confronting the Challenge of Change in Asia-Pacific International Relations

How has the end of the Cold War influenced the course of economic and security relations in the new era? Has the end of U.S.-Soviet competition provided a new foundation for regional relations? This chapter will attempt to identify the principal post-Cold War trends in the Asia-Pacific region and analyze their character in terms of possible linkages that exist between economic and security issues. More specifically, the chapter will consider from the perspective of Southeast Asian countries in the Association of Southeast Asian Nations (ASEAN), the strategic implications of regional economic and political institutions for future security arrangements in the region.

The chapter highlights how security concerns shape economic relationships. The picture it describes is a complex and somewhat contradictory one. On the one hand, the Cold War legacy is still felt by ASEAN—which was created primarily to protect Southeast Asian nations from communist aggression by strengthening security ties with the West, particularly the United States. Most of the Southeast Asian nations prefer forms of regional cooperation that bridge the Pacific and involve the United States in part because they seek to maintain a U.S. security presence in the region. On the other hand, the development of regional cooperation on both economic and security matters reflects changes in the security environment facing Southeast Asians. The Soviet threat disappeared and the United States may not be able to sustain a continued military presence in the region. Regional efforts that engage Japan and China in peaceful cooperation with their neighbors may help prevent new regional conflicts or the emergence of a new regional hegemon. Both the persistence of the Cold War and these new security concerns illustrate the influence of security concerns of regional governments on the way they cooperate on economic affairs. At the same time, economic interactions also influence regional security relations.

The Relevance of Existing Strategic Linkages for Post-Cold War Asia-Pacific Security

The patterns of political and economic cooperation and conflict characteristic of the Cold War continue to dominate the nature of international interactions. This broad generalization may be tested using regional phenomena that have emerged during the Cold War, and have developed and matured over the past three to four decades. All prevailing regional patterns and formations demonstrate the strong nexus between economic and security relations. It would be both relevant and useful to examine the major informal and institutionalized patterns of economic cooperation that have important consequences for Asia-Pacific regional security:

(a)   ASEAN or the Association of Southeast Asian Nations;

(b)   PECC (Pacific Economic Cooperation Conference), as an informal consultative mechanism for major Asia-Pacific economic actors;

(c)   APEC (Asia-Pacific Economic Cooperation) as an attempt to give more formal expression to regional economic processes; and

(d)   EAEG/EAEC (East Asia Economic Grouping/Caucus) representing more selective concerns of some states in the region.

ASEAN and Regional Security in Southeast Asia

The emergence of ASEAN[1] as a regional actor in Southeast Asia cannot be divorced from the principal strategic trends dictated by the Cold War (1947-89). This regional organization has, over the years, established conclusively that the motivating factors for regional cooperation are more ideological, political, and strategic, and less economic or social. The birth, development, and maturity of ASEAN regional cooperation represents a classic model of confidence building and conflict reduction in international relations—a model that continues to maintain its validity and vitality into the post-Cold War era. As I wrote in 1988, "perceptions by national actors that regionalism best serves the national interest in terms of enhancing domestic political and economic stability as well as regional security have strengthened trends toward greater regional cooperation in Southeast Asia."[2]

What then are the linkages that ASEAN has established that are relevant for regional economic and security management in Pacific Asia after the Cold War? First, ASEAN as a regional experiment cannot be discussed in isolation from three preceding regional arrangements, SEATO (Southeast Asia Treaty organization, 1954), ASA (Association of Southeast Asia, 1961), and MAPHILINDO (a loose ethnocultural alliance encompassing Malaysia, the Philippines, and Indonesia, 1962). Second, a dissection of all four regional patterns reveals the mix of endogenous and exogenous factors that are involved in the security scenario of Southeast Asia in particular, and the Asian region as a whole. ASEAN-based postindependence nationalism was a product of Western influence as much as of the Cold War. The micro-processes involved in national, post-independence consolidation invariably combined with the macro-processes unleashed by the politics of superpower rivalry between the capitalist-oriented United States and the communist-oriented Soviet Union. Third, regional conceptions of security reflected the growing impact of the alternative ideological systems available to mankind, and the inevitable necessity of choice. Economic and political security cannot be separated from the region's relationship with external powers. Finally, the balance of advantage in postwar Southeast Asia tended to favor the West over the Soviet Union and the Communist bloc—a trend invariably strengthened by the United States' preponderance in world affairs.

The ASEAN countries adopted a pro-Western orientation to ensure strategic survival. This basic pro-United States orientation in external relations, as well as the foreign and defense policies derived from it continue today and are likely to influence ASEAN approaches to regional security in the post-Cold War era. The two main features of this strategic link to the West can be identified in terms of (1) the bilateral and multilateral security relationships of ASEAN countries, and (2) the pattern of the regional entity's external economic links.

ASEAN's Security Relations

ASEAN members entered individually into bilateral and multilateral security treaties to augment internal and external security. SEATO served as the multilateral security framework although only two Southeast Asian states were formal members (Thailand and the Philippines). Except for North Vietnam, the rest of Southeast Asia fell within the defense perimeter envisaged by the Manila Pact of September 1954. The element of voluntarism was missing in the initial stages. Nevertheless, the military-oriented regionalism of SEATO created the necessary political and ideological foundation for future indigenously motivated patterns of regional cooperation. The 6-member ASEAN body represents this pattern of cooperation in the security, political, economic, and sociocultural dimensions.

That this pattern of strategic cooperation with strong linkages to the West will persist into the twenty-first century is borne out by recent evidence concerning how the U.S. strategic presence in the Western Pacific is being integrated into ASEAN defense planning. President George Bush's January 1992 visit to Singapore—

which earlier signed a Memorandum of Understanding (MOU) with the United States in November 1990 on the use of Singaporean territory by U.S. military forces—is an indication of the mutuality of interests and commitments by the United States and ASEAN. However, differences exist within ASEAN over the implications of the U.S. military presence in Singapore in terms of how it impacts upon the progressive implementation of ZOPFAN (Zone of Peace, Freedom, and Neutrality) and NWFZ (Nuclear Weapons-Free Zone). The Philippines welcomes the new deployment as a contribution towards burden sharing of regional security, whereas Indonesia views it as a contravention of the ZOPFAN principle.[3] Nevertheless, the closure of U.S. bases in the Philippines enabled greater security cooperation between U.S. and ASEAN security officials through the provision of repair and replenishment facilities to support the presence and maintenance of U.S. strategic power in Southeast Asia.[4] ASEAN would prefer the continuity of the economic and political balance provided by U.S. trade and investments in the region as well as the network of U.S. and Western security commitments to reduce the element of uncertainty in the post-Cold War regional balance of power.[5] This element of uncertainty stems from the prospective role of major Asian powers (China, Japan, and India) in the post-Cold War era in the wake of a declining Pax Americana.

This ASEAN consensus on the strategic importance of maintaining a U.S. security umbrella in Southeast Asia may be diluted by the sheer pace of global change (the Gulf War, collapse of the Soviet Union and its empire, emergence of the United States as the single superpower, and the European Community's (EC) increasing size and potential).[6] Additionally, the Sino-Soviet, Sino-Vietnamese, and ASEAN-Vietnamese rapprochements, the prospect of a more benign Japanese political and security role, and a global retrenchment by the United States, could encourage the ASEAN states to adopt a more multilateral approach to security to complement their traditional security ties to the west.

A reflection of this reassessment is found in ASEAN's move to broaden in regional and global security ties. At the Fourth ASEAN Summit (27-28 January 1992), Singapore proposed that the five permanent members of the UN Security Council accede to the Treaty of Amity and Cooperation (TAC) signed at the First Summit in 1976 held in Bali, Indonesia. The hosts even suggested that ASEAN consider multilateralizing security arrangements using the machinery of the PMC (Post Ministerial Conference). The PMC mechanism symbolizes the regional body's informal approach to regional security in which all the major external actors have the opportunity to provide inputs in a presumably non-confrontational atmosphere. ASEAN's reluctance to formalize security arrangements in the post-Cold War era stems from a desire to avoid polarizing the Asian security environment. The Singapore Summit also approved India and China as ASEAN's new dialogue partners, in addition to the existing seven (USA, Japan, Canada, EC, Australia, New Zealand, and South Korea).[7] Partially in response to the ASEAN initiative, the Clinton administration at first was ready "to drop its policy of seeking a sole leadership role in Asian security and instead form within five years a multinational system which like the CSCE seeks to secure regional peace and stability."[8] But since then, the United States lead on signing the 1994 accord with North Korea and its decision in 1995 to postpone initial troop withdrawals from the region indicate this policy may have changed.

U.S. approval of the Conference on Security Cooperation in Asia (CSCA) framework would, in a very important sense, address ASEAN concerns that post-Cold War security in Asia must involve the greater participation of Japan as a major strategic actor. A certain degree of progress in linking political, economic, and security issues was seen in the creation via the PMC mechanism at its annual foreign ministers meeting in Singapore (23-24 July 1993) of a regional security forum—the ASEAN Regional Forum (ARF)—to address the common concerns of extraregional and intraregional powers. In July 1994, ASEAN held the first ARF meeting, demonstrating that it had finally dropped its reluctance to discuss regional security concerns in official multilateral settings. The three-hour meeting established agenda items for future ARF discussions: "preventive diplomacy," increased transparency, confidence and security building measures (CSBMs), nuclear non-proliferation, regional peacekeeping, exchange of military information, maritime security, and preemptive prevention of conflict.

Thus, For the first time, concrete security issues are to be considered by the ASEAN Six, its seven dialogue partners, three observers, and two consultative partners-comprising a total of 18 participants.[9] Particularly significant is the fact that the inclusion of China and Russia "has brought together for the first time all the major powers in the Asia-Pacific region."[10]

The major problem of a multilateral forum that includes so many members as ARF is the lack of discussion of existing problems, notably those involving a more assertive China (Taiwanese independence; Spratly Islands dispute). The regional entity's resolve to assert some control over the uncertain post-Cold War regional security order first found expression in the ASEAN Declaration on the South China Sea, adopted at its annual ministerial meeting in Manila (July 1992). Fearing China's military assertions and desire for control over the contested Spratlys, the ASEAN ministers "wanted to lay down a political statement to arrest any possible military takeover by one of the claimants, particularly China."[11] Thereafter, Chinese Foreign Minister Qian Qichen announced at the July 1995 meeting of ASEAN ministers that while the PRC maintained "indisputable sovereignty" over the disputed Spratly Islands, for the first time it expressed a willingness "to work together with the countries concerned to resolve appropriately the relevant disputes according to the recognized international law....Joint development is the most realistic and practical way of handling the dispute."[12]

There is also evidence of growing regional confidence to expand ASEAN to include all ten Southeast Asian states, that is, the ASEAN Six plus Cambodia, Laos, Vietnam, and Burma. With all ten states in ASEAN, there is also the stronger possibility of indigenizing regional security management with minimal outside (Western) assistance or interference, and increased participation by the three major Asian powers: China, India, and Japan.[13] Thus a post-Cold War Southeast Asia might well exhibit close linkages between conflict reduction, conflict settlement, self-reliance, and enhanced confidence in regional security management.

ASEAN's External Economic Orientation

The linkages in Southeast Asian-Pacific economic and security relations can also be observed from the pattern of ASEAN's external economic relations. The regional entity's major trading partners (accounting for more than 80 percent of total ASEAN trade) are invariably the Western countries (United States, European Community, Canada, Australia, and New Zealand) and Northeast Asia (Japan, South Korea, and Taiwan). In 1991, intra-ASEAN trade accounted for only 18.8 percent of total trade, whereas trade with the United States was 16.3 percent, with the EC (14.3 percent), Canada (one percent), Australia (2.6 percent), New Zealand (0.4 percent), Japan (21.0 percent), while the newly industrialized economies (NIEs) (China, Hong Kong, Taiwan, and Korea) constituted 13.3 percent of ASEAN's total trade.[14] Northeast Asia is also closely linked to the United States via economic and security relationships. Economic ties to the United States and Japan will continue to significantly influence the pattern and direction of Southeast Asia's external political, economic, and strategic relations into the twenty-first century.

PECC AND INFORMAL ECONOMIC REGIONALISM

The economic dynamism and interdependence in Asia has also driven the development of regional cooperation. The demand for regional consultations on economic issues had already emerged in the early 1980s, even while the Cold War still simmered. The tripartite consultative process among the Asia-Pacific economies grouping together three segments (government officials, businessmen, and academics), began in the midst of the revival of the Cold War following the Vietnamese invasion of Cambodia in December 1978 and the Soviet invasion of Afghanistan in December 1979. That these two major Cold War developments did not stifle initiative for broader economic consultations testified to the fact of increasing economic integration of the Asia-Pacific economies. For instance, the share of Asia-Pacific destinations in the exports of Asia-Pacific countries rose significantly from 54 percent in 1970 to 66 percent in 1987, while the volume of intra-regional trade in terms of both imports and exports increased more than ten times during 1970-87.[15] In 1950, East Asia was only one-sixth the size of the U.S. economy, but by 1980, the total GDP of East Asia was 59 percent that of the three NAFTA countries (USA, Canada, and Mexico) and of Western Europe (EC plus AFTA). However, by 1990, East Asia's economy was 66 percent as large as the NAFTA countries and 73 percent that of Western Europe.[16]

The role of the NGOs (nongovernmental organizations) in building and strengthening linkages beyond the economic realm became more central to broader security considerations. The depoliticized atmosphere created by NGOs is more conducive to less emotive discussions of sensitive issues affecting international relations than official arenas such as the ASEAN Regional Forum (ARF).

The PECC forum, which began in Canberra in 1980 with the objective of encouraging tripartite consultations among government officials, business leaders, and academics, "has successfully mobilized forces that really count in the region to chart out a new course towards what the participating countries believe to be the Pacific Century."[17] The organization's original membership of 12 was increased to 21 at the tenth international general meeting of the Pacific Economic Cooperation Council in Kuala Lumpur, Malaysia (22-24 March 1994).[18] Significantly, this meeting adopted the Kuala Lumpur Concord on Open Regionalism, emphasizing the need to "establish processes and instrumentalities for studying and monitoring the development of protectionism and liberalization in the Pacific and elsewhere."[19] As a barometer of the nature of evolution of Pacific economic relations, the PECC progressed on the discussion of several trade issues which have an important bearing on security for several key regional actors such as ASEAN. Underdevelopment is viewed as a condition of insecurity, so that the concept of economic development became closely associated with national and regional security in the developing world. As one analyst observed: "the search for economic development was a cohesive factor in the region in thinking about economic cooperation, not just for its own sake but as a major security concern."[20]

The original PECC agenda (1980) established five priority areas of cooperation in the context of challenges arising from growing regional economic interdependence: (1) trade, including market access problems and structural adjustment associated with industrialization in developing countries; (2) direct investment, including guidelines for investors and harmonization of foreign investment policies; (3) energy, including access to market assurance of continued supply, alternative forms, conservation, and research exchanges; (4) Pacific marine resources; and (5) international services such as transportation, communication, and educational exchanges.[21] These areas of functional cooperation are expected to strengthen institutional linkages between policymakers, traders, and academics whose experience and expertise are brought into a common forum to address common issues. The PECC process was preceded by an awareness of the critical need to build consultative mechanisms and processes to address the anticipated phenomenal expansion of the Pacific economy. The Pacific Trade and Development (PAFTAD) idea (1968) of establishing a free trade area in the Pacific region, and the Pacific Basin Economic Council (PBEC, 1969) represent earlier private attempts to expand information flows and professional contacts with a hope of influencing governmental policies.

The PECC can be viewed as an ongoing CBM (confidence building measure) that provides a vehicle for the convergence of diverse regional perceptions, interests, and projects to foster multilateral free trade and outward looking rather than defensive forms of cooperation.[22] In the Asia-Pacific region after the Cold War, the PECC is positively viewed as a vehicle that facilitates "Pacific partnership for cooperative peace and prosperity" as the primacy of economics puts a premium on political cooperation for economic development.[23] The region's continued economic dynamism will serve as a platform for new and expanded forms of cooperation as envisaged in the original PECC agenda. The formation of the Triple-T (tourism, telecommunications, and transportation) task force by the PECC at its annual project meeting in Kuala Lumpur (22-23 June 1993) is aimed at "easing the flow of goods, people, money, information, and technology across the Pacific."[24]

Another NGO, the PBEC is steadily upgrading its role as a major actor for the post-Cold War era. At its twenty-sixth international general meeting in Seoul (May 1993), this multinational organization comprising more than 900 companies located in the 15 member countries emphasized "the basis of cooperation in the Pacific region should be compatibility rather than exclusivity so as not to jeopardize extra-regional ties."[25]

APEC AND THE BROADENING OF INSTITUTIONAL LINKAGES

Initiatives for the creation of institutionalized forms of economic cooperation among Asia-Pacific countries were launched in apparent anticipation of changing global trends. One of these principal trends in the Pacific region is the economic vitality of pro-United States regimes—governments that initially could not have survived without the United States' support, but which were able to demonstrate impressive economic and political resilience using the capitalist-democratic framework as an instrument in their development. By the decade of the 1980s, the Four Tigers (South Korea, Taiwan, Hong Kong, and Singapore) had begun to have a significant economic impact upon the Asia-Pacific. Following the same path, the ASEAN states (with the possible exception of the Philippines) proved to be success stories of development, stability, and prosperity based on the same free enterprise model. Meanwhile, the war in Cambodia following the Vietnamese invasion in 1978 rendered the socialist model less and less attractive to Southeast Asians, who were inclined to link socialism to war and misery, and capitalism to peace and development. It is not surprising that APEC and PECC would incorporate the ideas of free market economies while isolating command economies. This market orientation dominated Asia-Pacific economic regionalism and reinforced existing security ties with the United States.

APEC groups together the most dynamic economies of the Asia-Pacific region.[26] Initially, the APEC forum comprised 12 countries: 10 from the region (Japan, South Korea, Australia, New Zealand, and the ASEAN six), and two members from outside the region (the United States and Canada). However, in light of growing economic liberalization in the PRC and the impressive performance of Taiwan and Hong Kong, APEC membership was expanded to 15 at the Third APEC Ministerial meeting in Seoul (November 1991). The inclusion of China, Taiwan, and Hong Kong into APEC cannot be divorced from the political consideration of encouraging a peaceful resolution of Hong Kong's return to China's jurisdiction in 1997. Economic regionalism, it is hoped, will stimulate attitudes and patterns of interaction away from conflict and towards confidence building and conflict reduction. Leadership in APEC provided through Japan and the United States is directed towards influencing the democratization process within the PRC, thereby enabling China to integrate more fully into the APEC process.[27] And at the fourth APEC Ministerial meeting in Seattle in November 1993, the organization's membership was increased to 17 with the inclusion of Mexico and Papua New Guinea.

APEC's open regionalism reflected Asians' desire to retain their links with the United States while strengthening economic and financial links amongst themselves. In 1992, the G4 (Japan, Australia, Singapore, and Hong Kong) held talks in Hong Kong to underscore "the growing interdependence of financial markets and economies" in the Asia-Pacific region.[28] Singapore's Minister of Trade and Industry, Lee Hsien Loong remarked at the second APEC Ministerial meeting in Singapore (July 1990) that "the idea of APEC is to prevent the formation of a dollar bloc and a yen bloc, and to keep the links across the Pacific intact."[29]

Nevertheless, the end of the Cold War provides greater scope for dissent and disagreement within the Western alliance system, and underlying economic frictions are expressed more openly and assertively with a view to altering the post-Cold war economic balance of power in favor of regionalism. Economic dynamism and regional assertiveness complement each other in the absence of other cohesive factors. Malaysia refused to participate in the U.S.-sponsored meeting of Heads of State of APEC countries in Seattle (November 1993) because the United States, and some other APEC countries, did not accept its proposal for an East Asian Economic Caucus (EAEC, a regional consultative trade forum that excluded the United States).[30] Increased political-cum-economic activism may characterize future APEC gatherings as market-driven forces encourage centrifugalism in the Asia-Pacific economic order.

At its annual summit meeting in Bogor, Indonesia in November, 1994, APEC agreed to the momentous Bogor Declaration, which set forth a timetable for establishing free trade within the Asia Pacific region by 2020. After negotiations in which Malaysia and China finally dropped their objections to the free trade timetable, the representatives from the APEC countries committed APEC's "industrialized economies" to free trade by 2010, with the remaining countries to be integrated by 2020. It also declared APEC's opposition to this process leading to an inward-looking trading bloc such as the European Economic Union.

EAEG/EAEC: The Prospect of Alternative Trade Regimes

Marked increases in resources, wealth, and prosperity in the Asia-Pacific are paralleled by trends to protect these assets based on the perception that other regions are in the process of creating trade blocs. As economic development is directly linked to political stability and regional security, Asian leaders perceive a need to collectivize regional energies to strengthen the trading interests of the East Asian nations. Existing multilateral trade mechanisms are viewed by the leaders of certain countries like Malaysia as being deficient in terms of effectively addressing the structural problems of international trade faced by developing countries. Countries that have a certain geographical proximity to one another and whose levels of economic performance promote a closer identity of interests can benefit from institutionalizing their external economic relations, especially when dealing with powerful trading blocs like the European Community. The EC set 31 December 1992 as its deadline for the completion of the internal market, with the aim of achieving a singularly high level of integration in economic, as well as political and security matters. Nevertheless, while this might be a positive development for Europe, EC integration heightened fears of rising world protectionism—a trend that is clearly detrimental to the national and regional aspirations of the newly industrialized economies (NIEs) in Asia which rely on open American and European markets. This apprehension is founded on the premise that linkages exist between economic stability and prosperity and market access in the West for the manufactures of East Asian countries. The Single European Act (1986) and the North America Free Trade Agreement (NAFTA) threaten trade diversion away from ASEAN and have triggered concerns about "the emergence of an economic cold war, a vastly complicated global struggle for economic influence where the powerful seek to dominate, even exploit the weak."[31]

The East Asia Economic Grouping (EAEG), which presumably groups together the ASEAN Six and Japan, Taiwan, South Korea, Hong Kong, and China, was proposed by Malaysian Prime Minister Dr. Mahathir Mohamad in December 1990. Serious discussion has taken place exploring its feasibility in the context of the overall Asia-Pacific regional order in the post-Cold War era. Is the idea relevant to the needs and challenges of the Asia-Pacific region after the Cold War? There is no consensus, even within ASEAN, on the composition or the timing and objectives of the East Asia Economic Grouping (which has now been renamed East Asia Economic Caucus (EAEC) to accommodate the divergent views of member states). The Fourth ASEAN Summit (January 1992) at best endorsed the idea in principle but clearly refrained from enunciating concrete measures such as committing itself to a time frame for its implementation. The perceived linkages between Asia-Pacific economic and security relations after the Cold War shaped the debate over EAEC concerning the nature of regionwide comprehensive security. Economic factors increasingly determine the concept and content of regional security in Pacific-Asia under the concept of "comprehensive security." Such a concept incorporates the notion that both national and regional security depend both upon national and regional economic resilience and sociopolitical stability.[32] This new conceptualization of security stems from ASEAN's post-Cold War fears about its traditional security reliance on the United States, as well as recognition of nonmilitary threats (cross-boundary pollution and illegal migration) and black market cross-border activities (arms smuggling and drug trafficking).

The growing interdependence of the Asia-Pacific economies in the last 15 years is giving rise to new concerns pertaining to the protection of markets, sources, and supplies. A hierarchy of dependence is clearly discernible among Japan, the NIEs, and ASEAN. The rising proportion of NIE investments in the four ASEAN states of Indonesia, Malaysia, Thailand, and the Philippines, coupled with the traditionally dominant economic role of Japan in ASEAN (relative to the U.S. and Western economies) is the new trend shaping the Asia-Pacific regional economic order. As one analyst notes, "the accumulation of foreign direct investment (FDI) has been so rapid that, by 1990, the major foreign investors in the ASEAN countries of Malaysia, Indonesia, and Thailand were Taiwan, Japan, Korea, Hong Kong, and Singapore, and had displaced the United States and Europe."[33] Contributory factors to this trend include rising wages, stronger exchange rates, land scarcity, and environmental concerns in the NIEs—all of which compel NIEs to relocate their labor-intensive industries in the ASEAN region. Dramatic increases in FDI from the NIEs to ASEAN stimulated domestic economic reform, liberalization, deregulation, and privatization in the recipient ASEAN states. These contemporary economic trends are likely to continue into the twenty-first century, reinforcing the nexus between economic growth and political stability in the Asia-Pacific region.

The overall pattern of trade and investments in the ASEAN region in favor of a larger NIE and Japanese role strengthened regional desires to build mechanisms to ensure continued political stability via rising economic prosperity. For instance, during 1987-91, investments from Japan and the Asian NIEs combined, accounted for 61.9 percent of the total $84 billion of investments into ASEAN, compared with the industrial countries' share of 15.9 percent.[34] Nevertheless, ambiguities in political and security considerations are the key factors constraining the formation of the EAEC. Key Asia-Pacific actors such as Japan and South Korea have strong security and economic ties to the United States which, along with other APEC members (Australia, New Zealand, and Canada) were excluded from Mahathir's agenda. The long-term security implications of the formation of an East Asian Economic Group that excludes the United States may be stated as follows: (1) The new regional grouping/caucus will confer legitimacy and pre-eminence to the role of Japan. (2) Japanese economic and political dominance could undercut the hitherto established role of the United States as a credible security manager of this vast region. During the last decade, Japan was the largest provider of aid to Southeast Asia, especially ASEAN, with $2.2 billion or 33 percent of total ODA (Official Development Assistance) given to Southeast Asia in 1989, as compared to $440 million in economic and military aid provided by the United States (of which $350 million went to the Philippines).[35] And given Japan's structural advantage in production, capital, and investment, the bulk of intra-ASEAN trade is accounted for by the growth of horizontal trade among Japanese offshore subsidiaries more than by export promotion by ASEAN governments.[36] (3) Additionally, existing regional economic institutions might lose their *raison d'être* in the wake of growing pressures for the creation of geographically oriented trade blocs in which Japanese dominance will be virtually unchallenged. (4) The resulting shifts in strategic perceptions of competitive rather than complementary alternative futures could precipitate trade wars which can ultimately lead to political and military conflicts—as evidenced by the U.S. economic embargo against Japan in the 1930s.

It is this fear of economic and political rivalry between Japanese and U.S.-led economic blocs which generated a congruence of perceptions and policy vis-à-vis the EAEG on the part of the United States, Japan, South Korea, as well as some ASEAN states (especially Indonesia and Thailand). Indonesia for instance would prefer the strengthening of existing regional processes (ASEAN, PECC, and APEC), as they represent concentric levels of integration of the Asia-Pacific economies without enhancing the danger of trade wars between global economic blocs. Furthermore, a continued American economic presence is considered to have a salutary effect on the economic balance of power in the region. Thailand on the other hand, prefers to renew regional efforts in the direction of establishing an ASEAN Free Trade Area (AFTA)—a scheme that is now moving towards full implementation by the turn of the twenty-first century. The EAEG concept ignores the vital and inseparable economic role, as well as the continued security role, of the United States in East Asia. Further devaluation of the American economic role in the Asia-Pacific region through the creation of exclusive trade regimes could endanger the regional economic balance. A more prudent course of action would entail the participation of both the United States and Japan as the two key political-cum-economic-cum-security actors in Asia-Pacific after the Cold War, whereby the joint and separate involvement of both best provides peace, stability, and development. However, it is pertinent to consider whether the ultimate goal and strategy of the EAEC is to activate the United States' national interests to stem the tide of isolationism and withdrawal, and ensure the United States' continued political, economic, and strategic presence as well as participation in the unfolding economic dynamism of the Asia-Pacific region.

Nevertheless, the EAEC may materialize in the not too distant future as a subregional caucus within the broader framework of Asia-Pacific regionalism, thus posing no threat to existing processes. Indeed, definitive progress was made in this direction at the July 1993 meeting of ASEAN foreign ministers in Singapore. The regional grouping achieved consensus that the EAEC will function as a caucus within APEC, but whose (EAEC) agenda would be set by the ASEAN economic ministers' meeting and not by APEC.[37] While the duplication in membership seems unavoidable in view of similar objectives pursued by APEC, an EAEC that is APEC-compatible would help stem the potential for dissent produced by the dissipation of Cold War political certainties.

LINKAGES IN CONFLICT REDUCTION AND SETTLEMENT IN SOUTHEAST ASIA

Major developments in international relations over the past seven years significantly influenced prospects for confidence building and conflict settlement in Pacific Asia. The Soviet leader's Vladivostok Speech (28 July 1986)—de-emphasizing the role of force in international relations while stressing the importance of economic relations—can, in retrospect, be viewed as a positive CBM (confidence building measure) for Asia-Pacific security and economic development. The link between changes in superpower relations at the global level and their manifestations at the regional level is evidenced by progress in Cambodia. The removal of Cambodia as a threat in the regional security agenda enabled the formation of economic linkages between ASEAN and Indochina after 1989, that is, following the formal military exit of Vietnam from Cambodian soil. ASEAN's concept of security management during the Cambodian conflict (1978-91) was supplanted by a program of conflict settlement and economic development of Indochina. All ASEAN countries, especially Thailand (given its geopolitical proximity to Indochina), are in the process of expanding and intensifying economic cooperation with Vietnam in particular, and Indochina in general. Current international participation via the United Nations is expected to create and strengthen institutional structures to produce a permanent *modus vivendi* on the part of all four Khmer factions in a postelection Cambodia.[38] To the extent that external participation in Cambodia's internal institutional processes can imbue national (Cambodian) and regional (ASEAN) confidence in the future security, stability, and development of Indochina, the linkage between security and economic development is self-evident.

The prospect of superpower restraint on one hand and a higher United Nations involvement in regional security and development reflect the changing scenario in Southeast Asia and the Asia-Pacific. UN involvement in the Cambodian peace process demonstrates the interface between international organization and international politics in the "new world order" in terms of the opportunities and constraints inherent in the post-Cold War international system. Old security linkages built upon the Cold War international system are being redefined or replaced by new linkages in the context of strategic unipolarity and economic multipolarity. For instance, the emergence of "Growth Triangles" and "Economic Cooperation Zones" describes subregional economic processes that transcend national boundaries, reflecting economic complementary at subregional and micro levels—which in turn can affect broader regional and macro processes. Examples of this phenomenon in Southeast Asia are (1) the Singapore-Johor-Riau Growth Triangle; (2) the Indonesia-Malaysia-Thailand Triangle involving northern Sumatra, northern Malaya, and southern Thailand; and (3) "Souvanaphoum" involving Thailand, Cambodia, Laos, Vietnam, and Burma.[39] Furthermore, an enlarged version of the growth triangle is the UNDP's Tumen Delta Project, sprawling over the boundaries of China, Russia, and North Korea.[40] Through these growth triangles, East Asians are augmenting regional integration "by pooling their capital, labor, manufacturing expertise, raw materials and other crucial inputs in order to further exploit the region's growth potential through a modular strategy."[41]

Politically, the effective decoupling of the Soviet-Vietnamese relationship following the U.S.S.R's death compelled Vietnam to redefine its national and regional security agenda in accord with ASEAN's conceptions of regional order. The waning of the Cold War in Southeast Asia undoubtedly boosted prospects for genuine regional cooperation involving all 10 nations. And the impetus given to Southeast Asian regionalism through Japanese capital, investments, and entrepreneurship enables Tokyo to play a more effective political and security role that might be more acceptable to Asia-Pacific after the Cold War. In fact, Japan already signaled a desire to assume a higher profile in post-Cold War Asia's international relations by sending troops to participate in UN peacekeeping operations in Cambodia.

Tokyo is preparing for a more definitive political/security role in the new strategic environment, albeit within the framework of the time-tested U.S.-Japan alliance. Former prime minister Kiichi Miyazawa stressed in a speech to the National Press Club in Washington, DC (July 1991) that "in Asia, not only do we intend to continue economic cooperation, but we also hope to play a positive role in promoting political stability."[42] This formulation of Japan's security policy or the Miyazawa Doctrine, like the Nixon Doctrine, is essentially predicated on U.S.-Japan "global partnership"—a sort of joint Pax Americana-Pax Nipponica to manage international security and economic stability in the post-Cold War era.

CONCLUSION: ECONOMIC REGIONALISM, TRIPOLARISM, AND ASIA-PACIFIC SECURITY

Any discussion of the linkages between Asia-Pacific economic and security relations must consider the many complexities involved in attempts to forge cohesive levels of economic cooperation and integration. Factors which impede higher levels of regional economic integration include:

(1) substantial diversity based on country characteristics (especially between the developed and developing Asia-Pacific economies) in terms of size, level of development, trade composition, trade dependence, and indebtedness; and

(2) heterogeneity within countries in terms of producer and consumer interests, as well as interests of labor and environmental groups.[43]

Some of these factors have been instrumental for the discussion of issues in the recently-concluded Uruguay Round of Multilateral Trade Negotiations.[44] Differences in the attitudes of ASEAN leaders about optimal strategies for promoting regional economic cooperation reflect not only regional economic diversity but also the varied legacy of Cold War security ties. ASEAN's failure to endorse the EAEC concept at its fourth summit, coupled with its reaffirmation of its own relevance to the post-Cold war era, are indicative of the political sensitivities stemming from structural differences toward prospective forms of regionalism. Just as political considerations dominated the formation of ASEAN, similar perceptions lie at the root of proposals to form other regional blocs in an era marked less and less by ideological cleavages.

The dominant trend in Asia-Pacific regional economic processes is an open regionalism compatible with GATT, which can be viewed as essential CBMs in a time of dramatic change and uncertainty.[45] But rising protectionism and "trade blocism" in Europe and America, coupled with the decline of the United States' hegemonic power, could cause Asian regionalism to turn inward in preparation for a U.S. withdrawal from the region. The Asia-Pacific region is still coming to grips with the loss of an international hegemon (United States), with no acceptable replacement.

In the interim, the United States-Japan alliance may be the best vehicle to balance competing political, economic, and security interests in Asia-Pacific relations, and to provide stability and continuity within the context of change.[46]

The U.S.-Japan alliance removed the necessity for Japan to acquire offensive military capabilities while forestalling "traditional rivalries among Asian powers that otherwise could unravel into unrestrained military competition, conflict, and aggression."[47] In the absence of a comprehensive multilateral security arrangement for Asia, the ASEAN-PMC (Post-Ministerial Conference) mechanism would at this juncture serve as a plausible forum to discuss the political and institutional mechanisms that are needed to replace the security order of the Cold War. The annual ASEAN-PMC forum is held to discuss economic issues between the ASEAN Six and the seven dialogue partners immediately after the annual meeting of ASEAN foreign ministers. In July 1991, Japanese foreign minister Taro Nakayama supported the ASEAN proposal to convert the PMC into a security dialogue.[48] The Clinton administration also proclaimed its support for a security dialogue. In this regard, it is noteworthy that the first meeting of the ASEAN Regional Forum was held in Bangkok on 25 July 1994. In keeping with ASEAN diplomatic style and tradition, the ARF can be expected to avoid or postpone discussion of security issues that are controversial or divisive in nature (for example, Spratly Islands).

As a key dialogue partner of ASEAN, the U.S. role in influencing the emerging security order is critical. Although American power is not preeminent in the post-Cold War era, any regional economic and security order that attempts to exclude the United States is bound to falter on principle as well as performance.[49] In this regard, Professor James Rosenau's observation bears relevance for U.S.-managed security systems in the Pacific: "the dramatic moments of history are those marked by turbulent change, but most of its moments, an overwhelming preponderance of them, are suffused by continuity, by systems moving through time very much as they have always done."[50] Moreover, regional foreign policy realists know that the Asia-Pacific region's remarkable economic growth "would not have been possible without the geopolitical stability assured by the United States' security commitment over the past half century."[51] As the only remaining superpower, the United States is the linchpin of Asia-Pacific security.[52] Nevertheless, the United States will encounter greater difficulty in formulating "grand strategy" for the post-Cold War world, as opposed to the bipolar world in which threats and enemies were more readily identifiable.[53] Similarly, Japan will be unable to use its economic superpower status to create an exclusive security regime in East Asia in view of the very high levels of global and regional interdependence characterizing the Asia-Pacific economy. Moreover, an "exclusivist regional option would run counter to the interests of Japanese business in maintaining access to the trilateral economy" (U.S., Europe, and Japan).[54] The centrifugal tendencies inherent in the region—manifested by the rivalry between North and South Korea, between China and Japan, South Korea and Japan, the United States and Japan, as well as divisions within the 6-member ASEAN on a common external policy—invariably militate against the formation of an East Asian trading bloc.

Post-Cold War Asia is beginning to demonstrate "new thinking" on political and security issues based on a strengthening foundation of political stability and economic success. The obvious power vacuum accompanying a declining Pax Americana is being filled by high-level diplomacy and dialogue, with ASEAN spearheading efforts to multilateralize regional security. The regional grouping's nonthreatening posture bolstered confidence in the credibility of ASEAN to initiate dialogue on regional security involving great and small powers. Furthermore, Pacific Asia's commitment to open regionalism precludes the emergence of a formal trade bloc like the European Community. This may contribute to tripolarism at the global level (involving the United States, Germany, and Japan as the key players) being increasingly co-opted to enhance regionalism. It also will augment new linkages arising in the economic and security relations of the Asia-Pacific region after the Cold War.

NOTES

1. The Association of Southeast Asian Nations (ASEAN) was established by the Bangkok Declaration of 1967, comprising Indonesia, Malaysia, Thailand, Singapore, and the Philippines. Brunei joined as its sixth member upon gaining independence from Britain in 1984.
2. K.S. Nathan, "The Role and Significance of ASEAN in World Politics," *Foreign Relations Journal* 3:4 (December 1988), p. 76.
3. *Far Eastern Economic Review (FEER)* 155:2 (16 January 1992), p. 22.
4. K.S. Nathan, "Vision 2020 and Malaysian Foreign Policy: Part II: The New World Order," *Asian Defence Journal* (February 1992), pp. 16-20.
5. See for instance the article by Chin Kin Wah, "Changing Global Trends and Their Effects on the Asia-Pacific," *Contemporary Southeast Asia* 13:1 (June 1991), pp. 1-16.
6. *Asia 1992 Yearbook* (Hong Kong: Far Eastern Economic Review, 1992), p. 63.
7. *FEER* 155:5 (February 6,1992), p. 11. The Singaporean security proposal is partly a reaction to pressure on ASEAN from Australia, Canada, and Japan "to think more multilaterally about defence." See *FEER* 155:2 (January 16,1992), p. 23.
8. *New Straits Times*, 2 March 1993, p. 22.
9. The ASEAN Regional Forum comprises the foreign ministers of the 6 ASEAN countries (Brunei, Indonesia, Malaysia, The Philippines, Singapore, and Thailand), plus the foreign ministers of the seven dialogue partners (Australia, Canada, Japan, New Zealand, South Korea, the U.S. and EC), plus three observers (Laos, Papua New Guinea, and Vietnam), plus two consultative partners (China and Russia). *FEER* 156:31 (5 August 1993), p. 10.
10.*Asia 1994 Yearbook* (Hong Kong: Far Eastern Economic Review, 1994), p. 73.
11.*Asia 1993 Yearbook* (Hong Kong: Far Eastern Economic Review, 1993), p. 66.
12.Philip Shenon, "China Signals Willingness to End Island Dispute," New York Times, 31

July 1995, p. A3.

13. *FEER* 155:4 (30 January 1992), pp. 19-20.

14. International Monetary Fund, Direction of Trade Statistics Yearbook, various issues.

15. Mohamed Ariff, *The Malaysian Economy: Pacific Connections* (Singapore: Oxford University Press, 1991), p. 148.

16. Noordin Sopieee, *Economic Integration and Economic Cooperation in Pacific Asia* (Kuala Lumpur: Institute of Strategic and International Studies (ISIS), 1994), p. 4.

17. Mohamed Ariff, *The Malaysian Economy: Pacific Connections* (Singapore: Oxford University Press, 1991), p. 168.

18. The ten PECC meetings held to date are as follows:
    (1) Canberra, Australia (15-17 September 1980),
    (2) Bangkok, Thailand (3-5 June 1982),
    (3) Bali, Indonesia (21-23 November 1983),
    (4) Seoul, South Korea (29 April-1 May 1985),
    (5) Vancouver, Canada (16-19 November 1986),
    (6) Osaka, Japan (17-20 May 1988),
    (7) Auckland, New Zealand (12-15 November 1989),
    (8) Singapore (20-22 May 1991),
    (9) San Francisco, USA (23-25 September 1992), and
    (10) Kuala Lumpur, Malaysia (22-24 March, 1994).

19. The Kuala Lumpur Concord on Open Regionalism was signed by the 21 members of PECC, namely: Australia, Brunei, Canada, Chile, China, Chinese Taipei, Columbia, Hong Kong, Indonesia, Japan, Malaysia, Mexico, New Zealand, Peru, Russia, Singapore, South Korea, Thailand, The Philippines, United States, and South Pacific Forum (Fiji) on 24 March 1994. Source: *ISIS Focus* no. 101 (Kuala Lumpur: Institute of Strategic and International Studies (ISIS) Malaysia, August 1993).

20. Stuart Harris, "Varieties of Pacific Economic Cooperation," *The Pacific Review* 4:4 (1991), p. 304.

21. *Pacific Economic Cooperation: Issues and Opportunities* (Report of the Fourth Pacific Economic Cooperation Conference, Seoul, 29 April-1 May 1985), Seoul: Korean Development Institute, 1985, p. 186.

22. Andrew Elek, "The Challenge of Asian-Pacific Economic Cooperation," *The Pacific Review* 4:4 (1991), p. 324.

23. See Kuala Lumpur Concord On Open Regionalism, tenth PECC meeting, Kuala Lumpur, Malaysia, 22-24 March 1994.

24. *ISIS Focus*, op. cit., p. 32. ISIS Malaysia's Director-General, Dr. Noordin Sopiee was chairman of the tenth PECC. The new chairman for the eleventh PECC is Mr. Li Luyi of China.

25. *ISIS Focus*, op. cit., p. 31. The current membership of the Pacific Basin Economic Council (PBEC) is drawn from 15 countries: Australia, Canada, Chile, Colombia, Fiji, Hong Kong, Japan, South Korea, Malaysia, Mexico, New Zealand, Peru, the Philippines, Taiwan, and the United States.

26. Five APEC ministerial meetings have been held to date:
    (1) Canberra, Australia (6-7 November 1989),

(2) Singapore (29-31 July 1990),

(3) Seoul, South Korea (12-14 November 1991),

(4) Bangkok, Thailand (10-11 September 1992, and

(5) Seattle, United States (17-19 November 1993).

27. The views of Australia's Foreign Minister, Gareth Evans, Japanese Foreign Minister, Taro Nakayama, and U.S. Secretary of State, James Baker, as expressed at the second APEC Ministerial meeting in Singapore (July 1990) seem to converge on the strategic role of APEC vis-à-vis China. See *Asiaweek* (10 August 1990), pp. 24-26.

28. *New Straits Times*, 6 May 1992, p. 20.

29. *Asiaweek* (10 August 1990), p. 25.

30. Malaysian Prime Minister, Dr. Mahathir Mohamad speaking in New York prior to addressing the 48th UN General Assembly. See *New Straits Times*, 1 October 1993, p. 4.

31. "Malaysian Foreign Policy in the 1990s." Address by Malaysia's Foreign Minister (Abu Hassan Omar) to the Malaysian International Affairs Forum (MIAF), on 3 May 1990. *Foreign Affairs Malaysia*: 23:2 (June 1990), p. 7.

32. Professor David P. Dewitt, Director of the Centre for International and Strategic Studies (CISS) of York University, Canada elaborates on this concept in his paper on "Concepts of Security for the Asia-Pacific Region in the Post-Cold War Era: Common Security, Cooperative Security, and Comprehensive Security," delivered at the Seventh Asia-Pacific Roundtable, Kuala Lumpur, 6-9 June 1993. See commentary by Farish A. Noor, "Another Step Forward for Multilateralism" in *ISIS Focus*, op. cit., p. 7.

33. Linda Low, "The East Asia Economic Grouping," *The Pacific Review* 4:4 (Winter 1991), p. 378.

34. *Economic Report* 1993/94 (Kuala Lumpur: Ministry of Finance Malaysia, 1993), p. 66.

35. Richard P. Cronin, "Changing Dynamics of Japan's Interaction with Southeast Asia," *Southeast Asian Affairs 1991*, (Singapore: Institute of Southeast Asian Studies, 1991), p. 53.

36. Ibid., p. 59.

37. *FEER* 156:31 (5 August 1993), p. 11.

38. UN-supervised elections were held in post-Cold war Cambodia between 23-28 May 1993, after which a new constitution creating a constitutional monarchy restored Prince Norodom Sihanouk as King of Cambodia on 24 September 1993.

39. For details, see Noordin Sopiee, "The New World Order: Implications for the Asia-Pacific," in Rohana Mahmood and Thangam Ramnath, eds., *Confidence Building and Conflict Reduction in the Pacific*, proceedings of the sixth Asia-Pacific roundtable, Kuala Lumpur, 21-25 June 1992 (Kuala Lumpur: Institute of Strategic and International Studies (ISIS) Malaysia, 1993), pp. 4-29.

40. *FEER* 155:2 (16 January 1992), pp. 16-17.

41. *Economic Report* 1993/94 op. cit, p. 68.

42. *Asiaweek* 18:30 (24 July 1992), p. 21.

43. See for instance John Whalley, *The Uruguay Round and Beyond* (Ann Arbor, MI: The University of Michigan Press, 1989), pp. 9-10.

44. The Marrakesh Declaration also marked the end of GATT and the birth of its successor,

the World Trade Organisation (WTO). See *New Straits Times*, 17 April 1994, p. 16.

45. Singapore's foreign minister, Wong Kan Seng noted with reference to the EAEC that "No one has ever suggested that there should be a closed East Asian economic bloc. This is a self-created nightmare of some Americans and Europeans who are troubled by developments in East Asia." See *Asiaweek* 19:16 (21 April 1993), p. 24.

46. For details, see Julius Caesar Parrenas, "China and Japan in ASEAN's Strategic Perceptions," *Contemporary Southeast Asia* 12:3 (December 1990), 198-224.

47. Alberto R. Coll, "Power, Principles, and Prospects for a Cooperative International Order," *The Washington Quarterly* 16:1 (Winter 1993), p. 8.

48. For details, see Leszek Buszyinski, "ASEAN Security Dilemmas," *Survival* 34:4 (Winter 1992-93), p. 90-107.

49. See for instance the conlusions reached by Joan Edelman Spero in her work, *The Politics of International Economic Relations*, fourth edition (London: Routledge, 1993), p. 353.

50. James N. Rosenau, *Turbulence in World Politics: A Theory of Change and Continuity* (Princeton, NJ: Princeton University Press, 1990), p. 87.

51. Robert B. Zoellick, "Economics and Security in the Pacific," in Ronald N. Montaperto, ed. *Cooperative Engagement and Economic Security in the Asia–Pacific Region* (Washington, DC: National Defense University Press, 1993), p. 141. For a similar Asean view, see Lee Lai To, "Beyond Containment: The Future Utility of the U.S. Presence in the Asia-Pacific-A View from Southeast Asia," in op. cit., pp. 119-136.

52. Lee Lai To expresses an ASEAN viewpoint in his essay "Beyond Containment: The Future Utility of the U.S. Presence in the Asia-Pacific-A View from Southeast Asia" in Montaperto, p. 119-136.

53. Samuel P. Huntington, "America's Changing Strategic Interests," *Survival* 33 (January/February 1991), p. 3.

54. Joseph S. Nye, Jr., "Coping With Japan," *Foreign Policy* 89 (Winter 1992-93), p. 108.

5 Lines of Fracture, Webs of Cohesion: Economic Interconnection and Security Politics in Asia

John Zysman and Michael Borrus

INTRODUCTION

This chapter considers whether the expanding web of economic ties in Asia will mute national conflicts in the region, creating a more stable security environment, or whether those ties will define new lines of conflict, reinforcing or exacerbating regional security problems. It is part of a broader story in which a steady redistribution of economic capabilities has been defining new arrangements of power and interest since well before the collapse of the Soviet Union.[1] The system of relations most hope will emerge is *managed multilateralism*, an adjusted version of what we have now. In this case the security problem dwindles or vanishes. But the emerging distribution of economic capabilities also suggests *regional rivalry*, a twenty-first century form of mercantilism where the drive for autarky would be fueled not by welfare concerns but by aggressive beggar-thy-neighbor economic strategies to accumulate state power at the expense of others. Security in that world would be a very different game from what we have become accustomed to over the past 45 years. We fear such an era in which military threats to territory and society recede, only to be replaced by new more sophisticated threats; an era in which "security threat" no longer refers just to tanks and missiles but also to the control of markets, investment, and technology; an era that recycles the old security vocabulary to fit such new issues as market share, protectionism, and relative gains from trade.[2]

East Asia, which stands out in today's world as the only region with a consistently high trade surplus and strong growth, encapsulates the same story of alternate security futures. Remarkable growth in trade and extraordinary expansion of foreign direct investment within Asia are together restructuring and expanding interconnections among the region's companies and countries.[3] Will this astonishingly rapid development of economic interconnections lead to increased regional stability by increasing the stakes that each country has in the continuation of peaceful relations? Certainly, these expanding economic connections can weave webs of political cohesion. More pessimistically, they can also define new lines of conflict. Economic rivalry can beget political confrontation. Those confrontations may be within Asia, for example, as mid-tech countries attempt to upgrade their position. Or political and economic cohesion within Asia could create rivalry and confrontation with the United States and Europe. Our objective in this chapter is to show that the emerging structure of trade competition within the Asian region does in fact contain economic rivalries that may create or exacerbate lines of conflict.

There are two vantages from which to view expanded economic interconnection and more rapid growth. One face looks on the mutual *absolute* gains from trade. This is the world in which each country will be a winner if only it has the nerve to make the adjustment that competition will compel. The possibilities of these gains will induce governments and the private firms who reap profits to support expanded trade and avert wasteful, unprofitable, and inconvenient political conflicts. The second vantage looks on the *relative* gains that trade produces. Here the shift in position of different countries motivates action. Governments concerned by the growing economic and technological resources of a rival or the risks of dependency—whether real or perceived—may fixate on the possibility of a loss of position and power. Private sector actors seeking government support in their market rivalries against other national firms may highlight the national risks of technological dependency or relative loss of position. Since these two vantages look on the same economic process, the interpretation, the explanation of the significance of expanding trade and investment, is a political act. Neither government interests nor private interests, let alone the more amorphous national interests, are intrinsically defined. Rather they are created. It is that story which concerns us.

A GLOBAL ECONOMY WITH A REGIONAL GEOGRAPHY

There may be a global economy but it has a regional geography. Asia is one of three distinct, though interconnected, regional economies each with its own economic and technology base. The significance of the Asian regional story turns on its particular internal economic structure and distinct relation to the other regions.[4]

The economic world consists of three powerful trading groups: Asia, North America, and Europe.[5] These three groups together constitute close to 70 percent of global GDP, with the U.S. and European shares each at about a quarter of global GDP and Asia's share growing very rapidly.[6] Contrary to the common perception that trade is spread widely among the nations of these regions, a large part of trade takes place within the regions. For example, interregional trade makes up only a small part of GDP of the Asian and European regions. For the United States, foreign trade as a part of the GDP has grown in the last quarter century, but Canada and Mexico still are its top two trading partners respectively.[7] Moreover, the percentage of intraregional trade grew in each of these three groups in the decade since 1980.[8]

Of course, trade is certainly not the only activity that connects the regions. Consider the often talked-about multinational corporations and financial institutions. Though these firms roam the globe, each has a home—a country that necessarily shapes its character and both constrains and directs its choices. Multinational corporations may someday be able to act without national constraint, but not yet. Firm strategies and tactics are formed within particular institutional arrangements and supply bases that at once constrain and direct their choices.[9]

The regional base of multinational corporations is suggested by patterns of foreign direct investment (FDI). FDI grew much faster than world trade between 1983 and 1989, expanding at a rate of almost 30 percent compared to less than 10 percent for world exports.[10] Roughly 80 percent of the flows during this period took place among the advanced industrialized countries, suggesting simple integration. But if we look closer, a regional pattern reemerges. As Sylvia Ostrey notes,

> a significant aspect of the 1980s FDI wave is what appears to be the emergence of regional strategies by the triad's MNCs, leading to the likely formation of investment blocs and thereby also hastening intra-regional trade integration. The clustering pattern which is emerging among the countries shows each region dominated by investment from a single triad member: the Americas by the United States; Asia by Japan; and Eastern Europe as well as selected African countries by the EC.[11]

That is, the transnational corporate investment flows are themselves shaping three global regions.[12]

In sum, though the three major regions are interconnected, each also commands an independent industrial and technological base, vast financial resources, and a developed "domestic" regional market capable of sustaining growth. This combination provides each region with the economic foundations for independent action. There may be a more global international economy, but that does not end the importance of place—community, district, nation, or region. Economic strategies and responses to new competition are generated within particular places, rather than by world corporations that stand outside a home base.

That these regional groupings exist is not in dispute. What is in question is how they were formed and how they will connect in the future. These groups were not formed by politics; that is, they are not the product of political decisions or restrictions. Rather they reflect the attraction, the gravity, of proximity.[13] The question is whether these economic groupings which emerged naturally will become the basis of political blocs in which policy rivalries amplify and accentuate the natural economic tendencies. To avoid inappropriate argument, we must distinguish between economically driven trade *groups* and politically driven trade *blocs*.[14]

In Asia, the significance of regional trade is ever more important. Moreover, the foundations for its steady increase are firmly in place. Trade within Asia, the fastest growing of the three regions, grew faster since the second half of the 1980s than trade with other regions. The major source of imports for each Asian economy is usually another Asian economy, usually Japan.[15] In the late 1980s, for example, Japan supplied on average about 25 percent of the newly industrialized countries' (NICs) imports versus 16-17 percent from America.[16] Japan supplied more than 50 percent of Korea's and Taiwan's total imports of technology products in the late 1980s, more than double the U.S. share of technology imports to either. Conversely, these NICs increased their share of Japan's imports of manufactured products from 14 percent to 19 percent between 1985 and 1989. Over that time, increased intra-Asian trade permitted the NICs to reduce their dependence on the U.S. market, with U.S.-bound exports falling from one-half to one-third of total exports.

Specific sectoral stories make even clearer the meaning of these general statistics. In textiles the share of exports from the five leading textile producers (China, Hong Kong, Japan, Korea, Taiwan) to themselves increased from 34 percent to 51 percent of total exports.[17] Note that part of this volume is accounted for by reexport out of the region, but the percentage of exports to North America and Western Europe stayed roughly stable.

In electronics, the expanding sector, the story is even more dramatic. Based on a recalculation of trade figures by Paolo Guerrieri as part of his work on trade integration in Asia, the share of Asian trade that was intraregional increased substantially for both exports and imports from 1970 to 1991. In fact, the data suggests that there is a substantial reorganization of production within Asia while it maintains its classic position of exporting product out of the region. Imports in electronics within Asia rose from 26.4 percent to 57.7 percent in this period. The United States and Europe absorbed about 60 percent of exports, down from 70 percent in the early 1970s.[18] When we look at particular countries, we find the same pattern. Consider Korea. In 1985 three-quarters of Korea's exports went to North America and Europe, but in 1992 the figure had dropped to 35 percent. Exports to Asia exclusive of Japan had risen from 12 percent to 27 percent. If, as some anticipate, the populous country markets in Asia like China grow dramatically, Asia may become an even more important final market.[19]

Note that even as intra-Asian trade grows, Asia remains an export factory shipping to Europe and the United States. By contrast European-American trade relations were balanced in terms of exports, imports, and direct investment. Both American and European trade with Asia is growing very rapidly, with Asian trade exceeding their total trade with the other. This reflects the increase in the Asian region's share of world merchandise trade from 20 to 24 percent in the last decade.[20] But the Asian trade for both Europe and the United States is quite imbalanced. Both massively import from and have a massive deficit with Asia.

The same imbalance that exists in trade also exists in foreign direct investment (FDI). Japan and Asia more generally are not as open to FDI as Europe and the United States. The result of the imbalance in FDI will likely be an enduring imbalance in trade.[21] Let us consider why. FDI influences much more than simple ownership or corporate position in several markets. FDI powerfully drives trade as well. FDI is not just a substitute for trade in which cars or video casette recorders (VCRs) that were once produced in Japanese factories or American factories are now produced in European factories. Rather FDI opens up a wedge which often expands trade as subsystems and production equipment are shipped from the home country of investing corporations to the host country where production subsequently takes place. Equally, additional products not produced by the investing corporation in the host country are then still imported from elsewhere. It is essential to note, as Dennis Encarnation makes clear, that majority-controlled FDI is an impetus to exports from the home country of the investor.[22] However, certainly in Japan, minority investment in a firm often involves a foreign firm buying into a source of product. Consider Ford's investment in Mazda as a means of obtaining models to fill out its product range in the United States.[23]

In sum, patterns of trade, finance, and FDI indicate that there are three significant regional economic groups, not a homogeneous global economy. Several questions concern us here. First, will the Asian region remain dependent on access to markets in Europe and the United States? Export dependence is declining for Japan, but growth in the region still seems linked to exports. It is not simply a question of whether there will be disruptions, for assuredly there will be. Rather it is most crucially a question of whether a substitute for the demand for consumer durable products that now drives Asian industrialization could be found, and if so, how quickly and on what terms. Rapid growth of the more populous countries may provide markets and make Asia more autonomous.

With the rise of the Japanese yen in the last half of the decade of the 1980s, Asian exports have been associated with an internal production reorganization. In the decade from 1979 to 1989 the deficit of Europe and the United States with Asia expanded.[24] This occurred despite a substantial increase in North America's exports to the region.

> It seems that the exchange rate changes since late 1985 had a significant impact on the geographical distribution of trade surplus within Pacific Asian economies (i.e. from Japan to [newly industrialized economies] (NIEs) and NNIEs), but not necessarily the size of trade imbalances between the two regions.[25]

Asian exports to Europe and America powerfully shaped the character of the region's industrial reorganization. The large outside market helped generate a pattern of international regional specialization and trade.[26] Then, of course, all of Asia has a deficit with Japan, as Japanese components and subsystems are assembled throughout Asia into final product for export out of the region.[27] Japan then ends up with a surplus with virtually everyone, a global structural imbalance that expresses itself as a series of bilateral quarrels. The trade imbalances, both those directly between Japan and Europe/America, and indirectly through other Asian exporters, generate a more fundamental structural problem that in our view makes the international trading system unstable and risks the objectives of multilateralism. In any case, the reorganization of production and trade within Asia is dramatic and significant.

The character of the production reorganization, and the Asian security consequences of the reorganization, that occurred in Asia while the region maintained its critical European/American export markets will concern us in the remainder of this chapter.

ECONOMIC COMPETITION AND CONFLICT IN ASIA

Asia's Japan-Centered Industrial Economy

Expanding investment and trade in the 1980s and 1990s created a Japan-dominated market hierarchy. The American economic presence was diminished if not marginalized, which at present reduces the choices for Japan's Asian rivals. Japanese preeminence in basic technologies, its investment throughout Asia in markets and production, and the importance of the Japanese domestic market all give Japan increasing economic influence within the region. One now conventional metaphor for Asia is a squadron of flying geese, each positioned behind Japan in a form of sequential development as industrial learning spreads, technology spreads, and wages rise. The expanding trade and investment ties that this relationship implies are, in the view of many, also "likely to promote greater interdependence among the Asian economies and make the region a more cohesive entity in the world economy."[28] This cohesion would be one of dominance in which the other geese are held in position as suppliers to Japanese firms and final product assemblers for export using high value-added Japanese components, subsystems and equipment.

Japanese domination could, alternatively, define national rivalries. Economic dependence on Japan could set the lines of conflict as its rivals in the region seek to build autonomous industrial and technological positions from which they could challenge Japan and break loose from their positions in that formation of flying geese. Efforts to break out of position in the squadron could pit country against country. That struggle for position in Asia might, then, define how the region as a whole interacts with the other principal regions, the United States and Europe.

Japan is for now the industrial center of the Asia region. Direct foreign investment over the last decade in Asia constructed a Japan-centered industrial economy and pushed the United States out of its position of preeminence. By almost any significant measure Japan, rather than the United States, is now the dominant economic player in Asia. Japan is the region's technology leader, its primary supplier of capital goods, its dominant exporter, its largest annual foreign direct investor and foreign aid supplier, and, increasingly, a vital market for imports (though the United States remains the largest single import market for Asian manufactures). By 1990, Japanese industry was investing about twice as much in Asia as was American industry. From 1984 to 1989, there was as much direct Japanese investment in Asia as in the previous 33 years, thus doubling the cumulative total. Japanese investment in the Asian NICs grew by about 50 percent per year, and by about 100 percent per year in the Association of Southeast Asian Nations (ASEAN) nations. Perhaps even more indicative, in several emerging Asian economies cumulative NIC direct investment in the second half of the 1980s surpassed the cumulative U.S. total (by as much as five times greater in Malaysia). Moreover, the use in Asia of the yen as a reserve currency is expanding.

Technology is at the heart of an increasingly complementary relationship between Japan and its major Asian trading partners, but the complementary rests on Japanese dominance of the relationships. Japanese companies supply technology-intensive components, subsystems, parts, materials, and capital equipment to their affiliates, subcontractors, and independent producers in other Asian countries for assembly into products that are sold via export in third-country markets (primarily in the United States and other Asian countries). Conversely, nonaffiliated, labor-intensive manufactures and affiliated low-tech parts and components flow back into Japan from other Asian producers. Summarizing these trends, the Ministry of International Trade and Industry (MITI) noted in 1987 the "growing tendency for Japanese industry, especially the electrical machinery industry, to view the Pacific region as a single market from which to pursue a global corporate strategy."

Patterns of Japanese investment in the region reflect this strategy. In auto-making and electronics, there appear to be two key elements. One is to spread subsystem assembly throughout Asia, while persuading each government to treat subsystems originating in other Asian countries as being of "domestic origin." The second element is to keep tight control over the underlying component, machinery, and materials technologies by regulating their availability to independent Asian producers and keep advanced production at home. The two elements together tend to deter too rapid a catch-up by independent producers to the competitive level of leading Japanese producers, while simultaneously developing Asia as a production base for Japanese exports to the United States and Europe to avoid bilateral trade frictions.

In sum, advanced products and most of the underlying technologies are thus dominated by Japan, with labor-intensive and standard technology production in the periphery of the region and often under the control of Japanese industry. As a result, there is resistance to these patterns by other Asian countries. In a sense, there is a competition of corporate and national development strategies. The Koreans seek to break their technological dependence with national technology programs implemented by the large *chaebol* firms. The Taiwanese, Thais, and Malaysians, among many others, tailor policy to their local circumstances in an attempt to reshape the existing regional division of labor. To some extent, all of the region's economies seek to emulate some of the developmental policies and business strategies responsible for Japan's success. Our instinct is that this developmental competition is likely to reinforce Asian autonomy even if it relaxes Japan's control over the division of labor.

Can Other Asian Economies Challenge the Japanese Industrial Position?

The Asian competitors of Japan must find an independent source of technology. They require a supply base of the parts, components, subsystems, materials, and equipment technologies that is not tied to their regional competitor. The supply base can be thought of as an infrastructure for any given firm, in the sense that it is external to the firm but broadly supports the firm's competitive position by helping to delimit the range of its possibilities in global markets. The supply base affects producers by enabling or deterring access to appropriate technologies in a timely fashion at a reasonable price. Any relative decline in the American technological position, and any subsequent weakness of its supply base (particularly in autos and electronics), makes the mid-tech Asian firms more dependent on their Japanese competitors.

The architecture of the supply base powerfully influences technology access, timeliness, and cost. The architecture of the American supply base is much more open than that of Japan, by almost any definition. Easier technology access for the companies in Asia makes it all the easier to build domestic technology competencies and challenge Japan.

An industry that is significantly dependent on a foreign supply base (that is, on imports of key inputs) will not be overly constrained wherever markets are open and competitive, and foreign suppliers are numerous, geographically dispersed, and not in the same lines of business as their customers. This was essentially the case for European electronics systems producers from the 1950s to the 1980s. They relied primarily on U.S. components suppliers, who were themselves competitive, numerous, located in both Europe and the United States, usually not in competition with their customers, and accessible through relatively open markets for trade and investment. Indeed, it was not until the competitive problems of U.S. chip producers threatened a much more constraining architecture of supply for Europe in the 1980s that European companies moved at great cost to recreate a locally controlled supply base.

By contrast, producers should be concerned where the architecture of supply is characterized by closed markets, oligopolistic and geographic concentration, and, especially, wherever such concentrated suppliers compete directly with their customers. When suppliers have the ability to exercise market power or to act in concert to control technology flows, or when markets and technologies are not accessible because of trade protection, then the architecture of supply significantly constrains competitive adjustment to the disadvantage of domestic industry. Such an architecture is emerging today in Asia, and this is creating problems for American and NIE producers. A small number of foreign suppliers, principally Japanese, are more and more driving the development, costs, quality, and manufacture of the technological inputs critical to all manufacturers. Most of these suppliers of electronic components, manufacturing equipment, and subsystems are also competitors in a range of electronics systems from TVs and portable phones to computers. These firms are then increasingly in a position to dictate the degree of access U.S. and certainly Asian mid-tech producers have to essential technologies, the speed at which they can bring new products incorporating them to market, and the price they pay for the privilege.

Asian governments and companies believe there is a problem of access to Japanese technology. The evidence of a number of studies suggests that access to Japanese components and subsystem products as well as underlying technology is in fact difficult. Given the industrial structure of Japan, this is not surprising.[29]

The Erosion of the American Technology Supply Base

Without entering into the broad debate about the troubled American adjustment to international competition in the late 1970s or the real comeback in certain electronics sectors, we note simply that far more has been lost during the past decade than market position in specific sectors. The risk is that the supply base of the economy is unraveling: The components and parts technologies, materials and machinery sectors, and related industrial skills necessary to sustain competitive manufacturing and development are eroding, or in some cases, are already gone. For example, competition in the past decade has devastated domestic producers of manufacturing machinery, including advanced industry segments such as computer-numerically controlled machine tools, robotics, and semiconductor photolithographic equipment. U.S. dependence on foreign supply of such machinery increased dramatically since 1988, with imports rising from 14 to 40 percent of domestic consumption. The equipment dependence reflects a broad change in the manufacturing position of Japanese industry. Guerrieri showed that in the broad category of capital goods that embody production know-how across a wide range of industries, American industry lost market position in the past decades relative to their German and Japanese competitors.

Let us consider the case of electronics in more detail. U.S. producers are broadly dependent on foreign supply of a huge and growing list of essential component, materials, and machinery technologies.[30] Most U.S. computer firms can no longer produce consumerlike products (for example, laptop and smaller PCs) without an alliance with Japanese firms to provide the necessary components, micro-design know-how, and relevant manufacturing skills—Compaq with Citizen Watch, Apple with Sony, Sun with Fujitsu and Toshiba, and Texas Instruments with Sharp. Even IBM is not immune from this trend. The U.S. General Services Administration recently noted that IBM's RISC System 6000 model 7013-540 computer has foreign content in excess of 88 percent.

In electronics, existing dependencies appear slowly to be creating a cumulative knowledge gap that is profoundly disturbing: Even when they can procure technology inputs from abroad, U.S. firms no longer retain many of the design and manufacturing skills necessary to use them in a competitive fashion. For example, Japanese producers painstakingly acquired over several product generations the precision mechanical design expertise embedded in products such as VCRs, or the precision machining know-how in auto-focus camcorders. A leading U.S. industrial laboratory recently reverse-engineered such products and concluded that the embedded precision mechanical skills probably no longer existed anywhere in the United States.

Perhaps the most troubling development is the emergence of the new, high-volume, high-technology development trajectory in Japan. In this case, the development and application of a broad range of subsystem, component, machinery and materials technologies are increasingly driven by high-volume commercial applications that boast leading-edge sophistication and extremely high quality at remarkably low costs.[31] The significance of this development for our story is twofold. First, America is further diminished as an alternative to Japanese component and production technology. Second, the dependence of the NIEs on Japanese technology for the export of consumer durable products is augmented.

Access to Markets

Along with competitive technologies, Asian firms outside Japan require access to sophisticated markets. For mid-tech rivals to become high technology players they need not just markets, but markets that will pay for cutting-edge products. There are three such markets: Europe, the United States, and Japan. Expansion of demand in China, no matter how great, is not an alternative in the short run. For at least a while, China's market will largely demand only mid-tech, standard products. Recall that a notebook computer (of whatever sophistication) that is two years behind the leader is a mid-tech product; an automobile that uses imported components for transmission, active suspension, antilock brakes and the like is similarly a mid-tech assembly product. The exception may be in military goods, but as we have argued elsewhere, military demand no longer drives technology innovation. Rather, increasingly high-volume civilian technologies are pushing the technological frontier.[32]

The European and American markets will be essential to these Asian firms trying to establish independent position. Each region, however, is increasingly restricting access. As is widely observed, the mid-tech NICs cannot count on rapidly expanding markets or steadily increasing market shares in either region. In any case, the Japanese market, the most proximate, is in many domains the most sophisticated. Access to that market will prove crucial to higher tech ambitions. But that market has been difficult to access, particularly in cutting edge segments where the Japanese compete. Efforts to access Japanese technology will likely generate one set of tensions. Efforts to enter the Japanese market will generate another.

The Japanese market will become increasingly central to the region's pattern of growth and dependence. The issue is not strictly whether the level of manufactured imports will rise. It will. The question is not, then, whether Korean or Taiwanese products will be sold, but how rapidly demand will expand. Even more important is the question of whether the NIE firms will be pushed into the more standard commoditylike, lower end of the market, or whether they can break into higher end segments. Fukasaku is pessimistic for simply economic reasons:

> Japan is unlikely to become the major absorber of manufactured exports from other Pacific Asian economies, partly because of the size of her economy (it is less than half the American counterpart), and partly because Japan will continue to keep technological edges over her neighboring competitors and remain cost-competitive in human-capital and technology intensive products for many years to come.[33]

Politically, there is a more difficult matter: Will the Japanese control their markets (leaving ambiguous whether the control is a natural product of corporate strategy or an intentional policy of government) to prevent NIE firms from leveraging themselves into a position where they could independently compete with Japan? Technology management is one mechanism for doing this. Indigenous development of technology as a central commitment of government and companies in Japan cannot be dismissed as the warnings of fearmongers. Richard Samuels, the noted scholar of Japanese political economy who has long been critical of exaggerated views of Japan, traced the broad Japanese drive toward technology indigenization and the policies that involve protection, diffusion, and domestic promotion. Market management is another method that Japan can use against NIE and U.S. competition. For our concern—the implications of industrial competition for security politics—the perception of political intention in the management of access to technology and markets may be as important as the reality.

Japan may in fact be wide open and the market available to all comers. This is not, though, the popular perception. In trade, for example, Japan still tends not to import in sectors in which it exports and, despite progress, its overall level of manufactures imports is still quite low. Although manufactures have doubled to account for about 50 percent of Japan's imports, that is still far below the level of the United States and Germany, each with 75-80 percent. Moreover, the recent upsurge in imports can be seen as a regional adjustment of Japanese industry to the yen shock as as much an opening of the Japanese economy. Quantitative studies of Japanese imports suggest that in technology-intensive sectors, imports are tied to Japanese firms, a finding backed up by MITI surveys indicating that perhaps half of manufactured imports reflect intra-firm transfers between Japanese companies and their affiliates in foreign countries. Comparing equipment purchases by subsidiaries of Japanese, European, and American firms in Australia is likewise revealing. European and American firms buy equipment widely on global markets; Japanese firms buy almost exclusively from Japanese suppliers, returning to Japan for equipment. The econometric evidence will not settle this. Saxonhouse would argue that the Japanese pattern is not distinct. Belassa has argued that the Saxonhouse methodology is wrong and that the pattern is distinct. Some point to rising levels of manufactured imports. But Ed Lincoln, formerly head of the Japan Economic Institute, argues that the bulk of such imports into Japan are very low-value, initial processing activities.

Nor is Japan fully open to direct foreign investment. Though Japan is an increasingly prolific foreign investor, it has not permitted comparable foreign ownership of its domestic economy. Restrictions on takeovers, while serving the important domestic purpose of maintaining social peace and order, are still enormous barriers to foreign investment. Though direct investment into Japan has increased substantially over the past decade, by the late 1980s foreign direct investment in manufacturing accounted for less than one percent of Japanese manufacturing sales, employment, and assets. The comparable figures for the United States and Germany were 7-10 percent and 13-18 percent, respectively.

For the United States, the asymmetry of access to technology, markets, and investment opportunities is substantial whatever the mix of causes—policy, market structure, business practice, or consumer preference. For the Asian NIEs, let us simply say that access is difficult and Japanese markets and technology are unlikely to play the same role in their development as American markets and technology once did (or still do, depending on one's perception). Asymmetrical access maintains a strategic advantage for Japanese firms. Even foreign firms with technology or product advantage still enter licensing arrangements they would not consider either in the American or European market. Where once the government forced technology licensing (and foreigners accepted it because they perceived Japan as weak), now financial muscle and market strength ensure a flow of foreign technology into Japan. The insulated domestic market permits firms to compete intensely among themselves, honing product and processes, and then pour exports onto foreign markets. Other countries are then forced to absorb the excess capacity that Japan's market-share strategies generate. These two strategies— asymmetrical access and overbuilding of capacity—help preclude or at least slow the independent technology development of technology by foreign producers. This is a serious handicap for American and European firms. It may be decisive for the firms from the Asian NIEs. This strategic advantage can be demonstrated both in particular sectors and across industries.[34]

Can Other Asian Economies Challenge the Japanese Industrial Dominance?

Efforts to wrench free from Japan's economic domination of the region will certainly generate political and industrial rivalries. But the Japanese position is deeply entrenched and will be hard to loosen. No one of the mid-tech countries are able to break loose on their own. The lines of autonomous development require alliances, within Asia or with Europe and the United States, or a broad development of income and demand across the region that generates technology markets.

Asian firms outside Japan find themselves in difficult market positions; they often play the role of a second-tier supplier of standard product or the role of a low value-added final assembler. Even cases of apparent success, such as the entry by the Korean firm Samsung into the semiconductor memory business, are suspect. The Japanese transferred technology to Korean partners to move away from profitless or low value-added market segments of the industry. They retained the core technologies and the development position in next generation product that would prevent their partners from catching up and establishing position in more attractive market segments. Mastery of direct random-access memory (DRAM) technology has won the Korean firms only the "bleeding edge" position of the semiconductor business and the opportunity to suffer huge losses. And Korean firms are still dependent on Japanese (and, for now, American) firms for equipment. The leading edge of the business is shifting to arenas such as systems-level/chip-level design and applications expertise where American firms and Japanese firms are strong.

To break loose from the Japanese production network, Asian firms outside Japan need to enter high value-added segments of the industry that demand innovative technological content. They must do so without depending on Japanese competitors for core technologies, or at least insure that they can secure those elements from Japanese suppliers on a competitive basis. The access to sophisticated components on a timely and cost competitive basis is in fact a serious problem for many mid-tech Asian firms.[35] Many complain of being denied critical components in the volumes they require or that their supply is unreasonably delayed. These firms must internalize vital technology critical to the value they would add, which means they certainly cannot give up value-added to their suppliers, or remain dependent on their competitors. It will not be easy for these firms to establish independent positions that would allow them to compete with the Japanese in high value-added segments. Let us consider why by reviewing two possible strategies for achieving this.

First, these firms might try to define dramatically new market segments. This has been the distinct strength of American firms in the past decade, keeping them in markets where they had seemingly lost position. In consumer electronics, for example, American firms are redefining the character of the industry and creating entire new markets with innovative products. The Apple Macintosh and, more recently, the Apple Newton are good examples. Control of product design, definition and marketing often allowed American firms to force component and subsystem technology, no matter how sophisticated, to be sold as commodity products. Similarly, other U.S. firms such as Motorola or Intel created proprietary standards in a supposedly open system world that allowed them to capture monopoly or semi-monopoly rents. Korean and Taiwanese firms do not have the technological or market skills and power to define and create such break-out products. Significantly, their home markets are neither large enough nor sophisticated enough to generate demand for such products. Their position in the American and Japanese market might suggest such products, but more likely their efforts to survive in low-margin, intensely competitive segments will distract them. The emerging Chinese market, with its blossoming demand for low price, standard products will likely further deflect their attention from breakthrough strategies. Dedicating themselves to the tempting Chinese market could simply entrench countries such as Korea and Taiwan in a mid-tech position.[36]

Alternatively, firms might produce differentiated, high quality products that permit them to capture a piece of new markets or a share of the high value end of established ones. The trouble is that Japanese firms control the production systems with components and subsystems that allow a sophisticated differentiation of products. They may not make these available to other Asian firms. In fact, the new high-volume, high-technology development trajectory has been created and defined entirely by Japanese firms. Japanese firms intelligently and carefully manage their technology position to maximize what they control and minimize their potential dependence on outside sources. The vertically integrated character of major Japanese firms means that firms selling components and equipment are often competing with their clients in the final product markets. Given this industrial structure, Japanese firms behave as we might expect and as firms such as IBM or Boeing behave. They attempt to limit the transfer of critical technology to potential competitors or possible suppliers to competitors.

Any non-Japanese firm in the region will find it difficult to develop internally the technological resources either to define new markets or to differentiate products within an existing market. The home countries simply do not support the sheer range of technologies and the scale of investment that in fact differentiates the truly advanced from the mid-range countries. These firms must seek out alliances and partnerships. Japanese partnerships are not likely to cumulate into an independent position. Partnerships among mid-technology rivals such as Taiwan and Korea would be difficult to organize and would not, at least directly, permit a technology jump. Governmental and corporate alliances with the United States are a possibility; indeed the United States has long been the first or second largest investor in the region. But such alliances are difficult, for the moment, because of trade conflicts and the growing concern among American firms over transferring technology to competitors. Investments in American firms by mid-tech players is an option, of course, but in itself it will unlikely break these countries out of their trap.

Lines of Fracture: Confrontation of Development Strategies and the case of Korea

The Korean case points to a possible confrontation of development strategies that can emerge within Asia as a response to Japanese technological and industrial prowess. Japan is not alone in Asia to give priority to industrial development and domestic technology development as a means to achieve national goals of security as well as wealth. But what happens when developmental strategies collide?

To sustain its industrial development, Korea must now break out of a well-understood trap. That effort may generate lines of regional fracture. Over the past couple of decades Korea became a major industrial producer (it now has the fifteenth largest GNP in the world). The position was built with heavy investment in basic industries such as steel (Korea has the two largest steel companies in the world) and scale production in consumer durables (Korea is the sixth largest producer of electronics—$32.75 billion).[37] Korean firms have borrowed technology, effectively applying and improving what has been developed by more experienced companies in the advanced world.[38] The limits they now confront are: (1) risks of market closure in the advanced world; (2) rising wages that push up production costs and compel them to compete by product and technology differentiation; and (3) limited sources of technology caused, first, by advanced firms restricting access as Korea closes the technology gap, and second, by turning to more guarded Japanese firms as the American supply base weakens. Arguably, the Korean ability to sustain its development is influenced more and more directly by Japanese choices; its pursuit of stronger position in the economic world will more and more confront Japanese ambitions.

There are certainly strategies out of these traps, but the problems are real and the confrontation between developmental strategies not simply a stretch of the rhetorical imagination. The bulk of Korea's exports now go to the Asia-Pacific region. Exports to China have grown to nearly $9 billion, but that market could, as Dennis Simon argues, produce a degree of technological complacency. The Japanese market is difficult, in part because in sectors such as steel, autos, and electronics, the Koreans face world-class competitors from Japan, and in part, as some argue, because Japanese trade restraints are now aimed more at the NICS than at the United States. Indeed, Korea imports components and subsystems from Japan (26 percent of Korean imports) and exports final product assembled from them. The American market remains the critical outlet for manufactured goods. It is important not only in quantitative terms, but as one of the leading-edge markets that forces Korean firms to succeed at product differentiation and production quality. Firms such as Samsung and Goldstar have invested in America to ensure market access, but there are strains, even tears, in the trading relation as a result of charges of dumping and intellectual piracy.

Korean wage costs rose above those in Hong Kong and Mexico, although they certainly remain far below those of the advanced countries. Korean firms may seek some production capacity elsewhere in Asia.[39] But this further pressures Korea to seek ever-higher technology to create distinct capabilities. In that effort, Korea must struggle to keep ahead of its rivals in the push for higher value-added products, although there is some specialization within the region.[40] Korea may expand its investment in domestic technology development but for the moment such strategies will really serve to expand the capacity to absorb technology, not create fundamental product innovation. The Koreans face, as Dieter Ernst argues, a "successful technology catching-up trap." The closer a country comes to the technology frontier, the more reluctant foreign companies will be to share their technology.[41] There are, of course, multiple forms of obtaining technology running from contract manufacturing through licensing, with the host country's capacity to absorb being the key to its success.[42] However, Korean firms must increasingly obtain their technology from the advanced countries, particularly from firms that are their rivals.

The increasing dependence on Japan is perhaps clearest in semiconductors, in which 10 years ago the United States supplied nearly all production equipment for Korea. Today, Japan supplies 75 percent of that equipment.[43] More generally, Japan is the primary source of technology; that is, Japan is Korea's primary supply base. Korea has for nearly a decade sought to upgrade its relationship with the United States, to forge a technology alliance to decrease its dependence on Japan. American firms have been reluctant to support such initiatives, however; partly because of the attraction of Japanese technology and markets and, partly, because of the technology and dumping charges that loom over American-Korean conversations. The Koreans complain that Japan only transfers technology that is well established or that only partial technology is provided. That is hardly surprising since Japanese firms are competitors, and in turn Japanese firms express reluctance to do ventures with Korea because of the intensifying pressure for technology transfer. Simon argues the point very clearly:

> The valve of technology movement from Japan to Korea will, in all likelihood, open no faster than the specific needs of the Japanese economy—which basically still leaves Korea caught up in a pattern of articulation with Japan that promises little in terms of supporting the high technology thrust of the government and local industry.[44]

Korea may well be able to extract itself from its dependence on Japan for markets and technology. A combination of corporate technology alliances, domestic technology investments, government technology partnerships, and investment in foreign markets may suffice. But years of uneasy partnership and dependence almost certainly lie ahead. We may witness a confrontation of development strategies.

China and the Overseas Chinese Economy: Webs of Cohesion or Counterweight to Japan?

Someday, China may become the economic counterweight to Japan and could generate a confrontation between the region's richest and highest tech power and its most populous and soon largest economy. But China's entry into international trade and the overseas Chinese community contributes to the web of economic interconnection in the region and the general expansion of markets that permits a focus on absolute gains from trade.

China's expanded participation in international trade since 1979 has augmented intraregional trade, since its trade has been predominantly with neighbors such as Japan, Hong Kong and Singapore.[45] The special economic zones and open cities in coastal China have become major producers of manufactured goods. As a result, Hong Kong has taken on the role of entrepôt for this production. In the decade from 1979 to 1988, the share of Chinese exports to Hong Kong subsequently re-exported jumped from roughly one-third to three-quarters. Such figures do not include goods that are simply transshipped, which means that the Hong Kong traders are adding value in a variety of forms. The Chinese demand for such Hong Kong services reflects both the increase in trade and the increase in manufactured trade. Manufactured goods require more extensive commercial services. Yet China's tough stance regarding Hong Kong's future certainly suggests that politics of power and control rather than narrowly defined economic gains will set the lines of policy. Economics will remain a servant of the sword.

The overseas Chinese community is a symbol of the economic interconnection that weaves webs of cohesion in the region. The overseas Chinese, some argue, have begun to rival the Japanese as traders and investors in Asia.[46] Difficult to quantify, one estimate suggests that taken as a whole, this community that spreads across Asia would constitute a GNP of $200 billion. What is significant here is that communities of small- and mid-sized firms, complemented by some intraregional business groups, create a web throughout the region. The implication is that such a community, embedded as it is across Asia, is more tied to trade and profit within the region than to the development or power of any particular national component.

WHAT CONCLUSION: LINES OF FRACTURE? WEBS OF COHESION?

We return, finally, to the guiding question of this chapter: what is the consequence of expanded economic interconnections in Asia for regional security? Will the focus be on relative gains? In that case rivalries over economic position will reinforce existing cleavages and define new lines of political fracture and confrontation. Governments concerned by the growing economic and technological resources of a rival and the risks of dependency—whether real or perceived—may fixate on the possibility of a loss of position and power. Private sector actors seeking government support in their market rivalries against other national firms may highlight the national risks of technological dependency or relative loss of position.

Examining the dynamics of the Japan-centered industrial hierarchy in Asia reveals how easily economic conflicts could sharpen in the near future. From our discussion that began with the Japanese-centered industrial hierarchy, there appear to be three lines of potential conflict.

First, there will be efforts by the middle power, mid-tech countries such as Korea to break loose from their position in the hierarchy and move toward higher value-added products built on more advanced technology, creating a rivalry of developmental strategies. If the developmental strategies of the mid-tech NIE's involve a broad Asian drive toward technology indigenization, that is, substitution of national for European or American products, then such strategies will also involve interregional rivalries and conflicts over a wide range of issues.

Second, China, or possibly other populous countries like India or Indonesia, may provide an alternate and competing line of development in Asia. That would make industrial competition a means of security competition within Asia.

Third, whatever the arrangements within Asia, there may be conflicts between Asia and the other two industrial regions. The core issues of regional conflicts are likely to be market access, particularly to Japanese markets, and secondarily access to Japanese technology.

Alternatively, can the possibilities of absolute gains bridge existing conflicts— or at least constrain them? Do the market connections—in the form of trade, investment, subcontracting, technology exchange, product development and the like—represent webs of cohesion? Three major developments would push in the direction of cohesion, would set the terms of debate firmly about mutual advantage. First, the emergence of new markets for sophisticated and high income products and production equipment would reduce dependence on Japanese, European, and American markets. Second, if these markets become large enough, they even may open sufficiently to permit balanced regional trade, that is, to absorb exports of American and European production and production services. This would require the opening of the Japanese and other regional markets. Third, the drive by the mid-tech and populous countries to match Japanese technology may encourage both intra-Asian alliances and mutually advantageous ties to America and Europe.

We seem no closer to an answer to our question of whether expanding economic interconnection will produce lines of fracture or webs of cohesion. The situation is very ambiguous. To suggest the ambiguity of the objective situation, we very cursorily sketched the position and choices of two of the actors: Korea and China, including the overseas Chinese community. Korea overtly wishes to break loose from its position in the industrial hierarchy but is deeply woven into the fabric of the Asian industrial production machinery. China's market-oriented policies represent a decision to drive development by becoming entangled in the production web but alternately it represents a true rival to Japan. Consequently whether China's visions of its security will be influenced by that involvement in the region's production is unclear.

No analysis of the economic dynamics alone can answer questions about security relations. The consequences of the economic situation are open to be defined by politics.[47] Observe the European case where the security politics determined the meaning of market connections. The European Community forged an intimately bound market with expanded political connections precisely because the several governments faced common threats. The implication is that in an Asia politically divided, economic connections are perhaps more likely to reinforce lines of fracture than heal them.

NOTES

1. See the Berkeley Roundtable on International Economy (BRIE) project by Wayne Sandholtz, et al., *The Highest Stakes: The Economic Foundations of the Next Security System* (New York: Oxford University Press, 1992).
2. San Francisco Chronicle, April 27th, p. 6: "CIA warns U.S. FIRMS of French Spying." Our concern has been that the extensive role of governments in directly shaping trade outcomes combined with the intellectual justifications for such roles which suggest that the stakes in particular trade conflicts are entire trajectories of economic development, and the limits of the existing approaches to trade conflict would push U.S. toward the dangerous outcome in which the central interests of the major countries are defined in terms of winners and losers.
3. Kiichiro Fukasaku, *Economic Regionalisation and Intra-Industry Trade: Pacific Asian Perspectives* (Paris: OECD Development Centre, 10 June 1991). The paper cites the Asian Development Bank Outlook of 1990.
4. Winfried Ruigrok and Rob van Tulder, "The Ideology of Interdependence," unpublished dissertation, University of Amsterdam, 1993.
5. This argument is widely disputed. For a view parallel to ours, see Lawrence B. Krause, "Trade Policy in the 1990s: Good-bye Bipolarity, Hello Regions," *World Today* 46:5 (Royal Institute of International Affairs, May 1990). For skeptical views, see Gerald Segal, *Rethinking the Pacific* (Oxford: Clarendon Press, 1990), and Jeffrey Schott, "Is the World Developing into Regional Trading Blocs?" (Washington, DC: Institute for International Economics, 1989). In our view, the difference is largely one of vocabulary.
6. In 1987, Japan alone accounted for 12.4 percent of global GDP, and Japan plus the East Asian NICs accounted for 15.8 percent. (These figures are based on data in Bureau d'Information et Prevision Economique, *Europe in 1992* (Paris: BIPE, October 1987).
7. Gerard Lafay and Colette Herzog with Loukas Stemitsiotis and Deniz Unal, *Commerce International: La Fin Des Avantages Acquis* (Paris: Economica, 1989).
8. Calculations by Dieter Ernst on the basis of figures provided in the *UN Monthly Bulletin of Statistics* 45:6 (June 1991).
9. See for example "Everybody's Favorite Monsters" *The Economist*, 27 March 1993.
10. "Foreign Direct Investment in East Asia," prepared by Sylvia Ostry for a joint research project designed by Sylvia Ostry, Center for International Studies, University of Toronto, and the Berkeley Roundtable on the International Economy, 1992.
11. Ibid.
12. See "Everybody's Favourite Monsters," op. cit.
13. Jeffrey Frankel and Miles Kahler, eds., *Regionalism and Rivalry: Japan and the United States in Pacific Asia* (Chicago: National Bureau of Economic Research, University of Chicago Press, 1993). See Section 1 and the work of Jeffrey Frankel in particular.
14. Note that the view here is consistent with the position of Frankel. His question is

whether the groups have been formed by politics, while our analysis reverses the question to ask whether these economic developments will become the basis of new political alignments.

15. "The Rising Tide: Japan in Asia," special supplement, *Japan Economic Journal*, 1990, p. 4. See also Takashi Inoguchi, "Shaping and Sharing Pacific Dynamism," *The Annals of the American Academy of Political and Social Science* 505 (September 1989).

16. Yung Chul Park and Won Am Park, "Changing Japanese Trade Patterns and the East Asian NICs, paper prepared for the National Bureau for Economic Research Conference, 19-20 October 1992.

17. GATT Database, Textile Working Group, 1991.

18. Paolo Guerrieri, data prepared for this paper. See Guerrieri and Milana, "Technological and Trade Competition in High-Tech Products," BRIE Working Paper #54 (Berkeley, CA: University of California, 1991).

19. Dieter Ernst, "Export Performance and Technological Capabilities—The Korean Electronics Industry under Pressure," in Ernst and Mytelka, eds., *Catching Up, Keeping Up, and Getting Ahead: The Korean Model Under Pressure* (Paris: OECD forthcoming). Based on figures provided by the Electronics Industry Association of Korea.

20. Fukasaku, op. cit., p. 6.

21. A decade ago the United States was the principal source of FDI in the world. Today, after Japan (principally) and Europe (secondarily) have spent the 1980s entrenching themselves in the American market, the United States has become the most prominent recipient country for FDI. This in part mirrors America's huge trade deficits. Japan's investment mirrors its large and entrenched trade surplus. The United States is now no longer a country whose companies use their technology and organizational advantages to implant themselves in host markets, but a host country itself. Sylvia Ostry, op. cit.

22. See Dennis Encarnation, *Rivals Beyond Trade: America versus Japan in Industrial Policy, 1925–75 (Tokyo: Charles E. Tuttle, 1982).*

23. The significant role of FDI as a source of, rather than substitute for, trade creates several real policy problems. *First*, it undermines the classic role of exchange rates in creating trade equilibrium. An enduring national trade surplus should induce a currency appreciation. That appreciation should, according to the coassical model, create a new equilibrium by raising the prices of exports and reducing those of imports. However, that appreciation also increases the value of funds to buy foreign assets, or, put differently, reduced the prices of those foreign assets to the surplus country. The resulting investment can contribute to the trade imbalance rather than resolve it. This is particularly important, since there are similar imbalances in FDI in Asia, Europe, and North America. Consider Japan. Though FDI in Japan has increased substantially over the past decade, by the late 1980s foreign direct investment in manufacturing accounted for less than one percent of Japanese manufacturing sales, employment, and assets. The comparable figures for the United States and Germany were 7-10 percent and 13-18 percent, respectively. Second, FDI's promise to increase access to technology and diminish risks of technological dependence may be hollow. FDI may, in fact, lock countries into a subordinated (the French might say subjugated) position.

24. Guerrieri, op. cit.

25. Fukusaku, op. cit., p. 11.

26. Ibid., p. 4.

27. Japan's trade with the rest of Asia in 1989 surpassed her trade with the United States, more than doubling since 1982 to over $126 billion. "The Rising Tide: Japan in Asia," op. cit., p. 4.

28. Asian Development Bank cited in Fukusaku, op. cit.

29. Denis Fred Simon "The Orbital Mechanics of Korea's Technological Development: An Examination of the 'Gravitational' Pushes and Pulls," March 1993. Paper prepared for the conference "Redefining Korean Competitiveness in An Age of Globalization" (Berkeley, CA: Center for Korean Studies, University of California, 24 April 1993).

30. Gaps in the U.S. Technology Supply Base:
Precision-mechanical

- Motors—flat, high torque, sub-miniature

- Gears—sub-miniature, precision machining

- Switch assemblies—sub-miniature

Packaging

- Surface mount, plastic

Media

- Magnetic disk

- Optical disk

Displays

- Electroluminescent

- LCD, color LCD, LCD shutter

- CRT—large, square, flat

- LED—arrays

- Projection systems

Optical

- Lens

- Scanners

- Laser diodes

Feromagnetic

- Video heads

- Audio heads

- Miniature transformer cores

Copier-printer

- Small engines for laser printers

Source: National Advisory Committee on Semiconductors.

31. Borrus develops the case for electronics in "Reorganizing Asia: Japan's New Develoment Trajectory and the Regional Division of Labor" (Brie Working Paper 53, March 1992).

32. Borrus and Zysman, in Sandholtz et al., op. cit.

33. Fukasaku, op. cit. p. 4

34. In semiconductors see Borrus. In automobiles see the very interesting essay by Jay Tate that compells a re-evaluation of the lean production notions.
35. Takashi Hikino and Alice H. Amsden "Staying Behind, Stumbling Back, Sneaking Up, Soaring Ahead: Late Industrialization in Historical Perspective" in William J. Baumol, Richard R. Nelson, and Edward W. Wolff, eds., *International Convergence of Productivity, With Some Evidence From History* (New York: Oxford University Press, 1993)
36. Hikino and Amsden, op. cit.
37. Simon, op. cit.
38. Hikino and Amsden, op. cit.
39. Ernst, op. cit., p. 3.
40. Simon, op. cit.
41. Ernst, op. cit.
42. The absorption capacity must be differentiated. The distinctions Ernst and others make among investment capabilities, production capabilities, minor change capabilities, marketing capabilities, linkage capabilities, and major change capabilities are useful.
43. Simon, op. cit., p. 10.
44. Simon, op. cit., p.
45. Fukasaku, op. cit. p. 12.
46. "Overseas Chinese Set Region's Trends: Report" South China Morning Post Weekly, 30-31 January 1993, p. B4. "The Chinese Dealmakers of Southeast Asia" *BusinessWeek*, 11 November 1991, p. 61
47. Weber and Zysman, in Sandholtz et al., op. cit.

Part II
The Security-Economic Linkage: China

6 Understanding China's Asia Connection

Wang Jisi

INTRODUCTION

As the end of the 20th century approaches, the People's Republic of China is engaged in extraordinary economic and political reform. While state security and self-reliance preoccupied Chinese foreign policy in the pre-reform period (1949-78), the last 15 years witnessed China's opening to the outside world for purposes of economic modernization. As a result, economics now rates as high as security concerns on Beijing's foreign policy agenda. This trend of giving economic modernization high priority will continue as economic reform further penetrates Chinese society.

Three important domestic policy considerations will affect Chinese foreign policy within Asia: concentrating on economic development; building a new political model while resisting political pressures from the West; and dealing with decentralization and initiatives taken by localities. This chapter analyzes these three factors and their impact on China's relations with other powers in the region.

CHINA'S PRIORITY ON ECONOMIC REFORM AND ITS RELATIONS WITH ITS ASIAN NEIGHBORS

Despite the political reform tensions that led to the Tiananmen incident of 1989, the PRC leadership determined that economic development should remain the central task to guarantee the success of China's modernization program. This central concern suggests a diminished role for old-style ideological indoctrination and a greater need for political democratization.

Beijing's determination to adhere to reform stems from the recognition that the PRC economy still lags far behind those of some of its smaller neighbors, including Taiwan and Hong Kong. Moreover, Beijing desires that both economic powers reunify with the mainland. Setting economic growth as the top priority is motivated largely by the communist leadership's belief that its own longevity depends directly on its ability to improve the standard of living for the Chinese populace. If the PRC failed to compete with the capitalist economies surrounding the mainland, how could it convince its people of the virtue of "socialism with Chinese characteristics?" The idea and process of reunification with Taiwan and Hong Kong might suffer as a result. The PRC also clearly sees the experiences of the Soviet Union and Eastern Europe as demonstrating a causal relationship between economic backwardness and political instability.

The dramatic changes in the Soviet bloc naturally generated great apprehension in Beijing. American rhetoric about the global transformation toward Western-style democracy added worries that the United States would refocus the West's effort away from thwarting the Soviet Union and toward undermining the Chinese communist regime. In 1991, some leading Chinese observers described the world situation ominously. Calls for suppressing bourgeois liberalization surfaced, with blame squarely laid on political infiltration from the West.

In early 1992, following Deng Xiaoping's talks during his tours of south China, this dismal international situation was reassessed. In an officially edited version of his talks, later made available to the Chinese cadres, only one sentence involved Chinese foreign relations. But the meaning of that sentence was significant: The international environment was advantageous to China. Since then, a number of setbacks occurred, notably Washington's decision to sell F-16 fighters to Taiwan in 1992, Hong Kong Governor Chris Patten's plans for political reform that miffed Beijing, and U.S. sanctions against Beijing in August 1993 stemming from alleged Chinese sales of M-11 missiles to Pakistan. Nevertheless, Beijing still considers the international climate to be in its favor.

Under Deng Xiaoping, China achieved the longest stable period of foreign relations in its history. As in the 1980s, China's current foreign policy centers on creating an international environment conducive to the successful implementation of China's economic reforms. Because military security is basically assured, successful economic development requires that China's diplomacy mobilize to serve its economic interests. Another rationale for "economic diplomacy" lies in the belief that only a prosperous socialist society can resist political contamination from Western concepts of democracy.

China's expanding economic ties with the outside world hastened structural reforms and expanded Chinese knowledge of the international arena. In 1992, China's import and export volume totaled $165.63 billion, a 22.1 percent increase over 1991.[1] Whereas in 1978 China's foreign trade volume ranked the country thirty-fourth in the world, by 1992 it surpassed the Republic of Korea and Spain and had moved up to eleventh place.[2] China's foreign trade in 1992 constituted 41 percent of its gross domestic product (GDP), which reached $403.44 billion that year.[3] In 1992, total contracted foreign investment from new projects reached $58 billion, tripling that of 1991. Actual investment of foreign funds in 1992 was more than $16 billion, up more than 50 percent from 1991.[4]

The PRC is undergoing basic changes in the private, cooperative, foreign, and joint venture sectors of the economy, which are growing at two to eight times the rate of the state-owned sector.[5] As market-oriented economic activity outpaces state-planned activity, China is submerging the old planned economic system without formally declaring its abandonment.

The domestic economic, foreign trade, and investment reforms are more advanced in South China, especially in the Special Economic Zones of Shenzhen, Zhuhai, and Hainan, where the degree of local economic autonomy is pronounced. Flexible investment policies and economic performance in those areas attracted foreign investment and generated increased consumer income. Bestowed with privileges from the central government and their proximity to Hong Kong, these zones provide models that encourage enterprise reforms leading to a full-fledged market economy.

The absorption of management skills, entrepreneurship, and other capitalist experience makes many areas in South China resemble their neighbors in the Asia-Pacific region. What is more, the north is now trying to catch up with the south in many aspects of socio-economic life. As a Chinese commentator remarks,

> after more than 10 years of reform and opening the south has become the most vigorous and forward-looking economic region. Every experiment became a motive power to influence the future trend of Chinese development. In view of the importance of economic construction, the south will undoubtedly rapidly raise its status, and its political influence will certainly grow....The Northern Expedition at the beginning of this century was the joint overthrow of the rule of feudal warlords by the Communist Party and the Kuomintang. Now, at the end of the century, a second Northern Expedition has been launched by the South's new economic model.[6]

To be sure, there are, in Deng's words, "those who don't support reform," but a wide coalition of vested interests stands against conservative critics. Along the coastline, rivers, and borders, a chain of prosperous centers are linked by common gain through the open door reforms. Moreover, the PRC State Council approved more than 300 open cities.[7] Resembling Special Economic Zones (SEZs) in their policies toward foreign trade and investment, these open cities contain a host of municipal, provincial, and central ministerial officials whose power base and promotion potential are directly tied to these economic zones, which are dependent on the reform process. Access to foreign advice, technology, and capital has also helped to nurture a scientific, technological, and managerial elite. As a result, more highly trained people are less committed to ideology and increasingly cosmopolitan in their outlook.

Economic ties between the PRC and other parts of the Asia-Pacific region (including the United States) are extremely important, representing some 80 percent of China's foreign trade.[8] Because of U.S. sanctions against the PRC after Tiananmen, strong political incentives exist to reduce what some Chinese officials perceive to be an undue dependence on U.S. trade and technology. However, Beijing is more likely to do so by expanding and diversifying commercial relations with the rest of Asia and elsewhere, rather than by cutting economic links with the United States.

Previously, Beijing's desire to avoid excessive dependence on economic ties with the United States was balanced by concerns that Japan could gain too great a command over the Asian economy. Chinese complained that Japan was overly interested in selling commodities, yet too reluctant to export technology and capital investment. Privately, China encouraged American investment to prevent Japanese economic hegemony. However, more recent Japanese willingness to finance trade infrastructure such as roadways is abating these concerns.

China's desire to bolster overseas economic relations promises a strong interest in participating in the process of economic globalization rather than solely in that of East Asia. Despite their conscious identity as a developing Asian power, the Chinese discarded the old notion of regarding the General Agreement on Tariffs and Trade (GATT) as a "club of rich nations" and are intent on re-entering it. "Government officials, economists, merchants and entrepreneurs have all been studying how to conduct business in accordance with international practice, integrate domestic and world markets, and meet the requirements of various GATT clauses."[9]

The resumption of the PRC's GATT membership assumes not only a vigorous effort to embrace market principles and economic rationality but also an improvement of its political image in East Asia and the world. China's external policies toward the rest of Asia must be made compatible with these economic and political necessities. In the security dimension, these policies will remain focused on reducing existing or potential tensions with its neighbors.

In areas of potential military conflict, China has systematically sought to reduce the probability of armed conflict on its periphery—with Southeast Asia, India, and Japan. There are territorial disagreements in the South China Sea with a few Southeast Asian states, lingering border disputes with Vietnam and India, and a territorial dispute with Japan over the Diaoyu islands. Over the past few years, the PRC has played down its assertiveness in territorial claims, and has taken specific diplomatic actions to minimize the apprehension that Beijing will try to employ military force over any of these issues. Beijing has reiterated that disputes in the South China Sea should be settled peacefully, and that its policy is to shelve the sovereignty issue and cooperate with the countries of Southeast Asia.[10]

In addition, although the question of Taiwan's reunification with the mainland remains unsettled and could trigger intense political struggle, the extensive economic ties between the two sides developed during the reform era bode well for a peaceful settlement. The PRC leadership has reiterated the position of realizing reunification through peaceful means, although it warns Taipei that "resolute measures" would be taken against "Taiwan independence."[11]

Despite these positive trends in its relations with its neighbors, the PRC seeks advanced technology to modernize its armed forces. Throughout China's recent history, including the decades since the founding of the PRC, the Chinese were in a position of great military inferiority vis-à-vis the other great powers, and they have been acutely aware of this fact. In China's military confrontation with weaker neighboring countries like Vietnam and India, its rivals were perceived to be supported by either the United States or the Soviet Union. China's national security problem was dealing with militarily superior and threatening powers from a position of weakness. In the light of China's historical experience, its assertion of national defense—which has always had a sensitive domestic dimension—does not reflect expansionary desires but survival instincts. But it is unlikely that a dangerous military threat to China exists comparable to the Soviet Union. Despite recent increases in China's defense budget, military requirements continue to receive a low place in China's development priorities since military power is now only a hedge against unanticipated events requiring the use of military force.

Domestic political and economic forces in China, especially since early 1992 when Deng's ideas of reform regained the upper hand, moved the country irreversibly toward opening to the outside world. Although any exclusive economic grouping would be detrimental to China's economic interest, and its security interest is not confined to the Asia-Pacific, Chinese foreign policy seeks an "Asian identity." The PRC is enhancing its position by expanding contact and building confidence with virtually all of its neighbors.

CHINA'S POLITICAL VALUES AND ITS ASIA POLICY

Economic security interests are not the only underpinnings of China's Asia connection. Internal political stability remains a key concern in the PRC's domestic and foreign policies. Especially since the political storm of Tiananmen, the Chinese leadership has denounced any schemes aimed at transforming China's political system on a pluralist, multi-party basis. Chinese ambivalence about turning abroad for political institutions represents a unique combination of ethnocentric cultural pride and a recognition of the nation's relatively backward economic and technological development.

There is an emotional controversy among Chinese intellectuals and in Chinese society about how to approach and evaluate China's cultural heritages. Faced with the challenge of irresistible commercialization, even many of those who support a more open policy often warn that China might lose its cultural values, become economically dependent upon its foreign patrons, or become vulnerable to foreign pressures. Some surrounding societies provide what some Chinese regard as models more relevant to China's modernization program because of similarities in terms of history and culture. These societies (for example, Japan and Singapore) attained rapid economic growth and political stability while still retaining their indigenous culture and value system.

Chinese concerns about political order and cultural identity produced a fashionable school of political thought, neither endorsed nor criticized officially. Those who support "neo-authoritarianism," "neo-conservatism," or "enlightened authoritarianism" make positive references to the political and economic experiences of Japan, South Korea, Taiwan, Hong Kong, Singapore, and a few other ASEAN states. According to these analysts, politics in those countries are characterized by (1) relatively uncorrupt political leadership not subservient to foreign capital or indigenous interest groups; (2) strong government following market principles but actively intervening in socio-economic life; and (3) combination of state ownership and private ownership with a cooperative relationship between the government and the enterprises.[12]

This reasoning implies that the PRC should be more selective in borrowing Western knowledge and learn more from Japan and the newly industrialized countries and areas in Asia. Some observers openly assert that political democracy is not a prerequisite for economic and social progress. However, it should also be noted that there are resolute counter-arguments opposed to any attempt to adopt neo-authoritarianism in China—opponents accuse such thinking as espousing a anachronistic totalitarianism.[13]

No matter what evolves from this controversy, Chinese elites will track political developments in South Korea, Thailand, and the Philippines very closely, as developments there might have some spillover effects on China's domestic politics. Beijing will be interested in strengthening political ties, promoting cultural exchange, and expanding institutional linkages with other Asia-Pacific states.

The PRC's political characteristics also reflect its views on domestic events in more closed societies in Asia (Vietnam, North Korea, Laos, and Burma). On the one hand, China may welcome these countries' moves in a more open, market-oriented direction because that will tend to increase Chinese economic opportunities. On the other hand, Beijing's interest would not be served by any political upheaval in these states that would help magnify Western influence surrounding the PRC. Chinese analysts sometimes express their mixed feelings about dilemmas in this context.[14]

Chinese policies toward the remaining socialist-oriented states in Asia are also influenced by domestic ideological considerations. In expounding Beijing's objectives in aiding Laos, a Chinese writer cites remarks by communist leaders of both countries on the necessity of guarding against the "peaceful revolution" strategy, an alleged Western scheme to undermine communist regimes. In defending Chinese aid, the writer states, "the maintenance of a stable, developing People's Democratic Republic of Laos is undoubtedly conducive to preserving a stabilizing international environment for our domestic construction and to our fighting against the infiltration and subversion by hostile forces."[15] Another writer, when analyzing the situation in Burma, praises the military regime's "consistent vigilance against the Western powers headed by the United States to prevent them from conducting subversion and infiltration."[16]

The PRC's regional policies, like its overall foreign policy, serve to resist Western (especially U.S.) political pressure by defending its fundamental institutions and values at home. One means of doing this is to support other regional governments' defiance against Western values and influences. To some degree, Beijing's efforts to improve relations with other regional powers, including Japan, can be explained by wanting to avoid American dominance in this region.

The Chinese are aware of a broad consensus in Asia that there is an "Asian model of development," a path in which economic takeoff proceeds fundamental political change. In addition, "there is a general sense in Asia that Americans are not sufficiently mindful of what instability in the PRC would mean in very direct terms for China's neighbors....A strategy of American economic sanctions that aims to make economic life in the PRC more precarious is a strategy that makes China's neighbors profoundly nervous."[17] Beijing agrees. The Chinese official press gives great publicity to such Asian leaders as Lee Kuan Yew, former Prime Minister of Singapore, and Datuk Seri Mahathir Mohamad, Prime Minister of Malaysia, whenever they harshly criticize the United States for its human rights diplomacy.

Similarly, Chinese attitude toward Japan reflects domestic political considerations. Despite the long-standing ambivalence toward Japan's role in the region, Beijing has recently expressed cautious support for Japan's larger role in international affairs. The damage of Tiananmen on Japanese-Chinese economic ties was temporary and limited. Japanese leaders are much less assertive than Americans in asking for political reform in the PRC. Rather, Tokyo is seen as playing the role of moderating American criticisms of China's human rights record. In other words, as far as China's domestic stability is concerned, Japan is not identified as a threat.

Therefore, some Chinese have found reasons to extend limited backing for Japan's role as a great political power while trying to restrict its military capabilities. As one Chinese observer suggests, "we should take advantage of the contradictions between imperialist powers, give conditional and appropriate support for Japan to have a larger say in international affairs as a great political power, so as to strive for a good international environment favorable to our economic construction. However, it is also possible for Japan to become a great military power when, or after, it moves into a political power. To this we should be steadily opposed."[18]

China increasingly associates itself with other Asia-Pacific countries in economic and political terms while expressing suspicions of U.S. intentions. Recent U.S. clamor about increased Chinese defense spending reinforced the Chinese impression of growing American hostility. In contrast, the Chinese now describe regional states as "benign" players in regional affairs. Chinese official media have not responded directly to Asian concerns similar to those expressed by U.S. media about a potential Chinese military threat. Rather, many Chinese newspaper reports accused Americans of deliberately inflaming anti-PRC feelings and manipulating them to achieve a U.S. strategic objective, that is, weakening China and thwarting its modernization drive.[19]

Although Chinese resistance to Western influence is likely to lead China to follow the "Asian model of development," it cannot and will not abandon its open door to the industrialized countries of the West. Despite political similarities among remaining Asian socialist states (China, North Korea, Vietnam, and Laos), China's Asia connection will be oriented to the economically more advanced societies. If Beijing continues to maintain a reasonably stable relationship with Japan, South Korea, and ASEAN countries, its attitude toward the West will be partly contingent on these countries' relations with the West. The most important and relevant variable in this connection is the future of U.S.-Japanese relations.

ECONOMIC DECENTRALIZATION AND CHINA'S ASIA TIES

Another key factor in China's relations with the Asia-Pacific is the economic momentum on its periphery. The decentralization of the Chinese economy presents profound policy implications for dealing with neighboring states.

The Chinese economy in the reform period has demonstrated strong long-term factors at work that will likely sustain a high growth rate for at least the remainder of this decade. Nonetheless, for both structural and policy reasons, this growth was unevenly distributed.[20] It is vitally important for Beijing to deal competently with the relationship between the center and the localities, and to maintain a balance between centralization and decentralization. In reality, whether the central leadership is capable of doing so depends largely on its ability to develop responsive political institutions that can better reflect the views and interests of a more assertive society.

In the past few years, a major shift of economic power devolved from Beijing to the provinces. This derives partly from deliberate delegation of decision-making authority to local levels to boost economic incentives. But the process of decentralization was also propelled by external economic forces, especially in Guangdong, Fujian, Hainan, and the Yangtze Valley. Inland areas possess far less power, with those in the far northwest remaining largely dependent upon central government subsidies.

In the future, the fastest developing regions will be those which successfully establish external economic links. In addition to those regions mentioned above, export-oriented economic centers may emerge in the future from provinces and autonomous regions along other coastlines and borders. Possibilities include Heilongjiang (bordering with Russia), Jilin (with North Korea and Russia), Yunnan (with Burma, Laos and Vietnam), Guangxi (with Vietnam), and Shandong (across the sea with South Korea). This geographical redistribution of power and wealth should have important social and political impacts in China. Meanwhile, vigorous local initiatives for developing economic ties with neighboring countries also creates new Chinese policies toward the Asia-Pacific region.

A number of Southwestern provinces already expressed their ardent aspirations to catch up with more advanced coastal areas. He Zhiqiang, Governor of Yunnan, promulgated the slogan, "Open the south door, and face Asia-Pacific."[21] Looking beyond neighboring countries, he claimed that all of Southeast Asia is a "bridge and hub" for Southwestern China to enter international economic circles.[22] Governor He's remarks were echoed by Yang Rudai, former Party Secretary of Sichuan Province and currently a Politburo member of the Communist Party's Central Committee. Yang called for coordination of efforts made by the southwest provinces to "march toward Southeast Asia for developing the Great Southwest." People in this region have vigorously advocated the establishment of export-oriented economic zones that would enjoy preferential treatment like that of Shenzhen in the central government's policy.[23]

Furthermore, it is argued that the Southwest provinces' economic ties with states on the Indochinese Peninsula, "to some extent," already became closer than those with the Chinese inland.[24] Previously, the opening of southwest China (comprising Yunnan, Guizhou, and Sichuan Provinces, the Guangxi Zhuang Autonomous Region, and the Tibetan Autonomous Region) to the outside world was accomplished via coastal regions. However, many complain that this approach did not serve the region's best interests, thus enlarging the economic gap between coastal and Southwest China. To respond, the Southwest provinces should make full use of their advantages in resources and geographical location and develop their own projects for opening to other regional economies.[25]

Some contend Southwest China is competing with Indochina and Thailand for foreign investment, but remains disadvantaged at this stage of development. On the other hand, Southwest China is competing with ASEAN in exporting commodities to Indochina. Because Vietnam wants to join ASEAN, and because Laos and Burma are also interested, it is now urgent for these Chinese provinces to become more competitive and strengthen their connection with these neighbors.[26] Some experts call for sub-regional economic cooperation between China, Laos, Thailand, and Burma.[27] A more ambitious scenario proposes that Southwest China serve as a "Eurasia Corridor" through which Southeast Asia would be linked with Central Asia and Europe.[28] Specifically, proposals have envisioned the provinces and autonomous regions coordinating their efforts to establish export-processing free zones.[29]

Ambitious plans for developing economic ties between Northern China and adjacent foreign regions are found in the Chinese press. One chapter describes the emergence of a "Northeast Asia Economic Cooperation Region" which embraces North China, Japan, the Korean Peninsula, Mongolia, and the Russian Far East. The author divides this economic region into "three circles and one area": the Tumen River Circle, the Vladivostok Circle, the Yellow Sea Circle, and the Chinese-Russian-Mongolian Borders Area.[30]

Other reports are more specific in discussing concrete steps toward closer economic interaction between China's northern provinces and the neighboring countries in Northeast Asia. Suggestions are made for establishing privileged economic zones and further decentralization, much like those proposals for Southwest China. Shandong Province regards its booming economic relations with the Republic of Korea (ROK) as a vehicle for "participating in the division of labor in the Asia-Pacific region," which will "activate the economic takeoff of the whole province."[31] From 1988-91, Shandong's exports to South Korea increased 113 percent annually, more than doubling the 49.9 percent increase of the PRC's total exports to South Korea. The report proposes a number of measures to attract South Korean investment in Shandong, including the founding of "ROK Industrial Parks" in the cities of Qingdao, Yantai, and Weihai.[32]

Taking notice of this local enthusiasm and potential, some authors advocated diversification of China's participation in Asia-Pacific regional economic cooperation. They argue it is not enough for the PRC to take part in regional bodies such as APEC—southern provinces should also join the South China Common Market (obviously referring to the close association among Guangdong, Fujian, Taiwan, and Hong Kong), and the nine provinces and municipalities in North and Northeast China should enter into Northeast Asian regional cooperation.[33]

The development of economic cooperation with bordering states requires a peaceful international environment and further easing of international tensions. It is recognized, for instance, that the territorial disputes between Japan and Russia, as well as the tensions on the Korean Peninsula, constitute impediments to regional economic cooperation on a multilateral basis.[34] Additionally, the unfolding plans for the Tumen River economic zone in China's Jilin Province depend partly on the political stability of North Korea and its policies toward South Korea, Russia, and China.[35] The growing economic links between Southwest China and Southeast Asian countries are contingent on Beijing's relations with their governments, and a negotiated settlement of the disputes over Nansha (the Spratlys) will be conducive to economic cooperation in the region.[36]

Although there is no hard evidence that Beijing now has to consult provincial and local governments before readjusting its foreign policies toward concerned neighboring countries, the continued decentralization, with the growing assertiveness of provincial and local interest in China, is likely to drive Beijing in that direction. Diversified interests in China will not only serve as a catalyst for strengthening Beijing's ties with other Asian-Pacific countries, but will, hypothetically, also become a lubricant in case these ties are jeopardized by territorial, ethnic, or other disputes.

The burgeoning economic ties between China's provincial areas and their neighboring countries stimulated an unprecedented interest among local officials, scholars, and entrepreneurs in these foreign countries, deepening Chinese understanding of the Asia-Pacific region. A new generation of China's international "area specialists" are emerging from provincial capitals and elsewhere. They seem to be more open-minded in perceiving the outside world. Often representing local interests, they are introducing new perspectives which differ sharply from those of the international analysts and area specialists working directly for the central government in Beijing.

New Chinese interests in investigating the conditions of other regional countries tend to narrow the existing perception gaps between Chinese and other Asian peoples. Several years ago, a Southeast Asian specialist put it bluntly, "what is seen by China as its opportunities or assets in dealing with Southeast Asia may well be actually its limitations or liabilities from the Southeast Asian perspective."[37] This situation is now changing.

For example, in their own observations, some writers in South China recognize that Indonesia is still on its guard against the ethnic Chinese in that country, who play an economic and commercial role out of proportion to their numbers. The Indonesian government is concerned that some ethnic Chinese business people are reducing their investment in Indonesia in order to put more capital in China. The Chinese, it is pointed out, should be more sensitive to issues related to the ethnic Chinese problem in Southeast Asian countries so that economic relations with them can be smoothly enhanced.[38] For another example, contrary to the general impression created by the Chinese media, a local researcher stresses the decline of the Chinese cultural tradition in Singapore.[39] These kinds of perceptive remarks were rarely found in Chinese publications a few years ago.

In the past, it was feared that nostalgic feelings about China's past grandeur and cultural superiority in Asia might be mobilized to heighten its nationalistic posture. The often misleading references to other cultures in this region as "subcultures of the Han culture" could imply the relative insignificance of China's smaller neighbors and impede China's understanding of its own image and position in the region. Now with the rapidly expanding exchanges of consumer goods, personal visits, and information at various levels and across the vast geographical areas, misperceptions between the Chinese and other peoples are being reduced, although they cannot be removed easily.

CONCLUSION

China's policies toward the Asia-Pacific region are consistent with its domestic agenda of focusing on economic development along the road toward a "socialist market economy." Energetic economic drives by both the central leadership and local officials dictate a strong interest in furthering good relations with other countries in the region. This general policy orientation facilitates China's expanded participation in the world economy and enhances the image of a responsible power willing to contribute to regional peace and cooperation.

In the years to come, initiatives taken by China's local governments and enterprises will assume a more systematic and outspoken form, injecting new momentum and new influences into the central leadership's foreign policy decision-making. The local influences on the center will be generally positive. Meanwhile, the prospects for national disintegration along regional lines are very remote, if not totally inconceivable.

The motivation behind China's reaching out for closer Asia-Pacific connections include a desire to learn from the economic and political experiences of the regional societies and a need to fend off Western interference in the PRC's domestic affairs. A commitment to economic and political reform should make Beijing more pragmatic in its foreign policy in general and its regional policies in particular, whereas a retreat from reform or a failure to maintain domestic stability would create more uncertainties and pitfalls. China's neighbors, and indeed the whole world, have a stake in the success of China's ongoing reform.

NOTES

1. Tong Zhiguang, "China Heading Toward a Trade Power," *Beijing Review* 36:3 (18-31 January 1993), p. 10.
2. Li Ning, "China Moves Closer to GATT," *Beijing Review* 36:6 (8-14 February 1993), p. 13.
3. *Beijing Review* 36:2 (11-17 January 1993), p. 5.
4. Ibid, p. 5.
5. The Atlantic Council of the United States and the National Committee on United States-China Relations, "United States and China Relations at a Crossroads," policy paper, February 1993, p. 23.
6. Chen Xuegen, "The Wind From the South," *Nexus*, no. 23 (Spring 1993), pp. 15-16.

7. Wu Naitao, "From Planned to Market Economy," *Beijing Review* 36:2 (11-17 January 1993), p. 16.

8. Cheng Jingbiao, "Asia-Pacific economic ties grow closer," *Beijing Review* 36:6 (8-14 February 1993), p. 10. According to another account, the PRC's trade volume with the major countries and areas in the region amounted to $103.8 billion in 1991, or 76 percent of its total foreign trade volume. See Wang Zhile, "Zhongguo Canjia Yatai Quyu Hezuo de Mubiao Xuanze" [Setting Objectives in China's Participation in the Asian—Pacific Regional Cooperation], *Yatai Jingji* [Asia-Pacific Economics], no. 5 (October 1992), p. 1.

9. Li Ning, op. cit., p. 13.

10. See Frank Ching, "Scientific Meetings Being Held to Reduce Spratlys Tension," *Far Eastern Economic Review*, 27 May 1993, p. 30.

11. For example, during the Taiwanese elections in 1994, when independence once again became a campaign issue, Beijing reasserted its position that any Taiwanese declaration of independence will be equivalent to a declaration of war and met with a military invasion. China also responded vigorously to U.S. President Clinton allowing Tawainese President Lee to visit his alma mater, Cornell, in 1995. The planned resumption of cross-Strait talks in the summer of 1995 was postponed indefinitely, while U.S.-Chinese military contacts, which had been increasing steadily since 1994, were temporarily suspended. Beijing's strong diplomatic rhetoric regarding Taiwan's proposal for UN entry and President Lee's visit to a few European countries in 1995 illustrated the leadership's sensitivity regarding the "one China" policy.

12. Shen Huasong, "Kaiming Qiquan Zhuyi Yu Shichang Yuanze Xiangjiehe" [The Combination of Enlightened Authoritarianism and Market Principles], *Shijie Jingji Yu Zhengzhi* [World Economics and Politics], no. 8 (August 1992), p. 34.

13. See Xi Shuguang and Yang Ping, eds., *Kua Shiji Duihua* [A Dialogue Standing on the Century-dividing Point] (Chengdu: Sichuan Renmin Chubanshe, 1992), pp. 420-422.

14. For a very insightful analysis of North Korea's considerations about establishing the free economic zone, see Yan Shi, "Lun Chaoxian de Ziyou Jingji Maoyi Qu" [On the DPRK's Free Economic and Trade Zone], *Dongbeiya Yanjiu* [Northeast Asian Studies], no. 3 (June 1992), pp. 42-45.

15. Wen Song, "Zhongguo Yuanzhu Laowo de Xin Xuanze" [A New Choice in China's Assistance to Laos], *Dongnanya Yanjiu* [Southeast Asian Studies], no. 2 (April 1992), p. 55.

16. Wei Tianqi, "Jinnian Miandian Jushi Zongshu" [A Survey of Burma's Situation in Recent Years], *Dongnanya Yanjiu*, no. 6 (December 1992), p. 36.

17. The Atlantic Council and the National Committee on U.S.-China Relations, *United States and China Relations at a Crossroads* (policy paper, Barber B. Conable, Jr. and John C. Whitehead, co-chairs, and David M. Lampton and Alfred D. Wilhelm, Jr., co-rapporteurs), February 1993, p. 40.

18. Cheng Ye, "Riben Zhengzai Cong Jingji Daguo Zouxiang Zhengzhi Daguo" [Japan Is Moving from an Economic Power to a Political Power], *Waiguo Wenti Yanjiu* [Foreign Studies], no. 4, (December 1992), p. 34.

19. See, for instance, Chen Te-an, "Zhuguan Yixiang Daiti Bu Liao Keguan Xianshi: 'Zhongguo Weixie' Lunxi" [Subjective Fabrication Cannot Replace Objective Reality: A Comment on 'China Threat'," *Renmin Ribao* [People's Daily], 27 March 1993.

20. For instance, by 1990 some 60 percent of all foreign investment in China was in Guangdong Province, a fact which helped it achieve explosive growth rates, some of the highest living standards in China, and export production roughly one fifth of China's total. See Robert Kleinberg, *China's "Opening" to the Outside World: The Experiment with Foreign Capitalism* (Boulder, CO: Westview Press, 1990), p. 233.

21. Shen Xu, "Fazhan Xinan Diqu Yu Zhongnan Bandao Jingmao Guanxi de Jidian Sikao" [A Few Suggestions About Developing Economic and Trade Relations Between the Southwest Region and the Indochinese Peninsula], *Yunnan Shehui Kexue* [Yunnan Social Sciences], no. 4 (August 1992), p. 14.

22. *China Daily*, "Business Weekly," 11-17 April 1993, p. 6.

23. Shen Xu, op. cit., pp. 14-20.

24. Ibid., p. 14.

25. Wang Chongli, "Daxinan Kaifa de Duiwai Kaifang Shijiao" [The Opening Angle for Developing Great Southwest], *Yunnan Shehui Kexue*, no. 1 (January 1992), pp. 10-15.

26. Shen Xu, op. cit., pp. 14-15.

27. Tan Guolin and Su Wenjiang, "Zhong, Lao, Tai, Mian Pilin Diqu de Jingji Jishu Hezuo" [The Economic and Technological Cooperation in the Border Area of China, Laos, Thailand and Burma], *Yatai Yanjiu* [Asia-Pacific Studies], no. 3 (June 1993), pp. 68-72.

28. Wang Chongli, op. cit., p. 15.

29. Bao Kunming, "Jiejian Dongnanya Guojia de Jingyan Kaichuang Woguo Xibu Diqu Xiyin Zhijie Touzi de Xin Jumian" [Draw on the Experiences of the Southeast Asian Countries and Create a New Situation in Absorbing Direct Investment for Our Country's Western Regions], *Yatai Yanjiu*, no. 3 (June 1993), p. 66.

30. Luo Bengu, "Lun Dongbeiya Jingji Hezuo Qu de Zouxiang Ji Hezuo Fangshi Yu Buzhou" [The Northeast Asia Economic Cooperation Region: Its Prospects, Pattern, and Process], *Dongbeiya Yanjiu*, no. 4 (August 1992), pp. 7-13.

31. Han Jianguo and Xu Ningjiang, "Shandongsheng Tong Hanguo Kaizhan Guoji Maoyi Jingji Hezuo de Kaocha Yu Sikao" [Observations and Considerations of Developing Shandong Province's International Trade and Economic Cooperation with the ROK], *Yatai Jingji* [Asia-Pacific Economics], no. 5 (October 1992), pp. 56-63.

32. Ibid.

33. Wang Zhile, op. cit., p. 6.

34. Luo Bengu, op. cit., p. 11.

35. Yan Shi, op. cit, pp. 40-45.

36. He Shengda, "90 Niandai Zhongguo Xinan Yu Dongnanya d Jingji Hezuo" [Economic Cooperation Between China's Southwest Region and Southeast Asia in the 1990s], *Yunnan Shehui Kexue*, no. 5 (October 1992), pp. 18-19.

37. Chang Pao-Min, "China and Southeast Asia: The Problem of a Perceptual Gap," *Contemporary Southeast Asia* 9:3 (December 1987), p. 189.

38. See, for example, Wen Beiyan, "Jiji Fazhan Guangdong Dui Yinni de Jingmao Guanxi"

[Actively Develop Guangdong's Economic and Trade Relations with Indonesia," *Dongnanya Yanjiu*, no. 5 (October 1992), pp. 20-23; Zheng Renliang, "Guanyu Yinni Huaren Caituan Yinqi de Zhenglun" [Controversy Over the Ethnic Chinese Financial Groups in Indonesia], *Dongnanya Yanjiu*, no. 2 (April 1992), pp. 40-45.

39. Huang Songzan, "Xinjiapo Huaren de Shengcun Daolu" [The Road of the Ethnic Chinese in Singapore], *Dongnanya Yanjiu*, no. 5 (October 1992), p. 49.

7 The Interaction Between Economics and Security For China's External Relations

Tai Ming Cheung

INTRODUCTION

In the post-Cold War order, the relationship between economics and security is virtually inseparable. Prosperity and stability is crucially dependent upon exports to foreign markets and the unimpeded import of raw materials, technology, and capital. For China, however, this interdependence was not always accepted. Before the 1980s, Chinese leaders prided themselves on economic self-reliance. Maoist radicals believed that the country's national security was best secured by relying on its own resources and internal markets. But the overriding result was the sacrifice of economic development as the Chinese economy stagnated. Chinese leaders eventually realized that maintaining security without development was not a feasible long-term option. When more pragmatic leaders assumed power in the late 1970s, these radical policies were overturned and replaced by those that stressed economic modernization. Policymakers also began to rethink their views of the relationship between economics and security. Past dogmas that stressed the superiority of ideology over professionalism and self-reliance over interdependence were rejected.

But Chinese policymakers are finding the division between economics and security increasingly blurred. China's rapidly growing external trade means that security planners are focusing more attention on how to safeguard this trading environment. The search for economic resources, particularly in the country's surrounding seas, means a broadening of China's national security realm, particularly into the maritime sphere. Even in Beijing's foreign policy activities, economic and security dimensions are more related in several key relationships, such as Sino-Russian ties. Finally, the sweeping conversion of the Chinese defense industry from military to civilian production included its integration into the rest of the economy.

This growing interaction between economics and security in China's external relations is the focus of this chapter. Attention will be paid to the shifting attitudes of Chinese policymakers towards the relationship between economic and security policies. Next, a discussion of a number of developments with potentially far-reaching ramifications for China's long-term security posture and its impact in Asia and beyond will be included. One issue is how economic development is redefining and broadening China's national security realm. Chinese officials are making it clear that they view large areas of the seas surrounding China as being under their control. This includes disputed territories such as the Spratly islands in the South China Sea. How far will China's national security realm extend? How far will China go to defend its interests?

Another issue is how economic and security issues help to define China's foreign relations. Of particular concern are China's ties with key neighboring and regional powers, including the United States, Japan, and Russia. What is the primary impetus behind Beijing's ties with these states? In the post-Cold War order, have security and military relations taken on a secondary role to trade and other economic imperatives? What is the importance of arms sales in China's foreign relations and in its dealings with other developing countries?

Attention will be paid to what the country's economic development means for the military and defense-industrial establishments. Rising prosperity and technological levels undoubtedly allow China's military capabilities to become more advanced and powerful. But what is the likely pace and scale of this transformation? Where will resources be allocated and spent in the overhaul of the massive but backward People's Liberation Army (PLA) and the defense industry? How much will defense spending grow and to what extent will the government provide increases or will they come from the military's own money-making activities?

HISTORY OF ATTITUDES TOWARDS THE RELATIONSHIP BETWEEN ECONOMICS AND SECURITY

One of the main conundrums that Chinese policymakers tackled in the past 45 years of nation-building was finding a balance between maintaining a strong national security posture while pressing ahead with economic development. But achieving this balanced approach was elusive. Policies alternated between favoring either security or economic priorities, rather than paying equal attention to them.

This lack of symmetry is because of the compartmentalized nature of the policymaking process in which the military and economic bureaucracies are kept separate from one another. This meant military and economic planners paid scant attention and had little understanding of each others' needs and outlooks, and it generated fierce institutional rivalries, in particular in the competition for limited national resources.

More significantly, top leaders were torn in their attitudes toward the importance of the relationship between security and economic priorities. Their views were primarily dictated by the drastically changing external challenges that China faced. These different attitudes can be separated into two periods. The first phase spanned the period from the founding of the People's Republic to the passing of Mao Zedong and his followers from power in the late 1970s. During this period, security considerations were of paramount concern because of the perceived threat of imminent conflict with the United States in the 1950s and then with the Soviet Union in the 1960s and 1970s. With the country fighting for its survival, security interests and policies were defined in narrow military terms. Maintaining a strong defense posture to safeguard the country's border was emphasized. This meant not only building up a massive military establishment supported by a large defense-industrial complex, but also that much of the rest of the population and the economy were geared toward playing a supporting role. Efforts at boosting economic development were concentrated in areas that were considered strategically important, such as heavy industry. China's leaders downplayed modern military power, instead emphasizing the economic and social basis of national capacity to survive an attack.

China was isolated from the rest of the international community, including economically. Although a heavy economic price was paid for this, Chinese leaders at the time believed that autarky was essential to the country's national security and at the same time, it boosted China's image as a global power independent of the U.S. and Soviet-dominated global balance of power. One of the main reasons for Beijing's decision to turn to self-reliance was the painful lesson of its overdependence on Soviet assistance in the 1950s. Although much of Moscow's help was devoted to building up China's military-industrial complex, the abrupt pullout of Soviet specialists following the rift in relations at the end of the 1950s showed Chinese leaders the dangers of looking abroad for economic assistance. The entrenched radicalism and xenophobia within China throughout the 1960s and much of the 1970s ensured that self-reliance became a chapter of official faith.

Only when Deng Xiaoping took power in the late 1970s and purged radicals from the leadership did a new perspective emerge. It was a turnabout as security and military issues were relegated to a secondary position and policies aimed at promoting economic development assumed central importance. This was spelled out in the Four Modernizations program, in which the reform of the agricultural, industrial, and science and technology sectors took precedence over defense modernization.

Policymakers were also revising their notions of what constituted the country's national security goals and how they should be safeguarded. Many of the new views were put forward by Deng, who said that China was no longer threatened by an imminent or large-scale threat of conflict. This meant that defense planners could relax from their heightened state of military preparedness and concentrate on slimming the PLA's size and become more involved in helping to realize the country's economic reforms.

However, changing long-held notions of security was not an easy matter, especially given the entrenched conservatism within the military-dominated security policy-making apparatus. PLA chiefs, aware of the importance of economic reforms, still were not keen to lessen their role in protecting the country's national interests. These concerns were expressed in the early 1980s debate within the senior civilian and military leadership over the need for substantial cutbacks in the PLA. Eventually, this debate resulted in a decision at the enlarged meeting of the Central Military Commission (CMC) in July 1985 to cut one million troops from the PLA payroll, about a 25 percent reduction in troop numbers.[1]

The debate saw different numbers put forward over the need to drastically scale back the number of soldiers in favor of a smaller but better trained and equipped force. Most civilian leaders supported this move because it reduced the military's heavy economic burden at a time when large-scale investments were needed to sustain the rapid momentum of economic reforms. Military chiefs also endorsed the need to consolidate, at least for the short-term. But they pointed out that this should only be a temporary expediency and more resources should be made available to the military industry within a few years as the economy grew. As Defense Minister General Zhang Aiping pointed out in 1983, "modernization of our national defense must be based on the construction of our national economy." But, he added that with the country's economic development, "more favorable conditions will be created in turn for our national defense modernization. This means not only funds for building national defense will be increased, but more fine scientific and technological personnel and newer scientific and technological results will also be shifted to the military industry to promote the development of national defense modernization."[2]

Military chiefs, therefore, accepted the cutbacks, but only in return for assurances that they would be granted more resources later. Defense spending between 1979 and 1989 declined steadily in real terms by an annual average of approximately seven percent. At the same time, the military-industrial complex underwent sweeping reform aimed at converting most of its production from military-related goods to civilian products. This scaling back of the defense-industrial complex and defense spending drastically curtailed Chinese foreign military assistance programs.

But the earlier promises that the military eventually would be rewarded with more resources began to be met at the end of the 1980s. The defense budget increased by more than 12 percent annually since 1990. Appropriations almost doubled in absolute terms between 1989 and 1993, rising to $42.5 billion in 1993. Hidden allocations are estimated to have grown by the same amount. The additional resources now being set aside for the PLA indicates that with a rapidly expanding economy and good prospects for continued growth throughout most of the 1990s, policymakers are finally seeking to achieve a balance between economic development and the building of a strong security posture. Recent remarks by senior Chinese officials confirm this thinking. At the eighth National People's Congress in Beijing in March 1993, Communist Party General Secretary and CMC Chairman Jiang Zemin pointed out that only by "building up a strong army that is commensurate with our national status can we guarantee that our national security will be safeguarded and that socialist modernization can progress smoothly."[3]

To underline how resistant the military was to changes in national priorities, another debate in 1992 about further PLA cutbacks was rejected. The issue was discussed since the late 1980s, when it became apparent that only 800,000 troops were demobilized from the target figure of one million. With the end of the Cold War and improved relations with many of China's neighboring one-time foes, including Russia, India, and Vietnam, the need for a sprawling military establishment with more than three million troops was seen as excessive. An enlarged CMC session in April 1992 included military chiefs discussing whether and how large the cutbacks should be. A total of 300,000-500,000 troop cuts were under consideration, including the consolidation of the military command structure and support facilities.[4]

However, military chiefs eventually decided against a major demobilization and approved a more modest plan to close 20 military academies and schools and streamline the PLA general staff headquarters. Around 100,000 positions were eliminated. The decision against further sweeping cutbacks was taken because military officials believed that the PLA's present size represented the minimal level of forces necessary because of China's large size and diverse security needs. In terms of the ratio of soldiers to the overall population, China has one of the lowest figures in the world. They did not mention, however, that a large proportion of military units today spend more time engaged in money-making activities than undertaking professional duties.

Although economic development continues to remain the government's central priority, security issues are likely to assume higher prominence in the coming years even though China is relatively secure. So why does China need to build up its military? The primary reason is that Chinese leaders continue to regard military power as one of the most important instruments to achieve their objectives and defend their interests. Since 1949, Chinese leaders did not hesitate to use military force on numerous occasions, including the Spratly Islands in March 1988 as a warning to Vietnam to stop pressing its territorial claims, and against its own people in the streets of Beijing in June 1989.

This does not mean, however, that Chinese policymakers take any decision to use force lightly. But they are more open to consider military options at an earlier stage than their counterparts in the West. This tendency is because military power used to be one of the only levers of influence that Chinese leaders had at their disposal in the pursuit of external objectives. The country's economic might was inconsequential and its diplomatic muscle limited. While the rapid expansion of the Chinese economy will increase the country's economic importance in world affairs, China's main claim to global power status will still be based on its possession of a massive and increasingly potent military establishment. As these other non-military levers of influence become gradually more effective, Chinese policymakers will at least have a wider choice of options to choose from in the pursuit of their national interests.

CHINA'S EVOLVING NATIONAL SECURITY REALM

The extent to which Chinese decisionmakers are ready to use force will be determined by what they consider their most critical national security interests. Almost all of these interests fall within the boundaries of what policymakers perceive as their national security realm. Chinese views of this realm today are significantly different than they were only a decade ago. The difference is not what policymakers see as the geographical extent of this realm, but rather in how they perceive their ability to be able to secure control of it.

The national security realm can be broken down into several parts that radiate from the Chinese heartland. The core component is continental China as acknowledged on official maps. Some of the border regions in Western China may be in dispute with a few of its neighbors, but Chinese security planners are not worried these days about any serious threat to China's territorial integrity. Any possibility of invasion almost completely disappeared with the breakup of the Soviet Union.

The next part of this security realm is the waters surrounding China. It is here where more serious problems and conflicting interests between China and several of its neighbors exist. Until the beginning of the 1980s, the maritime realm did not figure highly in security planners' priorities because they were still preoccupied with the threat of a land invasion from the Soviet Union. Policymakers had not fully recognized the vast economic potential of the offshore maritime realm. But views on the significance of these waters quickly changed and they began to receive top-level attention from senior leaders in the mid-1980s.

The leaders were impressed by some of the estimates of the economic value that lie within China's maritime waters. By the year 2000, according to one forecast, the value of marine exploitation will be more than two percent of the country's gross national output.[5] The importance of offshore oil deposits to the country's economy is likely to grow substantially within the next 10 years because of the tapering off of production in some of China's long-time onshore oil fields. At present, offshore oil output accounts for only 2.5 percent of the country's oil production (3.5 million tons), but officials from the China National Offshore Oil Corporation, which is in charge of offshore activities, estimate that this could grow to 10 million tons in 1997 as new offshore fields are developed in the East and South China Seas. Total offshore "oil in place" reserves are estimated to be up to 850 million tons, although not all of this is cost-effective to recover.[6]

The riches fall within the three million square kilometers of maritime territory the Chinese claim. Chinese officials, however, say about one million kilometers of this territory is occupied or being illegally exploited by other countries, with the Spratly Islands and its surrounding waters considered the most serious violation.[7] At present, the Chinese navy lacks the ocean-going capabilities to stop this encroachment, but efforts are being made to correct this. Since the mid-1980s, the navy adopted an offshore defense doctrine to replace a more narrow and passive coastal defense strategy. This new naval doctrine is intended to effectively control territorial waters extending to the boundaries of its 200 mile exclusive economic zone and more than 1,000 miles into the South China Sea to include the Spratlys. This strategy is directed primarily against Vietnam and, to a lesser extent, other Southeast Asian states which are seen as the main trespassers. As China's navy chief Admiral Zhang Lianzhong has pointed out, "in order to effectively defend China against attacks from the sea, it is necessary to extend the depth of defense into the oceans and to have a naval capability of intercepting and destroying the enemy."[8] Since the early 1990s, Chinese law enforcement authorities and the navy vigorously patrolled their territorial waters to fend off suspected pirates or smugglers. There were numerous instances where Chinese ships fired upon foreign ships as they passed by Chinese or even international waters.[9]

China's maritime realm is now being codified into law by the Chinese government. In April 1992, the National People's Congress passed a law concerning its territorial waters that claimed all of the Spratlys and control over much of the adjacent waters. This action sent shock waves around the region as neighboring littoral states speculated whether or not this action signaled a more belligerent Chinese policy. Chinese maritime officials also are drafting a law on the delineation of the exclusive economic zone to mark out vast stretches of the waters around China considered to be under its control.[10]

Naval capabilities are being steadily upgraded, enabling the military to carry out these more aggressive, long-distance missions. Chinese shipyards in Shanghai and other port cities have rarely been so busy. New classes of more capable destroyers, frigates, and logistical support ships are coming off production lines to replace outdated 1950s and 1960s Soviet-designed warships that still make up most of the navy's front-line combatants. Warships are also being deployed further afield to provide training and experience for naval personnel as well as to display the Chinese flag and naval muscle. Not surprisingly, one area with particular emphasis is the Spratly Islands. But Chinese warships also sailed and exercised as far south as the Straits of Malacca and near Iwo Jima Island in the Western Pacific.[11]

Closely associated with the growing significance of the offshore maritime realm are the sea lanes where a rapidly expanding proportion of China's trade is being transported. Chinese security planners include the defense of sea lanes as one of the primary missions in the navy's offshore defense strategy. This protection is primarily limited to 200 miles off of China's coastline, which constitutes the extent of the Chinese navy's effective long-range capabilities. This protection is likely to extend farther as Chinese naval capabilities expand, although the country's legally defined exclusive economic realm will remain at the 200 mile mark (as stipulated in the International Law of the Sea convention).

Safeguarding Chinese seaborne trade beyond the country's immediate maritime borders will be one of the navy's future tasks as the present strategy evolves to become a blue-water naval strategy. Naval planners are unambiguous that this is their ultimate goal, especially as they discuss long-term warship building plans. One development plan publicly advocated by naval analysts calls for a three-stage evolution to a blue-water navy. The first stage, extending through the end of the century, places emphasis on construction of major warships equipped with guided missiles and advanced electronic hardware. This is already taking place. The second stage, in the first two decades of the next century, calls for the building of several light aircraft carriers of around 20-30,000 tons displacement as well as the acquisition of vertical take-off aircraft and warships to form carrier task forces. In the third stage, from 2020 to 2040, the Chinese navy plans to begin to approach the former Soviet or even U.S. naval capabilities and be able to conduct sizable naval operations anywhere around the world.[12]

While these grandiose plans are still decades away from being realized, Chinese security planners pay attention to developments among other regional naval forces that threaten China's maritime interests. Policymakers in Beijing pay particular attention to the naval and maritime policies of Japan and to a lesser extent, India. While these naval forces are focused on securing their territorial waters, their long-term outlook eyes more expansive notions of regional defense and influence. India's present sphere of influence stretches from the Arabian Sea north through South Asia, and southeast to the Andaman and Nicobar Islands less than 100 miles from Indonesia. Some Indian defense analysts say that the country's strategic domain eventually will extend to Southeast Asia.

Japan's naval build-up is keeping pace with China and India. The Japanese

Maritime Self Defense Force (JMSDF) boasts 60 destroyers and frigates, more than either China or India, although it has fewer coastal combatants and submarines. The extension of the JMSDF's security responsibilities in the early 1980s to 1,000 nautical miles from the Japanese coast, is motivated both by Japan's dependence on critical raw material imports and U.S. pressure to assume a burden-sharing role in regional security. While this build-up was further expanded when Japanese mine sweepers were sent to the Persian Gulf following the end of the Gulf War in 1991, Tokyo stressed that the strengthening of the JMSDF presents no threat to the rest of Asia.

Chinese security planners consider the potential Japanese threat in vague and futuristic terms. There are few perceived sources of tension that could provoke military confrontation, at least over the next decade. But one time bomb is the territorial dispute over the Senkakus (Diaoyudao Islands) 120 miles northeast of Taiwan in the East China Sea. Japan has possession of the islands, although Beijing and Taipei claim sovereignty. The islands are important in delineating the ownership of the continental shelf and seismic surveys have indicated that the waters around the islands are oil-rich.[13]

With the establishment of Sino-Japanese diplomatic relations in 1972, both Beijing and Tokyo agreed to shelve the dispute for, as paramount leader Deng Xiaoping said, "the next generation" of leaders to ponder. By acknowledging this status quo, Beijing tacitly conceded its claims to the Diaoyudaos in return for closer relations. Military planners, acknowledging they hold different views from Foreign Ministry counterparts, say the dispute remains unsettled and foresee naval tensions in the future, especially if Japan continues to build up its military capabilities.

Pragmatism in China's Bilateral Relations

When Deng Xiaoping assumed power and threw open the country's doors to outside economic ties at the end of the 1970s, China's external relations underwent vast changes. Ideology was cast aside, and trade, investment, and other economic contacts were actively encouraged, in particular with Western countries. Economic imperatives became a chief motivating force behind China's external relations. Even trade with the former Soviet Union and South Korea developed rapidly before China normalized relations with these two countries during the late 1980s.

Sino–American Relations: Economics Divorced from Security Issues

One of China's most important bilateral relationships is with the United States. But today's ties are substantially different and less significant than they were a decade ago when Beijing and Washington had close contacts and common interests in many areas, the most important being economic and security links. The June 1989 military crackdown in Beijing, however, resulted in an abrupt severing of almost all security exchanges. Although the two countries have maintained a limited dialog on international security matters, in particular in multilateral forums such as the UN Security Council, they have been steadily drifting apart strategically in the past few years until 1994, when military meetings were resumed. However, Taiwanese President Lee's visit to Cornell University in 1995 once again exacerbated tensions in U.S.-Chinese security relations. The strongest aspect of these relations, military exchanges, were suspended.

Interaction on security issues between China and the United States is characterized by strong differences even after President Clinton decided against linking human rights and the extension of most favored nation (MFN) status for China in 1994. Washington is concerned that China may still be flouting international conventions with covert exports of nuclear and missile-related arms and technology to unstable regions, in particular the Middle East and Southern Asia. This issue ranks as one of the top irritants in today's bilateral relations, along with human rights violations and a huge and widening trade deficit. From Beijing's perspective, however, the United States' attitude towards arms sales is duplicitous because of the high volume of U.S. weapons exports to these regions. This annoyance at perceived U.S. hypocrisy turned into outrageous indignation in September 1992 when Beijing learned of the U.S. administration's decision to authorize the sale of up to 150 early generation F-16 fighter aircraft to Taiwan. Chinese officials furiously condemned the deal and said it was in contravention of past communiqués and understandings signed between the two governments when they agreed to establish diplomatic relations in the late 1970s and wind down U.S. arms sales to Taiwan.

The sale underlined how far the Sino-U.S. strategic relationship changed in the post-Cold War era. Although U.S. President George Bush was considered sympathetic to Beijing, he still authorized the sale because of domestic political considerations linked to his presidential re-election campaign and to demonstrate his commitment to help the U.S. defense industry.[14] Although there were other reasons for Bush's decision, including Russian fighter aircraft sales to China and the deteriorating quality of Taiwan's front-line fighters, it was domestic U.S. political and economic imperatives that were more instrumental in changing one of the cornerstones of U.S. policy on China. Washington was no longer concerned about Beijing playing the "Moscow card," which in the past caused the United States to respect China's actions.

Although China threatened to disrupt economic ties immediately following the F-16 announcement, this proved to be largely empty rhetoric as few, if any, deals involving U.S. companies were canceled. Instead of a slowdown, Sino-U.S. economic ties have surged. U.S. companies are rushing to take advantage of the booming Chinese economy, and Chinese demand for high-quality U.S. goods, from airliners to cars, is also growing.[15]

The foreseeable trend in Sino-U.S. relations was one of increasingly important economic ties but a widening gap in the security and strategic arena. This state of affairs had many U.S. military and security policymakers and specialists worried that a lack of engagement with their Chinese counterparts would produce adverse effects on U.S. and international security interests over the long term, especially as China becomes a regional actor to be reckoned with. The resumption of high-level contacts between the U.S. and Chinese military establishments is an attempt to nurture channels of communication to foster a higher level of understanding between the world's largest armed forces. The cultivation of personal and working ties between senior U.S. and Chinese military officers is seen as one of the main achievements in the development of security and military contacts between Beijing and Washington from the late 1970s to the late 1980s.

Sino–Russian Relations: Economically Driven Security Relations

While Sino-U.S. security ties are in the doldrums, China's security and military relations with Russia have been developing at remarkable speed in the past few years. Indeed, it was the cut-off in Sino-U.S. military relations in the aftermath of the June 1989 crackdown that was one of the major factors that caused Beijing to decide to turn to Moscow. The first military delegations were exchanged toward the end of 1989 and relations began in earnest the following year.[16] The pace and scale of working ties today are frenetic, with Russian and Chinese military delegations from almost every branch of the armed forces and military-industrial complexes frequently exchanging visits.[17]

A critical factor affecting Sino-U.S. relations may be the Sino-Russian security relationship, which has three main objectives: seek reductions of troop levels and develop confidence-building measures along the Sino-Russian border, foster friendly exchanges between Russian and Chinese armed forces, and sell Russian arms and defense technology to China. Russian and Chinese officials downplay the significance of these ties, saying they can never return to the military alliance of the 1950s. However, judging from the level of exchanges taking place, both the troop exchanges and their pace extend well beyond any military and security interactions that China undertakes with other countries, even with Pakistan, where China is involved in several projects to help jointly produce trainer aircraft and a new generation of tanks. Even the height of the Sino-U.S. security relationship in the late 1970s does not match the current level of Sino-Russian defense ties.

The main motivating factor behind this military rapprochement is not strategic but financial. The Russian government, desperate for money to bail out its massive but insolvent military-industrial complex, regards China as one of the most lucrative markets today. Faced with the stark alternative of selling the best Russian arms and technology to almost anyone willing and able to buy these products or closing down much of its military-industrial complex, Moscow chose the first option. The Chinese bought $1.8 billion worth of arms, including 26 Sukhoi-27 fighter aircraft and the S-300 advanced air defense missile system.[18] Other projects are under discussion and a few crucial deals are likely to be made. The Chinese showed particular interest in a few high-technology areas, in particular the design and development of advanced fighter aircraft.[19]

Russia's willingness to assist in China's modernization of its military-industrial complex for short-term financial gains represents a golden opportunity for China. Although the initial costs of at least several billion dollars would be high, it would be a real long term bargain for China's defense technological and industrial establishments. The acquisition and integration of the latest Russian technology and know-how would initiate the improvement of China's technological levels within a short period of time. Although the financial costs involved are substantial, they are by no means crippling for the Chinese. A large proportion of the payments are believed to come from extra outlays outside of the officially announced defense budget. Payments are also easier because Russia is willing to accept barter for a large portion of the contracts. The Chinese only had to pay hard currency for 35 percent of the more than $1 billion for the Su-27s it purchased in 1991. The remaining 65 percent was paid with consumer and agricultural goods.

The weaving together of economic and security strands in Sino-Russian ties points to the forging of a close, stable, and long-term relationship. Economic ties between Russia and China also have been developing rapidly. Official trade between the two countries exceeded $6 billion in 1992.[20] This figure does not include the high volume of unofficial border trade conducted by individuals along the Sino-Russian border.

Although the value of Sino-Russian trade is recorded in hard currency figures, much of it is arranged in barter payment terms. This trading relationship is mutually complementary for both countries. China has an abundance of consumer products that Russia would like, while the Russians can offer industrial and technological goods, as well as potentially vast oil sources, that the Chinese economy lacks.

Sino–Japanese Relations: Strong Economic Ties Unable to Restrain Security Friction

China's relations with Japan are likely to become one of the pivotal bilateral relationships within the Asia-Pacific region in the coming years. How these ties develop will have a crucial bearing on the stability of the regional balance of power. Compared to China's relations with other major powers, the Sino-Japanese relationship is reserved and lacks maturity. This is in part because of the deep-seated historical resentments and distrust that China harbors toward Japan, in particular Japan's invasion and brutal occupation of large parts of China in the 1930s and 1940s. The Chinese government used Japanese Emperor Akihito's visit to China in 1992 to signal its willingness to put these past historical enmities aside, although strong undercurrents of anti-Japanese feelings still exist.

These historical animosities have limited the development of Sino-Japanese security ties. Even when both countries faced the common threat of a massive buildup of Soviet military forces in the Far East, there were no attempts to forge any strategic dialogue. Both countries preferred to deal indirectly with each other through their bilateral security ties with the United States. But with the severing of SinoñU.S. military ties in 1989, following the Tiananmen Square crackdown, a vacuum appeared in the Beijing-Tokyo-Washington triangle. Tokyo, which had refrained from expressing any serious criticisms of the Chinese leadership over the crackdown, stepped into the void and began to approach Beijing and open a security dialogue. The Chinese agreed to this because Tokyo was one of the largest donors of development assistance.[21] Japanese officials' main goal was to encourage the Chinese to curb military spending and weapons proliferation, and to involve them in efforts to work out a multilateral security framework in Asia. These contacts were confined to foreign ministry officials. The defense establishments remained distant from this process until 1994.

Short-term prospects of a more regular and institutionalized security relationship between the region's two powerhouses is limited. Even though they are neighbors with many overlapping security concerns, ranging from the Korean Peninsula to the Russian military presence in the Far East, security planners do not see any pressing need to develop a close dialogue. With the Soviet Union's demise, Tokyo and Beijing no longer share a common foe and look at each other in more threat-oriented terms. Japanese concerns are growing over Russian arms sales to China, in particular over reports of China's intended acquisition of an aircraft carrier and other naval purchases. With Japan dependent on access to sea lanes for most of its trade as well as energy and food resources, the prospect of China amassing naval capabilities that can cut off this lifeline worries Japanese security planners.

Can the expanding economic ties between these two Asian giants provide the impetus for security contacts in the future? Not really, since these two elements of the relationship have had little bearing on each other. This compartmentalization of ties means that in the security realm, the two countries will keep a respectful distance. Even if today's tentative security dialogue evolves into a more permanent arrangement, it will remain perfunctory. With the U.S. presence in Asia in gradual decline, Japan is assuming a more independent and assertive foreign policy posture. It is interested in expanding its influence through primarily economic means. This worries Chinese policymakers who are also eager to make their influence felt regionally. The prospects, therefore, for strategic competition between China and Japan are high and are certain to breed suspicion and rivalry.

GROWTH OF CHINA'S MILITARY AND DEFENSE-INDUSTRIAL CAPABILITIES

One of the most important long-term consequences of China's economic development is the modernization of China's military and defense-industry capabilities. Although the size of the PLA and the defense-industrial complex is unrivaled, these institutions are woefully backward technologically. Arms produced by Chinese defense factories are 20-30 years behind U.S. or Russian weapons. Almost all of the PLA's weapons systems are hopelessly outdated. But China's growing economic prosperity and access to foreign, and in particular Russian technology, can lead to an upgrade of China's defense industrial base. This would have a major impact on the regional balance of power.

The defense-industrial complex is currently in the throes of a sweeping consolidation that is aimed at shifting most of its output from military to civilian production. This conversion program forced the vast majority of defense plants to halt or drastically reduce their output of military equipment since the late 1970s. By the end of 1992, the total output value of civilian goods manufactured by defense plants accounted for almost 65 percent of the industry's total production as compared to eight percent in 1979.[22] The defense industry is one of the country's largest producers of motorbikes, cars, refrigerators, and other high-end consumer goods. Defense industry officials say that by the end of the Eighth Five-Year Economic Plan in 1994, they are aiming for civilian production to account for as much as 80 percent of the value of the defense industry's output. This will leave 20 percent of the defense-industrial complex devoted primarily to military production.

There are no official figures on the size of the defense industrial complex, but it is estimated to include more than 50,000 factories, research institutes, and other enterprises with perhaps more than five million personnel. These plants vary enormously in size, with several hundred being medium and large-sized enterprises, employing thousands of workers. There are also a number of huge complexes located deep in China's hinterland that are self-contained communities with their own schools, railway lines, and hospitals.[23]

This shake-up should allow those parts of the defense-industrial complex remaining in military production access to more and better resources. The financing of defense-industrial projects during the 1980s was woefully lacking and poorly planned. One report points out that investment in research and development (R&D) in the defense industry lagged well behind spending on weapons. Because of the specialized and highly technological nature of weapons R&D, "defense research requires a large investment, usually two and three times as much as research for civilian projects," says the report.[24] But actual per capita spending on defense R&D is lower than in the civilian sector. China's per capita investment in defense R&D in the mid-1980s was only one-eighth of what the United States spent. But because of the huge size of the defense R&D establishment, a large proportion of the limited funds were "used largely to keep the huge workforce in this sector in existence." The huge scaling down of the defense industrial complex will allow a more efficient and more capable one.

The defense industry had a dismal record in indigenously developing weapons systems. Almost all arms currently being produced are modifications of obsolete Russian equipment that date back to the 1950s. Chinese fighter-aircraft such as the A-5 ground attack aircraft or the F-7 interceptor fighter are based on Russian designs of the MIG-19 and MIG-21 fighters. Several of China's efforts to design and develop its own aircraft foundered because scientists and engineers have been unable to master the technology and the techniques.[25]

There are some signs that the Chinese defense industry's technological capabilities are steadily improving. In less technologically demanding areas such as tank and warship design, the Chinese were able to put out new generations of products. They also showed notable progress in the highly advanced field of missile technology. They are developing a new series of intercontinental ballistic missiles as well as tactical range missiles that have Western countries concerned because China intends to export them. Chinese efforts to upgrade its defense-industrial complex were substantially boosted by their access to Western technology and know-how during the late 1970s and late 1980s. Chinese defense industry and military delegations went on extensive shopping trips to the United States and Western Europe during this period to gather information and buy some of the most advanced technology. Particular attention was paid to aerospace technology, and China entered into several agreements to acquire Western avionics equipment to be fitted into Chinese airframes. The largest was a $550 million deal signed with the U.S. Grumman Aerospace Company in the mid-1980s to refit 50 Shenyang F-8II Peace Pearl fighters with U.S. avionics and fire-control systems. However, this and other projects were suspended following the June 1989 crackdown, when China's window to Western defense-industrial assistance was temporarily closed.[26]

Nonetheless, within a matter of months, China found an even more accommodating partner in the Soviet Union. Although the Soviets were reluctant to sell advanced technology to China, they were willing to sell Beijing the latest Soviet arms. Following the Soviet Union's breakup, the Russian government, with a military-industrial complex in economic malaise, was ready to meet Chinese demands for state-of-the-art defense technology. There is evidence that the Russians are beginning to provide the Chinese with information and designs for the development of sophisticated fighter aircraft, and the Chinese have extensive shopping lists for other types of hardware and technology (missiles, radar systems, and helicopters). Russia also helped refurbish more than 250 Chinese industrial plants equipped with 1950s era Russian machinery, some of which are located in the defense-industrial sector.[27]

The ability of the Chinese defense-industrial establishment to integrate and make use of Russian technology is strong, although it will be a daunting task as the systems and processors involved are several generations ahead of present Chinese levels. China's past experience in working with the Russian military-industrial complex during the 1950s will be of considerable benefit. Although the technology is new, thousands of Chinese scientists were trained in the Soviet Union in the 1970s and understand the Russian approach to science and technology. It will take at least another few years before new weapons systems begin to roll off Chinese production lines. A new generation of fighter aircraft will not begin to be ready for full-scale production for another decade.

The upgrading of the defense-industrial complex also means that China can afford a faster pace of weapons modernization for the PLA. This is likely to have a major impact on neighboring countries which are already watching China's modest military modernization efforts with apprehension. Chinese defense expenditures have been growing steadily since 1990 and this trend appears to be continuing into the near future.[28] The PLA's requirements are huge. Most of the 5,000 combat aircraft in the air force inventory are outdated and need to be replaced, as do most of its warships and tanks. Rather than an across-the-board re-equipment program, however, which would take decades to achieve, military chiefs are focusing their efforts and resources on upgrading a small number of elite units. They form the nucleus of a rapid deployment and power projection force that military planners regard as more suitable in dealing with China's present and future military needs. With the country no longer threatened by large-scale confrontation, military doctrine is directed towards dealing with limited local contingencies that take place either along China's borders or beyond. China's current ability to spend more on new weapons acquisitions will see these forces, which number several divisions, develop more quickly. It will also cause China's naval and air reach to grow more substantially towards the end of the 1990s.

New generations of locally made arms may cause China to re-emerge as a major seller in the international arms bazaar, although prospects still look bleak. During the 1980s, China exported billions of dollars worth of weapons, in particular to the Middle East and Asia. But sales dropped drastically after the late 1980s as many clients and prospective customers were enticed away by higher quality discount weapons systems from the United States, Soviet Union, and other advanced Western arms manufacturers. Some clients, initially attracted by low prices, were disappointed by the unreliability of the equipment and poor after-sales service. By the beginning of the 1990s, arms exports were no longer seen as a "cash cow" by the Chinese arms industry. A few new clients were found, like Burma, but its needs are considerably smaller than past customers (Iraq, Iran, and Thailand). Tough international restrictions on long-range missile exports also meant that lucrative sales made during the 1980s to Saudi Arabia and Syria are no longer possible. To partly compensate for this decline in business, the defense industry turned to exporting its civilian products. The nuclear industry was particularly active in exporting its nuclear technology and signed contracts with Pakistan, Iran, and other countries to build nuclear power stations for several hundred million dollars each.[29] China's arms exports only will become attractive again if it can substantially improve the technological standards of its weapons, and this will depend on whether China is able to acquire and master foreign technology.

CONCLUSIONS

After several decades of oscillating between economic and security priorities in the formulation of its national policies, China is now finding a balance that allows for economic development while also ensuring security interests are protected by a modest, but accelerating build-up in military capabilities. As China becomes an established and influential regional power, how will it use its newly acquired economic and military power to achieve its external objectives? Will the growing nexus between economic and security interests see policymakers take a more comprehensive and measured view of how to exercise their influence?

Whereas in the past Chinese policymakers were often limited to using military-related measures, such as providing arms or using force to achieve their external goals, they now have economic levers at their disposal. These economic instruments cannot be compared to the levels of aid and assistance Western countries are able to provide. As a major recipient of international economic assistance, China's foreign aid program is tiny. China's foreign assistance reached its peak during the 1960s and 1970s when China helped to build a number of high-profile infrastructure projects for African and Asian countries, such as a railway linking Tanzania to land-locked Zambia or roads in Laos. Since then, this assistance was cut substantially.

But as China grows more prosperous, it may again be willing to distribute its largesse to win influence. Beijing had been providing modest amounts of aid to some African and Asia-Pacific countries in an effort to stem efforts by Taiwan to win their diplomatic recognition. In 1990, China provided $800 million worth of agricultural export credits to the Soviet Union to allow it to import Chinese grain and other agricultural foodstuffs. Beijing may decide again to provide cheap weapons in return for influence, although these transfers also may be because of efforts by Chinese arms manufacturers to win new customers. One example is a burgeoning Sino-Burmese military relationship; China is giving sizable amounts of arms to Burma. Although these arms are costing Rangoon more than $1 billion, they are attractive to Burma because of the flexible terms of payment, such as barter, trade, and hefty discounting.

However, it appears that Beijing has not been willing to give free arms to gain influence—resulting in a drastic slump in Chinese arms transfers to North Korea. It is believed that Chinese leaders refused North Korean requests for large amounts of free arms following that country's cut-off from Soviet military assistance.

The primary economic card that China can play in expanding its external ties is access to its large and growing market. Few countries in Asia or major trading states outside of the region can afford to ignore the economic attraction and potential of Chinese trade. Fear of affecting trade relations with Beijing was the main reason countries such as Germany and the Netherlands refrained from selling arms to Taiwan. Southeast Asian states are also scrambling to develop economic ties with China. Singapore and Indonesia established diplomatic relations with China in 1990 after a long hiatus, and the Singapore government is now hoping to develop economic ties with China.

But China's economic importance as a trading partner works both ways. China cannot afford to damage economic relations with major economic powers, even if its relations with them are not good. This is particularly the case with the United States. Despite the sale of F-16 fighters to Taiwan, Beijing did not undertake any economic retaliation. Although the Chinese government closed down the French Consulate in Guangzhow when Paris decided to sell its fighters to Taipei, this was a mild step compared to Beijing's downgrading of diplomatic relations with the Netherlands in the early 1980s. And, although Chinese officials have threatened that Sino-British trade could be affected if London's row with Beijing persists over constitutional reforms in Hong Kong and the colony's return to Chinese sovereignty in 1997, no concrete steps were taken beyond these warnings.

Chinese policymakers increasing awareness that their political and security actions often have economic repercussions may result in a tempering of their attitude towards some of their territorial disputes. One important test will be the Spratly Islands. The use of force over the Spratlys could affect Chinese interests in its southern waters and in Southeast Asia. It might scare away potential foreign investors, including oil companies, which are reluctant to prospect for oil in an unstable region. In addition, it would heighten the already wary security concerns of Asian countries towards China, in particular Malaysia and the Philippines. This will damage Beijing's efforts to build up diplomatic influence in the region.

China began to focus attention on ways to settle the Spratlys dispute through negotiation. As Chinese Foreign Minister Qian Quchen said during a visit to Jakarta in June 1991: "We hope we do not see [the Spratlys dispute] become a root cause of tension in this region. On the contrary, we hope to see a common development in the common interests of this region."[30] While the common development is still a more theoretical than concrete concept, especially as Beijing's demand over sovereignty remains unacceptable to other claimants, more modest steps toward building confidence and understanding appear to be in the "pipeline." As a first step, Chinese specialists began to participate in academic and government-sponsored forums involving Southeast Asian states on issues relating to the South China Seas.

But these steps toward conflict resolution remain tentative. As China grows more powerful it also can behave more arrogantly. One of the developments to follow will be how much confidence China gains from its economic growth and how this will impact policymakers' views of the country's place in the world. There are strong assertive nationalistic feelings on the rise that could breed a more aggressive Chinese approach to the execution of its external priorities. If these views dominate, there will be grave consequences for China's overall national security.

NOTES

1. See Tai Ming Cheung, "Disarmament and Development in China," *Asian Survey* (July 1988).
2. "Zhang Aiping on Defense Modernization," Red Flag, 1 March 1983, in BBC, *Summary of World Broadcasts, The Far East* (hereafter SWB/FE), 18 March 1983.
3. Willy Wo-Lam, "Bid to Boost Military," *South China Morning Post* (SCMP), 23 March 1993.
4. See Tai Ming Cheung, "Fit to Fight," *Far Eastern Economic Review* (FEER), 3 May 1992.
5. Yang Jinsen, "Understand the Ocean, Exploit the Ocean," *Hongqi* (Red Flag), 1 April 1988.
6. Interview with Chen Bingqian, Vice-President, China National Offshore Oil Corporation, Beijing, October 1992.
7. Yi Yuanqiu and Wang Zhuanyou, "Establish Strong Border Defense Thinking," *Liberation Army Daily*, 6 October 1989.
8. "Interview with Navy Commander Zhang Lianzhong," *People's Daily* (Overseas Edition), 1 August 1983.
9. Lincoln Kaye, "Signal Guns," *FEER*, 18 February 1993.
10. Interview with Yan Hongmo, a senior administrator at the State Oceanic Administration of the People's Republic of China, Beijing, October 1992.
11. For the Iwo Jima exercise, see "Navy Reportedly Completes 'Extensive' Exercises," *Agency France Press*, 3 June 1986, in *Foreign Broadcast Information Service* (FBIS), China, 4 June 1986, p. Kl. See also "Report on Deep-Water Naval Exercise," Quinghai

Provincial Radio, 1 June 1987, in *SWB/FE/8585/BII/9*, 4 June 1987 which tells of an exercise by warships off the East Sea Fleet off of the Miyako Straits, several hundred kilometers to the East of Taiwan. Exercises in this area flex naval might in a demonstration to Japan over its competing claims against China over sovereignty of the Senkaku or Diaoyudao Islands near Taiwan, and also show the Taiwanese authorities that the PLA navy has the ability to blockade that island should that option be taken. On the exercise to the Straits of Malacca, see "First Naval Ocean Cruise," *Jianchuan Zhishi* (Naval and Merchant Ships), 8 March 1990. On the Senkaku (Diaoyudao) dispute, see Ji Guoxing, "The Diaoyudao (Senkaku) disputes and Prospects for Settlement," *The Korean Journal of Defense Analysis*, 6:2 (Winter, 1994), pp. 285-311.

12. Bai Kemin, "Orientation for Naval Development," *Naval and Merchant Ships*, 8 December 1988. Although such a plan is overly ambitious, its essential elements conform with the perceptions and aspirations that many naval planners hold.

13. China is at present actively inviting foreign oil companies to search for oil in areas in the East China Sea that is adjacent to the Senkakus, although in what China regards as its territorial waters. Interview with Chen Bingqian, Vice-President of the China National Offshore Oil Corporation, Beijing, October 1992. See also, Carl Goldstein, "Crude Optimism," *FEER*, 11 February 1993.

14. See Susumu Awanohara, "Election Dynamics," *FEER*, 20 August 1992.

15. Although the U.S. escaped Beijing's wrath over the F-16 deal, a French decision to allow the sale of 600 Mirage-2000 interceptor aircraft to Taiwan resulted in Beijing retaliating by closing the French Consulate in Guangzhou and excluding French participation in major infrastructural projects. Beijing did not want to risk the possibility of a trade fallout with the U.S., so the message of disapproval was sent over the arms sales to Taiwan by retaliation against France. But even these measures are relatively mild compared to Beijing's downgrading of diplomatic relations following the Netherlands' decision to supply submarines to Taiwan in the late 1970s.

16. For details of the relationship, see Tai Ming Cheung, "Ties of Convenience: Sino-Russian Military Relations in the 1990s," in Richard Yang, ed. *China's Military: The PLA in 1992/93* (Taipei: Chinese Council of Advanced Policy Studies, 1993).

17. Chinese military and military-industry delegations visit Moscow and many other Russian cities on a virtually continuous basis today. The Chinese Embassy in Moscow has considerably expanded its military representation to be able to handle this heavy volume of traffic. A military trade office has been added to the embassy's economic section to deal with weapons and technology transfer. This has been repeated in the Russian Embassy in Beijing. Besides the official diplomatic representations, one senior Russian Defense Ministry official says there are almost 100 Russian defense scientists and engineers n China at any one time and more than 300 Chinese defense specialists in Russian cities. Interview, Moscow, April 1993.

18. Russian President Boris Yeltsin announced this figure during a visit to Beijing in December 1992. But Russian Foreign Ministry officials were divided as to what this figure included. Some officials said that the figure was for contracts signed in 1992 while other officials involved in handling arms sales to China said it was a rough estimate for all arms sold to China since 1991. The differences indicate the confusion within the Russian

government bureaucracy in the country's political transition to accountable rule. Interviews, Moscow, April 1993.

19. A senior Russian Defense Ministry official said that Russian and Chinese aerospace companies and research institutes were beginning collaboration on the research and development of a new generation of Chinese fighter aircraft that would be in the performance range of between a MiG-29 and MiG-31 combat aircraft. If successful, this would represent a remarkable generational leap for the backward Chinese aerospace industry. The project is estimated to complete its development stage towards the end of this decade. Interview, Moscow, April 1993.

20. Interview, Moscow, April 1993. Russian and Chinese Railway Ministry officials forecast that the amount of freight traffic, which is the main means of transport for Sino-Russian trade, going across their borders will almost double in 1993 over 1992.

21. Japan has set out several principals to guide its Overseas Development Aid program, including calling on recipients to reduce their defense spending. The Chinese government gave some symbolic face to Japan by announcing during a visit by Japanese Prime Minister Toshiki Kaifu to Beijing in August 1991 that they were going to sign up to the nuclear Non-Proliferation treaty after almost 25 years of opposing it. Beyond this success, Japanese officials say that they have had little success in persuading the Chinese to cut back their defense spending. Tai Ming Cheung and Louise do Rosario, "Seal of Approval," *FEER*, 22 August 1991.

22. "Defense Industries to Shift Production Mix," *China Daily*, 8 December 1992, p 1.

23. Of the industries considered to be under the defense-industrial umbrella, the nuclear industry employees more than 300,000 personnel, the aerospace industry has more than 800,000 workers and the China North Industries Company, which is the country's largest arms conglomerate under the control of the Ministry of Machine Building and Electronics Industry, has nearly one million employees. State enterprises in the Third Line industrial region, which are primarily defense-related plants established deep in China's interior during the 1960s and 1970s because of the threat of invasion from the Soviet Union, total 29,000 plants employing more than 16 million workers. See Zhu Huiyi, "Despite the Difficulties Confronted by China's Nuclear Industry in Advancing Toward Peace, The Prospects are Broad," *China News Service*, 12 December 1988, in FBIS/China, 15 December 1988, p. 19; *China Daily*, 3 July 1991, Zhou Peide, "Development and Modernization of Defense Industry in China," *Defense Journal*, May-June 1986.

24. Zhang Jianshu, Ma Dangsheng and Liang Zhenxing, "Analysis of the Present State of the National Defense Scientific and Technical Corps and an Exploration of Policies for its Development," *Zhongguo Keji Luntan* (Forum of Chinese Science and Technology), no. 5 (18 September 1989), in *Joint Publications Research Service*, 25 January 1990, p. 77.

25. See Kenneth W. Allen, *People's Republic of China People's Liberation Army Air Force* (Washington, DC: Defense Intelligence Agency, 1991).

26. See Jim Mann, "China Cancels U.S. Deal for Modernizing F-8 Jet," *Los Angeles Times*, 15 May 1990.

27. John Kohut, "Russia Hopes to Boost Arms Sales," *South China Morning Post*, 15 December 1992.

28. Annual increases in the defense budget of at least 10 percent were agreed by military

chiefs in negotiations with the Finance Ministry and other economic panning organizations during the drafting of the Eighth Five Year Plan in 1990. This increase is also likely to be extended into the Ninth Five Year Plan beginning in 1995. Interviews, Beijing, December 1990 and March 1991.

29. Pakistan signed a contract in December 1991 for a Chinese 300-MW pressurized water reactor for around $500 million. See Tai Ming Cheung "Nuclear Ambitions," *FEER*, 23 January 1992. A similar deal was also signed with Iran in late 1992.

30. Beijing Claims Sovereignty Over Disputed Islands," *South China Morning Post*, 8 June 1991.

8 Economic Interdependence and Political *Détente:* The Evolution of Relations between the China Mainland and Taiwan

Jia Qingguo *and* Susan L. Shirk

After more than three decades of economic separation and political antagonism, the relationship between China and Taiwan has shown significant improvement in recent years. The first initiatives to open contacts made by the mainland government in 1979 were motivated by the political objective of reunification and not economic objectives.[1] However, the economic relationship drove the political relationship thereafter. Trade and investment across the Taiwan Strait eased political tensions between the mainland and Taiwan. While economic interdependence produced political *détente*, it also produced a whole range of problems complicating future relations.

The evolution of relations between China and Taiwan is an example of what Nye and Keohane called the trend toward "complex interdependence."[2] In the past, the two countries engaged each other only through their governments; but now they interact through multiple channels. In the past, Taiwan's fear of invasion was the dominant issue in the relationship, but now the agenda of the relationship consists of multiple issues, and military security does not always dominate the agenda. In the past, threats of military force were the main currency in the relationship, but now the incentives to use force are reduced.

The evolution of relations between China and Taiwan illustrates how asymmetries in a relationship serve as dynamics of integration as well as incentives of continued separation. An interstate relationship is usually an asymmetric relationship in which strengths and vulnerabilities are unevenly distributed between two parties. One type of asymmetry results from disparities of physical endowment: territory, population, military strength, natural resources, and so on. Another type of asymmetry is relative dependency on the economic relationship (this has to do with the comparative proportions of total trade, the dependence of investors with sunk costs on the host country, as well as what other options the countries have to substitute for their trade and investment with that country). And a third type of asymmetry concerns disparities in domestic political vulnerabilities.

In all these three aspects, the relationship between China and Taiwan finds the latter more vulnerable than the former. In terms of the physical endowment, the mainland is stronger than Taiwan. In terms of economic dependence on the other party, despite the huge surplus in favor of Taiwan, China as the larger economy is less vulnerable, as will be shown later in the chapter. And in terms of political autonomy, the authoritarian mainland is also less vulnerable to political demands than the democratizing Taiwan. Generally speaking, an authoritarian government is more capable of resisting societal pressures than its democratic counterpart. Consequently, economic integration between an authoritarian state and a democracy tends to create more direct political risks in the democracy than in the authoritarian state. Thus, as Taiwan democratizes, Taipei is becoming increasingly more vulnerable than Beijing to demands from economic and political interest groups that have vested interests in profiting from the economic integration of the two sides.

In an asymmetric setting, although the stronger party has the option to coerce and the weaker party finds good reasons to resist integration, they often choose to cooperate since it is usually more beneficial than confrontation. The degree of complementarity of the economies creates powerful incentives to cooperate. An economy with capital and technology has great incentives to invest in an economy offering cheap labor and a large domestic market. Recognizing that its cheap labor and large market represented a powerful economic magnet to Taiwan and that as the stronger party, it could push the economic relationship toward reunification, Beijing initiated a conciliatory policy toward Taipei in 1979. Taiwan, although the weaker party, responded, albeit belatedly.

With two economies that are highly complementary, once a cooperative option is taken, the economies involved begin to integrate, and the number of economic and social interests and institutions built on the basis of that option grows. The growth of interests and institutions helps reduce the incentives to use coercion. In order to regulate economic exchange activities, both sides set up institutions whose existence depends on the continuation of these activities and which by bureaucratic instinct oppose any actions that might reduce or put a stop to these activities. A positive cycle begins.

As economic interests take hold and translate into political considerations, the nature of the relationship changes from separation to interdependence, from exclusion to acceptance, from confrontation to *détente*. For the economic interests, confrontation and isolation is a mutually destructive game. Only competition and contacts can produce profits and development.

Interdependence is, of course, double-edged. Just as Morse pointed out many years ago, it generates new conflicts while displacing the old ones.[3] As military confrontation fades away as a real possibility, conflicts generated from economic exchanges become numerous and prominent. Quarrels over balance of trade, tariffs, market access, taxation, and so on become commonplace.

Such conflicts combined with political issues raise the specter of political and even military confrontation, however remote a possibility that may seem. Under asymmetrical situations, the party that feels vulnerable tends to over-react to conflicts and fear often hinders efforts for the establishment of mechanisms to regulate the relationship. Unless something positive is done to reduce the tensions, overreactions may lead to further overreactions, to the detriment of the interests of both parties.

Our chapter will explore the consequences of growing economic interdependence for political relations between China and Taiwan. First we briefly describe the dramatic increases in trade and investment between the two sides. Then we analyze the political consequences: The proliferation of social-economic interests in the mainland-Taiwan connection, the multiplication of concerned institutions, the growing pragmatism in their respective policies toward each other, and the emergence of a *détente* regime in the relationships. Finally, we look at the types of new conflicts produced by asymmetries in the interdependent relationship.

CROSS-STRAIT TRADE AND INVESTMENT

Mainland-Taiwan trade grew from $77 million in 1979, the first year of Beijing's opening-up policy, to $9.3 billion in 1993 (see table 1).[4] (The Taipei government did not lift the formal ban on indirect exports to the mainland until 1984.) This dramatic increase in cross-strait commerce occurred despite Taiwan's ban on direct trade; most cross-strait trade goes through Hong Kong.[5] Taiwan exports to the mainland consist mostly of industrial raw and semifinished materials, and parts and equipment for the plants owned partially or wholly by Taiwanese. The three largest categories of Taiwan exports to the mainland are thread, cloth, and other textiles (amounting to more than 20 percent of the total in 1989); electronic parts and accessories, machinery equipment, and bicycle parts; and chemical raw materials for plastics.[6] The major categories of mainland exports to Taiwan are agricultural raw materials such as Chinese medicine, feathers, clay, and animal hair; and manufactured goods like cotton yarn, cotton fabrics, ferro-silicon, and leather. In 1989, the biggest item imported from the mainland to Taiwan was Chinese medicine (14.5 percent of the total mainland imports), followed by feathers (eight percent), fresh fish (5.4 percent), and cotton yarn (three percent).[7] Taiwan has a huge trade surplus with the mainland, in part because Taiwan's exports are higher value-added than the raw commodities exported by the mainland, and in part because of Taipei's import restrictions. If the foreign exchange earnings from Taiwanese tourists to the mainland are included, then the current account deficit might disappear or tip in China's favor.[8] China has a deficit in its trade account, but its current account deficit would be even smaller or perhaps become a surplus.

Table 8.1: Mainland-Taiwan Trade by Year
(*millions U.S.$)

Year	*Mainland to Taiwan	†Ratio %	Growth Rate %	Taiwan to Mainland	‡Ratio %	Growth Rate %	*Imports & Exports
1979	56	0.41	27.9	21	0.13	53.3	77
1980	78	0.43	39.3	242	1.22	1052	321
1981	76	0.35	-2.6	390	1.73	61.2	466
1982	90	0.41	18.4	208	0.94	-46.7	298
1983	96	0.43	6.7	169	0.67	-18.8	265
1984	128	0.49	33.3	476	1.41	181.7	553
1985	116	0.42	-9.3	988	3.22	107.6	1104
1986	144	0.47	24.1	811	2.04	-17.9	955
1987	289	0.73	100.1	1227	2.29	51.3	1516
1988	478	1.01	65.4	2240	3.65	82.6	2729
1989	587	1.12	22.8	2896	4.38	29.3	3483
1990	768	1.36	30.9	3280	4.64	13.3	4048
1991	1130	na	47.1	4670	6.00	42.4	5800
1992	1130	na	0	6280	na	34.5	7400
1993	1300	na	15.04	8000	na	27.3	9300

Sources: Japan External Trade Organization, China Newsletter, no. 69; Free China Journal, 28 February 1992; Renmin Ribao, 24 February 1993, p. 5.; Xinbao, 11 January 1994, p. 3.

† Ratio (1): M to T/total exports of Mainland

‡ Ratio (2): T to M/total exports of Taiwan

Note: The figure for 1990 is interpolated from the 1991 figures according to the ratios in *Free China Journal,* 28 February 1992.

As of 1993, Taiwan's exports to Mainland China had grown to $8 billion, according to the conservative estimate of Taiwan's Ministry of Economic Affairs.[9] Taiwan's substantial exports to the mainland have become an important source of the island's trade surplus. According to the same estimate of the Ministry of Economic Affairs, Taiwan's trade surplus in its trade with the Chinese Mainland came to $5.7 billion in 1993, close to the total of its global trade surplus.[10] Taiwan's exports to the mainland are also a significant factor in its economic growth. According to a Taiwanese study, every dollar's worth of Taiwanese exports to the mainland can generate two dollars' worth of domestic production in Taiwan.[11]

Taiwan's economic dependence on the mainland, however, stems more from its foreign investments there than from the share of its exports sold to it. Taiwanese businesses invested on the mainland even before the Taipei government authorized indirect investments in 1989. Taiwan investors increased their activity after Taiwan lifted the prohibition against travel to the mainland in November 1987, responding positively to China's 1988 regulations granting preferential treatment to Taiwan-funded enterprises, and to additional measures on preferential treatment issued in March 1989. Total Taiwanese investments on the mainland grew from an estimated $100 million in 1987 to $13.6 billion by October 1993.[12]

In recent years, the rapid appreciation of the Taiwanese currency, sharp increase of labor costs, continuing growth of international protection, drastic political changes, increasing awareness of environmental problems, and burgeoning foreign currency reserves, rendered Taiwan's investment environment much less attractive than before. Taiwanese business tried to find places outside the island for investment. Meanwhile, with its low labor costs but high quality labor, various tax incentives, relative political stability, primitive environment control measures, an enormous domestic market as well as language and cultural affinity and geographical proximity, the mainland is an attractive investment alternative for Taiwan business.[13]

The flight of Taiwanese capital to the mainland was motivated primarily by the increase in labor costs on the island and was concentrated in labor-intensive light industries. According to Taiwan's 1990 regulations, indirect investments in mainland enterprises are permitted only in products that either require raw materials in abundant supply on the mainland, are produced by labor-intensive methods, are commodities with a relatively low degree of inter-industry interdependence, or are otherwise relatively disadvantageous to produce in Taiwan. Most of the items on the list are products of traditional, labor-intensive industries.[14] While Taipei has lifted controls over some more products, it still bans many products as broadly defined in the regulation. Taiwanese businesses invested in enterprises producing umbrellas, shoes, handbags, nonferrous metals, toys, textiles, sports equipment, photographic equipment, furniture, aquatic products, ready-made clothes, plastic manufactures, electronics, rubbers, construction materials, and petrochemical products, as well as in service industries such as tourist facilities.

Taiwanese investment in mainland production makes economic sense. The China mainland offers abundant labor, raw materials, a strong heavy industrial base, and a large domestic market to complement Taiwan's financial resources and managerial and marketing skills; Hong Kong is the link that provides the financial and information systems. Taiwan-funded enterprises receive their orders from

Taiwan, process materials supplied by Taiwan, and export through Hong Kong to the international market.[15]

As a consequence of Taiwanese investment on the mainland, the Taiwan and mainland economies have become highly integrated in some specific industries and regions. Several industries involve a particularly close integration of the two economies. Shoemaking was one of Taiwan's leading export industries, while Fujian also has a good reputation for making shoes. In 1986, the shoe industry accounted for 2.9 percent of Fujian's total industrial output and 10.8 percent of its exports. During the 1980s, Putian city, located between Xiamen and Fuzhou, became the athletic shoe production capital of China, with more than 40 factories that employ more than 60,000 workers. Leading U.S. (Nike, Reebok) and German (Puma, Adidas) corporations entered co-production and joint venture agreements with Fujian, and Taiwan's shoe industry followed.[16] The mainland and Taiwan shoe industries essentially have merged so that by 1992, 38.1 percent of all shoes sold in the United States were made in China, in Taiwan-owned and managed factories.[17] Taiwan's food and timber industries also became integrated with their mainland counterparts.

In the early years of Taiwanese investment on the mainland, Taiwan investors cautiously put their money into joint ventures or processing arrangements that were short-term and small in scale. Having grown more confident, they now prefer wholly-owned enterprises and larger, more long-term projects.[18] More than 70 percent of Taiwanese investments in Fujian province are in wholly-owned enterprises, and more than 90 percent of the investment agreements signed in 1989 between Xiamen city and Taiwan involved wholly-owned enterprises.[19] In such enterprises the Taiwanese investor does not have to rely on the uncertain abilities of local Chinese managers nor share the profits with Chinese partners.

Another trend is the increasing number of midstream and upstream industries like petrochemicals, yarn spinning, and fabric printing and dying that began to follow the traditional labor-intensive processing industries to the mainland. The best-known example was Taiwan plastics tycoon Wang Yung-ching's plan to build a $10 billion naphtha-cracking facility for his Formosa Plastics Corporation in Fujian province, a plan that was shelved for the time being because of objections from both governments.

By moving production to the mainland, Taiwan created new competitors to challenge its products in world markets. Competition from Taiwan-funded mainland plants is a real threat for Taiwan companies producing toys, shoes, bicycles, textiles, garments, plastic goods, aquatic products, hardware and machinery, and chemical products.[20] On the positive side, Taiwan, by shifting export-oriented production to China, sloughed off a portion of its trade surplus with the United States, thereby easing its own, and intensifying Chinese, trade frictions with that country. What causes Taipei officials the greatest anxiety, however, is the fear that the shift in production to the mainland will "hollow-out" the Taiwan economy; that heavy and petrochemical industries will not develop on the island fast enough to fill the vacuum created by the departure of traditional labor-intensive industries and that the departure of these labor-intensive industries will rob the economy of financial resources needed to develop electric power and other infrastructure supplies for the next generation of industries.[21]

MULTIPLYING INTERESTS IN THE CHINA MAINLAND AND TAIWAN

Rapid expansion of cross-strait economic relations led to the proliferation of interests in the relationship: Before the development of economic relations across the Taiwan Strait, few people on the mainland other than those with Taiwan family connections actually had such concrete interests. Indeed, many with Taiwan connections suffered political prosecution political movements and lived as second-class citizens for many years because of them. This situation changed drastically as economic relations between the two sides of the Taiwan Strait expanded following Beijing's adoption of a more flexible policy toward Taiwan in 1979. Beijing's new Taiwan policy formally ended the second-class citizen status for those with relatives in Taiwan, expanding cross-strait economic relations and lifting them to economic and in many cases political importance. Their Taiwan contacts became useful assets promising trade and investment possibilities in the new open, reform-minded era of the PRC.

The end of official prohibition on cross-strait travel and communication (still indirect) opened up a flow of communication between people in the mainland and Taiwan that went beyond family ties. Shanghai's post office handles more than one million pieces of mail per month, 85 percent of which are forwarded to other provinces and cities; each month more than 200,000 indirect long-distance telephone calls and telegrams are handled between Shanghai and Taiwan.[22] In 1992 1.32 million people from Taiwan visited China.[23] Academic and cultural contacts also increased. In August 1991, to commemorate the forty-fifth anniversary of the victory of the anti-Japanese War, the Shanghai Symphony Orchestra and the Taipei Philharmonic Orchestra performed a concert together.[24] During the summer of 1991, several academic symposiums on cross-strait relations brought together mainland and Taiwan scholars.[25]

Cross-strait trade and investment activities also offered valuable opportunities for many mainland enterprises both in state and private sectors to expand and upgrade their production and market their products.[26] The Taiwan connection provides them with new access to valuable capital, technologies, and managerial and marketing expertise. This connection in turn contributed to the growth of other sectors of the local economy such as service industries, construction, real estate, and so on. Meanwhile, more and more mainland workers work directly or indirectly for firms with Taiwanese investment and depend for their livelihood on these firms.

Taiwanese investment is concentrated in Guangdong and Fujian provinces, especially in the Shenzhen and Xiamen special economic zones. 63 percent of all Taiwanese investment projects are located in Guangdong and Fujian.[27] Taiwanese investors' favorite spot for investing is Xiamen, where there is more foreign investment from Taiwan than from any other area, including Hong Kong.

Local governments of the regions with strong trade and investment links with Taiwan found the Taiwan connection not only beneficial but in some cases crucial to the economic development of their regions. This is especially the case with Fujian and Guangdong provinces. By January 1992, Fujian had approved 1,239 enterprises with Taiwanese investment amounting to $1.63 billion.[28] Guangdong, on the other hand, boasts of Taiwanese investment in more than 1,400 enterprises and total contracted investment exceeding $2 billion.[29] Taiwanese investment is concentrated in a few cities along China's southeastern coast not only because of the special concessionary terms offered by these cities but also because kinship ties open doors for Taiwanese investors in these cities.[30] The concentration of Taiwanese investment in two provinces and a few cities means that officials in these areas have a particularly strong economic stake in the continuation of political *détente* in the Taiwan strait. On the other hand, the recent expansion of Taiwanese investment into provinces beyond Guangdong and Fujian will broaden the political base for good relations with Taiwan.[31]

Economic interdependence with Taiwan created industrial and regional interests in the PRC that favor strengthening economic and political ties across the strait. But there is as yet no sign that representatives of the shoemaking industry or Fujian province pressure the Chinese government for particular policies toward Taiwan. When it makes its Taiwan policies, the authoritarian PRC government has more autonomy from group interests than does the democratizing Taiwan government.

On the other side of the Taiwan strait, social and economic groups have pushed government policies toward the mainland. Taipei's belated actions to relax prohibitions on travel, trade and investment in 1987 reflected both the government's inability to carry out such prohibitions in the face of rising popular demand for conducting visits and business and its realization that managed relaxation of control over cross-strait contacts served its economic and political interests better than the previous policy of outright prohibition. By 1987, a large and increasing number of Taiwanese defied the prohibitions to visit the mainland, to conduct indirect trade, and to make investments there. Even the highly publicized trial of Chen Kuo-hsun in 1985 failed to arrest this trend.[32] Taipei's ban on interactions proved to be both futile and counterproductive.[33]

Following the lifting of the ban, Taiwanese began rushing to the mainland in large numbers. Tourism, indirect trade, and investment boomed. Although few reportedly Taiwanese were impressed with the mainland's living standards or its political system, they did enjoy their new rights to travel to, trade with, and invest in the mainland. For many, the mainland connection also became an increasingly important source of income. Many enterprises produce exports to the mainland, and many Taiwanese investors need imports from Taiwan to maintain their production.[34] Most Taiwanese entrepreneurs doing business in the PRC appear to be profiting from their mainland operations.[35]

Politically, increasing popular demand for visiting and conducting business with the mainland, reunification advocates' criticism of Taipei for dragging its feet on reunification, and the opposition Democratic Progressive Party's (DPP) call for an end to mainland-Taiwan confrontation also compelled Kuomintang leaders to realize that gradual relaxation of control over such matters would help ameliorate popular dissatisfaction over its previously rigid mainland policy and defeat the DPP's attempt to manipulate the issue to its advantage.[36] Combined with economic interests, the political considerations contributed to the lifting of the ban on indirect trade and visits in 1987 and subsequent relaxation of control on indirect interactions across the Taiwan strait.

MULTIPLYING CONCERNED INSTITUTIONS

The growth of economic ties led both China and Taiwan to expand their institutional infrastructure for managing cross-strait relations. Beijing's efforts to support various kinds of Taiwan-related interests (economic, cultural, academic, political, etc.) led to the involvement of an increasing number of mainland institutions at various levels of government. At the center, in addition to the few traditional institutions dealing with Taiwan affairs such as the military, the Chinese Communist Party (CCP) Central Committee (CC) United Front Department, the CCP CC Department of Propaganda, the Ministry of Defense, Xinhua News Agency, and the Ministry of Foreign Affairs, many other ministries including the Ministry of Foreign Trade and Economic Relations, Ministry of Post and Telecommunications, Ministry of Education, and Ministry of Law, are in one way or another now involved in the Taiwan relationship. The Chinese Academy of Social Sciences has an Institute on Taiwan Studies, and there are a number of non-governmental associations like the Society of Taiwan Studies and the All-China Association of Taiwan Compatriots who also play a role. At the local level, many provinces, municipalities, and counties set up offices to handle Taiwan affairs. To provide policy guidelines for these institutions, Beijing set up the Small Group on Taiwan Affairs under the CCP CC at the end of 1987 and the Office of Taiwan

Affairs in the State Council in 1988.[37] To accommodate Taipei's wish to deal with practical matters arising from increasing cross-strait interactions on a quasi-official basis, the PRC formed the Association of Relations Across the Taiwan Strait (ARAT).

A similar trend of organizational elaboration has been occurring on the other side of the Taiwan Strait, though on a much smaller scale. Previous monopolization of the mainland policy by top decision-makers and party and security organizations is being broken up as more and more government institutions like the Legislative Yuan and various ministries, especially the Ministry of Economic Affairs, get involved in handling cross-strait interactions. The democratization process added yet another concerned institution, the Democratic Progressive Party. The government body coordinating the Taiwan government's policy toward the mainland is the Cabinet Mainland Affairs Council, while the nongovernmental body founded to negotiate with the mainland on issues arising in economic interchange is the Strait Exchange Foundation (SEF).

THE GROWTH OF PRAGMATISM AND EMERGENCE OF A *DÉTENTE* REGIME

Economic interdependence transformed the political relationship between the mainland and Taiwan. A *détente* regime, created in the place of political confrontation, is characterized by (1) political commitment to peaceful international environment to promote domestic economic development; (2) development of a non-zero sum, pragmatic approach to relations; (3) emergence of a framework for competition and coexistence; and (4) acceptance of incrementalism in the development of relations.

First, both Beijing and Taipei are making economic growth their foremost priority, and therefore have to avoid confrontation as much as possible. Beijing never abandoned its emphasis on economic development. A recent upsurge in economic reforms following Deng Xiaoping's speech in Shenzhen in early 1992 further underscores the importance Beijing attaches to economic development. Taipei's determination to push its economy up to a new level is equally forceful. As Lee Teng-hui said in a *Washington Times* interview, "We also need a peaceful environment for our six-year, $300 billion economic development plan, which will raise per capita income from $8,000 to $14,000, double our GNP, with emphasis on the quality of life and the environment."[38] Since the economies of the mainland and Taiwan are complementary, the economic emphasis encourages cross-strait trade and investment activities.

Second, both sides moderated their previous zero-sum approaches to their relations. Increasingly, they chose to subscribe to the wisdom that what is good for the other side is not necessarily bad for oneself. In this spirit, Beijing tolerated the indirect, one-way, nonofficial and gradual cross-strait contacts despite its repeated criticisms of this state of affairs.[39] It also permitted the big imbalance of indirect trade with Taiwan and looked the other way as many Taiwanese businesses evaded taxes while reaping profits on the mainland.[40]

A pragmatic interest in preserving the economic relationship with Taiwan motivated Beijing leaders to compromise when conflicts arose about organizational and regulatory issues. The most striking example of such flexibility was Beijing's abandonment of its long-held insistence that cross-strait relations be on an official or party-to-party basis. In 1991, it created a nongovernmental institution, the Association of Relations Across the Taiwan Strait, as a counterpart to the Taiwan Strait Exchange Foundation. A less momentous issue arose when the Hong Kong branch of the PRC China Travel Service issued an order that Taiwan visitors must show passports and household registration certificates, not just their Taiwan identification cards. When many Taiwan industrial groups protested, PRC officials quickly backed down, preferring to lose face instead of losing Taiwan business.[41]

Taipei also found that under economic interdependence, trouble for the mainland no longer is in its interest. Under the previous regime of confrontation, it was happiest when the mainland had political or economic troubles since these troubles might offer an opportunity for it to return to the mainland. Nowadays, it shows great caution in promoting dissent on the mainland. During the 1989 protests and crackdown in China, the Taiwan authorities exercised restraint in their reaction.[42] When the issue of most favored nation trade status for the PRC came up in Washington, Taiwan did not try to hide its interest in continuing MFN status for Beijing.[43] In 1991, when the PRC appealed to the international community for assistance to fight a huge flood that engulfed several Chinese provinces and destroyed the livelihood of millions of people, Taipei allowed major donation efforts on the island to help mainland flood victims. In 1991, Taiwan Premier Hao Po-tsun, when asked to speculate about mainland power struggles following Deng Xiaoping's death, said that "as a Chinese, he does not hope to see Mainland China thrown into turmoil because that would affect the well-being of the mainland compatriots."[44] The new approach represents nothing less than a major perceptual shift among the decision-makers on both sides in their thinking about policies toward the other side.

This new cooperative attitude between Beijing and Taipei has come into play in the arena of international organizations. The South Korean government helped mediate an agreement between the two to enter the Asia-Pacific Economic Cooperation (APEC) organization as equal, full-fledged members in November 1991 (Hong Kong joined at the same time). Taiwan compromised by entering the regional economic organization as the customs union of Taiwan, Penghu, Kinmen and Matsu, and the PRC compromised by accepting equality with Taiwan in an international organization despite its concern about *de facto* recognition of "two Chinas" or "one China, one Taiwan." While Beijing leaders vehemently object to efforts by Taiwan president Lee Teng-Hui to achieve international diplomatic recognition for Taiwan through membership in political organizations like the United Nations or by visiting the United States, when it comes to economic organizations, they have shown a flexible attitude toward Taiwan membership. Their increasingly pragmatic attitude underscores their desire to accelerate their own accession to membership in crucial institutions such as GATT.

Third, as economic and other interactions increase, the two sides increasingly find it necessary to engage the other side to cope with a whole range of practical issues. The two sides met through their designated parties, the airlines, the Red Cross organizations and more recently the Strait Exchange Foundation (SEF) and Association of Relations Across the Taiwan Strait (ARATS) to discuss and negotiate such issues as the return of a defected Taiwan cargo liner, fighting cross-strait criminal activities, repatriation of illegal immigrants from the mainland, and so on. Out of such engagement, they reached a number of agreements to serve as both a solution to the problems and a beginning of a framework for a normal relationship. On 12 September 1990, the Red Cross organizations of the two sides met in Quemoy and concluded an agreement on repatriation of illegal migrants and wanted criminal suspects following direct consultation. Between November 3 and 8, the Office of Taiwan Affairs of Beijing's State Council and the SEF consulted and reached consensus on the issue of joint efforts to cope with crimes at sea in the Taiwan strait. In March 1992, ARAT and SEF consulted about issues concerning notarization of documents and registered mail.[45] Direct talks between the heads of the ARAT and SEF were held in Singapore in April 1993, thus elevating the quasi-official contacts between Beijing and Taipei to a higher level. Although Beijing cancelled resumption of high-level talks between SEF and ARATS in the summer of 1995 in response to Taiwan President Lee Teng-hui's visit to the United States, the increasing level of contacts and cooperation between participants on both sides of the strait will increase the level of interdependence between China and Taiwan, even in the absence of high-level discussions.

Finally, the growth of economic interdependence in the mainland-Taiwan relationship also enhanced the preference for incremental change over drastic transformations of the current relationship. People on the two sides of the Taiwan strait may disagree over whether Taiwan should move toward reunification or independence, but an increasing number appear to be taking the view that whatever happens had better be gradual and incremental.

While Beijing encouraged economic and other nonofficial exchanges in the early 1980s in the hope of rapid reunification, it is now shifting its position to allow a longer period for the interaction between economic and political and between nonofficial and official forces to build up the momentum for ultimate national reunification. The recent PRC policy to encourage the "three exchanges" (direct mail, travel, and trade) instead of immediate official dialogue reflects this new attitude.[46]

Increasingly, decision-makers on the mainland are taking a moderate position on the Taiwan question. While the older generation of leaders are still and perhaps even more anxious than ever to get the reunification process started, their attitudes are increasingly complicated by their awareness of the economic and political stakes involved in pressing Taiwan too hard on the reunification issue.[47] Consequently, although they still repeatedly appeal to Taipei to negotiate and still threaten the use of force in the event of Taiwanese independence, they have refrained from taking more assertive actions. They even maintained silence over the failure of the fulfillment of one of the three strategic tasks of the 1980s, namely reunification. The younger generation of leaders have life experience after the founding of the PRC and CCP-KMT struggles and therefore less historical baggage. While it is equally important politically, if not more so, for them to adhere to the principle of reunification, they take a more pragmatic approach in handling mainland-Taiwan relations. Beijing's recent emphasis on three exchanges in handling the cross-strait relations reflects the current state of mind of both the senior and junior generations of leaders.[48]

On the mass level, after several years of private and economic-centered interactions with Taiwan, although few mainlanders have given up their desire for reunification, their personal contacts and economic interests probably encourage them to favor peaceful settlement of the issue. Reunification by coercive means would come at the expense of their own interests: family reunion, jobs, income, and so on. For a similar reason, various local governments benefiting from the Taiwan connection are likely to share this position. Also, since reunification by force promises to wreck China's diplomatic and foreign economic relations, advocates and supporters of the open policy in both local and central government also prefer peaceful settlement of the Taiwan problem. To an increasing number of people, therefore, nothing short of Taiwan's official declaration of independence warrants settlement of the problem by force.[49]

Ironically, the success of Beijing's policy of offering incentives to expand economic activities across the Taiwan Strait to facilitate China's reunification encouraged an increasing number of mainlanders to support the current state of the cross-strait relationship. As long as the reunification issue remains unsettled, those with Taiwan connections continue to benefit from their current privileged economic and political position. The enterprises with Taiwanese investment continue to enjoy special tax shelters. And local governments continue to be in a position to offer more attractive terms than those with fewer or no connections to Taiwanese businessmen to attract them to do business in their regions. To these groups, the threat to their interests comes not only from Taiwan independence but also from immediate reunification, which would create new uncertainties.

In Taiwan, decisionmakers have already abandoned their previous unrealistic policy of unilateral reunification. Instead, they have chosen a more practical approach to deal with the mainland. No longer do they claim legitimacy to rule the rest of China. No longer do they insist on calling Beijing a "bandit" or "rebel" government.[50] And no longer do they insist on one official representation for China in the international arena. Instead, they have publicly acknowledged that they do not have the authority over the mainland, that Beijing is the *de facto* government there, and that although China is still one country, it is ruled currently by two separate and equal governments.[51]

Taipei persists in its one-China policy goal despite the Democratic Progressive Party's opposition to the notion of reunification and the nativization of the KMT. But while its National Reunification Program puts reunification as its ultimate objective, the KMT views reunification as a long-term enterprise. As Lee Teng-hui said, Taiwan will proceed at its "own pace with three phases toward unification— first, exchanges and reciprocity; second, mutual trust and cooperation; and third, consultation and unification."[52]

Although for various reasons many people in Taiwan are less concerned about China's reunification than mainlanders are, their stake in the manner of the settlement of the mainland-Taiwan issue is high and their preference for a peaceful solution increasingly obvious. More and more Taiwanese interests are tied up with cross-strait economic relations. These people are fully aware that Taiwan independence has the potential to trigger military actions on the part of the mainland and hurt their personal welfare. Although they do not want to share wealth with the mainland nor do they like its political system, they do wish to prevent the independence issue from disrupting their personal welfare and profit-making pursuits.[53]

An increasing number of Taiwan businessmen are taking a longer perspective on the question of cross-strait relations. They have begun to see the mainland with its huge market and rich material and labor resources as the future of Taiwan's economic development.[54] Even people who are not in any way involved in mainland business appreciate how much damage conflict with the mainland could cause to Taiwan's economy. In light of the fluidity of international capital and investors' preference for putting their money in safe places, tensions in the Taiwan Strait could induce sudden flight of capital from the island and discourage new investment on the island even if nothing else happens.

The preference for incremental change in the current cross-strait relationship is obvious among the Taiwan public. Given the gap in living standards and difference in political systems, few Taiwan citizens see immediate reunification serving their interests. Meanwhile, in the light of the mainland's threat to use force and the potential domestic problems associated with it, they also find outright declaration of Taiwan independence dangerous and unacceptable.

Consequently, they reacted negatively to the two extreme positions of reunification and independence. Instead, they opt for maintaining the current state of the relations, that is, neither reunification nor independence, but *détente*.

Such a state of mind provides some clues to the important elections in Taiwan in recent years. During the National Assembly election in Taiwan in December 1991, the KMT, which had revised its policy from hostile confrontation and reunification to peaceful coexistence and *de facto* independence, won 71 percent of the votes while the DPP, which was further radicalized in its pursuit for independence, suffered a humiliating defeat.[55] A public opinion poll conducted in 1992 by a private polling firm commissioned by the Mainland Affairs Council of Taiwan's Executive Yuan showed that 71.5 percent of those interviewed favor maintaining the current state of the cross-strait relationship and moving toward reunification later when the time is ripe; 4.9 percent favored immediate KMT-CCP negotiation on reunification; and 7.8 percent advocated Taiwan's permanent separation from the mainland and the establishment of a new and independent Taiwan state.[56] Other public opinion polls appeared to confirm these findings.[57] During 1992s election of Taiwan's Legislative Yuan, when DPP played down the issue of independence, the result of the elections was quite different than in 1991. The KMT won a 53 percent share of the popular vote, reflecting a very poor performance, and the DPP managed to obtain 31 percent share, the highest on record.[58]

In the 1992 election of local governments in Taiwan, the two rival political parties again downplayed the independence issue. As the DPP maintained its relatively moderate policy stance on the question of Taiwan's independence in an attempt to improve its electoral performance, the KMT edged toward a policy of *de facto* Taiwanese independence for the foreseeable future, while still claiming that China's reunification remains to be its ultimate goal.[59] Through this and other socio-economic policy adaptations to meet the DPP half way, the KMT managed to retain 15 out of 23 seats, despite a recent political crisis in which one of its factions openly split from the KMT and formed the New Party, leading to widespread speculation that it would lose in the election.[60] By continuing their support of the ruling party, Taiwanese voters demonstrated their concern for stability and security in the island. The December 1994 nationwide elections saw a resurgence of the DPP sounding an independence theme. The DPP did not benefit from this platform—except for success in the Taipei mayoral race, where its candidate played down the independence issue, the DPP did not achieve major electoral victories.

The proliferation of interests in the mainland-Taiwan relations broadened support for the present relationship, and the multiplication of institutions dealing with mainland-Taiwan affairs on both sides of the Taiwan Strait institutionalized such support. Involvement of more institutions in handling the relations broadened channels of information, increased checks and balances, and encouraged more professionalism in policy deliberations. This in turn helps policymaking participants make a comprehensive analysis of the relationship and formulate policies on a more rational (especially in economic terms) and less emotional basis. This development also favors peace and incrementalism in the settlement of the Taiwan question.

CONFLICTS CREATED BY INTERDEPENDENCE

Economic interdependence promoted political *détente* but it also generated new conflicts in relations between China and Taiwan. Rapid economic development in the mainland, especially along China's coast, posed a challenge to Taiwan's exports. Mainland exports, including those produced by Taiwan-funded enterprises, are squeezing Taiwan products out of some of their traditional international markets. Moreover, some mainland products of higher technological level are also posing a new threat to Taiwan products in the world market.[61] Although the latter situation is not very serious for the time being, it has great potential and promises to influence Taiwan's perception of the mainland and its strategy in regulating Taiwanese investment to the mainland.

Secondly, as the reunification issue declines in immediate importance, the unequal distribution of benefits in the cross-strait relations is likely to receive increasing attention on the mainland. Increasingly, people running China's economy question the wisdom of tolerating a chronic large cross-strait trade imbalance. While the benefit of increasing Taiwanese investment on the mainland as well as concerns for reunification may have muted such criticism from Beijing for the time being, the moderating influence is likely to be reduced in the future for two reasons: First, Taiwanese investment is contributing to tension between Beijing and Washington by increasing China's trade surplus with the United States; and second, because alternative foreign investment sources are becoming available to Beijing as the international furor over the 1989 Tiananmen suppression subsides and Chinese economic reforms make China an increasingly attractive investment location.[62]

Third, the current structure and practice of Taiwanese investment on the mainland also aroused some controversy there. Partly as a result of Taipei's policy on limiting Taiwanese investment on the mainland to low-tech industries, Taiwan investors concentrate on labor-intensive and service-oriented enterprises in contradiction to Beijing's economic development priorities as well as those of the local governments. Critics also found Taiwan businesses competing unfairly for China's scarce technological resources and skilled labor pool. They point out that the Taiwanese firms have an unfair advantage because, unlike the mainland firms, they bear little social welfare burden and enjoy special tax breaks, as well as evading taxes.[63] Mainland critics of Taiwanese investment also argue that some Taiwanese firms are creating potential social welfare problems by failing to chip in as much as local firms do for education, housing, compensation for unemployment and other social services.[64]

Fourth, although the issue of ideological pollution is losing its appeal, some people on the mainland are still concerned with the vices of commercialization emerging in the localities. To them, Taiwanese businesses are responsible for the excessive materialism, gaudy life style, spreading prostitution, and so on. that plague their regions. Local authorities feel the subversive nature of the Taiwanese influx to their authority.[65]

Finally and perhaps most importantly, the growing integration of the two economies has accentuated the fear arising from the asymmetries in their relationship. Cross-strait trade occupies a much larger proportion of Taiwan's foreign trade than of China's foreign trade. On the foreign investment side, China has alternative sources of investment, and Taiwan could shift its capital from China to other countries such as countries in Southeast Asia. But now that Taiwanese investors have committed funds to mainland projects already in operation, they cannot pull out without paying a heavy price.[66] As a smaller economy, Taiwan worries about being vulnerable to manipulation by the mainland more than the mainland worries about being manipulated by Taiwan. Taiwanese officials worry that if the expansion of trade and investment is allowed to continue unchecked, it would lead to Beijing's political domination of Taiwan through control of Taiwan's economy and a weakening of Taiwan's leverage to negotiate with Beijing over reunification when that time eventually comes.[67]

Their concern is not completely without foundation. Since 1979, cross-strait indirect trade expanded rapidly and Taiwan's dependence on such trade grew steadily. Taiwan's exports to the mainland in 1991 represented 9.8 percent of its total exports, nearing the officially designated ceiling of 10 percent.[68] In some months of 1991, Taiwan exports to the mainland exceeded 10 percent (in large part because recessions in Japan and the United States reduced their demand for Taiwanese goods).[69] Some manufacturers have reached a "dangerous level" of 70—80 percent dependency on mainland markets.[70]

Trade dependence on the mainland and the vulnerability of their mainland investments to political manipulation and extortion worry Taiwan leaders who still distrust the communists. Taiwan Economics Minister Chen Li-an said in 1990, "The Peking regime will always try to use trade and other such ties to the detriment of the ROC and the people of Taiwan."[71] Although this suspicion of communist intentions may be weakened by increased economic and social interactions, it is also reinforced by the structural asymmetries of economic interdependence between the large mainland economy and the smaller Taiwan one and the political asymmetries of an authoritarian regime bargaining with a democratic one. Such distrust led to a series of self-protective measures by Taipei.

Economically, Taipei tried to regulate Taiwan's trade and investment with the mainland, and to delay moving from indirect to direct trade and investment.[72] In 1991 the Taiwan Board of Foreign Trade commissioned the Chung Hua Institute of Economic Research to design a monitoring system to give advance warning of overheated mainland trade; the system focuses on 205 export items and 218 import items.[73] In November 1992, Taipei announced that it would continue to prohibit foreign firms with mainland Chinese capital from investing in Taiwan or joining in public construction projects.[74] Meanwhile, facing unabating Taiwanese interest in trade and investment in the mainland, Taipei's Mainland Affairs Council publicly announced in late 1992 that it was considering financial measures to redirect Taiwan's trade and investment from the mainland to other destinations.[75]

Politically, Taipei has attempted to consolidate its political status by adopting a "dual sovereignty" approach. While persisting in the one-China principle, it now stresses the need to recognize the reality of China's separation and to treat the two parts of China as two equal political entities. To put this strategy into practice, Taipei sought to establish diplomatic relations with countries that have diplomatic relations with Beijing. It also made it known that it wishes to join the UN if that is possible.

In 1995, Taipei stepped up diplomatic efforts for international recognition of "dual sovereignty." Moves such as diplomatic trips to European Community countries, President Lee's trip to the United States, and calls for UN reentry were met with fierce resistance by Beijing's leadership. Sino-U.S. relations reached their lowest point in years with the withdrawal of China's ambassador and the cancellation of most high-level contacts in response to President Clinton allowing President Lee to attend his alma mater's reunion. The unprecedented July 1995 announcement by the PRC of missile testing off the northern shores of Taiwan caused the Taiwanese stock market to fall more than seven percent in one week, creating the biggest threat to Sino-Taiwanese interdependence since the 1980s and making the "dual sovereignty" goal seemingly not feasible.

Militarily, it has stepped up efforts to purchase advanced weapon systems from the West. Such efforts, coupled with the Bush administration's electoral interests during the U.S. recession, finally led to U.S. agreement to sell 150 F-16 advanced fighters to Taiwan despite Beijing's strong opposition. Following the U.S. decision to sell F-16s to Taiwan, Taipei also obtained permission from the French government to buy 60 Mirage 2000 fighters and permission from the Dutch government to build submarines in Taiwan.[76]

Taipei's efforts to manage risk associated with asymmetric interdependence did not pay off and instead generated new uncertainties in the cross-strait relationship. In the economic area, despite Taipei's efforts to control the level of trade with and investment in the mainland, both continued to grow at a rapid pace. Whereas the volume of transit trade grew by 25.5 percent in 1993, Taiwanese investment simply took off.[77] The increasing direct trade and travel across the Taiwan Strait in recent years and the large gap between official figures and actual figures of Taiwanese investment on the mainland underline the failure of Taipei's efforts at controlling Taiwanese trade with and investment in the mainland.[78]

As the two economies become more and more integrated, new issues arise and raise politically difficult regulatory policy questions. Should Taiwan relax its prohibition on high-tech cooperation with the mainland, even in areas like satellites and electronics engineering in which the mainland is stronger?[79] Automobile parts manufacturers are eager to penetrate the mainland market with joint ventures there, and Hyundai, Toyota, and Ford are ready to expand their Taiwan operations to achieve the same goal. Should Taipei change the rules to allow the high-tech automobile firms to invest on the mainland?[80] As China creates stock markets, should Taipei permit Taiwanese securities firms to assist eager Taiwanese investors?[81]

In politics, despite strenuous efforts, little progress was achieved in terms of establishing equal status with Beijing. Despite increased unofficial contacts between Taiwan and other countries in recent years, major states simply ignored Taipei's plea for diplomatic recognition. Partly to retaliate against Taipei's actions, Beijing hastened the process of establishing diplomatic relations with South Korea which severed rather than continued diplomatic relations with Taipei. At the time, Korea was the most important of the few states that maintained diplomatic relations with Taipei. Recently, the Japanese foreign minister refused to meet with Taipei's Foreign Minister Frederick Chien who was visiting Tokyo in an unofficial capacity.[82] Although dual sovereignty remains the aim of Taipei, its realization still appears remote.

In terms of military security, Taiwan's recent gains in purchasing advanced weapons are obvious. In the long run, however, such gains may not be as significant as they appear. As its economic development proceeds, the mainland also stepped up military modernization. Taiwan's active shopping spree only furnishes additional reasons for the continuous rise in the mainland's defense spending. Beijing's recent purchase of advanced weapons from Russia also helps to offset Taiwan's new military edge.[83]

In varying degrees, all these issues became hot domestic political controversies in Taiwan because they affect the interests of different economic groups who are well-organized and vocal and who may have contradictory preferences. Democratization complicates the task of formulating mainland policies and may put Taiwan at a disadvantage in its bargaining with the mainland. In a democracy, the policy process is more transparent, and political leaders are vulnerable to electoral opposition. Unlike their PRC counterparts, Taiwanese political leaders have to design a policy package that obtains popular support at any given time. Because the mainland and Taiwan economies are highly complementary, most economic groups pressure Taipei for less, not more, regulation of mainland trade and investment. A 1991 Gallup poll found that although Taiwan residents still see China as a hostile regime (44.1 percent) and favor a strong national defense (83.2 percent), the majority favors talks between the KMT and the CCP (68.2 percent) and a shift from indirect to direct economic links with the mainland (67.3 percent).[84]

Taiwanese government officials complain that Beijing is taking advantage of Taiwan's democracy to enhance its bargaining leverage. PRC authorities have established local groups of Taiwanese investors to press Taipei for deregulation and direct economic links. Beijing has promoted a triangular "Beijing-Taiwan investors-Taipei" relationship as a tactic of "using civilians to force the government."[85] Taipei authorities sought to manage the domestic politics of cross-strait regulatory policies by including industrialists on committees that advise the Ministry of Economic Affairs when it makes new rules.[86]

Taiwan is more vulnerable than the mainland to the potential for exploitation in economic interdependence as well as to domestic political pressures. As the stronger party, Beijing can keep dangling more direct economic and political ties in front of Taipei at no risk to itself.[87] The economic complementarity between the mainland and Taiwan produces powerful pressures on Taipei, despite its qualms, to eventually succumb to these enticements. For the time being at least, none of the conflicts generated by interdependence, including those provoked by Taiwan's attempts to reduce the asymmetric vulnerabilities of dependence, seem likely to derail the trend toward economic integration and political *détente* across the Taiwan strait.

NOTES

1. Beijing first announced its new Taiwan policy of peaceful reunification on 1 January 1979. The announcement urged that both sides develop trade as well as other exchanges, but it does not mention the idea of Taiwan investment in the mainland. Beijing's willingness to encourage Taiwan investment first appeared in Ye Jianying's nine-point speech nearly three years later on 20 September 1981. Among the incentives that Beijing provided in Ye's speech was Beijing's willingness to *subsidize* (emphasis added) Taiwan if Taiwan's local economy met difficulties. The first State Council regulation to encourage Taiwan investment throughout China was announced on 7 July 1988. This history indicates that Beijing did not stress the Taiwan connection in economic terms during the first few years after the adoption of its new Taiwan policy. Chen Guoshao et al., eds., *Tai Gang Au Shouce* 1 (Handbook on Taiwan, Hong Kong and Macau) (Beijing: Huayi Publishing House, 1990), pp. 464-467, 471, 475. For Ye's 1981 speech see Third Bureau of the United Front Work Department of the CCP Central Committee, ed. *Yi Guo Liang*

Zhi [One Country, Two Systems] (Beijing: Zhongguo Wenshi Publishing House, 1988), pp. 102-105.

2. Robert O. Keohane and Joseph S. Nye, *Power and Interdependence, World Politics in Transition* (Boston: Little, Brown and Company, 1977).
3. Edward L. Morse, "Transnational Economic Processes," *International Organization* 25:3 (Summer 1971), 380; also see Morse, "The Transformation of Foreign Policies: Modernization, Interdependence, and Externalization," *World Politics* 22:3 (April 1970), pp. 373-392.
4. *Xinbao* (Australian Chinese Daily) 11 January 1994, p. 3.
5. Direct merchandise trade, although forbidden by Taipei, is conducted by Taiwanese fishing boats to Fujian ports. According to one source, this illegal trade exceeded $300 million in 1988 (Ricky Tung, "Mainland China in Taiwan's Economic Future," *Issues and Studies* 26:5 (May 1990), p. 43; more recently, Taiwan's Ministry of Economy acknowledged that about 30 percent of Taiwan's exports to Hong Kong were shipped directly to the mainland. "Haixia liangan guanxi dashiji" (Major Events in Cross-Strait Relations), *Taiwan Yanjiu*, no. 4, 1992, p. 83.
6. Ai Wei, "The Development and Limitations of Taiwan-mainland Economic and Trade Relations," *Issues and Studies* 27:5 (May 1991).
7. Ai Wei, op. cit.
8. In 1989, approximately 540,000 Taiwan tourists visited China. The figures for the first half of 1990 were 35 percent higher than the corresponding 1989 numbers. Mitchell A. Silk, "Silent Partners," *The China Business Review*, September-October 1990, pp. 32-40; also see Chen Xiangming, "New Spatial Division of Labor and Commodity Chains in the Emerging Greater China Economic Region," in Patricia Roe, *Emerging Regions in the Pacific Basin*, (Austin, TX: ICCC Institute, 1994), pp. 127-154.
9. Another Taiwanese estimate puts it at a much higher level: $18.2 billion, see *Xinbao*, 11 January 1994, p. 3.
10. Ibid.; another study puts Taiwan's trade surplus with the mianland much higher than Taiwan's total trade surplus, see *Xinbao*, 5 January 1994, p. 3 and *Xinbao*, 10 January 1994, p. 4.
11. *Renmin Ribao*, 7 January 1994, p. 5.
12. Ibid.
13. Yu Fengzhu, "Taishang fu dalu touzi jizhong xintai de sikao (Psychological states of Taiwan businessmen who invest on the mainland)," *Guoji Maoyi* 6 (1991), pp. 52-53; Peng Tianxiang, "Fazhan dalu yu xianggang he taiwan zhijian de sanbian jinmao hezuo," [Develop the trilateral economic and trade cooperation between mainland, Taiwan and Hong Kong] *Guoji Maoyi 10* (1992), p. 29.
14. Yen Tsung-ta, op. cit.
15. Taiwan-funded projects tend to be more export-oriented than other foreign funded businesses; the export ratio of Taiwan-funded enterprises in Fujian is in excess of 80 percent. Yen Tsung-ta, op. cit.
16. Yen Tsung-ta, op. cit., p. 20.

17. David M. Lampton, The National Committee on U.S.-China Relations, personal communication.

18. *Renmin ribao*, 21 April 1992, p. 5.

19. Yen Tsung-ta, op. cit.

20. Yen Tsung-ta, op. cit.

21. *Free China Journal*, 16 April 1990. A survey of Taiwan foreign investment on the mainland conducted by the Chung-hua Institute for Economic Research warned that "becoming reliant on investing them could eventually hinder the island's industrial upgrading and spark competition between mainland and Taiwan goods in the international market," *Free China Journal*, 1 May 1992.

22. *Liaowang Overseas Edition*, 13 January 1992, in *FBIS*, 4 February 1992, p. 66.

23. *Renmin ribao*, 29 January 1993.

24. *Liaowang Overseas Edition*, op. cit.

25. *Liaowang Overseas Edition*, 19 August 1991, in *FBIS*, 28 August 1991, p. 62; *Chengming* (Hong Kong), September 1991, pp. 62-64.

26. Carl Goldstein, "Strait Ahead," *Far Eastern Economic Review*, 5 March 1992, p. 54; Peng Tianxiang, "Fazhan dalu yu xianggang he taiwan zhijian de sanbian jinmao hezuo," [Develop the trilateral economic and trade cooperation between mainland, Taiwan and Hong Kong] *Guoji Maoyi 10* (1992), p. 29.

27. Chen Xiangming, op. cit., p. 10.

28. *Remin ribao*, 6 March 1992, p. 5.

29. *Renmin ribao*, 3 March 1992, p. 5.

30. Ibid., p. 16.

31. Sichuan now has 55 Taiwan-invested enterprises, Dalian has 65, and Qingdao has approved 40. These figures reflect "a new trend: The reach of Taiwan businessmen has extended from the coastal areas to the hinterland, and from the south to the north." *Xinhua*, 23 June 1991, in *FBIS*, 28 June 1991, p. 79.

32. In December 1985, Chen was sentenced for twelve years in jail for his involvement in trade with the mainland. Chang Chien-feng, *Tai-wan hai, Shen-chen ho* (Taiwan sea and Shenzhen river) (Hong Kong: Baixin Publishing House, 1987), pp. 174-185; Li Ta *Tai-wan yu san t'ung* (Taiwan and the "three exchanges") (Hong Kong: Guangjiaojing Publishing Company, 1988), pp. 152-155. In 1987, 15,700 people from Taiwan visited Fujian. *Fujian Statistical Yearbook* (Peking: Chung-Kuo t'ung chi ch'u pan she, 1990), p. 298.

33. According to a 1988 Taiwan study of those who had visited the mainland, 68.3 percent of those interviewed wished to visit the mainland again. Chu Hai-yuan et al., *Ta lu t'an ch'in chi fang wen ti ying* [The impact of visiting relatives and friends traveling to the mainland] (Taipei: Caituan Faren Zhang Rongfa Foundation and Guojia Zhengce Yenjiu Zhongxin, 1989), p. 49.

34. According to a survey conducted by Charles H.C. Kao at the request of the Economic Affairs Ministry of Taiwan, Taiwanese firms shifted to the mainland "obtained 54 percent of their raw materials from Taiwan." Carl Goldstein, "Strait Ahead," *Far Eastern Economic Review*, 5 March 1992, p. 54.

35. According to a privately sponsored study in Taiwan, among those Taiwan entrepreneurs

who have investment in the mainland, 57.5 percent turn a profit over 10 percent. *Renmin ribao*, 6 March 1992, p. 5. A survey organized by Taiwan's Ministry of Economic Affairs also finds that one third of the Taiwan investors have already made money; 85 percent of the firms with Taiwan investment are running well; on average, these firms become profitable within a year; and their production cost is 24.3 percent lower than in that in Taiwan while their average profit margin is 13.2 percent. *Renmin ribao*, 11 April 1992, p. 2; also see *Free China Journal*, 1 May 1992 and Carl Goldstein, "Strait Ahead," op. cit.

36. By 1987, popular demand for the government's lifting its ban on visiting the mainland was very high. Some organizations organized various activities to push the government toward this direction. For example, the Waishengren fanxiang cujinhui (Association for promoting the policy to allow people from other provinces to visit their home towns) held a ceremony under the name of "missing mothers far away" in front of Zhongshan Memorial Hall on Taiwan's Mother's Day, 10 May 1987. Li Songlin, ed. *Guomindang zai taiwan sishi nian* [Forty years of KMT's rule in Taiwan], (Beijing: PLA Publishing House, 1990), p. 421. The Democratic Progressive Party proposed on the day of its founding on 10 November 1986 that Taiwan should make efforts to end the cross-strait confrontation. Zhang Shanke, ed. *Taiwan wenti dashi ji* [Chronology of major events on the Taiwan question] (Beijing: Huawen Publishing House, 1988), p. 753.

37. Li Ta, op. cit., p. 1; Chen Guoshao, op. cit., pp. 474-475.

38. *Washington Times*, 10 July 1991, p. A8.

39. For a description of such contacts, see Jia Qingguo, "Changing relations across the Taiwan Strait: Beijing's perceptions," *Asian Survey*, March 1992.

40. Wu Xingdu, "Taiwan dui dalu touzi de fenxi (Analysis of Taiwan's investment on the mainland)," *Guoji Maoyi*, May 1991, p. 14.

41. *Free China Journal*, 17 April, 21 April, 24 April, and 12 May 1992.

42. *Liaowang Overseas Edition* (Hong Kong), 23 October 1989, *FBIS*, 17 November 1989, p. 50. When the Goddess of Democracy, a radio ship used by West-supported Chinese dissidents to broadcast their views to the Chinese mainland, reached Taiwan to load radio transmission equipments there in May 1990, its passengers found not only a tepid reception, but also the government's refusal to load the equipment onto the ship for fear of antagonizing the mainland. *Far Eastern Economic Review*, 24 May 1990, p. 13; ibid., 31 May 1990, pp. 19-20.

43. According to Gu Liansong, a Taiwan business tycoon and also known as Taiwan's underground financial and economic ambassador, Taiwan would be the real victim of U.S. suspension of MFN to the mainland. *China Times Weekly*, 5 April 1992, p. 71; *FBIS*, 4 March 1992, p. 58; Taiwan's shoe manufacturers lobbied against U.S. imposition of Super 301 measures against China. According to a report, 90 percent of shoes China exported to the U.S. in 1991 were produced by enterprises with Taiwan investment on the mainland. *Chinese Daily News*, 16 December 1991, p. 2.

44. *China News Analysis* (Taipei), 27 February 1992, *FBIS*, 27 February 1992, p. 62.

45. Wen Yu, "Zhonggong duitai lingdao tiaozheng zhenrong (CCP leaders in charge of Taiwan affairs reshuffle)," *Guangjiajing Monthly* (Hong Kong), November 1990, p. 9; "Liangan

xieshang daji fanzui [The two sides of the Taiwan Strait consult on fighting crimes],"
Haiwai Xueren [Overseas Scholar], December 1991, pp. 9-10; *Central Daily News,* 24
April 1992, p. 1.

46. *FBIS,* 9 March 1992, p. 79; Yang Shangkun recently said that national reunification
would be impossible during this century. *FBIS,* 7 April 1992, p. 36.

47. Jia Qingguo, op. cit.

48. According to Wen Yu, the CCP has realized that national reunification will take a long
time and decided to place its emphasis of its work on encouraging "three exchanges" and
other direct and indirect interactions so as to facilitate mutual understanding and
communication and enhance the consensus of national reunification. Wen Yu,
"Zhonggong duitai lingdao tiaozheng zhenrong (CCP leaders in charge of Taiwan affairs
reshuffle)," *Guangjiaojing Monthly* (Hong Kong), November 1990, p. 9.

49. This viewpoint is reflected in Beijing's current official policy.

50. In his talk at a news conference in April 1991, Lee Teng-hui, President of the Nationalist
Government, said that his government had decided to regard Beijing as "authorities"
instead of a "rebel organization." "From now on, we must accept the reality that the
communists control the mainland." *The New York Times,* 1 May 1991, p. A15.

51. On 8 July 1991, Taipei placed an ad in *The New York Times.* The crucial section of the ad
reads, "Today, the ROC has replaced the war of words with a business-like approach to
the issue of China's division. For example, the ROC has formally declared its willingness
to accept temporary dual recognition from other countries (although Peking has not
accepted this principle yet)." *Shijie ribao,* 12 July 1991, p. 3.

52. *The Washington Times,* 10 July 1991, p. A8. The recent KMT decision to duck a decision
on how to elect the next president in order to avoid its implications for Taiwan's
political future also reflects such incrementalism.

53. This mentality probably contributed to over three hundred parties and political groups
issuing a declaration at the end of 1991 in reaction to DPP's sudden inclusion of the
Taiwan independence clause into its party program, demanding that the government take
serious measures to punish Taiwan independence advocates. *Renmin ribao,* 24 December
1991, p. 5.

54. Top executives of the Formosa Plastics, a multibillion dollar company, recently publicly
stated that Taiwan depends on the mainland for its future economic growth and
development. *Shijie ribao,* 12 March 1992, p. A6; in its March 1 editorial, Taiwan's
Gongshang ribao (Industrial and Commercial Daily) urges Taiwan authorities to open up
its mainland economic and trade policy further to meet the challenges of the new
situation. *Renmin ribao,* 4 March 1992, p. 5. According to a study by Taiwan's *Tianxia
zazhi,* five out of seven executives of Taiwan's manufacturing industries favor the
mainland for further investment. *Renmin ribao,* 6 March 1992, p. 5; also see ibid., 21
March 1992, p. 5; ibid., 25 March 1992, p. 2.

55. 71 percent of voters supported the KMT, 24 percent the DPP and the remaining five
percent other parties. *Washington Post,* 22 December 1991, p. A37; for DPP's radical
activities prior to the election, see Jia Qingguo, op. cit., p. 283.

56. *Central Daily News,* 25 March 1992, p. 1.

57. Ying-jeou Ma, "The Republic of China's Policy Toward the Chinese Mainland," *Issues & Studies*, June 1992, pp. 25, 32.

58. Julian Baum, "The Hollow Centre," *Far Eastern Economic Review*, 7 January 1993, p. 14.

59. On 22 November 1993, Taiwan's minister of Economic affairs, Chiang Ping-kun, surprised many people in Seattle by stating that Taiwan and China are two sovereign states. Taibei quickly qualified Chiang's remark and reaffirmed its goal for China's reunification, see *Chung Yang Ji Pao*, 24 November 1993, p. 1.

60. *The Economist*, 4 December 1993, p. 35.

61. Chen Jiaqi, "Haixia liangan canping de guoji shichang jingzheng fenxi [Analysis of competition for international market between the products from the two sides of the Taiwan Strait]," *Guoji Maoyi*, February 1992, pp. 20-24.

62. On the issue of surplus transfer see Wu Xingdu, "Taiwan dui dalu touzi de fenxi (Analysis of Taiwan's investment on the mainland)," *Guoji Maoyi*, May 1991, p. 14; Sun Zhenyu, "Zhongmei jingmao guanxi xianzhuang ji cunzai de wenti," [The status and problems of current Sino-U.S. economic and trade relations], *Guoji maoyi*, July 1991, p. 5. According to Beijing's State Statistic Bureau, in 1992, China manage to contract $57.5 billion and actualize $11.16 billion foreign investment in China. *Renmin ribao*, 20 February 1993, p. 2.

63. Wu Xingdu, op. cit., pp. 14-15; Yu Fengzhe, "Taishang fu dalu," op. cit., pp. 53-54.

64. Wu Xingdu, op. cit., May 1991, p. 15.

65. Wu Xingdu, op. cit., pp. 15-16.

66. It is worth noting that if the Taiwan ventures were confiscated, the PRC would lose a larger percentage of its exports than Taiwan would lose of its exports.

67. Zhonghua Jingji Yanjiuyuan (Institute of Chinese Economic Studies), "Haixia liangan maoyi jinzhan zhi pinggu (Estimate of the development of cross-strait trade)," supplement, August 1989, pp. 8-9; Chu Yun-han, "Taiwan yu dalu jingmao guanxi fazhan de zhengzhi zhangai (Political obstacles in the development of economic and trade relations between Taiwan and the mainland)," Liao Kwang-sheng, ed. *Liangan jingji fazhan yu yatai quyu hudong [Economic development in both sides of the Taiwan Strait and interactions in the Asia–Pacific region]* (Hong Kong: Hong Kong Chinese University, 1991), pp. 125-128; Julian Baum, "The Mainland Dilemma," *Far Eastern Economic Review*, 18 October 1992, p. 29.

68. *Renmin ribao*, 17 April 1992, p. 5.

69. *China News Analysis* (Taipei), 17 June 1991, in *FBIS*, 26 June 1991, p. 66.

70. *China News Analysis* (Taipei), 20 March 1991, in *FBIS*, 22 March 1991, p. 58.

71. *Free China Journal*, 16 April 1990.

72. Taiwan's economic affairs minister Hsiao Wan-chang said that Taiwan would not allow cross-strait commercial exchanges to endanger Taiwan's political stability and security. *FBIS*, 24 March 1992, p. 85.

73. *China News Analysis* (Taipei), 19 June 1991, *FBIS*, 26 June 1991, p. 67; *Free China Journal*, 2 July 1991, p. 3.

74. *Free China Journal*, 12 November 1992.

75. *Free China Journal.*, 23 October 1992.

76. Julian Baum et al., "Ancient Fears," *Far Eastern Economic Review*, 3 December 1992, p. 9; Julian Baum, "Prepare to Surface," *Far Eastern Economic Review*, 4 February 1993, p. 10.

77. Calculated according to the estimate of Taiwan's Ministry of Economic Affiars as reported in *Xinbao*, 11 January 1994, p. 3.

78. Ricky Tung, "Mainland China in Taiwan's Economic Future," *Issues and Studies* 26:5 (May 1990), p. 43; "Haixia liangan guanxi dashiji" [Major Events in Cross-Strait Relations], *Taiwan Yanjiu*, no. 4, 1992, p. 83; *Free China Journal*, 15 January 1993; also see the previous footnote.

79. *Free China Journal*, 20 March 1992, p. 8.

80. *Free China Journal*, 14 April 1992, p. 8.

81. *Free China Journal*, 8 May 1992, p. 3.

82. Robert Defts, "Accidental tourist," *Far Eastern Economic Review*, 4 March 1993, p. 17.

83. Tai Ming Cheung, "Sukhois, Sams, Subs," *Far Eastern Economic Review*, 4 April 1993, p. 23.

84. *China News Analysis* (Taipei), 6 April 1991, in *FBIS*, 8 April 1991, p. 82. The new option of exiting to Taiwan also gives big industrialists, who are important for funding political parties as well as for the island's development, a powerful lever over domestic regulatory policies. Y.C. Wang of Formosa Plastics reportedly received a promise of less stringent environmental regulations in exchange for locating his new plant in Taiwan instead of the mainland.

85. *Free China Journal*, 17 April 1992, p. 3.

86. *Chung-kuo shi-pao* (Taipei), 18 June 1990, in *FBIS*, 3 July 1990, p. 57.

87. At its first formal meeting with the Taiwan Straits Exchange Foundation in April 1993, the PRC Association for Relations Across the Taiwan Straits threw Taiwan off balance by urging a move to direct foreign investment across the straits. *Los Angeles Times*, 29 April 1993, p. A11.

9 Transitions in and Interactions between the Chinese Mainland, Taiwan, and Hong Kong

He Di

INTRODUCTION

The Chinese mainland, Taiwan, and Hong Kong are undergoing processes of fundamental change.[1] The Chinese mainland is experiencing economic and political changes, both reinforced by a generational transition; Taiwan a "nativizing" transition; and Hong Kong a sovereignty transition. All three transitions are sweeping in nature. They reflect not only the ending of the Cold War era but also basic changes in economic development, politics, and popular sentiment in each of the three geographical areas. While each transition has its distinctive characteristics, all three share one common problem—how to relate to one another in light of the regional trend toward integration. How will their political futures be shaped? How will they interact? Will there be a unified China or a Chinese federation (or confederation)?

Because of their distinctive characteristics, the three transitions are taking place at different speeds, in different forms, and in different directions. Meanwhile, because of the problem they share—regional integration—their transitions must influence each other. This is especially the case with the transition on the Chinese mainland, where economic and political change and generational turnover will determine future relations between China, Taiwan and Hong Kong. In view of these prospects, the present chapter examines the following issues:

(1) the nature, special characteristics, and internal dynamics of the three transitions;

(2) the external dynamics affecting the interactions between the three sides during the transition period; and

(3) the interests—both common and divergent—likely to affect future relations among the three parties.

ECONOMIC-POLITICAL REFORM AND THE GENERATIONAL TRANSITION ON THE CHINESE MAINLAND

When people view China today, they concentrate on generational changes in leadership, the departure of the founder generation of communist leaders and their replacement by a generation educated since 1949. Such a view is understandable, since the "man-rule" convention of the Communist Party makes the appointment of its paramount leaders a crucial factor of the Party's policy formulation. However, the economic-political changes and generational transition are taking place in China synchronically, and the fundamental societal changes are occurring in areas other than leadership. There is a Chinese saying *"xingshi bi ren qiang"* ("the situation is more forceful than the man"). This illustrates the influence that societal changes exert on the behavior, principles, and policies of the new generation of leaders coming to power in China.

Fundamental change in China is evident in the economy, in politics, and in the popular mentality. China's reforms started in the economic sphere. After 14 years of uneven, punctuated evolution and many debates, the goal of establishing a "socialist market system" was firmly set at the CCP's fourteenth National Congress in the fall of 1992. Since then, China's centrally planned economy is undergoing a rapid transformation into a market economy. Though this transition is not complete, the direction of change is irreversible. Several factors combine to ensure that China's economy will continue to move in this direction:

- China's economic transformation is driven by the commercialization of three production factors: labor, capital, and real estate. Markets for these production factors expanded greatly, especially in China's coastal areas.
- China's system of public ownership is being transformed into private (or semi-private) ownership. The private economic sector is expanding at an accelerated rate, already exceeding 50 percent of China's total GNP.
- China's closed economy is transforming into an open economy, and the Chinese economy is being gradually integrated into the international economy. The volume of imports and exports for 1993 reached $195.72 billion, amounting to an increase of 18.2 percent from the previous year. In a breakdown of the trade figures in 1993, the total number of newly-approved foreign investment projects nationwide came to 83,265, with their contractual value standing at $110.852 billion, and actually-injected foreign investment value at $25.759 billion. These figures represent increases of 70.68 percent, 90.7 percent, and 134 percent, respectively. They are almost identical with the total for the first 14 years since the beginning of the reform drive. By the end of 1993, the cumulative number of approved foreign investment projects

across the country amounted to 174,056, with pledged investments at $217.216 billion and the real investment value reaching $60.042 billion[2]

- During the past 14 years, Hong Kong and Taiwan played an extremely important role in China's economic transformation. Although many are concerned that the imminent return of Hong Kong to Chinese sovereignty will destroy the vitality of the Hong Kong economy, these fears have been groundless. The main direction of influence since 1982 has been just the reverse. Hong Kong's free market economy exerted immense influence on the mainland, fostering the rise of new economic interests and speeding the transformation of the mainland's economic system. The Hong Kong "tail" was wagging the Chinese "dog," rather than vice versa. In similar fashion, the transfer of large amounts of Taiwanese capital to the mainland in the past four years accelerated the economic transformation of China's coastal areas. Deng Xiaoping's 1992 remark that China should strive to create "several Hong Kongs" vividly illustrates that in the relationship among the Chinese mainland, Taiwan and Hong Kong, the primary flow of influence has gone from Hong Kong and Taiwan to the mainland. Hong Kong and Taiwan not only are the economic windows and commercial partners of the mainland economy but also continue to provide examples to guide the mainland's transition toward a market economy.

In comparison with this profound economic transformation, the mainland's political transition is ignored. For the past decade, foreign observers paid more attention to the frequent power struggles and periodic shifts in political line and leadership than to the gradual emergence of secular changes in China's political system. Although political struggles continue on the mainland, and aftereffects of the "June 4th Incident" persist, important and irreversible changes in the political system also occurred for the following reasons:

- Economic development is the principal aim of national policy. Economic development replaced class struggle as the leadership's highest priority; attention to political consciousness clearly receded to second place and continues to diminish in importance.
- Changes in leadership involve not only changes in personnel, but also in leadership style. The dictatorial practices of the Maoist era are gone. Although Deng Xiaoping is in an extremely powerful position, balance-of-power mechanisms already exist. After Deng dies, the latter modality is expected to prevail.
- China's centralized administrative system was weakened while local governments increased their powers, particularly in the coastal areas. This decentralization process is expected to continue after Deng's death.

- The Chinese Communist Party (CCP) is beginning to change from a revolutionary/military party to an administrative/bureaucratic ruling party. One consequence of this is that its cadres' functions in the future will be concerned more with public administration than with political and ideological education. Civil service reform was successfully introduced on an experimental basis in Shenzhen.
- The era of isolation in China's foreign relations ended. Ideology is no longer the primary factor influencing China's decision-making, and participation in international society is the main tenet of Chinese diplomacy. Somewhat paradoxically, fallout from the "June 4th Incident" further accelerated these trends.
- The emergence of proto-democratic regimes in East Asia, particularly in Taiwan, South Korea, and Singapore, presented the younger generation of Chinese leaders with an alternative model. The concept of "neo-authoritarianism," although it fell out of favor in the post-June 4 period, is expected to exert increasing influence on China's political development.

Underlying China's political and economic reforms are changes in popular modes of thinking, especially in the coastal regions. People became more open and practical in their thinking. Economic interest-centered thinking began to supplant the traditional mentality centered on ideology, power struggle and class conflict. Given this situation, Maoist-style political movements are not likely to gain significant popular support, but the ways of thinking and the life styles of Hong Kong and Taiwan are exerting greater influence on the mainland's coastal population. Such influence is expected to spread to China's interior regions.

Although China is in transition in a comprehensive sense, with great change taking place in economic development, politics, and ways of thinking, many questions remain. Uncertainty over the scope and pace of reform and leadership change after Deng passes from the scene will affect the speed, degree, and manner of these comprehensive changes. The political disturbances at the end of 1986 and in the spring of 1989 led to the downfall of such bold reformers as Hu Yaobang and Zhao Ziyang. These events illustrate both the complexity and the urgency of China's political transition. The rise of Asiatic "neo-authoritarianism" directed people's attention to the emergence of a new generation of Chinese leaders and to their potential impact on the PRC's future development. But the Chinese path to political development nevertheless remains lined with uncertainties.

THE "NATIVIZING" TRANSITION IN TAIWAN

The end of the Chiang Ching-kuo era and the beginning of the Lee Teng-hui era marked the entrance of Taiwan into a process of nativizing transition. This transition is a response to growing demands on the part of native-born Taiwanese for a redistribution of political power. The rise of an articulate Taiwanese middle class and the growth in native Taiwanese economic development more generally played major roles in fomenting these demands. This transition is reflected in the Taiwanese authorities' efforts to seek international recognition of Taiwan as a sovereign political entity, a claim made more credible by Taiwan's expanding economic influence. The development of the Taiwan independence movement as represented by the DPP (which won its first major election for the first time in 1994) also contributed to this nativizing transition, albeit along a different track.

Economic development was the foundation for Taiwan's nativizing transition. Taiwan's foreign exchange reserves reached $80 billion, making them the largest in the world. In 1992, Taiwan's exports amounted to $81.8 billion, imports $72.3 billion, and total foreign trade $154.1 billion, occupying the twelfth, fourteenth and thirteenth places in world exports, imports, and foreign trade, respectively. At the same time, its per-capita income reached $10,196. Overall, the Taiwanese economy is one of the fastest growing in Asia, having expanded by 80 percent in the 1980s.

The impact of these economic successes on Taiwan's nativization was strongly reflected in the political arena. Since Chiang Ching-kuo lifted martial law on 15 July 1987, Taiwanese authorities permitted formation of new political parties, abandoned newspaper censorship, allowed Taiwanese to visit the mainland, and began the democratization process in Taiwan. In 1988, Lee Teng-hui became the first Taiwanese native to become KMT chairman and president of the "ROC." At the end of 1991, the election of the "National Assembly" and the mass resignation of senior assembly members (who had been elected on the mainland more than four decades ago) furthered the nativization process. In 1992, "Constitutional Reform" was completed following the abolition of the "period of mobilization against rebellion." Recent elections of the Legislative Yuan pushed the process of political nativization forward. In 1993, after mainland-born Premier Hau Pei-tsun was replaced by Lien Chan (a native Taiwanese) as the head of the Executive Yuan, the process of political power transition from mainlanders to natives was almost completed: Taiwanese natives occupy a dominant position within both the ruling KMT party and the government. The political force represented by Taiwan natives also became quite "mainstream" in Taiwanese society. One impact of these changes was to raise the two-sided (and internally conflicting) question of how to gain international recognition while continuing to "normalize" relations with the mainland.

Taiwan's nativization process widened the cultural and emotional gap separating the younger generation of Taiwanese from their older, mainland-born compatriots. Most of the former identify themselves with Taiwan rather than with the mainland, and many wish to gain international recognition for Taiwan. On the other hand, as more and more Taiwanese people visit the mainland, and as economic ties between the two sides increase, the bonds between the Taiwanese and Chinese grew visibly. A "greater China" consciousness emerged and appears to be growing steadily. One example is widespread support reported in Taiwan for Beijing's recent Olympic bid.

Even though the nativization process appears irreversible, redistribution of power in Taiwan is not complete. Nativization and democratization are taking place simultaneously. The struggle for power among various political parties and factions, both within the KMT and between it and the rival DPP, is likely to be more intense in the future. The question of reunification versus Taiwanese independence is a primary focus of the power struggle in Taiwan. In order to attract votes and thereby gain power, the DPP publicly included a Taiwan independence clause in its Party Program. It also organized activities designed to promote Taiwan's return to the UN, and it has demanded an immediate plebiscite to determine Taiwan's future. Its aim is to create problems for the ruling KMT. Whether the politicization process in Taiwan will lead to Taiwanese independence—and a new crisis in the Taiwan Straits—remains to be seen. However, notwithstanding such uncertainty, Taiwan's policy toward China is becoming a central focus of political debate in Taiwan and the outcome of this debate will have a great impact on Taiwan's future.

THE SOVEREIGNTY TRANSITION IN HONG KONG

In 1997, Hong Kong will be transformed from a British colony into a Chinese "special administrative region." During the transition, how to maintain Hong Kong's current level of prosperity and stability while affecting a transfer of sovereignty in accordance with the Basic Law on Hong Kong enacted by the Chinese legislature (the National People's Congress) will remain highly controversial. On 7 October 1992, Hong Kong Governor Chris Patten initiated a proposal (eventually passed by the Hong Kong legislature in mid-1994) for greater democratic home rule in the period leading up to 1997. This initiative brought the question of Hong Kong's transition to the point of crisis. The Sino-British negotiations on Hong Kong have become a battlefield, with both sides seeking to protect their own interests. How this conflict is resolved—through dialogue and mutual accommodation or through confrontation and threat—will deeply affect Hong Kong's economy, politics, and popular confidence level.

On the one hand capital outflows and a substantial "brain drain" since the signing of the Sino-British Joint Declaration in 1984 reflected a lack of confidence regarding Hong Kong's future. On the other hand, the mainland's adoption of economic reform and open policies in its urban and coastal areas, especially in

Guangdong province (bordering Hong Kong) injected new vitality and opportunities into the Hong Kong economy. The uncertainties inherent in the sovereignty transition are thus counterbalanced by stability stemming from the ongoing economic integration of Hong Kong and the coastal areas of South China.

Since 1985, the Chinese mainland has been Hong Kong's largest trading partner. Total trade between the two grew more than 11 times between 1981 and 1991. In 1992, Hong Kong-China trade reached its height, totaling $80.56 billion and accounting for 53 percent of Hong Kong's total foreign trade (as compared to only 15.54 percent as recently as 1981). The Chinese mainland is also the leading beneficiary of Hong Kong's booming transit trade, accounting for more than 80 percent of all such transit trade (which totaled $88.6 billion in 1993). In this connection, Hong Kong was the transit point for 51 percent of Taiwan's exports to the Chinese mainland, 65 percent of Japan's exports, and 57 percent of U.S. exports. Hong Kong is, moreover, China's largest "foreign" investor, and vice-versa. From 1979 to the first quarter of 1992, Hong Kong businesses signed contracts calling for $74.5 billion in investment in China, accounting for 64 percent of all contracted foreign investment in that period.[3] By the same token, mainland China's investment in Hong Kong reached $12 billion in 1992, thereby enabling China to supplant Japan as Hong Kong's largest Asian investor. Because of these close economic relations, Hong Kong dollars flowing into the mainland reached $15 billion in 1992, accounting for fully 30 percent of China's money supply that year.

This trend of economic integration between Guangdong and Hong Kong also helped to lay a more stable foundation for Hong Kong's 1997 sovereignty transition. It is interesting to note that contrary to past experience, the Sino-British dispute over Chris Patten's 1992 democratization proposal and its subsequent ratification did not significantly affect Hong Kong's economy—one clear sign of this is that Hong Kong capital continues to flow into the mainland. At the same time, increasing internationalization of Hong Kong capital is expected to contribute to Hong Kong's future stability and prosperity, both during and after the 1997 sovereignty transition.

In contrast to economic integration, the political side of the Hong Kong sovereignty transition equation generated substantial friction. Because of Hong Kong's colonial status, it had neither a democratic tradition nor democratic institutions. But in 1992, the British government decided to accelerate the democratization process. This produced an immediate, hostile reaction from the Chinese government, which claimed that all arrangements for Hong Kong's future must be accord with the Basic Law of Hong Kong. Moreover, since Hong Kong's sovereignty transition is regarded as an irreversible *fait accompli*, China insisted on its right to determine the direction of Hong Kong's future political development. Despite a number of victories for pro-democratic movements in the colony, the future of local autonomy and self-government in Hong Kong remains problematic. Given these circumstances, the ongoing Sino-British dispute over Patten's reforms became a barometer for predicting Hong Kong's probable future political climate.

Since the return of Hong Kong to China is irreversible, many Hong Kong residents already began to identify more closely with the mainland. The political behavior of Hong Kong residents before and after the June 4th Incident in Beijing in 1989, their donation activities on behalf of victims of the catastrophic floods that inundated East China in 1991, and their generally strong support for Beijing's recent Olympics bid reflect this tendency. As 1997 approaches and as the Hong Kong people's perception of their common nationality and common interests with the people of mainland China increases, it is expected that there will be a gradual diminution in their perception of common interests with Great Britain. Indeed, support for this hypothesis can be gleaned from the popular reaction in Hong Kong both to the deadlocked negotiations over the construction of a new Hong Kong international airport and to the dispute over Patten's democratization proposal. In both cases, more Hong Kong residents began to side with Beijing. The common thread of shared nationalism linking the people of Hong Kong with their compatriots on the mainland appears to be gaining strength. Both these facts are expected to contribute to the formation of a shared national consciousness between the two peoples, facilitating their peaceful reconciliation beyond 1997.

INTERACTIONS AND COMMON INTERESTS

Each of the three transitions examined above is taking place at its own pace, in its own manner, and within its own unique policy context. Such differences inevitably create or exacerbate misunderstandings between the various parties. For example, the more open and flexible international orientation and negotiating style of the new generation of Taiwanese leaders is barely comprehensible to the older generation of Chinese leaders in Beijing. Consequently, any articulation of demands for Taiwanese independence and any other political maneuvers on the question of reunification and independence initiated by Taiwan's various political parties and factions was met with negative reaction from the mainland, including thinly veiled threats of military action. This situation will change when the generational transition on the mainland is complete. The new generation of mainland leaders may be more open to flexible solutions to the Taiwan Straits problem.

Timing is crucial. It is difficult to conceive of Beijing not taking military action against Taiwan if the latter were to declare its independence. On the other hand, if the Taiwan problem were left to a later generation of leaders to handle, less confrontational interactions are likely. To ameliorate inevitable frictions engendered by generational (and other) differences, all sides need to be prepared to: (a) give high priority to issues currently amenable to flexible response and accommodation; and (b) put off for future consideration issues that cannot be negotiated. Only in this manner can the emergence of new transitional crises be avoided.

The impacts of differences in the manner of transition are evident. For example, political transition on the mainland is from Leninist totalitarianism to Asiatic "neo-authoritarianism," while the transition on Taiwan is from neo-authoritarianism to multiparty democracy. In terms of focus, the transition on the mainland represents a change from one generation of leaders to another, while that in Taiwan reflects a change from leaders of mainland origin to those of Taiwanese origin. If these differences are not appreciated, this can lead to misunderstandings and overreactions.

In the short run, political transitions in Taiwan and Hong Kong are the main factors complicating their relations with the Chinese mainland. For example, the development of a movement for Taiwanese independence, together with Taipei's recently accelerated efforts to "return to international society," have unavoidably generated friction between the mainland and Taiwan. In similar fashion, recent tendencies toward the political democratization and economic internationalization of Hong Kong also posed fresh challenges to the Chinese mainland.

In the long run, the results of the generational transition on the Chinese mainland will heavily influence future relations between the three sides. According to estimates of China's political development after Deng Xiaoping's death, if China follows the Soviet Union's footsteps and degenerates into political-military fragmentation and civil war, then Taiwan's independence is virtually unavoidable. Hong Kong's future is even more difficult to predict.

If China's generational transition goes smoothly (that is, if Deng's reform and open policies are maintained and the mainland manages to achieve a market economy while also affecting a smooth transition from a totalitarian system to a neo-authoritarian one), then China's peaceful reunification is more likely. If, on the other hand, China's political situation remains ambiguous and volatile for an extended period of time, the effects on Hong Kong and Taiwan will be very different. Under such a scenario (and assuming that the central government in Beijing retained its ability to govern), Hong Kong's sovereignty transition might still be accomplished, while mainland-Taiwan relations would remain highly uncertain. With so many variables involved, it becomes extremely difficult to predict what kinds of crises are likely, between which parties, and with what ramifications.

Because of the manifold particularities and uncertainties inherent in the transition processes described above, the three sides are becoming more cautious and circumspect in their dealings with one another. Notwithstanding such circumspection, the following general propositions summarize their dominant patterns of interaction:

- During the period of transition, each side is making internal affairs its top priority. For this reason, before the mainland and Taiwan complete their respective transitions, it will be very difficult for them to conduct meaningful talks on reunification.
- Economic exchanges are the main focus in the developing relations between the three sides. Because of China's economic backwardness and developmental needs, economic incentives are the trump card held by Taiwan and Hong Kong in their relations with the mainland. However, as economic development is increasingly regionalized, the economies of Taiwan and Hong Kong will become more closely integrated with the mainland's coastal areas.
- Pragmatism prevails in their mutual interactions. Issue-by-issue practical negotiations and step-by-step gradual development of mutual economic benefit and peaceful exchange are the preferred methods on both sides of the Taiwan Strait. Out of such practical, gradual, beneficial, and peaceful contacts may arise a set of shared norms, expectations, and corresponding institutions. Such convergence, in turn, may pave the way for the peaceful resolution of China's reunification question.
- Following the end of the Cold War, the influence of external forces in East Asia (principally the United States, Russia, and Great Britain) declined, while that of Japan is increasing. Under these circumstances, reunification becomes primarily an internal Chinese affair.

Despite the many unstable factors in the transitional equation, and despite the special characteristics exhibited by each of the three sides in this equation, a set of common regional interests and policy preferences are taking shape, and it may provide a suitable foundation for the resolution of conflict. The main components of this emerging regional consensus include the following:

- Maintenance of regional stability;
- Promotion of economic cooperation and integration;
- Promotion of a wide range of exchanges to facilitate mutual understanding and trust;
- Control of arms competition and adherence to the ultimate goal of peaceful reunification;
- Mutual acceptance of the principle of gradualism as the preferred means of developing relations.

Barring new and unforeseen regional political, military, or economic traumas, these shared interests should suffice to ensure a continued, steady flow of capital, goods, ideas, people, and information across the increasingly open boundaries of "greater China." By the same token, these shared interests also may ensure gradual convergence among the three transitions.

NOTES

1 . The views expressed in this chapter are the author's own and should not be construed as representing those of any Chinese institution. The author wishes to acknowledge Professor Richard Baum of UCLA for his stylistic revision.

2. See *The Bulletin of the Ministry of Foreign Trade and Economic Cooperation of the People's Republic of China*, Beijing, 25 January 1994.

3. Yun-Gwing Sung, "Hong Kong and the Economic Integration of the China Circle," in *The China Circle: Evolving Relations among Taiwan, the People's Republic of China, and Hong Kong–Macao*, Susan L. Shirk and Christopher P. Twomey, eds. (forthcoming, c1996).

Part III
The Security-Economic Linkage:
Northeast Asia

10 The Russian Economic Crisis: Implications for Asian-Pacific Policy and Security

James Clay Moltz

INTRODUCTION

The ongoing crisis in the Russian economy has been viewed by many analysts in the security field as a deplorable but not particularly threatening course of events.[1] After 1991, the standard argument of those interested in the future of Pacific security relations—in the United States and Japan, as well as other countries—has been that as long as Russia remains preoccupied with its current economic crisis, it will be unable to pursue adventurist policies in East Asia and will be more malleable in future regional negotiations.[2] The basis for this perspective is what observers see as an inherent Russian vulnerability: its need for economic aid and debt relief from the Group of Seven (G-7) countries and other Western nations.

The field of international relations theory provides considerable support for this policy perspective. Rational choice approaches, for example, portray Russia as a self-interested actor facing a tradeoff between linked options of "military adventurism/economic hardship" and "foreign policy restraint/foreign aid." It is presumed that in this time of economic crisis, the latter choice will be the preferred one because of the incentive structure facing the Russian government. At the same time, cognitive theories picture Russia as a country moving towards economic liberalization and democracy: processes driven by intellectual shifts among its leaders that will result in more accommodative foreign policies. In this scenario, domestic political changes and the restraints imposed by international economic institutions should increase the common interests Russia shares with other democracies and therefore induce moral self-restraint in foreign policy.

The problem with conventional wisdom regarding Russia and its supporting theoretical bases is that the evidence of Russian policy in East Asia since 1991 contradicts them. Specifically, this "benign decline" approach fails to account for the disruptive effects of the ongoing Russian political and especially economic crises on its Asian-Pacific policy. Rather than following the presumed direction of post-Cold War "cooperation," Russia has been forced by its economic and political crises to pursue a policy of short-term "self-interest" in East Asia. While the Cold War has not been restarted, a number of signs are troubling. The Yeltsin government has taken an increasingly recalcitrant policy on the Kurile Islands dispute with Japan. In search of hard currency, it has engaged in large-scale arms sales to China, including front-line ships, tanks and modern fighter aircraft. Moreover, Russia's incomplete economic reforms promoted illegal smuggling activity as well as unwise environmental policies in the Russian Far East. Finally, the central government has shown itself to be unable to provide financially for its existing military forces in the region. These conditions have brought about a dangerous rise in discontent and criminality within the Russian military, threatening discipline and lending instability to East Asia as a whole.[3] Left unaddressed, the range of possible harmful scenarios is sobering: the further expansion of high-tech arms sales to the region, unsanctioned nuclear aid to North Korea by destitute scientists, and, most seriously, a breakdown of the domestic political and military situation to a degree that could render the Russian Far East ungovernable from Moscow. As David Holloway argues, while we used to worry about the problem of a "strong" state in the U.S.S.R., today we are finding that a weak Russian state is perhaps a greater danger.[4]

It is this multidimensional Russian crisis—rather than the popular image of a safe and steadily reforming Russia—that faces East Asian elites as they contemplate the possible implications of Russia's continued economic difficulties. While many of these trends may be reversible, they have created new problems that have begun to sour the taste of the post-Cold War world in the Asian-Pacific region. The more we learn about these problems, the less we seem to be able to do about them, at least within the realm of traditional Cold War foreign policies.

The aim of this study is to examine the nature of the current crisis and suggest new policy prescriptions aimed at improving the Russian situation. I begin by examining the effects of Russia's economic crisis in three important areas: (1) Russian military policy in the region; (2) the economic situation in the Russian Far East; and (3) the regional political scene. Drawing on this evidence, I then examine the broader East Asian policy environment and suggest some possible solutions for regional actors interested in maintaining Russia as a reliable partner in East Asian economic and security cooperation. This involves developing a series of linked policy proposals aimed at alleviating the crisis and integrating Russia into the developing Asian-Pacific "community."[5]

RUSSIA'S ECONOMIC CRISIS AND ITS EFFECTS ON THE RUSSIAN MILITARY

The decline of the former Soviet economy since 1989 has been dramatic. The break-up of the old system created a fragmented and impoverished collection of industrial regions. With the end of the centrally directed supply network, what bonds remained stemmed largely from tradition and personal ties. Based on aggregate measures of economic performance, the country plunged into deep recession, suffering a 25 percent drop in output in 1992[6] and inflation rates of nearly 30 percent per month.[7] Some leading observers have described the Russian economy as being in worse condition than that of the United States during the Great Depression of the 1930s.[8] Meanwhile, the failure of Western economic aid to arrive in significant amounts and the lack of a domestic political consensus necessary for successful "bottom-up" reform within Russia has halted both the processes of economic integration internationally and of cognitive change toward the popular acceptance of capitalism domestically. Private foreign investment has also failed to live up to expectations.[9] Under these conditions, massive unemployment is avoided only through a widespread policy of enterprise subsidization of redundant workers.

In its sociological and psychological impact, Russia's crisis goes beyond typical economic depressions because it involves not only a sharp decline in the living conditions of most people, but also the destruction of a whole system of economy. While it is true that most Russians do not understand the underlying principles of a system struggling through birth amidst adversity, some factions oppose the reforms outright as inequitable, inappropriate, or even anti-Russian. The rise of petty theft, robbery, swindling, and organized crime created a negative impression of capitalism among a significant portion of the population, especially the elderly and those on fixed incomes.[10] In these circumstances, it is hard to convince people that things will get better. One recent newspaper report states that living standards have now declined from conditions of "poverty" to those of "misery."[11]

The current economic crisis is affecting all levels of society, but perhaps none more so than the Russian military. With the armed forces struggling to undertake simultaneously state-mandated cuts, defense conversion, and force restructuring, top brass and officers alike are trying to deal with an unprecedented threat to their survival.[12] In order to maintain even a basic level of readiness in the face of these severe budgetary shortfalls, the military has been forced to engage actively in blatantly "commercial" activities, as well as domestic politicking (violating a long tradition of non-involvement in politics). Unfortunately, as we analyze the overall impact of these practices on security in East Asia, the trends are highly negative and threaten to become even more unstable.

As perhaps the most visible symbol of Soviet power, the Russian military has been one of the primary victims of the break-up of the Soviet Union and the economic crisis. Not only was it forced to accept major reductions in its troop size and strategic weaponry, but it also lost key military bases, training facilities, housing units, repair facilities, and industrial enterprises in Eastern Europe and in the former Soviet republics. The combined effects of these losses weakened the Russian military and reoriented it eastward towards the Pacific.

But while the role of the Pacific Fleet grew in relative importance within Russian military strategy, especially after the reductions slated for land-based missiles in START I and II, the economic situation in Russia made it difficult for it to handle its added responsibilities. Currently, the Pacific Fleet has only 35 percent of the funds needed for maintenance of its ships. Some ships are also without adequate crew. Its two largest vessels (the "Novorossiysk" and "Minsk") were withdrawn to second-category reserve status because of repair problems.[13] These conditions caused Russia to curtail intelligence gathering activities in the Pacific and cut patrols to a bare minimum.[14]

With the independence of the other former Soviet republics, Russia is now deprived of important naval factories, ship repair facilities, and bases along its (former) northwestern and southwestern seacoasts. The problem in maintaining naval operations in these waters is that remaining service facilities are overloaded, and Russia cannot afford to build new ones.[15] Therefore, the Baltic, Caspian, and Black Sea Fleets have been forced to accept disproportionate cuts. Thanks to its location exclusively within the Russian Federation, the Pacific Fleet remained (at least on paper) unscathed. Here, centrally directed budget cuts resulted not in outright force reductions but instead in the idling of ships and personnel. One reason is the loss of shipyards and unique service facilities now claimed by Ukraine, which the Pacific Fleet depended upon for the maintenance of its most advanced, short-deck aircraft carriers. As Rear Admiral Viktor Topilin, chief of the Pacific Fleet Directorate of Repairs and Operation stated: Ukrainian independence "has deprived the Pacific Fleet of its hope for survival."[16] The Fleet's aim is to replace these facilities locally. But the problem, once again, is one of funding.[17]

Another problem of assuming that the Russian military's loss of funding is a positive development for Asian-Pacific security can be seen in those areas where advanced technologies are required to maintain military safety. For example, in its current circumstances, the Pacific Fleet cannot afford to decommission the nearly 40 nuclear submarines scheduled to leave service due to obsolescence. At present only 18 have been decommissioned, while the rest float idly in various harbors, manned by skeleton crews.[18] Should political conditions in Russia change, they could be called back into service. In another area, after studies completed last summer, the Russian Defense Ministry concluded that Russian troops cannot be fully withdrawn from the southern Kurile islands because it would cost too much to replace the troops running the region's airports and seaports with civilian specialists.[19] Here again, the assumed benefits of Russia's economic difficulties have been rendered moot by other complicating factors.

Among average soldiers—draftees living on minimal wages under difficult conditions—theft and other crime has risen, as chains of authority have been broken by economic distress and the flight of a large portion of the officer corps to the private sector.[20] Similarly, the disruption of Russian society caused by the simultaneous economic and political crises has caused problems with recruiting, which is far below required levels, despite the recent institution of paid contract service for a portion of interested inductees. Meanwhile, for those leaving the service and those being forced from previously lucrative jobs in the defense sector, the option of using their old connections to engage in the smuggling of weapons or other military material, including nuclear technology, has become increasingly appealing.[21] In December 1992, Russian intelligence forces in Moscow caught 36 nuclear scientists aboard a plane destined for North Korea.[22] Given the progress of the North Korean nuclear and missile programs, speculation arises as to whether others already got through.[23] One expert on technology transfer even predicts that foreign terrorist groups (especially in the Middle East) may be the beneficiaries of Russian nuclear smuggling within the next five years.[24]

But the main threats posed by Russia's economic woes for East Asian security probably lie beyond the realm of the cloak-and-dagger world of arms smuggling. In terms of scale, a more troubling phenomenon facing cooperative security in the region is open Russian arms saleswith government orders for new weapons falling by an estimated 60 percent,[25] defense enterprises unable to move quickly into consumer goods production have faced a difficult decision of either laying off workers or seeking out foreign customers for their products.[26] The problem here is that many of the old veto-gates controlled by government ministries on such sales now have disappeared. In the past year, the Yeltsin administration shifted its policy from one focusing on control to one of actually promoting arms sales by its defense enterprises through a loosening of trade regulations. During recent trips to South Korea, China, and India, President Yeltsin overtly advertised for arms sales, in many cases, successfully.

While in absolute terms Russian weapons sales have declined from $19.6 billion in 1989 under Gorbachev to around $4 billion in 1992, much of this decline is because of Russia's termination of sales based on foreign aid credits, which made up most of Soviet-era weapons exports.[27] Direct cash sales and barter agreements are now the rule. But while a decline in overall sales is a positive sign, the negative corollary of the decline in Russian global reach is the end of Russian "leverage" over its customers. That is, today's arms clients no longer fear that the "long arm" of Moscow will remove them should they engage in activities that go against Russian policies. Nor do new hard currency customers fear the potential loss of Russian credits, since none are being extended. This often means that favorable Russian policies in support of United Nations actions or other international restrictions may be undercut by regional leaders seeking arms to promote their own policies, rather than those of Moscow.[28]

Geographically speaking, recent Russian arms sales (and barter deals) in the rapidly growing Pacific Rim have been especially brisk, with China snapping up

$1.4 billion in advanced fighter aircraft and tanks. new deals have included air defense systems, frigates, and diesel submarines.[29] Meanwhile, Russia sold 18 MIG-29s to Malaysia in 1993[30] and a "wide range of armaments" to South Korea in exchange for debt relief.[31] Moreover, at talks surrounding the Yeltsin-Roh summit in 1992, the two sides agreed to military co-production deals in a variety of weapons categories aimed specifically at improving Russia's ability to market its military products internationally.[32] Elsewhere, controversial arms sales to India (cryogenic missiles) and to an array of Middle Eastern countries (submarines to Iran) continued.

This suggests that the long-term effects of Russia's economic crisis on Asian-Pacific security may be very negative. But the effects of the Russian economic crisis for East Asia are not limited to military consequences. Instability in the Russian Far Eastern economy also may prove problematic for Russia's Pacific neighbors.

THE RUSSIAN CRISIS AND THE RUSSIAN FAR EAST'S ECONOMIC INTEGRATION WITH THE ASIA-PACIFIC REGION

The floundering national economy, combined with the failure of the Yeltsin government to stem the tide of regionalism, has created a situation wherin sub-economies have begun to dominate Russia. In the Russian Far East and elsewhere, increasingly powerful regional organizations are bargaining effectively for an expanding share of the economic pie, claiming a larger portion of the revenues gained from the sale of local resources. At the same time, the lack of an agreed-upon formula for economic reform at the center and the largely undocumented growth of private companies have wreaked havoc on old systems of government financing, namely the turnover tax and state deductions from enterprise paychecks. In the absence of political control over the regions, the center is able to collect only a fraction of required taxes from the growing private sector. Similarly, corruption has risen dramatically, frustrating many citizens because bureaucrats running state enterprises seem to benefit as much (if not more so) than they did under the old system.

In the Far East, for example, state wildlife protection officials are selling pelts and running illegal hunting trips for foreigners using military helicopters.[33] In the Primorskiy region near Vladivostok, local officials took bribes to allow South Korea's Hyundai Corporation to engage in illicit logging of protected species of trees beyond their allotted harvesting areas.[34] The ramifications of these practices are a worsening of environmental damage in this fragile region as well as growing cynicism about economic reform. The net effect of these uncontrolled market conditions is to cause many people to yearn for a return to the strong hand and order of authoritarianism.[35] One particularly tragic event recently tilted the scales even further against reformers among many people in and around Vladivostok. Because of cutbacks in already poor military rations and inadequate supervision by senior officers, four young naval cadets at the Russkiy Island facility died from malnutrition in early 1993, and hundreds of others were hospitalized.[36] Both the military and the local population reacted harshly to this news.[37] There is bound to be continued grumbling among conservatives and senior military leaders that the government has lost control and needs to be replaced.

On the positive side, the economic integration of the Russian Far East into the greater Pacific Rim is beginning, with trade growing between Russia and many of its neighbors (including China, South Korea, and Taiwan). But former partners, such as Japan, have restricted trade in the past year because of concerns about debts by Russian enterprises and the ongoing political disputes between the two countries over the southern Kuriles. Also hurting trade between Russia and its Asian neighbors is the skeptical attitude of Russian entrepreneurs towards contracts signed with foreigners and the inability of foreign corporations to seek effective legal recourse in cases of dispute or outright thievery. Economic pressures cause Russia's entrepreneurs to focus on the short term, making practices such as "shopping" the products of joint ventures to the highest bidder (regardless of previous agreements) commonplace.[38] Several optimistic foreign companies quit doing business in the Russian Far East as a result of these practices.[39] This suggests that if the economic decline is not stopped and financial order is not established, economic integration with the Pacific Rim may be in jeopardy.

Another regional problem that the current national economic crisis exacerbates is the crucial task of building a modern economic infrastructure in the Russian Far East. Despite grandiose plans in the last years of the Gorbachev government to invest heavily in Far Eastern development, progress has been minimal. The most serious problems are the lack of all-weather roads, inadequacies in the carrying capacity of the trans-Siberian and BAM railroads, poor port development (especially in the area of container facilities), lack of sewage and water purification facilities, unreliable electric power grids, and poor electronic data and telephone communications. Even with the widescale opening of Russian Pacific ports in 1992 and the opening of several international airports (including Vladivostok), there are still inadequate means for handling freight and passengers. The limited infrastructure development has originated largely from self-interested foreign investment.

While the resource-rich Russian Far East finds itself in a highly beneficial location for economic development (on the northern edge of the capital-rich Pacific Rim), the tightness of investment funding—from Moscow and local sources, as well as foreign countries and corporations—is slowing and corrupting this development. In terms of regional security, the long-term effects of Russia's failure to integrate economically into the Pacific Rim are serious. To the extent that Russia fails to benefit economically from its contact with the region, it will be less likely to support cooperative initiatives, especially as long as its only card is a military one.

THE RUSSIAN ECONOMIC CRISIS AND REGIONAL POLITICS IN THE FAR EAST

Current political trends within the Russian Federation are highly influenced by the failures of economic reform measures and therefore show a similarly unsettling pattern of disintegration. Constituent republics are negotiating with Moscow for more autonomy while smaller regions are seeking various forms of political and economic independence from *oblast-* and *krai-*level governments.[40] Throughout the country, nationalistic and conservative parties are gaining in strength.

In the Russian Far East, economic independence movements have gained power and persuasiveness. The huge Far Eastern republic of Yakutia (the Russian Federation's largest non-Russian administrative area) changed its name back to the aboriginal "Sakha" Republic and has gained considerable sovereignty within Russia.[41] Meanwhile, the Chukotka region (in extreme northeast Russia) gained administrative independence from its erstwhile superiors in the Magadan *oblast* government in order to increase its profits from local resources. A similar "upgrading" in status is being sought by the northern portion of the Kamchatka peninsula (the Koryak autonomous *okrug*) from the control of the *oblast* government in Petropavlovsk. Other pro-independence movements seeking more radical measures include various regional groups calling for a return to the independent Far Eastern Republic that existed in this area from 1920-22.[42] Finally, the formation of the Far Eastern Association for Economic Cooperation brought together the leaders of the region's Councils of People's Deputies in order to bargain collectively with Moscow over economic and political issues.[43] Should conditions in Russia worsen further, this body could become the nucleus for new political demands.

The one restraining factor on these movements is the presence of a majority of Russians in every so-called "minority" region, even in the Sakha Republic.[44] This means that as long as these governments continue to become more democratic, the weight of the Russian population should be a moderating factor.[45] However, as former Gorbachev advisor Aleksandr Yakovlev argues, it is not evident that democratization will continue in Russia's regions or that self-serving demagogues will be kept from exercising power over unwilling constituents.[46] In many respects, Yakovlev argues, conflicts among elite republic-level politicians, not popular sentiment, led to the break-up of the Soviet Union. Similar dynamics may be found in the Russian Far East, particularly as politicians deem Moscow an inviting target to blame for the worsening economic conditions. The increasing fragmentation of the country and the population's growing alienation from the center constitute threats to stability in the region and Moscow's ability to govern.

If it continues, the economic crisis in Russia could well create political and social conditions that would make the process of "Lebanonization" seen in Russia today almost irreversible, save by a repressive, ultranationalist regime.[47] Thus, as the economic crisis reduces the perceived benefits within the region of continued political subservience to Moscow, power is becoming more fragmented. For East Asian decisionmakers, acquiring Russian input and consent on international issues is complicated by having to communicate with conflicting local leaders, rather than with a unified government. The threat of the fragmentation and even regionalization of the Russian military cannot be discounted.[48]

PROPOSALS FOR ASIAN-PACIFIC POLICY INITIATIVES

Given the range of new threats developing as a result of the Russian economic crisis, new international policy initiatives must be developed. These initiatives should encourage the transformation of current Russian policy in East Asia from confrontation to one which will foster integration and regional cooperation. This transformation can be attempted through a variety of new means. The following proposals supplement a number of positive, but still very limited, efforts to integrate Russia into the region. At the same time, they recognize the limits of what foreign actors can do in Russia. Since high-level summits and subsequent newspaper columns have raised an abundance of proposals for Russia, my focus is those programs that impact specifically Russia's Asian-Pacific policy.

In the area of economics, Russia needs to both stabilize itself domestically and integrate itself internationally. Outside aid can help, but recent experience shows that tied credits have had little effect, except to cause greater Russian indebtedness. What foreign countries must do—both in order to placate domestic critics and to weaken the catcalls of Russian nationalists—is to support their own corporations' investment in Russia, especially in joint ventures aimed at improving the people's long-term ability to provide for themselves. In the Far East, such projects include the creation of for-profit companies in the area of infrastructure development (transportation, communications, water treatment, and power grid management), where user fees could be generated to cover the costs of foreign investment. These projects could enhance the integration of the Russian Far East into the Pacific Rim economy by making a more attractive business environment for foreign manufacturers. Some ideas already in-progress include the Greater Vladivostok Project and the multinational Tumen River Project, both aimed at the creation of new manufacturing zones with access to the Sea of Japan and the Asian continent.

A second and related area of new foreign aid to the Russian Far East might be the development of joint ventures to promote the value-added processing of the Far East's raw materials (timber, gemstones, precious metals, and fish products). These projects could help ease Russia's debt burden by increasing the value-added content of Russia's scarce hard currency exports.[49] They might also help support the creation of a proposed Far Eastern development bank to guarantee foreign investment and provide the means for ready exchange of foreign companies' ruble profits into hard currency.[50] The success of these efforts can help bring Russia into the Asian-Pacific economic community on the basis of new civilian industries, rather than weapons sales. In support of these efforts, foreign countries should redirect their aid packages in two directions: (1) away from Moscow-based agencies and to regional projects; and (2) away from state-run industries and to private ones. With the exception of the crucial government-to-government talks on rescheduling Russia's heavy Soviet-era debt, developed countries in the region should encourage their own corporations by channeling aid into increased loan guarantees for private investors and providing additional incentives to enter the Far Eastern market.[51] Although channeling aid to the regions might further destabilize the domestic political situation, developing greater prosperity in the regions will reduce the likelihood that current economic discontent develops into divisive independence movements.

Finally, in the economic realm, all states in the Pacific Rim can strengthen market forces in the Russian Far East by lowering trade barriers to Russian products. This would send a clear signal to prospective local entrepreneurs, while also making it easier for foreign corporations to develop manufacturing enterprises there. To the surprise of many not familiar with the region, the southern Far East has an abundance of highly-skilled but increasingly redundant workers in the military industries of Vladivostok, Komsomolsk-na-Amure and Khabarovsk. With improved foreign investment, these military-trained technicians could play a positive role in design, engineering, and production in the commercial electronics industry and other high-tech fields.[52] The alternative is an increasingly restive regional workforce that could begin to support growing reactionary forces in Russian regional politics.

One of the biggest security challenges of the post-Cold War era in the Pacific is preventing the possible isolation, politicization, and regionalization of the Russian military. Until economic conditions stabilize, the armed forces—like other groups in Russian society—will be under pressure to use illegal means to secure their personal well-being. Similarly, having borne the brunt of considerable public disapproval for its initial role in the August 1991 coup and the violent October 1993 attack on the Russian Parliament, the military needs to be reassured of its place in Russian society. East Asian nations should promote a role that is peaceful.

A number of mutually beneficial cooperative military programs can be proposed by the Asian-Pacific countries. One area of possible cooperation is in the crucial task of decommissioning the Pacific Fleet's older ballistic missile submarines. Despite the obvious interest of the United States in seeing these ships removed from service, there are no U.S. Navy programs to help the Russians do so.[53] But past Soviet practices of sinking damaged submarines and reactor cores (especially in the Kara Sea) argue for a more proactive regional policy to promote responsible Russian environmental policies in the Pacific region. Possible funding for such a program could come from programs such as the still largely unspent Nunn-Lugar funds. Other programs, such as exchanges of officers and training in civil-military relations in a democratic context may help the high command deal with its new place in Russian society.[54] Finally, active regional cooperation to promote trade and environmental protection of the Pacific Ocean, Sea of Okhotsk, Sea of Japan, and Yellow Sea may restore some of the Russian Navy's sense of purpose, while channeling it in a more positive direction. One incipient program is a cooperative project sponsored by the U.S. Coast Guard to introduce a new system of joint rescue operations in the Pacific.[55] Other areas where joint U.S.-Russian efforts may succeed include enforcement of regional bans on drift net fishing, as well as combating the growing incidence of piracy on the region's seas. These bilateral U.S.-Russian efforts, of course, do not exempt Japan and other regional naval powers from their responsibilities in promoting cooperative efforts aimed at integrating the Russian military into more positive functions in the region. The alternative— namely, a Russian military backlash in the Far East and return to traditional nationalistic behavior—is an outcome that all regional powers want to prevent. Such efforts also encourage the Russian government to look eastward for its new commercial future, a process that further benefits the development of Asia-Pacific.

CONCLUSION

In contrast to prevailing policy views and the predictions of various theories, viewing Russia's economic crisis as a "plus" for East Asian security is a very dangerous perspective. The simultaneous worsening of Russia's economic crisis and the rise of Russian conservatism undercut the hopeful predictions of many analysts. Recent events suggest that the uncontrolled effects of the on-going Russian economic decline could be the single biggest unknown in the Asian-Pacific security calculus, raising new dangers of regional conflict and a resurgent Russian military presence.

While Russia's current crisis renders the possibility of military aggression being launched against the Pacific Rim from the Russian Far East unlikely in the short term, its implications beyond the next few years threaten both direct aggression (by a possible revanchist government) and indirect destabilization of the

Asian-Pacific region (through arms sales and technology transfer). The break-up of the old union and the difficulties of economic reforms have led to the simultaneous rise of both ultra-nationalist groups and regional independence movements. These forces threaten internal stability and external turmoil. Without cooperative efforts among the region's powers, the Russian Far East may become dangerous: a region of warlordism, illicit arms dealing, and nuclear instability.

The current Russian economic crisis has reduced the level of traditional security threats emanating from the Russian military. But it also created a whole new realm of threats and sources of instability with which the United States and other regional powers are unfamiliar. While foreign countries can play only a supporting role in solving Russia's problems, their policies do have important practical and symbolic effects on Russia's development. Therefore, regional powers in the Pacific need to take Russia's economic problems seriously and, within the limits of their existing budgets, adopt long-term economic, political, and security policies that will integrate Russia into the Asia-Pacific community, rather than push it towards ultra-nationalism and economic autarky.

Notes

1. See, for example, Stephen M. Meyer's argument on the absence of a Russian military threat to the United States and the impossibility of its resurrection (*The New York Times*, 3 April 1993, p. 4).
2. For example, Vice Admiral David M. Bennett (U.S. Navy) has stated that he no longer considers Russia a threat in the Pacific due to its inability to maintain funding for a "blue water" navy. (Interview at Coronado Naval Base, San Diego, California, 9 June 1992).
3. Serious accidents have occurred in the fire-induced explosions of nuclear materials in Tomsk-7 (April 1993) and of conventional ordnance stockpiled near Vladivostok (May 1992). Both incidents bore the signs of a lack of supervision and increased carelessness among defense personnel.
4. David Holloway, "Military Security Implications of Imperial Disintegration—U.S.S.R.," speech at the 17th Annual Berkeley-Stanford Conference on "The Disintegration of Multinational Communist States," University of California, Berkeley, 12 March 1993.
5. By "community," I mean the various proposals and efforts aimed at creating norms and more regularized ties among members of the Asian-Pacific area. Some of these are limited as of yet to ASEAN, others include such region-wide efforts as APEC and the PECC. Finally, still others include the flawed, but potentially significant, efforts of states cooperating with the United Nations to solve the Cambodian crisis and with the IAEA to contain and stop the North Korean nuclear program.
6. It must be pointed out, however, that the sharp decline in Russian output is in part a result of the required overproduction of many goods under the communist system, especially steel, coal, and other heavy industrial products. Widespread wasting of resources typified Soviet industrial practice, thus conservation and production drops are

not necessarily bad in these areas of the economy. See interview with Vladimir Shumeyko, first deputy Prime Minister, *Nezavisimaya gazeta*, 6 October 1992, p. 2; FBIS-SOV-92-195, 1 October 1992, p. 14.

7. For inflation estimates, see T. Popova, "Na protsent kazhdiy den' pastut tseny v Primor'e," *Krasnoye znamya* (Vladivostok), 2 April 1992, p. 3.

8. See for example comments by Richard Nixon, "Clinton's Greatest Challenge," *The New York Times*, 5 March 1993, p. A15.

9. For example, despite all of the talk of new Russian-American business ties, U.S. companies have invested only $400 million in Russia from 1987-92. (*The New York Times*, 29 March 1993, p. C1.)

10. According to recent polls in Vladivostok, a plurality of 40 percent cites "the mafia" as the most powerful actor in the city's new economy. This compares to some 20 percent who cite "new businesses" and an embarrassing seven percent who believe that "government officials" are in control. (Figures from a survey conducted by the newspaper *Tikhookeanskiy zvezda* (Vladivostok), 3 July 1992; cited in *RA Report*, Center for Russia in Asia, University of Hawaii, no. 14 (January 1993), p. 20.)

11. Ye. Belykh, "Eto uzhe ne bednost', a nishscheta," *Krasnoye znamya* (Vladivostok), 23 February 1993, p. 2.

12. The position of the military can be said to be more precarious than during its last great threat (the Nazi German invasion) in that the armed forces today *lack* the broad support of the general population.

13. *Komsomolskaya Pravda*, 26 August 1992.

14. Interview with Vice Admiral David M. Bennett, Coronado Naval Base, San Diego, California, 9 June 1992.

15. Roman Zadunayskiy, "Bezopasnost': Stanet li Rossiya vnov' morskoy derzhavoy?," *Rossiyskiye Vesti* (Moscow), 5 January 1993, p. 2.

16. ITAR-TASS report, reprinted in FBIS-SOV-92-160, 18 August 1992, p. 3.

17. Some of these dire statements, however, may be carefully orchestrated efforts by the Fleet's command to attract additional funding from Moscow. Indeed, despite the Navy's complaints, the construction of new ships has not stopped completely. In December 1992, for example, a new anti-submarine vessel (the "Admiral Panteleyev") arrived in Vladivostok from a Baltic Sea shipyard. (ITAR-TASS report cited in *RA Report*, no. 14, January 1993, p. 129.) In fact, in the strategic nuclear area, one Russian officer reports that the Pacific Fleet has recently added a newly-developed sea-launched ballistic missile and that, overall, it is actually increasing its level of readiness. (ITAR-TASS report cited in *RA Report*, no. 14, January 1993, p. 129.) Thus, in some cases, "leaner" may actually mean "meaner."

18. Report by NHK television in *RA Report*, no. 14, January 1993, p. 128.

19. See military reports and interview with Maj. Gen. Sergei Sergeev (from *Svobodniy Sakhalin*, 23 May 1992, cited in *SUPAR Report*, no. 13, July 1992, p. 123); also reports (from *Krasnaya Zvezda* and *Nezavisimaya Gazeta*) in *RA Report*, no. 14, January 1993, p. 45.

20. On these issues, see interview "Pavel Grachev: Armii cegodnya trudno, kak i vsemu

narodu," *Izvestiya*, 23 February 1993, pp. 1, 5.

21. On these issues, see William C. Potter, "Nuclear Exports From the Former Soviet Union: What's New, What's True," *Arms Control Today* 23:1 (January/February 1993).

22. See Potter, op. cit., p. 8.

23. One recent report claims that 56 kilograms of plutonium were smuggled by train from the Russian Far East into North Korea with several shipments of scrap metal in early 1992. See *Eye on Supply*, no. 8, Winter 1993, Emerging Nuclear Suppliers Project (ENSP), Monterey Institute of International Studies, p. 41.

24. UN Inspector David Kay, cited by David Hughes, "Arms Experts Fear Nuclear Blackmail," *Aviation Week and Space Technology*, 4 January 1993, p. 59.

25. "Tough Conversion for Russia's Armsmakers," Daniel Sneider, *The Christian Science Monitor*, 27 November 1992, p. 6.

26. One positive sign of the military's consolidation is that the production of nuclear submarines in the Far East at Komsomolsk-na-Amure shipworks will halt at the end of 1993. However, the newly-privatized enterprises there will continue to produce diesel submarines for export abroad to willing buyers in China, India, and several other countries. (*Arms Control Today* 22 (November 1992), p. 39.)

27. On the first figure, see Peter Almquist and Edwin Bacon, "Arms Exports in a Post-Soviet Market," *Arms Control Today* 22, (July/August 1992), p. 12; on the latter figure, see estimates by 1992 by Daniel Sneider in "Russian Armsmakers Take Care of Their Own," *The Christian Science Monitor*, 25 November 1992, p. 6

28. It should be noted that Russia is not alone among today's arms suppliers in facing this dilemma. The experience of France, for example, in arming Iraq before the Gulf War is a case in point.

29. INTERFAX reports that the deal includes up to 60 SU-27s and up to 90 MiG 29s (*RA Report*, no. 14, January 1993, p. 131). Other information noted that Chinese pilots were being trained by Russian air force personnel to fly the aircraft during the fall of 1992. In an earlier deal, reportedly agreed to in late 1991, China purchased some 400 advanced T-72 battle tanks for delivery in 1992 (KYODO news report, *SUPAR Report*, no. 13, July 1992, p. 126).

30. Aleksandr Babitskiy, "A. Rutskoi ugovarivaet malayziytsev kupit' MiG-29," *Izvestiya*, 3 March 1993, p. 3.

31. FBIS-SOV-92-242 (16 December 1992), p. 18.

32. See reports from the South Korean press cited in *RA Report*, no. 14, January 1993, p. 55.

33. Information based on offers made to the author (as well as to a subsequent visiting journalist who confirmed this report) at the Far Eastern Institute of Wildlife Management in Khabarovsk.

34. David Gordon and Antony Scott, "Russia's Timber Rush," *The Amicus Journal* (Natural Resources Defense Council) 14, (Fall 1992).

35. One recent survey states that the Russian people would prefer a "strong leader" to continuing "democracy" by a 51 percent to 31 percent margin. (Poll cited by Steven Erlanger, "What Russia Wants: Less Pain, a Strong Hand," *The New York Times*, "Week

in Review," 18 April 1993, p. 5.)

36. In addition, various reports state that between 350 and 600 cadets were hospitalized. On these events, see Natal'ya Ostrovskaya, "Uzhe fevral', a my eshche zhivy! no ne vse," *Vostok Rossii* (Vladivostok) 5:79 (February 1993). For additional details, see "Malnutrition Kills 4 Cadets; Russian Officers Suspended," *The New York Times*, 3 March 1993, p. A6; also, ITAR-TASS report (FBIS-SOV-93-051, 18 March 1993).

37. Soon after the incident, Defense Minister Pavel Grachev angrily dismissed the commander of the Pacific Fleet (Admiral Gennadiy Khvatov) and several other senior officers on his staff. Khvatov was replaced by Vice Admiral Georgiy N. Gurinov, former chief-of-staff of the Black Sea fleet.

38. Some of these problems could be addressed through changes in the Russian legal system, but the weakening of central power and funding for law enforcement has fostered corruption here too.

39. These include Sunshine Foods of San Francisco, which in 1991 saw half of its packaged product (caviar) seized by export officials in Khabarovsk, and then, in 1992, the whole spring's production being sold off illegally by their partners to another foreign buyer. (See Matt Miller, "U.S. investor gets cold shoulder in Siberia," *San Diego Union-Tribune*, 3 April 1993, p. C-1.) A similar experience befell two Seattle-based fishing companies in a joint venture operating with a Russian crew on a U.S.-provided vessel in the Sea of Okhotsk. (*Seafood Leader*, January/February 1992).

40. *Oblasts* and *krais* are—in rough terms—equivalent to state-level governments in the United States.

41. This declaration came from the Sakha Parliament, a body which has a slight majority of native peoples, despite the republics overall Russian and Ukrainian dominance. Notably, there has been no popular referendum on full independence.

42. One of the most powerful leaders of this movement was Sakhalin's Governor Valentin Fyodorov, who frequently threatened to reestablish the Far Eastern Republic if the Yeltsin government tried to return the southern Kuriles to Japan. Ironically, the very regional independence that Fyodorov promoted led to his ouster from power in March 1993 when the Sakhalin *oblast* Congress of People's Deputies declared that his initial appointment by Yeltsin to the post was invalid. The *oblast*-level congress scheduled its own election to replace him. (See "Press-konferentsiya malogo soveta," *Gubernskie vedomosti* (Yuzhno-Sakhalinsk), 6 March 1993, p. 1.) This has now taken place. The new governor is a former industrialist with recent experience working for a foreign joint venture operation.

43. The group currently is chaired by a standing president, Nikolai Danilyuk, who maintains a permanent office and staff in Khabarovsk.

44. In the Sakha, to be more specific, Russians constitute a large plurality. Together with those of Ukrainian descent, they are a large Slavic majority compared to ethnic Yakuts.

45. Notably, the Sakha Republic's independence declaration remains an act solely of the minority Yakut-dominated legislature. A vote on full independence would likely fail in a popular election. But, leaders are already acting on it nevertheless.

46. Remarks in an address at the Institute of International Studies, University of California, Berkeley, 22 February 1993.

47. Moreover, as Stephan Sestanovich argues, the United States' own budget crisis and the unwillingness of Americans to support old-style Cold War military commitments to cover its prosperous allies will greatly *reduce* our ability to deal with such a threat, should it arise. See his op-ed column, "U.S. Power, Less Than Super," *The New York Times*, 23 March 1993, p. A15.

48. In the Far East, such a process could create the world's third largest nuclear power, with a population of only 10 million people serving an independent regional government. With its forces based in virtually unassailable submarines on the northern edge of the Pacific Rim, such a government might wield considerable leverage over both Moscow and its Asian-Pacific neighbors.

49. Under the Soviet system, very little was done to promote such industries. Instead, the focus was simply on harvesting larger quantities of unprocessed raw materials for quick export.

50. For more on this concept, see P. Minakir, "Ekonomika sovetskogo Dal'nego Vostoka: vyzov krizisu," *Problemy Dal'nego Vostoka*, no. 5, 1991.

51. For the United States, this would mean greatly increasing funding for the Overseas Private Investment Corporation (OPIC), which currently plays a very limited role in Russian projects due to its low funding caps.

52. One positive sign is August 1993 announcement that the U.S. government and McDermott International will jointly aid in the conversion of one of the Far East's largest military enterprises, the Amur Shipyard in Komsomolsk-na-Amure. (*Izvestiya*, 4 August 1993), p. 1.

53. Interview with Vice Admiral David M. Bennett at Coronado Naval Base, San Diego, California, 9 June 1992).

54. One cautionary note, however, is raised by General John Galvin (U.S. Army). He points out that such "pro-democracy" programs in the 1950s and 1960s with Latin American officers helped convince visiting officers that U.S.-allied dictators at home needed to be overthrown. (Remarks in an address at the University of California, Berkeley, 11 March 1993.)

55. See TASS article cited in *SUPAR Report*, no. 13, July 1992, p. 122.

11 Japanese-Russian Economic Relations and Their Implications for Asia-Pacific Security

Tsuneo Akaha

INTRODUCTION

From their very first encounter towards the end of the eighteenth century, the Japanese and the Russians saw each other more with anxiety and suspicion than with confidence and trust, with the demarcation of bilateral territorial boundaries a perennial concern to both sides. The 1855 treaty of commerce and the 1875 Karafuto (Sakhalin)-Chishima (Kurile) exchange treaty between the rising Asian power and the expanding Eurasian empire could not eliminate the political, legal, and psychological tensions between the two nations. Their mutual animosities and hostilities exploded in the Russo-Japanese war of 1904-05 and the Japanese intervention in Siberia in 1918-20. Moscow's abrogation of the 1941 neutrality pact with Tokyo, declaration of war against Japan, and seizure of the southern Kuriles in 1945 prolonged the hostility and suspicion between the two peoples, leaving obstinate legacies for the Cold War and post-Cold War eras.

In the Asia-Pacific region, what are the prospects that multilateral political, security, and economic regimes will emerge to facilitate collective leadership? On the economic front, there is movement, albeit slow and by no means trouble-free, toward the establishment of a region-wide economic community. The most notable in this context is the growing regional acceptance, facilitated by U.S. advocacy, of the strengthening of the Asian Pacific Economic Cooperation (APEC) process that will serve as a catalyst for economic liberalization and policy coordination among its member governments. Another example of regional cooperation is the ASEAN Free Trade Area (AFTA), which started the process of tariff reduction in January 1994 towards the eventual establishment of a free trade zone in Southeast Asia by 2010 for some countries, and 2020 for all countries. On the political front, the six ASEAN countries, Japan, the United States, China, Russia, Vietnam, and others formed a ministerial ASEAN Regional Forum (ARF) to consult on security issues.

In Northeast Asia, deep-seated suspicions, historical rivalries, and legacies of the Cold War have impeded regional cooperation. Little movement toward multilateral security consultations has been achieved, and most security dialogues continue through bilateral channels. Even on the economic front, Northeast Asian countries did not consider governmental schemes for multilateral policy coordination, with most cooperation taking place on a bilateral basis.[1] North Korea's economic ties with its neighbors were damaged by the demise of the Soviet Union, China's pragmatic modernization strategy, South Korea's rapprochement with the Soviet Union and China, and Pyongyang's growing international isolation over its noncompliance with the safeguard provisions of the Nuclear Nonproliferation Treaty (NPT) in 1994. This inspired North Korea's accord with the United States to start remedying the consequences of these circumstances.

Even more conspicuous are the distant economic relations between two neighboring countries which would seem to gain much from closer economic cooperation: Japan and Russia. The resource-rich but capital-poor Russia and the resource-poor but capital-rich Japan have many complementary economic needs, yet their economic ties are severely limited. The political and security cooperation between these "distant neighbors" is similarly wanting.[2]

At the end of the Cold War, Japanese-Soviet economic ties were severely limited, political relations were still strained, and security concerns (particularly in Tokyo) still loomed large. The Soviet presence in Asia-Pacific was still primarily military and Japan's power base remained largely economic. Neither side could claim to have found a trustworthy partner in the other.

The absence of stable and trust-based relations between Russia and Japan is one of the most important obstacles to peace and stability in the post-Cold War Asia-Pacific. The vicarious but predictable bipolar order of the region during the Cold War must now be replaced by multinational regimes for regional security and economic relations, requiring integration of Russia into cooperative security and economic ties in Asia-Pacific. What should and can the two nations do to transform the present strained relationship into a friendlier and more stable one?

The following analysis explains the implications of sour relations between Japan and Russia for security in the Asia-Pacific in the post-Cold War era, and what can be done to change the situation. A stable relationship between these neighbors and their contribution to the peace and stability in the Asia-Pacific requires expansion of bilateral economic ties and reduction of the destabilizing military dimension of power disequilibrium between them. I will emphasize the importance of successful economic reform in Russia, the development of its Far Eastern region, and this region's integration into the Asia-Pacific economy.

POST-COLD WAR REGIONAL SECURITY AND JAPAN-RUSSIA RELATIONS

The impact of the end of the global Cold War on Asia-Pacific was complex and mixed. Economic development became the centerpiece of domestic and foreign relations and a key dimension of regional security against the diminishing significance of military power.[3] This was dramatically exemplified by South Korea's political rapprochement with Russia and China. Behind Gorbachev's perestroika was the Soviet leader's recognition of the need to reduce the economic burden of strategic rivalry with the United States. Moscow's decision to reach rapprochement with Beijing and South Korea also was attributable to the Soviet need to reduce its defense burden and explore economic gains from improved relations with its neighbors. Moreover, Japan's transformation from a defeated militarist-imperialist power into a successful "trading state" was recognized as the most important catalyst of regionwide economic prosperity. The end of the Cold War accelerated the proliferation of various schemes for regional economic cooperation and integration, for example, the Asian Pacific Economic Cooperation (APEC) forum, the Pacific Economic Cooperation Council (PECC), ASEAN Free Trade Area (AFTA), East Asian Economic Caucus (EAEC), and the Sea of Japan economic zone concept.

However, the economic dynamism of the Asia-Pacific region unfortunately was not sufficient to eliminate all legacies of the Second World War and the Cold War. The Cold War division of East Asia between capitalist and socialist camps prevented full reconciliation between Japan and other Asian countries because of Japan's imperialist atrocities of 1910-45. Japan's economic dominance reawakened the specter of a Japan-centered East Asian political order. The Japanese and the Russians do not agree on a formula for settling their Northern Islands territorial dispute. The division of China and Korea continues, Japan and North Korea have yet to establish diplomatic ties, and the futures of Cambodia and Hong Kong are uncertain. Moreover, the end of the Cold War security framework in the region rekindled fears of regional hegemonic rivalries and concerns over other territorial disputes among East Asian powers.[4]

An important question for the post-Cold War Japanese-Russian relations is whether the two countries can move closer by expanding economic ties and reducing military investments. For a stable economic-security equation to emerge, the two countries need to reach common understanding about a desirable configuration of power. This is a particularly difficult task since their power capabilities vary substantially and their foundations of power are equally diverse.

On one hand, Japanese defense planners view with great concern Russian military presence in the region, particularly the policy of using the Sea of Okhotsk as a sanctuary for nuclear-fueled ballistic-missile submarines.[5] They maintain that in view of the small population and limited industrial capacity of Russia's Far East region, the military forces deployed in the region far exceed defense requirements.[6] The breakup of the Soviet Union and the precipitous withdrawal of forces from the European and Central Asian territories of the former Soviet Union also increased the relative importance of the Far Eastern forces within the reconfigured Russian military structure, with a naval buildup in this region a distinct possibility.[7] Finally, the Russian military leadership is concerned about a power vacuum that unilateral force reduction or negotiated U.S.-Russian arms control may create in the region.[8]

On the other hand, the United States declared Russia no longer a security threat but rather a partner in post-Cold War global politics. Some Russian diplomats now realize the need to develop a nonmilitary presence in the region.[9] In fact, Russian military activity in the region, particularly that of naval and air units, has declined recently. Moreover, during his visit to Tokyo in October 1993, Russian President Boris Yeltsin reaffirmed Moscow's plan to withdraw all its forces from the disputed island territories, although the timetable for troop withdrawal remains uncertain.[10]

Under these circumstances, the most realistic approach to the region's security in the immediate post-Cold War period would be a three-pronged approach combining (1) the residual hegemonic power of the United States in maintaining bilateral security alliances, including security ties with Japan; (2) the development of a multilateral framework for security consultations; and (3) the promotion of economic interdependence and acceleration of economic integration in the region, including eventual integration of the Russian Far East and China into the Asia-Pacific economy. Under this approach, a continued U.S. military presence in the region, albeit at a reduced level, will be required to prevent a possible Chinese-Japanese-Russian rivalry to fill the region's power vacuum.[11] Eventually, Gorbachev's proposal for Russian-U.S.-Japanese political consultations on confidence-building measures may be acceptable to Tokyo.[12] Japan's regional security role will continue to be based on its economic power, but a more explicit and active pursuit of its comprehensive security policy may be acceptable to Russia and other regional powers.

The multilateral approach envisaged here would include confidence and security building measures (CSBMs), arms control, and regularized security consultations among the participants. Admittedly, building an entirely new multilateral security structure would be difficult in the absence of any relevant historical precedent. The alternative approach, that is, unilateral pursuit of national security, would likely produce a very unstable balance-of-power system in the region, with national armaments at levels substantially higher than today.[13] A complex network of escalating arms races would also be a likely consequence. One scenario: the Japanese build arms in response to continued Russian force deployment in the Far East; the Chinese see this as targeted against them; this triggers yet another arms race; all these developments further complicate Japanese-Korean security relations; a complex network of arms transfers becomes an attendant phenomenon. Of course, the economic consequences of this scenario would be quite distressing.

In the three-pronged regional security scenario, the United States and Japan would take the lead in strengthening APEC's role as a forum for economic policy coordination, as well as security issues. This raises the question of Japan's role in Russia's integration into the Asia-Pacific economy.

INTEGRATING THE RUSSIAN FAR EAST INTO ASIA: HOW TO ACHIEVE IT AND THE VALUE OF DOING IT

How should the growing economic interdependence and economic integration in the Asia-Pacific be extended to include Russia? Although economic reform and development in Russia depend ultimately on its own initiatives, ideas, and resources, international cooperation is very important. Given the Russian Far East's geographical proximity and potential economic complementarity with its neighboring countries, Tokyo and Moscow must encourage the region to cooperate with both public and private entities in these countries. Private investment and public assistance from Japan and other countries are crucial to the economic development of the Far East region and to the promotion of private enterprises. The region's trade with its neighboring countries should be expanded. Any trade surplus would be an important source of capital for investment in the development of socio-economic infrastructure in this region. Although industrial production in the Russian Far East declined by two percent from 1990 to 1991 and by 12 percent from 1991 to 1992, the region's foreign trade is experiencing healthy growth, with total exports increasing by 30 percent in 1992, to $1.2 billion. This is partly because of increasing foreign investments in fisheries, timber, and other resource development, including joint ventures with U.S., Japanese, and Chinese partners.[14] Value-added industries gradually must be developed, with foreign assistance and private investment, and must be added to the extractive industry-dependent foundations of the current Far Eastern economy.

Ultimately, the region will become a part of what Scalapino calls a Natural Economic Territory (NET), that will encompass the Sea of Japan.[15] The Japan Sea region enjoys a highly complementary economic potential, but historical animosities among the Northeast Asian nations and a lack of cooperative experiences present major obstacles to the development of regional integration. The development of the Tumen River delta region can serve as a catalyst for the creation of the Japan Sea economic region, and the Russian Far East should participate actively in this scheme along with Japan, China, and Korea. "Open regionalism" can guide future cooperation among the Japan Sea rim countries, allowing opportunities for participation for countries outside of the region.[16]

There are four necessary conditions for eventual integration of Russia into the Asia-Pacific economy. The most important of these is political stability in the nation. Political stability in Russia would represent the sustained legitimacy of Moscow's leadership, enhance the leadership's ability to mobilize domestic support for market reforms, and engender confidence among foreign political and economic partners.

Unfortunately, Russia's political future remains uncertain. President Yeltsin may not possess the kind of leadership that is necessary to lead the nation out of the present political and economic crises. Although the June 1993 national referenda indicated a surprisingly high level of support for Yeltsin's reform policy, the economic crisis resulting from the radical reform policy gave political ammunition to Yeltsin's opponents in the Russian Parliament. Yeltsin's trusted reformist prime minister Yegor Gaidar was forced to resign in December 1992 as part of the President's compromise with the anti-Yeltsin forces in the Parliament. Political struggle escalated throughout 1993 and resulted in an armed clash in October 1993 between the Yeltsin government and the anti-Yeltsin forces, an incident in which more than 150 people died. Although the Russian President's resort to force and his rule by decree temporarily stopped the slippery slide toward political chaos, it deepened the political cleavages in the country and damaged the long-term relationship between Moscow and the increasingly restless regions (including the Russian Far East), where support for autonomous economic development is increasing.

As Moltz points out in chapter 10, the uncertain future of Russia's political and economic reforms is a potential source of instability for Asia-Pacific. The Japanese diplomatic bluebook for 1992 states, for example, that the optimistic prospects for peace and stability in the wake of the Cold War have been replaced by trends of increasing anxiety and uncertainty in the face of the unstable situation in Russia, the problem of nuclear and conventional arms proliferation, the outbreak of regional conflicts, and the dark clouds hanging over the global economy. Defining the Russian situation as "one of the most important issues facing the world in transition," the diplomatic report warns that the situation involves "destabilizing factors of hyperinflation, declining production, political confusion, and ethnic conflicts" and that the instability of Russia has "serious implications for the world" because the country possesses a huge nuclear arsenal and other weapons of mass destruction.[17] Japan evidently wants, but does not soon expect, a stable Russia.

There are currently many disincentives for Japanese financial and technological investments in Russia. The absence of a reliable (that is, both stable and enforceable) legal regime for foreign investment in Russia is a critical problem. Also problematic are the inconsistent and ambiguous bureaucratic rules and practices in the country, which forces foreign enterprises to change their business partners or incur unnecessary business expenses. Finding reliable Russian partners who understand the legal and operational implications of fast-changing laws and regulations on investment, export and import, tax, and ownership itself is no easy task for foreign businesses. For Japanese businesses, their Russian partners' inability to meet payment and delivery obligations is another serious problem. Although the Japanese government has provided for trade insurance to protect Japanese exporters, Russian importers' debts continue to climb. The hyperinflation in the country and the nonconvertibility of the ruble make potential business opportunities in Russia just that, "potential." As a result, Russian Japanese two-way trade dropped from more than $5 billion in 1990 to less than $4 billion in 1992.

Although the painful transition toward a market economy must proceed unabated, disruptive consequences of market reforms would not be conducive to political stability. Herein lies Moscow's political economic dilemma—how to move the nation forward on market reform without risking political instability? So far the fragile Russian political system has not produced a national consensus on this question, and this limits the scope of Japanese and other Western help and the effectiveness of assistance that is extended to Russia.

Third, Russia's integration into the Asia-Pacific economy demands that Moscow give priority to the economic development of the nation's Far Eastern region. The region is richly endowed with natural resources, including timber, fresh water, fish and other marine products, coal, oil, natural gas, iron ore, diamonds, gold, silver, tin, antimony, boron, fluor-spar, mercury, and tungsten. Their development could link the region's economy to the more advanced Asia-Pacific economies. However, neither Moscow nor the region itself has adequate capital to sustain the development of these resources. The region also suffers from a severe energy shortage and needs foreign assistance in developing its oil and natural gas reserves.

Japan can provide assistance for overhauling the superannuated oil and gas equipment and facilities in the Russian Far East. However, Moscow first must clarify natural resource ownership, control, operation, and marketing rights for the region, eliminate administrative and legal ambiguities and contradictions, and establish legal protection for foreign investors. Tokyo also can cooperate in introducing energy-efficient technologies for the region's industrial sector. Over the long term, Japan and Russia must be able to cooperate with other Northeast Asian countries in developing an international energy network linking producers in the Russian Far East and China to Japanese, Korean, and other markets.

A related issue of importance to the future Far Eastern economy is the region's lack of autonomy from Moscow in economic planning. Despite the enormous resource potential just mentioned, the region historically was heavily dependent on Moscow's economic subsidies and military protection for its survival. Moscow also prevented development of regionalism in the Russian Far East for fear it might seek political independence.[18] The region has developed international economic ties only with those Asian neighbors that Moscow would allow. This center-periphery relationship survived the end of the Cold War and the dissolution of the Soviet Union. Backward and underdeveloped, the Russian Far East does not

204 • The Security-Economic Linkage: Northeast Asia

have indigenous factors of development to break its tie to Moscow and must await central reforms, including the elimination of legal and other institutional barriers to foreign trade and investment.

A fourth obstacle to a smooth transition to a market-oriented economy in the Russian Far East is presented by the region's heavy dependence on the defense sector. This sector is one of the most important industries in the region, representing approximately 10 percent of industrial output and industrial employment in the region. In Khabarovskii Krai and Primorskii Krai, the military-industrial complex is even more important, where these figures are about 20 percent.[19] Therefore, any economic development program in the region must incorporate the short-term and long-term needs of the region's military-industrial complex. The immediate task is to contain the destabilizing impact of the ongoing force reductions, budget cuts, and reductions in defense production. However, as long as the region continues to depend on the military-industrial complex for its economic development, including weapons export, it will limit civilian production potential and be scrutinized by its neighbors as a source of arms acquisition races and a destabilizing factor. Over the long term, the region must undertake conversion efforts.

The process of defense conversion must be accelerated with a focused resource allocation for this purpose. What would be ideal for Russia would be if Japan and other members of the international community provided financial assistance to ease Moscow's burden for housing, job training, and other aspects of adjustment for the affected personnel and their families. However, the prospects of the United States and Japan doing so are still limited. And the process of conversion in the Russian Far East is extremely slow and is by no means assured.[20]

The needs and obstacles in Russian economic development and the integration of its Far Eastern region into the Asia-Pacific economy have been identified above. The premise was that interdependence and integration will promote better political relations and improved chances of international peace and security. Several qualifications need to be made, however.

Economic integration and extensive social contacts are deemed a necessary step toward the creation of a "security community," defined as a group of people which has become "integrated." "Integration" means the "attainment, within a territory, of a 'sense of community' and of institutions and practices strong enough and widespread enough to assure dependable expectations of 'peaceful change' among its population."[21] It is additionally contended by neointegration theorists that crossnational economic linkages promote peace if they bring visible and tangible benefits to the people concerned.[22] It is also usually believed that economic interdependence promotes expansion of human and social contacts across national boundaries that would otherwise not develop.[23]

However, economic interdependence does not necessarily bring about stable social integration between nations.[24] Asymmetric interdependence may cause frictions and even present security concerns if it generates an acute sense of dependence, relative deprivation, or vulnerability on the part of the weaker of the economies concerned. This is particularly true if the benefits of economic interdependence and integration are unequally distributed between the increasingly interconnected countries.[25] This probability is high between economies that are at different levels of development and as geographically proximate as Japan and Russia. It would be more productive for Japan to cooperate with other diverse Asia-Pacific countries in bringing Russia into the regional economic community. Multilateral cooperation provides the advantage of creating multiple positive-sum situations, enhancing the complementary nature of the economies involved. For example, the resources of the Russian Far East could be developed with capital input from Japan, but low-tech products manufactured in the region could be marketed more readily in China, North Korea, and Mongolia than in Japan or South Korea. Labor input from China and North Korea would be competitive in the Russian Far East manufacturing industries.

Moreover, domestic economic growth may or may not be conducive to peace and stability if the benefits of economic growth are not equally shared within the society. Disadvantaged groups may feel deprived relative to the others in the country. Such a possibility is particularly problematic in a society, such as Russia, that lacks democratic traditions and institutions. In the Russian Far East, there are growing signs of income and wealth disparity among its residents. Secondly, economic development raises people's expectations that may generate frustrations and anxieties. Third, industrial growth is often associated with enlarged defense spending, increased arms production, and expanded weapons purchases, particularly in those countries in which the military and the defense industries are an important element in the political structure.[26]

THE IMPORTANCE OF JAPAN GETTING PAST THE ISLANDS ISSUE

During the perestroika period, Soviet analysts recognized Japan's leading role in the development of a dynamic Asia-Pacific economic community as well as the nation's potential as a catalyst for the Soviet Union's successful entry into that community.[27] Today most Russian diplomats responsible for Asia-Pacific affairs believe their country should build a closer relationship with this leader in the Pacific dynamism.[28] Japan, with its economic power and its leading role in the Asia-Pacific economic development, holds greater potential for the development of the Russian economy and its integration into the region than it ever did during the Cold War.

Tokyo's willingness to support Russia's reform efforts was limited by its territorial dispute with Moscow. Although the Russian foreign ministry believes the two nations must find a solution to the territorial dispute before their relations can be normalized, President Yeltsin's tenuous position at home has prevented him from making any major concessions to Japan.[29] The territorial issue is now a pawn in the power struggle in Russia, with nationalists, conservatives, and antireform elements criticizing any sign of compromise on the part of the Yeltsin government.[30]

Until 1989, Tokyo rigidly maintained the policy of *seikei fukabun* (indivisibility of politics and economics) conditioning Japan's economic assistance on Russian concessions on the Northern Territories issue. In May 1989, Tokyo announced a new policy toward Moscow based on the principle of *kakudai kinko* (expanded equilibrium) improving economic and other relations with Russia while simultaneously seeking progress on the territorial issue. The new policy helped the Kaifu-Gorbachev summit in April 1991 produce a mutual acknowledgment of the territorial dispute and 15 modest agreements on economic-scientific cooperation and cultural exchange. However, Yeltsin's weakening domestic position and Tokyo's insistence on Russian recognition of Japanese sovereignty over the entire disputed islands forced Yeltsin to cancel his planned visit to Tokyo in September 1992 and again in May 1993.[31] The relations between Tokyo and Moscow soured and the policy of expanded equilibrium produced no major breakthrough.

Tokyo was in no position to take new foreign policy initiatives toward Russia when international support for the beleaguered Yeltsin and his reformist policy mounted in the spring of 1993. As chair of the G7 summit in July 1993, however, Tokyo could not ignore the international call for a major aid package for Moscow. Tokyo eventually agreed to extend more than $1.8 billion in loans and credits as a part of the G7 aid package worth $43.4 billion. The decision represented a *de facto* divorce of economics from politics (*seikei bunri*). Moscow welcomed Tokyo's decision to participate in the G7 aid package at this time as an important departure from its previous position, and Yeltsin expressed renewed interest in visiting Tokyo.

But the Northern Territories issue remains an obstacle surmountable only through patient negotiation and mutual compromise. Unfortunately, the weak position of both the Moscow and Tokyo governments precludes bold initiatives on either side and promises protracted talks on this issue.[32] Although essentially a bilateral issue between Moscow and Tokyo, the territorial dispute has broader regional and global implications. Most importantly, it limits the potential of trilateral cooperation among Russia, the United States, and Japan in dealing with broader regional problems, including Asia-Pacific security.

Settlement of the territorial dispute would require Moscow's unequivocal acknowledgment that the dispute over the Habomais, Shikotan, Etorofu (Iturup), and Kunashiri (Kunashir) islands is a legacy of the past that must be removed. Russia also would have to reaffirm the commitment the Soviet government made in 1956 to transfer the Habomais and Shikotan to Japan in return for the conclusion of a peace treaty, although the actual territorial transfer may take quite some time yet. However, it would help if Tokyo did not insist on Moscow's recognition of Japanese sovereignty over all four islands as a precondition for Japanese economic assistance for Russia. Rather Tokyo could flexibly apply its policy of "expanded equilibrium" and seek improvement in bilateral relations in the economic, social, scientific, and other spheres, with a view to developing a more receptive Russian public opinion. Tokyo risks limiting its international role if it takes a rigid, uncompromising position on this issue.

The summit between President Yeltsin and Prime Minister Hosokawa in October 1993 did not produce a major breakthrough on the territorial issue, but it marked an important step in the right direction. The talks produced two declarations, the political "Tokyo Declaration" and the "Economic Declaration."

The Tokyo Declaration stated that the two countries were determined to cooperate in the construction of a new international order and in the full normalization of bilateral relations. Specifically, the statement addressed the two leaders' discussion of the issue of sovereignty of Etorofu, Kunashiri, Shikotan, and Habomai islands, stating that the territorial dispute should be resolved on the basis of historical and legal facts in accordance with the principle of law and justice, and confirming that all treaties and international pledges between Japan and the Soviet Union applied to the bilateral relationship between Japan and Russia. To the surprise of many skeptical Japanese, Yeltsin even acknowledged in a press interview that the 1956 joint declaration was still valid. The political declaration also acknowledged the importance of bilateral dialogue over security and other broader issues of Asia-Pacific and expressed willingness to accelerate talks on these issues.[33]

The "Economic Declaration" stated that Japan would promote bilateral economic relations within the framework of "expanded equilibrium" and that successful Russian reform and integration into the world economy was an important matter. Although Yeltsin's priority was to obtain Japanese economic cooperation, Tokyo committed no new money. The declaration simply said that Japan would share its postwar experience in economic development, that the two countries would cooperate in energy, steel, transportation, and other areas, and that Japan would cooperate with Russia in the latter's bid to join international organizations.[34]

CONCLUSION

Neither the world's Cold War experience nor its brief post-Cold War record offers much help in the ongoing search for a new world order. It is an equally formidable task to establish a sustainable balance among the myriad of political, security, and economic interests and capabilities that exist in the post-Cold War Asia-Pacific region. Unfortunately, Japanese-Russian relations continue to be more of a hindrance than a facilitator in the development of a stable and just system of international relations in this region and in the world.

But if Japan, the second largest economy in the world, and Russia, with its enormous military capabilities, forge a new relationship of trust and confidence, they can participate constructively in the establishment of a stable system of international relations in the post-Cold War Asia-Pacific. Removal of the territorial dispute would certainly help Tokyo and Moscow move toward a more amicable relationship.

But the settlement of the territorial dispute may not be sufficient. What is required is the building of a comprehensive and robust relationship that can withstand short-term shifts in issues and concerns, much as Japan-U.S. relations have survived trade frictions. The region's legacies of the Second World War and of the Cold War extend beyond the territorial dispute. As long as structural power disparities continue between these important actors, their impact on the region's security is still destabilizing.

As Moltz points out in chapter 10, there are many hazards along Russia's path toward a modern, democratic society with a prosperous economy—hazards that could nullify any amount of international good will. The nation is experiencing a deepening internal conflict over its political and economic future, with the destructive forces of xenophobic nationalism and ethnocentrism threatening to tear down the already fragile social foundations of the multi-ethnic nation that is Russia. Further disintegration can be arrested only if its political leaders can agree on a new system of political legitimacy and a new model of economic development to replace the bankrupt Soviet system of coercive authoritarianism and bureaucratic centralization. Until internal reconciliation takes place, the effectiveness of Russia's foreign policy is severely limited.

Peace and stability in the Asia-Pacific requires Russia's successful transformation into a stable democracy with a market-oriented economy integrated with the Asia-Pacific economy. Russia's integration into the broader regional economy will require sustained economic development in the resource-rich but capital-poor Eastern Siberia, particularly the Russian Far East, and this in turn will require both the degree of regional autonomy and the level of international economic contacts that Moscow historically was unwilling to allow.

Particularly problematic is the uncertain and increasingly strained relationship between Russia's center and periphery. Until Moscow and the Russian Far East reach a mutually acceptable division of power, this region will not be able to develop sufficient indigenous foundations for economic development. The Russian Federation should recognize that self-sustained economic development of the region is in Russia's interest. A modern economic system in the region provides an essential link to the dynamic Asia-Pacific region.

Equally important will be the settlement of conflicts at the center. Unless and until Moscow solves the political impasse soon and does so in a democratic way, the government's legitimacy will be suspect in the eyes of increasingly restless political forces throughout the country. Moreover, political turmoil at the center further fuels growing independence movements such as Chechnya, with dire consequences for Russia's political and economic unity and for its role in the post-Cold War world.

Internationally, only by establishing itself as a reliable and trustworthy partner in regional cooperation will Russia be welcome to join those international economic institutions that could provide the region with badly needed access to financial resources, markets, and technical information. For example, it should cease all dumping of nuclear and other hazardous materials into the marine environment. Settlement of the territorial dispute with Tokyo would also go a long way toward establishing its credibility. Meanwhile, Tokyo must view its Russian relations in the broader regional, global, and historical context. If the two countries recognize this historic opportunity provided by the end of the Cold War for the construction of an entirely new regional and global order, then they can begin a long journey toward a potentially balanced and expanded relationship of trust and interdependence.

NOTES

1. The only exception would be the Tumen River Basin project which is beginning to see multilateral cooperation among China, Russia, North and South Korea, Mongolia, and the United Nations Development Program (UNDP). So far Japan has been taking a cautious "wait and see" approach. The absence of diplomatic ties between Tokyo and Pyongyang severely constrains Japan's potential role in this project.
2. The term "distant neighbors" is from Tsuyoshi Hasegawa, Jonathan Haslam, and Andrew Kuchins, eds., *Russia and Japan: An Unresolved Dilemma between Distant Neighbors* (Berkeley: University of California International and Area Studies, 1993).
3. Itaru Umezu, "Security in the Asia-Pacific Region and the Role of Japan," in *The United Nations Institute for Disarmament Research (UNIDIR), Conference of Research Institutes*

in Asia and the Pacific, Beijing, 23–25 March 1992 (New York: United Nations, 1992), p. 41; and Vladimir Fedotov, "Russia and the APR: Problems and Prospects," *International Affairs* (October 1992), p. 50.

4. For a Japanese view of the post-Cold War security environment in Asia-Pacific, see for example, Masashi Nishihara, "Northeast Asia and Japanese Security," in Danny Unger and Paul Blackburn, eds., *Japan's Emerging Global Role, Boulder* (Colorado: Lynne Rienner, 1993), pp. 85-98.

5. Alexei Zagorsky, "Russian Military Reform: Consequences for Asia-Pacific," unpublished paper, April 1993, p. 20.

6. Japan Defense Agency, *Defense of Japan, 1992* (Tokyo: Japan Times, 1992), p. 14. The Russian Far East accounted for a mere 4.9 percent of the industrial production of the Russian Federation in 1991. *Roshia Kyokuto Deta Bukku* [Russian Far East Data Book] (Tokyo: Roshia To'o Boekikai Roshia To'o Keizai Kenkyujo, 1993), p. 4.

7. Zagorsky, op. cit., p. 17-19, and 22-23, notes that 12 percent of the Russian military personnel are now stationed in Siberia and the Far East and that the Northern and Pacific Fleets will likely remain a core of the Russian navy, while the role of the Baltic and Black Sea Fleets will decline. Mochizuki notes 10,000 tanks have been transferred from Eastern Europe to east of the Ural Mountains. Mike M. Mochizuki, "The Soviet/Russian Factor in Japanese Security Policy," in Hasegawa et al., *Russia and Japan*, p. 132. See also Cai Mengsun, "Threat Perceptions and Security Requirements in the Asian and Pacific Region," in UNIDIR, *Conference of Research Institutes*, pp. 2-3.

8. See for example, V. Stefashin, "Varianty razvitiya voyenno-politicheskoy situatsii na Dal'nem Vostoke," *Problemy Dal'nego Vostoka* (Moscow) (1992): 88-89; cited in Zagorsky, op. cit., p. 25.

9. Fedotov, op. cit., p. 51.

10. In May 1992 Yeltsin mentioned 1993-94 for the removal of over 7,000 troops from the Northern Territories, but in August 1992 the Russian leader promised removal by mid-1995. Kyodo, 2 September 1992; reported in *FBIS-EAS* 92-175 (9 September 1992), p. 8.

11. For an expression of concern about an emerging strategic vacuum, see Dao Huy Ngoc, "First Response," in UNIDIR, *Conference of Research Institutes*, p. 53. For an argument that there is no power vacuum, see Nishihara, "Northeast Asia and Japanese Security," p. 86.

12. Gorbachev made this proposal in his speech to the Japanese Diet in April 1991. For a review of the Japanese debate on post-Cold War regional security and Japan's role, see Mochizuki, "The Soviet/Russian Factor," pp. 141-151.

13. Zagorsky notes the newly proposed Russian military doctrine prefers a unilateral option, continuing to view the United States as an adversary. Zagorsky, "Russian Military Reform," pp. 23-24.

14. Minakir, "Roshia Kyokuto Keizai no Genjo," pp. 1 and 4.

15. Robert A. Scalapino, "Diverse Perspectives on Assistance to Russia," paper prepared for presentation at the Monterey Institute of International Studies Center for East Asian Studies conference on "U.S.-Japan Cooperation in the Development of Siberia and the Russian Far East," 22-24 July 1993, Monterey, California.

16. Hisao Kanamori, "The Future Potential of the Japan Sea Economic Region for the U.S.,"

paper prepared for presentation at the Monterey Institute of International Studies Center for East Asian Studies conference on "U.S.-Japan Cooperation in the Development of Siberia and the Russian Far East," 22-24 July 1993, Monterey, California.

17. *Hokkaido Shimbun.* 2 April 1993, evening, p. 1.

18. Tsuyoshi Hasegawa, "Resiliency of Soviet Legacies: Political Environment and Far Eastern Economic Development," and James Clay Moltz, "Core and Periphery in the Post-Soviet Economy: The Changing Role of the Russian Far East," both papers prepared for the Monterey Institute of International Studies Center for East Asian Studies conference on "U.S.-Japan Cooperation in the Development of Siberia and the Russian Far East," 22-24 July 1993, Monterey, California.

19. *Dalnii Vostok Rossii Ekonomicheskii Ezhegodnik 1992* (Khabarovsk: Economic Research Institute, 1992), Tables I and II, reproduced in *Russian Far East Update* 3 (April 1933), p. 8.

20. See *Roshia Kyokuto Gunmin Tenkan Misshon Hokokusho* [Report of the military-civilian conversion mission to the Russian Far East], Tokyo: Roshia To'o Boekikai Roshia To'o Keizai Kenkyukai, 1993.

21. For the concept of "security community," see Karl W. Deutsch et al., *Political Community and the North Atlantic Area* (Princeton, N.J.: Princeton University Press, 1957), p. 5.

22. For a succinct summary of this hypothesis, see Bruce Russett and Harvey Starr, *World Politics: The Menu for Choice,* Third Edition (San Francisco: Freeman, 1989), pp. 429-433.

23. Ibid., pp. 421-429. Needless to say, Japan's postwar economic development along the capitalist path had very little to offer to the socialist economic development of the Soviet Union.

24. See for example, Jack Levy, "The Causes of War," in Philip Tetlock (eds.), *Behavior, Society, and Nuclear War* (Oxford: Oxford University Press, 1989); and Barry Buzan, "Economic Structure and International Security: The Limits of the Liberal Case," *International Organization* 38 (Autumn 1984), pp. 597-624.

25. Russett and Starr, pp. 432-433.

26. Harris, "The Economic Aspects of Pacific Security," pp. 24-25.

27. Gilbert Rozman, "Moscow's Japan-Watchers in the First Years of the Gorbachev Era," *Pacific Review* 3 (1988), pp. 257-275; and B. Klyuchnikov, "The Soviet Far East in the Pacific Century," *Far Eastern Affairs* 4 (1988), p. 8.

28. Author interviews with George E. Komarovskii, senior counsellor; Vassili I. Saplin, first deputy head, Asia-Pacific Department; and Andre M. Yefimov, chief of the Japanese Division, Russian Ministry of Foreign Affairs, 25 May 1992, Moscow. See also, Vladimir Fedotov, "Russia and the APR."

29. Author interviews with Komarovskii, Saplin, and Yefimov, 25 May 1992, Moscow.

30. Author interview with Vassili Istratov, deputy director, Bureau of Congressional Issues, Russian Ministry of Foreign Affairs, 1 June 1992, Moscow. According to Istratov, "justice and law," a phrase Tokyo euphemistically uses to refer to Russia's territorial concessions, does not mean anything to most Russians.

31. One Russian expert on Japanese affairs noted in June 1992 that a compromise might be possible between Foreign Minister Watanabe's proposal for a sequential resolution of the dispute (the 2+2 formula) and Yeltsin's proposal for a 5-stage settlement. Author interview with Konstantin Sarkisov, Institute of Oriental Studies, 3 June 1992, Moscow. Another Japan specialist was even more optimistic and stated that Yeltsin would be ready to concede the other two islands as well. He maintained the 1956 declaration was still valid. Author interview with Valery K. Zaitsev, Head, Center for Japanese and Pacific Studies, Institute of World Economy and International Relations, Russian Academy of Sciences, 1 June 1992, Moscow. His younger colleague agreed that eventually all the disputed territories should be transferred to Japan, but he remained quite pessimistic about Yeltsin's ability to achieve a major breakthrough on this issue. Author interview with Alexei V. Zagorsky, senior researcher, Center for Japanese and Pacific Studies, Institute of World Economy and International Relations, Russian Academy of Sciences, 1 June 1992, Moscow.

32. Robert A. Scalapino, "Diverse Perspectives," op. cit.

33. *Mainichi Shimbun*, 13 October 1993, evening, p. 1.

34. Ibid.

12 Japan's Concept of Comprehensive Security in the Post-Cold War World

Eiichi Katahara

INTRODUCTION

What are Japan's aims in the post-Cold War era? What part can Japan play in the large changes that are taking place in the world? For the last 40 years, Japan was a passive player in international political and security affairs, concentrating almost exclusively on economic growth and domestic affairs. With the rise of Japanese economic power, there emerged a consensus in the international community that Japan, as an economic and technological superpower, should play a more active role not just in the economic field but also in international political affairs. The Persian Gulf War sensitized Japanese leaders to the inevitable need to reassess Japan's postwar security policies and enable Japan to make a contribution to the maintenance of international order. Japan's decision to participate in UN peacekeeping operations (combat operations excluded) suggests that Japan is in search of a new international mission.

The debate on Japan's foreign and security issues has entered a new phase centering on Japan's role in the maintenance of international peace and order. Regarding Japan's contributions in the area of international peace and security and the question of Japan's role in the post-Cold War world, there are divergent perspectives, suggestions, and apprehensions.

At one end of the spectrum of the debate, Japanese liberals argue that Japan should define itself as "a global civilian power" and that there is much Japan can do for the welfare of the international community without resorting to military means. Yoichi Funabashi, a diplomatic correspondent for the Tokyo daily *Asahi Shimbun*, says, "Emergence of a more internationalist and actively engaged Japanese pacifism could play a constructive role in making Japan as a global civilian power."[1] Robert Barnett, the author of *Beyond War: Japan's Concept of Comprehensive National Security*, argues that Japan's comprehensive national security, with its important ingredients—Article 9 of the Constitution, the three nonnuclear principles, economic security, and restraints on military spending—can be a model for all countries.[2]

But Japanese neoconservatives want to make Japan a normal global power by scrapping or substantially reinterpreting its constitutional constraints to embark upon a leading role in international affairs, including military operations beyond Japan's borders.

The continuing debate on the Japanese Question should be welcomed and pursued in a cool-headed manner.[3] I argue that Japan should play a greater international role as a "global civilian power" for three related conclusions. First, Japan's concept of comprehensive security, with Article 9 of the Constitution and the United States-Japan alliance as its basic ingredients, remains effective in the post-Cold War world. Second, some aspects of Japan's comprehensive security policy require improvements and adjustments to better cope with a wide range of post-Cold War security issues. Third, a shift in policy approach is required—from largely bilateral to more multilateral dealings through forums such as APEC and the UN.

JAPAN'S CONCEPT OF COMPREHENSIVE SECURITY

Japan's concept of comprehensive security can be understood as an evolutionary policy concept with its philosophical roots in Article 9 of the Japanese Constitution. Unlike most countries' security policies, with military capability at the center of strategic plans and calculations, Japan denies itself the use of force in settling international disputes (Article 9 of the Constitution) and its defense posture is supposed to be "exclusively defensive." It behooves Japan to make maximum use of nonmilitary instruments such as diplomacy and foreign aid in promoting Japan's security interests, regional and global.

However, alongside this legalistic defensive posture, there is, embedded in the minds of Japanese policymakers, a deep sense of vulnerability in terms of energy and food supply as well as in the area of military defense.[4] Japan's lack of energy and food resources makes it imperative to maintain secure access to overseas energy and food resources as well as markets. Its small land mass and densely concentrated population of 120 million makes Japan vulnerable to large-scale, preemptive air attacks.

In this context, the concept of comprehensive security calls for an all-embracing, multidimensional and distinctively cooperative approach for ensuring both military and economic security. Within the basic framework provided by the Constitution and the United States-Japan alliance, the concept was refined, broadened and strengthened in response to changes in the international situation of the late 1970s and 1980s.

During the Cold War, Japan's security policy evolved in the context of tensions between Japan's "no-war" convictions and its entanglements with the Cold War military rivalry. The initial orientation of Japan's foreign policy and security was characterized by a narrow-minded, mercantilistic perspective (the Yoshida Doctrine). This directed Japan's security policy in three particular areas:

(1) Japan's economic reconstruction and political-economic cooperation with the United States;
(2) development of a modest defense force; and
(3) a stationing of U.S. forces on Japanese soil for Japan's own security.[5]

According to Kenneth Pyle, the doctrine was "the product of a carefully constructed and brilliantly implemented foreign policy. Japan's purpose in the postwar world was the result of an opportunistic adaptation to the conditions in which the Japanese leadership found their nation and a shrewd pursuit of a sharply defined national interest within the constraints that the postwar international order placed upon them."[6]

The doctrine's strong mercantilist content was clear, since it regarded the United States as the linchpin of Japan's foreign policy, while allowing Japan to pursue its economic interests singlemindedly in an international trading system guaranteed by the United States. Japan "was spared the psychological and material costs of participating in international politics," although it was a major beneficiary of the postwar international order.[7]

As Japan's economic power grew throughout the postwar years, and especially with Japan's recognition of the end of "Pax Americana" in the 1970s, a new kind of internationalism emerged in the minds of Japanese leaders, most notably Prime Minister Masayoshi Ohira, Foreign Minister Saburo Okita and Prime Minister Yasuhiro Nakasone.[8]

The "Report on Comprehensive National Security," initiated by Prime Minister Ohira, was Japan's response to a perceived economic leveling between the United States and Japan. The unprecedented policy document marked a departure from the self-serving perspective of the Yoshida Doctrine to a more internationalist and comprehensive approach to international problems. The 1980 Report observed:

> In considering the question of Japan's security, the most fundamental change in the international situation that took place in the 1970s is the termination of clear American supremacy in both military and economic spheres. Militarily...it has become necessary for the allies and friends to strengthen their self-reliant efforts, especially in the area of conventional forces, and the credibility of the U.S. nuclear umbrella cannot be maintained in the absence of cooperation with the United States....Economically, U.S. economic strength has declined both in absolute terms and in relative terms against the economic development achieved by Europe and Japan. As a result, it has become impossible to primarily rely

upon the United States as in the past for the maintenance of the international currency system and free-trade system.[9]

The Report argued that comprehensive national security policy was to be pursued at three different levels in two separate fields as shown in Table 12.1 below.

Table 12.1: The Elements of a Comprehensive Security Policy

Military Security

1. Multilateral	Efforts for peaceful international order; international cooperation; arms control and confidence-building measures.
2. Intermediary	Alliances with countries sharing common political ideals and interests
3. Self-reliant efforts	Consolidation of denial capability, that is, efforts to counter potential threats; protection of the state's independence.

Economic Security

1. Multilateral	Maintenance of the free-trade system; resolution of the North-South problem.
2. Intermediary	Strong relations with countries important to Japan's economy.
3. Self-reliant efforts	Stockpiling; reasonable level of self-sufficiency; maintenance of economic power through productivity and export; competitiveness.

Sources: Alan Rix, "Japan's Comprehensive Security and Australia," Australian Outlook 41: 2 (August 1987), p. 79 and Sogo anzen hosho senryaku [Comprehensive National Security] (Tokyo: Okurasho insatsukyoku, 1980), pp. 23–24.

In December 1984, the Peace Problem Research Council, set up by Prime Minister Yasuhiro Nakasone, put forward its policy report, "Comprehensive security policy for the international state Japan."[10] The report confirmed the basic elements of comprehensive security—Japan's greater political and economic role in the international arena, further strengthening of the United States-Japan alliance, maintenance of the open trading system, energy and food security, and most significantly, an accelerated defense build-up. The report reflected Nakasone's strong bid to eradicate the one percent of GNP ceiling on defense spending, which was abolished by Nakasone in January 1987.[11]

But this concept of comprehensive security provoked a number of criticisms. First, it was seen by some foreign policy experts as either a vague concept or an excuse for Tokyo's inactivity and passivity in the military sphere.[12] For example, the 1980 report on comprehensive security failed to mention the roles and missions for Japan's Self-Defense Forces in the context of U.S.-Japan defense cooperation. Masataka Kosaka, a prominent member of the Comprehensive National Security Group and the Chairman of the Peace Problems Council, observed that the concept could be judged as "underdeveloped." "Though excellent in theory, it has actually been an excuse, even a lie, to avoid greater defense efforts."[13] Second, the concept of comprehensive security as described in the official reports confirmed Japan's mercantilist orientation embedded in its international behavior. Alan Rix wrote:

> Japan's finely-tuned economic strength requires effective assurances of stable and reliable raw material supplies. It is to this end that comprehensive security is specifically aimed; it is the persuasiveness of the objective across multiple economic policy areas and across so much of Japan's foreign economic relationships, that stamps it as a neo-mercantilist instrument. The direct identification of the state's economic needs with the imperative of maintaining state power in the face of a potentially hostile international environment, and the extension of that perception into trade, investment, foreign aid and resources relationships in a non-passive role, also gives it a strong mercantilist flavor.[14]

Nevertheless, seen from the vantage point of the early 1990s, Japan's comprehensive security policy provided valuable guidelines for Japan's strategic planning and engagement in the international community. Comprehensive security helped Tokyo place all policies with significant international ramifications—defense, energy and food resources, and foreign aid—into a security context.[15] Measures for comprehensive security therefore include "not only the improvement of military capability but also research efforts for the advancement of science and technology, stockpiling of food and energy supplies, and assistance to developing countries. These measures are seen as contributing to the overall security of the nation."[16]

In the second place, the concept helped establish a consensus that Japan play a greater role in the international arena. Japan's foreign aid policy is a notable case in point. As William Brooks and Robert Orr note, "Japan's use of aid for comprehensive security reasons reflects in part its growing willingness to accept a wider political role in world affairs as well as an awareness of the potential of its economic strength and diplomatic influence."[17]

A final point is that comprehensive security was Tokyo's strategic response to the shifting balance of power in the Asia-Pacific region. With Japan emerging as an economic and technological superpower and U.S. power declining in relative terms, the comprehensive nature of Japan's security policy played a role in making the strengthening of the Japanese military force more palatable, both to other regional countries and to the United States

The crucial question then is whether or not Japan's comprehensive security policy can be viable and effective in the post-Cold War world.

JAPAN'S SECURITY CONCERNS IN THE POST COLD-WAR WORLD

From the perspective of Japanese policymakers, threats to Japan's security are manifold: they include potential security fears arising from Russia, China and the Korean Peninsula, the troubled relationship with the United States, the danger of losing access to overseas energy and food sources, and natural disasters such as the 1995 Kobe earthquake.

During the Cold War, Japanese policymakers viewed the Soviet military as the primary threat. The end of the Cold War and the ensuing political, military, economic and environmental developments at the regional and global levels are forcing Japan to revise its perceptions of the strategic environment.

First, Japanese policymakers are worried about the uncertainty of Russia's future, the chronically strained relationship with Moscow and Russia's offensive military capability deployed in the Far East. While Tokyo acknowledges the need to encourage reform in Russia by providing economic assistance, the Japanese attitude has been less than forthcoming, mainly because the Northern Territories conflict, a relic of the Cold War era, remains unresolved.

Second, the maintenance of peace and stability on the Korean Peninsula is essential to Japan's security. In particular, Tokyo is apprehensive of the possibility of North Korea developing nuclear weapons and long-range missiles.[18] This is evident from Japan's strong support of the United States-DPRK accords in 1994 that at least postponed the crisis.

Third, Japanese policymakers are watchful of the progress of China's reform and open door policies. They believe that the stability of China is essential to regional security as well as the security of Japan. China's nuclear capability, its substantial increase in defense expenditure, and its intention to develop a blue-water navy cause Tokyo considerable concern.[19] In Tokyo's view, China's constructive cooperation and participation in regional economic and political dialogues will be critically important, if the emerging new security order in the region is to be safe and stable.

Fourth, Japan has a persistent interest in promoting peace and stability in Southeast Asia through bilateral links and multilateral forums such as the United Nations and the ASEAN Post-Ministerial Conference. Japan's participation in UN peacekeeping operations in Cambodia proved to be a significant test case for its contribution to regional peace and order. Although Tokyo opposed the notion of creating an overarching security structure in the Asia-Pacific region (a new framework similar to the Organization for Security and Cooperation in Europe) efforts to construct multilateral mechanisms for regional security, such as ASEAN's Asian Regional Forum (ARF) loom large on Japan's security agenda.[20]

Fifth, Japanese policymakers are concerned about the future of the United States' commitment to Asian security and to the security of Japan in particular. They believe that the presence of U.S. forces in the region and the Japan-U.S. security arrangements are vital for peace and prosperity in the Asia-Pacific. Tokyo also stresses that most countries in the region, including Russia and China, recognize the critical value of the United States-Japan alliance as a stabilizing element in the post-Cold War security order.[21] The prospects for a further reduction in the U.S. military presence in the region are worrisome, despite Washington's continued assurance (for example, 1995 East Asia Strategy Report postponing U.S. troop withdrawal) that the United States will maintain its time-honored strategy of forward deployment.[22]

On balance, the most important factor contributing to a stable post-Cold War security order in the Asia-Pacific region is the United States' nuclear and maritime guarantee for Japan and Japan's commitment to the U.S. alliance. In the words of a Japanese diplomat:

> America's protective umbrella of nuclear deterrence is vital for Japanese security, particularly as long as Russia and China have nuclear weapons and North Korea has ambitions to develop them. So, too, is the U.S. naval presence in the Asia-Pacific region and the Indian Ocean. The security relationship between Tokyo and Washington is an important stabilizing element for the Asia-Pacific region.[23]

Perhaps an even more important concern to Japan is the troubled state of economic and trade relations with the United States caused by its huge, chronic trade surplus. During the Cold War, the United States subordinated economic concerns to geopolitical priorities. But the end of the Cold War and the trade imbalance between Japan and the U.S could adversely affect their security alliance and present the greatest destabilizing threat to the emerging new security order in the Asia-Pacific region.[24]

THE RELEVANCE OF JAPAN'S CONCEPT OF COMPREHENSIVE SECURITY TO THE POST-COLD WAR WORLD

The central policy issues for Japan's post-Cold War policy agenda: Article 9 of the Constitution, economic security, foreign aid, the United States-Japan alliance, multilateral efforts for collective security, and commitments to global issues, frame how relevant comprehensive security is in coping with the security issues affecting Japan's future.

Adherence to Article Nine of the Constitution

Article 9 of the Constitution proved to be a source of uniquely innovative security policies in postwar Japan. Its "exclusively defensive defense" posture—the ban on sending military units for combat abroad, the three non-nuclear principles, the ban on the export of arms, political constraints on defense spending, the denial of collective defense, the ban on conscription, and commitment to the peaceful use of space—all come from the interpretation of Article 9 of the Constitution offered by successive Japanese governments.[25] The concept of comprehensive security embraces all these policies as its essential ingredients.

Until very recently, the Constitution was ardently supported by a majority of the Japanese public. However, a sea change is swelling: an opinion poll conducted by the *Yomiuri Shimbun* shows that 50.4 percent of respondents favor revising the Constitution and 55.7 percent of those who supported constitutional revisions think that under the current Constitution, "Japan cannot deal adequately with the new international situation."[26]

This supports arguments advocating revision of the Constitution, in vogue in recent years.[27] During the Persian Gulf War, many Japanese were embarrassed by Japan's sitting on the sidelines with no physical role in settling the crisis, and it was widely felt that Japan's financial contribution of $13 billion fell short of international expectations. In the confusion and exasperation of the moment, Ichiro Ozawa, an influential neoconservative politician, sought to twist the established interpretation of the Constitution by saying that the idea of dispatching the Self-Defense Forces to the Persian Gulf would not violate the Constitution. In Ozawa's words,

> ...if we "desire to occupy an honored place in an international society," as written in the preamble to the Constitution, we need to decide that active cooperation is required. And one form of cooperation we have not yet employed is the dispatch of SDF troops.[28]

Advocates of constitutional amendment go further than this, believing that the present Constitution has some profound defects. They claim that Article 9 of the Constitution has been a major obstacle to Japan's full-fledged participation in UN peacekeeping operations, aggravating U.S.-Japan relations on one hand, and limiting Japan's greater role in international security affairs on the other; that the Constitution was forcibly imposed by the United States; that there is no clear stipulation of the right of self-defense in the document; and that it is mere hypocrisy to maintain the Self-Defense Forces while claiming nonpossession of war potential.

There are, however, some good reasons to preserve Article 9 of the Constitution. First and foremost, Article 9 defines a democratic and non-militarist orientation of the Japanese state. That is to say, the Constitution embodies Japan's postwar ideals—peace and democracy—which became the foundations of Japan's foreign and security policies during the postwar years.

Second, although the tide of public opinion may be turning, there is still no solid public consensus on the issue.[29]

Third, it is important to recognize the profound implications of Japan's Constitution for peace and prosperity in the Asia-Pacific region. Robert Barnett put it succinctly:

> I regard Japan's Article 9 (of the Constitution) and restraints on military spending as being one of the principal keys for the economic dynamism of the Pacific Region: other countries do not spend money on defense measures to answer a Japanese military threat. Nobody in the region believes that Japan is a threat. That is a huge contribution to arms control in the neighborhood.[30]

A final point is that Article 9 of the Constitution has the potential to inspire other countries in a world where the price of settling international disputes by force is no longer worth paying either for the vanquished or the victors. Edward Lincoln argues that:

> Japan today is a prototype of the desirable nation state of the future. Military force has no legitimate role except in a purely defensive posture...Japan should be in the mainstream of devising nonmilitary responses to international crises.[31]

If this line of argument is correct, Article 9 is not a declaration of irresponsibility in the international community, rather the opposite. The challenge for Japan in this regard is to act on its ideals in the international arena through the optimum use of non-military instruments for the maintenance of peace and stability.

Economic Security

The notion of economic security, a major defining element of Japan's concept of comprehensive security, is valid and necessary in coping with a host of new problems of the post-Cold War world. Japan's physical vulnerability and its vital necessity of keeping access to foreign food and energy resources remain a major preoccupation for Japanese policymakers. Thus Japan must make great efforts to support the open, multilateral economic and trading system.

The danger, however, lies in the possibility of Japan's policies for economic security taking on a mercantilist, protectionist or techno-nationalist character. As noted earlier, a deterioration in U.S.-Japan economic relations contains the seeds of breakdown of the multilateral economic order within APEC or the newly-created successor to GATT, the World Trade Organization (WTO), since the two countries are involved in such a vast amount of the world's trade.

Several trade disputes in 1994 and 1995 provide evidence of this deteriorating economic relationship. Most lasting was the U.S. threat in June 1995 to impose 100 percent tariffs on several luxury-size Japanese cars unless the two sides could agree on terms to help U.S. firms gain access to the lucrative Japanese automobile and auto parts markets. While the two governments reached a last-minute deal to avoid the tariffs (typical of the two countries posturing and threats regarding trade disputes), these highly publicized trade disputes are likely to continue. This agreement was immediately followed by another U.S. charge of unfair trade practices embodied in a Super 301 complaint from Kodak charging Fuji with unfairly restricting access to the Japanese film market. The U.S., in trying to achieve its trade agreements through unilateral and bilateral efforts such as tariffs and Super 301 disputes, threatens the efficacy of theWTO, and its appropriate role in the world trading system.

Foreign Aid

Foreign aid is a major foreign policy tool for enhancing economic security, thus constituting an essential component of Japan's concept of comprehensive security. Japan's current aid policy is predicated on the assumption that "national economic development in poorer and middle-income countries and international political stability are cornerstones of international trade, access to resources, and ultimately Japan's own well-being."[32] Many observers believe that official development assistance (ODA) is the "ideal" form of Japan's contribution to the international community. Koppel and Orr observed that "What [Japan's] ODA has done, first and foremost in Asia, and in recent years in the Pacific, the Middle East, Africa, and Latin America, is that it has further bound Japan to a non-military role in the international system."[33]

In terms of the quantity of ODA, Japan is unquestionably a global aid power. In 1989 and 1991, Japan was the world's largest donor of foreign aid with an $8.97 billion disbursement in 1989 and $11 billion in 1991.[34] Furthermore, the government has set its next five-year ODA target for 1993-97 at $70 billion, which would represent a more than 40 percent increase compared to the previous five-year period.[35]

Nonetheless, if we use measures other than just total sums of expenditure, Japan's ODA records are less than impressive: in 1991 Japan's ODA/GNP ratio was only 0.32 percent, ranking twelfth out of 20 Development Assistance Center (DAC) countries; in terms of ODA spent per capita Japan ranked eleventh; and its share of grants ranked last in the DAC list.[36] Along with these low rankings, there are deeper problems of Japan's aid policymaking and implementation: its lack of "a unified structure of political responsibility for aid policy";[37] understaffed administration and limited expertise with recipient needs; bureaucratic immobilism precipitated by the principle of "recipient request-basis" for aid; and heavy reliance on "yen loans."[38]

There have been some improvements in Japan's ODA policy. The argument that Japan uses its ODA primarily as an instrument for the self-serving economic interests of Japan may be less tenable today, since more than 90 percent of Japanese ODA is "untied."[39] And in June 1992, the Miyazawa cabinet adopted the so-called "ODA Charter."[40] This document, based on the guidelines of ODA announced by Prime Minister Toshiki Kaifu in April 1991, proposes to link economic aid with a wide range of considerations: political, security, economic, humanitarian and environmental conditions in the recipient country.[41] Although the Charter has no legal force, the new guidelines have already been applied to a number of countries in a somewhat flexible fashion. For example, Tokyo suspended aid to Burma in the wake of human rights violations in that country. Tokyo also suspended aid following the coup in Haiti. Tokyo expressed concerns through diplomatic channels but did not suspend aid in Peru, Indonesia, and Thailand, where political developments conflict with Japan's new aid guidelines. Tokyo extended aid, thereby supporting democratization and economic reform, in Mongolia, Zambia, and Nicaragua.[42]

How rigorously and effectively Tokyo will implement its new ODA guidelines in such recipients as China and Russia remains an open question. But Tokyo's ODA Charter represents a considerable broadening of the concept of comprehensive security and signals Japan's renewed willingness to bear its fair share of "global responsibilities."

Strengthening the U.S.–Japan Alliance

The U.S.-Japan alliance is an essential element of Japan's concept of comprehensive security. For Japan to be able to manage a host of security problems, global and regional, it is vitally necessary to maintain the United States-Japan alliance, which has been a key stabilizing factor in the Asia-Pacific region.[43] According to James Baker, "The keystone of our engagement in East Asia and the Pacific is our relationship with Japan. Nothing is more basic to the prosperity and security of the region and indeed to the effectiveness of the post-Cold War system, than a harmonious and productive U.S.-Japan relationship." This longstanding perspective of the United States remains intact, as President Clinton affirmed in April 1993:

> There is no more important relationship for the United States than our relationship with Japan. We are the world's largest economies with 40 percent of the world's GNP between us. Our security ties have fostered a generation of peace in the Asia-Pacific region, and remain critical to the region's continued stability and prosperity.[44]

A major rationale for the United States-Japan alliance disappeared with the end of the Cold War, and the United States-Japan alliance in its present form is becoming anachronistic.[45] The idea that the U.S. soldiers stationed on Japan's soil should serve to prevent the resurgence of Japanese military power is not sustainable in the long run, because it is predicated on distrust of Japan in the minds of Americans and Asians. The remarks made by Major General Henry

Stackpole III in March 1990 that "[no] one wants a rearmed, resurgent Japan. So we are a cap in the bottle, if you will..."[46] confirmed the persistent concern of Washington about Japan. As Kenneth Pyle has written,

> ...a continuation of this "cap in the bottle" approach presumes a virtual mercenary role for U.S. forces in Japan, playing the role of policeman in Asia while Japan's economic domination of the increasingly prosperous and self-assured region increases. Such an approach assures conflict with Japanese pride and its nationalist mood.[47]

In this connection, Tokyo's willingness to bear most of the stationing costs of U.S. forces in Japan gives the wrong impression that Japan wants to use U.S. soldiers as its mercenaries.[48] At a time when there is no unifying military threat, credibility of the United States-Japan alliance can only be strengthened, not by Japan's magnanimous use of "checkbook diplomacy," but by change in the relationship through "burden-sharing by devolution."[49]

Equally important is recognition of the uncertainty about the long-term U.S. commitment to regional security. One wonders how much longer the United States can afford to act as the global hegemon. Scalapino writes of some of the future prospects:

> At the end of this century the United States will have departed from most if not all fixed bases on foreign soil. The emphasis will be upon staging areas kept in readiness by those states aligned with the United States strategically, with a small number of American technicians in residence in some places. The premium will be upon lift capacity and rapid deployment, keeping in mind the contingencies most likely to occur. Moreover, its primary military forces [being] mobile, the reliance will be upon air and sea power; there is virtually no chance that large American ground forces will be sent into combat in Asia again.[50]

The real question then is, how can we affect change in the United States-Japan alliance through "burden-sharing by devolution" to strengthen credibility of the alliance in a changing world? Burden-sharing by devolution means sharing the responsibilities for the maintenance of a stable international order. Measures for devolution include: an enhanced self-reliance of Japan's defense force structure within the framework of an exclusively defensive force posture; Japan's efforts to develop an independent intelligence collection and analysis capability; Japan's active participation in international peacekeeping efforts under the aegis of the United Nations; the United States' handing over its bases and facilities stationed on Japan's soil to Japan; and the establishment of a new alliance relationship with the United States. Under this new alliance, the two countries should develop: a smooth host-nation support system for emergencies in Japan; effective air- and sea-lift capabilities; high levels of inter-operability between U.S. and Japanese forces; and coordination of contingency plans and crisis management measures.

However, there ought to be a number of crucial preconditions for effective devolution. There should be an array of multilateral mechanisms for maintaining peace and stability in the Asia-Pacific region, into which Japan must be firmly incorporated (see below). And much of the Russian military capability currently deployed in the Far East must be reduced to minimum levels. Ultimate resolution of the North Korean nuclear issue will also be a precondition for devolution in the United States-Japan alliance. The stationing of U.S. troops in Japan (and in South Korea for that matter) will be a necessity so long as there remains a possibility of military conflict on the Korean Peninsula. Finally, judicious management of economic and trade relations between Japan and the United States is vital. As noted earlier, worsening trade frictions between the two countries pose the greatest threat to the continuation of the United States-Japan security relationship in the post-Cold War era.

The U.S.-Japan alliance will remain an essential component of Japan's concept of comprehensive security, although it will require substantial readjustments. A breakdown of the United States-Japan alliance is highly undesirable not just for the two countries but for the entire world. It would cause a fundamental reordering of the balance of power in the Asia-Pacific region, creating enormous uncertainty. It could provoke the emergence of Japan as an unpredictable and militarily autonomous power which would alarm almost every country in the region, and finally, it would mean a collapse of the single most important pillar of the emerging global economic system.

Multilateral Efforts for Collective Security

The scope of Japan's comprehensive security can be broadened further by multilateral efforts for collective security. The ultimate challenge in East Asia would be the development of a concert system in which responsibilities for the maintenance of peace and stability are shared by all great powers. An East Asian concert system would require China's participation as a strategic partner, along with the reinvigorated U.S.-Japan alliance as the linchpin of the economic dynamism and political stability in the Asia-Pacific region. To expect the United States to remain the world's hegemonic superpower is unrealistic, and to pursue the idea of a U.S.-Japan condominium, or a condominium consisting of Japan, North America, and Europe, is illusory, since it ignores the inevitable rise of China.

There already are a wide spectrum of regionwide organizations or forums which promote economic policy cooperation, such as Asia-Pacific Economic Cooperation (APEC), the Association of Southeast Asian Nations (ASEAN), and the Pacific Economic Cooperation Council (PECC). There has also been a growing interest in developing multilateral mechanisms for political dialogue, coordination of security policies, and conciliation and peacekeeping. The use of the ASEAN Post Ministerial Conference (now ARF) as "the appropriate bases for addressing the regional peace and security issues" is an example which adds a new dimension to multilateral efforts for collective security.[51]

The most effective approaches to regional security issues may be best pursued in a subregional context.[52] For example, to encourage the process of reconciliation between the two Korean states, James Baker's proposal for the creation of a forum involving the two Koreas, the United States, China, Japan, and Russia is an important step towards such a multilateral forum on Northeast Asian security.[53] The ARF could be effective in promoting Southeast Asian security, such as in its dealings with the Cambodian peace process.

It is important to make the best use of existing bilateral and multilateral institutions to promote regional security, but existing institutions may be insufficient in the Asia-Pacific region. A stronger system of peace and stability will require a serious rejuvenation and strengthening of the United Nations and more prominent Japanese participation in UN activities for the maintenance of peace and security. It is worth noting that there was a shift in Japanese public opinion towards security issues. While a firm consensus has not yet emerged on the dispatch of the Self-Defense Forces (SDF) overseas, recent opinion polls show a growing public interest in Japan's participation in UN peacekeeping operations.[54]

Nevertheless, the idea of Japan's physical participation in UN peacekeeping remains problematic. It is possible to argue that Japan's decision to send SDF units for UN peacekeeping represents a significant departure from its long-standing policy of forbidding the dispatch of the SDF for settling international disputes. To justify the dispatch of the SDF abroad, the government set five conditions for Japan's participation in UN peacekeeping operations. These are (a) a cease-fire agreement; (b) advance consent of the countries involved; (c) maintenance of neutrality; (d) limits on the use of arms to the minimum necessary for self-protection; and (e) the right to suspend the activities of Japanese personnel should any of the conditions (a) to (c) not be met.[55] These conditions, however, deserve further study in light of the role the Japanese peacekeeping force played for the Cambodian peace process and many other situations where Japanese participation in peacekeeping is conceivable.[56]

Commitments to Global Issues

By using its financial and technological resources, Japan can play a constructive role in tackling emerging global problems—the population problem, environmental degradation, the spread of weapons of mass destruction, refugees, drugs, AIDS, terrorism, and ethnic conflict. The 1992 Tokyo Declaration can be viewed as an extension of Japan's comprehensive security to the United States-Japan relationship, since the Declaration "defines security in the broadest sense of the word, to include the environment, refugees, illegal narcotics trafficking, and development assistance for regions plagued with poverty, famine and disease."[57]

The question is how best to convert Japan's economic, financial and technological power resources to what Joseph Nye calls "soft co-optive power...the ability of a country to structure a situation so that other countries develop preferences or define their interests in ways consistent with its own."[58] Japan's comprehensive security, if creatively extended to such multilateral forums as the United Nations and APEC, could be a source of "soft co-optive power" to make a constructive contribution to these issues of transnational interdependence.

CONCLUSION

The central argument in this chapter is a defense of Japan's concept of comprehensive security. The two basic premises underlying it—Article 9 of the Constitution and the United States-Japan alliance—remain viable and effective in the post-Cold War world. Tokyo should neither be complacent about its postwar achievements and the present arrangements for security nor cynical about the limitations imposed by the Constitution on Japan's capability to play an active role in international security.

Japan's idea of comprehensive security, with its basic ingredients intact, should be further refined, broadened, and strengthened to cope with the new pressures of the post-Cold War world. In the short term, the management of U.S.-Japan economic relations is the most critical issue confronting Tokyo and Washington, because of its farreaching implications for the future shape of the international economic and security order. In the long term, the successful management of the complex threats of the post-Cold War world, spanning military, economic, social and ecological issues, requires a shift from largely bilateral to more multilateral dealings. This shift needs to be effected without corroding the two essential premises in which the concept of comprehensive security is founded. Multilateral forums such as APEC and the UN are the key to affecting this transition smoothly and providing frameworks in which the concept of comprehensive security can be creatively applied to a wide range of regional and global security issues.

NOTES

1. See Yoichi Funabashi, "Japan and the New World Order," *Foreign Affairs* 70:5 (Winter 1991/92), pp. 58-74.
2. Robert W. Barnett, "Japan's Concept of Comprehensive National Security in the Post-Cold War Era," seminar paper, (Tokyo: The Japan Institute of International Affairs, 27 November 1990). See also his *Beyond War: Japan's Concept of Comprehensive National Security* (Washington, DC: Pergamon-Brassey's, 1984).

3. Kenneth B. Pyle examines Japan's national purpose during the post-war period and suggests a new realism in the U.S-Japan alliance. See his *The Japanese Question: Power and Purpose in a New Era* (Washington, DC: The AEI Press, 1992). On the question of Japanese power viewed in an international context, see, inter alia, Chalmers Johnson, "Inquiry into Bases of Japanese Power" in *Leviathan: The Japanese Journal of Political Science* 2 (Fall, 1992), pp. 145-164. See also Karel van Wolferen's controversial book, *The Enigma of Japanese Power: People and Politics in a Stateless Nation* (London: Macmillan, 1989).

4. See, for example, Saburo Okita, *Japan in the World Economy of the 1980s* (Tokyo: University of Tokyo Press, 1989), p. 88.

5. In the early 1950s Prime Minister Shigeru Yoshida laid the foundation of Japan's postwar foreign and defense policies in what has since been labeled the "Yoshida Doctrine." See, for example, Pyle, op. cit., chapter 3.

6. Pyle, op. cit., p. 20.

7. Ibid., p. 43.

8. See Pyle, op. cit., Chapters 4-5.

9. See "Summary of the Report on Comprehensive National Security" reproduced in Barnett, *Beyond War*, Chapter 1. In 1979 Prime Minister Masayashi Ohira set up nine advisory task forces, one of which was called the Comprehensive National Security Group chaired by Masamichi Inoki, former President of National Defense Academy. This group's report was submitted to Acting Prime Minister Masayoshi Ito in July 1980 and was subsequently published in August 1980. See *Sogo anzen hosho senryaku* [*Comprehensive National Security*] (Tokyo: Okurasho insatsukyoku, 1980). See also Barnett, *Beyond War*, Chapters 1 and 2; *Heiwa mondai kenkyukai hokokusho: kokusai kokka nippon to sogo anzen hosho seisaku* [*Report by the Study Group on Peace Problems: Comprehensive National Security Policy for the International State Japan*] (Tokyo: Okurasho insatsukyoku, 1985); Shinkichi Eto and Yoshinobu Yamamoto, *Sogo anpo to mirai no sentaku* [*Comprehensive Security and Japan's Future Options*] (Tokyo: Kodansha, 1990); Alan Rix, "Japan's Comprehensive Security and Australia," *Australian Outlook* 41:2 (August 1987), 79-86; and Tsuneo Akaha, "Japan's Comprehensive Security Policy: A New East Asian Environment," *Asian Survey* 31:4 (April 1991).

10. *Heiwa mondai kenkyukai hokokush*, op. cit.

11. See Eiichi Katahara, "The Politics of Japanese Defense Policy Making, 1975-89," unpublished Ph.D. dissertation (Brisbane, Griffith University, April 1990).

12. See, for example, Barry Blechman's comments cited in Barnett, *Beyond War*, pp. 49-50.

13. See Masataka Kosaka, "Theater Nuclear Weapons and Japan's Defense Policy," in Richard H. Solomon and Masataka Kosaka (eds.), *The Soviet Far East Military Buildup* (Dover, Massachusetts: Auburn House, 1986), pp. 133-136.

14. Rix, op. cit., p. 79.

15. See ibid., p. 80.

16. Okita, op. cit., p. 88.

17. William L. Brooks and Robert M. Orr, Jr., "Japan's Foreign Economic Assistance," *Asian Survey* 25:3 (March 1985), p. 339.

18. See Japanese Foreign Ministry, *Diplomatic Bluebook 1991: Japan's Diplomatic Activities* (Tokyo: InfoPlus, 1992), pp. 13-14; Japanese Defense Agency, *Defense of Japan 1992*, pp. 50-52; and Research Institute for Peace and Security, *Asian Security 1992–93* (London: Brassey's, 1992), pp. 25-31.

19. See Japanese Foreign Ministry, op. cit., p. 65; Japanese Defense Agency, op. cit., pp. 47-50; see also *Nihon Keizai Shimbun* (8 March 1993).

20. For an analysis of the problems with the idea of developing an OSCE-type structure in the Asia-Pacific region, see Japanese Foreign Ministry, op. cit., pp. 69-70.

21. See ibid, pp. 68-69; Japanese Defense Agency, op. cit., pp. 68-70; Yukio Satoh, "The Changing Currency of Power: Paper II," in *America's Role in the Changing World Part I*, Adelphi Paper 256 (London: International Institute for Strategic Studies, 1990-91); and Kiyoshi Araki, "Japan's Security Policy in the Regional and Global Context," RIIA Discussion Paper No. 37 (London: The Royal Institute of International Affairs, 1991).

22. See, for example, U.S. Department of Defense, *A Strategic Framework for the Asia–Pacific Rim: Looking Forward to the 21st Century*, a report submitted to the Congress (April 1990), pp. 8-15; and Dick Cheney, *Annual Report to the President and the Congress* (January 1993), pp. 8-9.

23. Yukio Satoh, "A Grand Opportunity for a More Equal U.S.-Japanese Partnership," *International Herald Tribune* (20 January 1993).

24. See Edward N. Luttwak, "The Shape of Things to Come," *Commentary* 87:6 (June 1990), p. 19. See also his "The U.S.-Japanese Crisis," *The Washington Quarterly* 15:4 (Autumn 1992).

25. See, for example, Reinhard Drifte, *Japan's Rise to International Responsibilities* (London: The Athlone Press, 1990).

26. See *Yomiuri Shimbun* (3, 8 April 1993), and *Daily Yomiuri* (3, 8 April 1993). Constitutional amendments require a concurring vote of two-thirds of the members of the Upper and Lower Houses and the affirmative vote of a majority of the votes cast at a referendum. Another survey, conducted by the Japan Federation of Economic Organizations (Keidanren), investigated the views of the Japanese business community about Constitutional amendments. The results indicate that 45.9 percent of respondents think "the Constitution should be amended," while 45.9 percent believe "if necessary, the Constitution should be amended, but there is no such need at the present time." Only 3.3 percent think "the Constitution should never be amended." See *Asahi Shimbun* (22 April 1993); *Nihon Keizai Shimbun* (22 April 1993).

27. See, for example, *Yomiuri Shimbun* (3 April 1993); Tadae Takubo, "Kenpo kaisei no odo," ["The Royal Road to Constitutional Amendments"] *Shokun* (March 1993), pp. 26-40.

28. Quoted by Kiyofuku Chuma, in his "The Choice Is Clear: Diplomacy over Force," *Japan Quarterly* 38:2 (April/June 1991), p. 144.

29. See Shuichi Kato, "Goken no riyu"["Reasons for the Protection of the Constitution"], *Asahi Shimbun* (24 March 1993).

30. Barnett, "Japan's Concept of Comprehensive National Security in the Post-Cold War Era," op. cit.

31. See Edward J. Lincoln, "Japan in the 1990s: A New Kind of World Power," *The Brookings Review* (Spring 1992), pp. 12-17.

32. Bruce M. Koppel and Robert M. Orr, Jr., *Japan's Foreign Aid: Power and Policy in a New Era* (Boulder: Westview Press, 1993), p. 365; and *Sogo anzen hosho senryaku*, op. cit., pp. 38-41.

33. Koppel and Orr, ibid., p. 365.

34. See Akaha, "Japan's Comprehensive Security Policy," op. cit., p. 332; Takao Kawakami, "21seiki ni muketa nihon no enjo seisaku," ["Japan's aid policy towards the 21 century"], *Gaiko Forum* 54 (March 1993), pp. 4-15; and *Asahi Shimbun* (6 October 1992).

35. *Nihon Keizai Shimbun* (28 February 1993).

36. See *Asahi Shimbun* (6 October 1992); *Nihon Keizai Shimbun* (6 October 1992); and Alan Rix, "Japan's Foreign Aid Policy: A Capacity For Leadership?" *Pacific Affairs* 62:4 (Winter 1989-90), p. 464.

37. See Rix, ibid.

38. See ibid.; Takeshi Igarashi, ed., *Nihon no ODA to kokusaichitsujo* [*Japan's ODA and International Order*] (Tokyo: Kokusai mondai kenkyujo, 1990); and *Asahi Shimbun* (7 October and 4 December 1992).

39. The ratio of untied aid refers to "the procurement ratio of goods and services not restricted to those from the donor country." See Japanese Foreign Ministry, op. cit., p. 133. For a useful review of Japan's ODA policy, see Kawakami, op. cit.

40. Kawakami, ibid., pp. 8-9.

41. In the implementation of ODA, the new guideline will require the government to "pay full attention" to the following points of the recipient countries: (1) trend in military expenditure; (2) trend in development, production, etc., of weapons of mass destruction such as atomic weapons and missiles; (3) trend in the export and import of weapons; and (4) efforts for promoting democratization and introduction of a market-oriented economy and the situation on securing human rights and freedom. Japanese Foreign Ministry, op. cit., p. 131; Kawakami, ibid., pp. 11-12.

42. See Kawakami, op. cit. Koppel and Orr, p. 363; and *Nihon Keizai Shimbun*, 6 October 1992.

43. See Japanese Foreign Ministry, op. cit., pp. 67-68; Japanese Defense Agency, op. cit., pp. 68-70; Yukio Satoh, "The Changing Currency of Power: Paper II," in *America's Role in the Changing World Part I*, Adelphi Paper no. 256 (London: IISS, 1990-91); and Araki, op. cit.

44. See excerpts of press remarks by President Clinton, delivered April 14, following his meeting with Prime Minister Miyazawa, published in *Daily Yomiuri* (18 April 1993).

45. See Pyle, op. cit.; and Chalmers Johnson, "Japan in Search of a 'Normal' Role," IGCC policy paper no. 4 (La Jolla: IGCC, July 1992).

46. He was then the commander of Marine Corps in Okinawa. See *Washington Post* (27 March 1990).

47. Pyle, op. cit., pp. 145-146.

48. By 1995, Japan will pay about 70 percent of the total expenses of U.S. forces stationed on Japan's soil, excluding the U.S. military personnel and civilian components. See, Araki, op. cit., p. 22.

49. This term is borrowed from David P. Calleo, "Can the United States Afford the New World Order?," *SAIS Review* 12:2 (Summer/Fall 1992), p. 30.

50. See, Robert A. Scalapino, "The United States and Asia: Future Prospects," and Richard Holbrooke, "Japan and the United States: Ending the Unequal Partnership," in *Foreign Affairs* 70:5 (Winter 1991-92).

51. See statement by Foreign Minister Taro Nakayama to the General Session of the ASEAN Post Ministerial Conference, Kuala Lumpur, 22 July 1991, reproduced in Japanese Foreign Ministry, *Diplomatic Bluebook 1991*, pp. 463-471.

52. See Yukio Satoh, "The Changing Currency of Power: Paper II," op. cit., pp. 42-43.

53. James A. Baker, III, "America in Asia: Emerging Architecture for a Pacific Community," *Foreign Affairs* 70:5 (Winter 1991/92).

54. See, for example, *Yomiuri Shimbun* (3 May 1992).

55. Interview with a Japanese Foreign Ministry official, 24 December 1991.

56. Tokyo approved dispatch of 53 Self-Defense Forces personnel to take part in UN peacekeeping operations in Mozambique. *Yomiuri Shimbun* (29 April 1993).

57. Patrick M. Cronin and Lt. Col. Noboru Yamaguchi, "Japan's Future Regional Security Role," *Strategic Review* 20:3 (Summer 1992). For text of "Tokyo Declaration" issued by President Bush and Prime Minister Miyazawa in Tokyo, 9 January 1992, see *Foreign Policy Bulletin* (January-April 1992), 102-128, and *Yomiuri Shimbun* (10 January 1992).

58. Joseph S. Nye, "Soft Power," *Foreign Policy* 80 (Fall 1990), p. 168. See also his "Coping with Japan," op. cit.

13 The Post-Cold War Alliance Politics and Security-Economic Linkages: The Case of the United States and South Korea

Chung-in Moon

INTRODUCTION

The global transformation following the end of the Cold War fostered structural realignments within the Western alliance structure. The sudden evaporation of the common enemy, diverse threat perceptions, and ideological and fiscal limitations to common defense question the sustainability of the existing Western alliance system based on U.S. military leadership. Underlying the realignments is the diminishing capability of the United States to maintain its current level of security alliances.

Diluted military threats abroad and economic difficulties at home also are reshaping the hierarchy of values in the United States and its allies. Economic security is replacing the primacy of military security. The United States now is increasingly concerned about enhancing international competitiveness and ensuring jobs, welfare, and the quality of life at home. The same can be said of its allies. The shifting emphasis of national goals has produced new patterns of statecraft and diplomatic engagement. The primacy of economic interests over military ones has fostered a new form of alliance politics in which bilateralism and specific reciprocity are the prevailing norms and principles. Linkages between security and the economy are being dramatically re-altered, and the post-Cold War realignments in the Western bloc are likely to be more erratic and conflictual.

The security alliance between the United States and South Korea is an example of this profound realignment. The United States' security commitment to South Korea was predicated on the logic of strategic containment of the Soviet Union and the protection of Japan. In the name of common security goals, the United States facilitated South Korea's economic development and tolerated its mercantile free-riding. However, the collapse of the Soviet empire altered these strategic parameters. Institutional inertia still exists, and North Korea's volatile spoilership justifies continuing the United States' security commitment to South Korea. However, while North Korea poses a direct threat to Seoul, it may not be so to Washington, especially following the United States-DPRK accord of 1994.[1] Regardless of Seoul's intentions and preferences, the new macro-strategic landscape is bound to change the nature and direction of U.S.-South Korean security relations. Such realignments will also accompany formidable changes in bilateral economic relations.

This chapter explores newly emerging patterns of security-economic linkages between the United States and the Republic of Korea (ROK) in the post-Cold War environment.[2] The first section presents a brief overview of some salient analytical issues concerning security-economic linkages in the post-Cold War era. The next section examines the structure of specific security-economic linkages and bilateral conflicts in the United States-ROK relationship by focusing on defense burden-sharing and its macroeconomic implications, techno-nationalism and bilateral defense industrial conflicts, and the shifting of the security leverage in bargaining over economic frictions. Finally, the chapter addresses the overall implications of these security-economic linkages and the future of the United States-ROK alliance.

SECURITY-ECONOMIC LINKAGES IN U.S.-ROK RELATIONS: THREE CASES

In this section, several bilateral economic conflicts between the United States and the ROK will be analyzed. In each, the end of the Cold War and changes in U.S. alliance strategies had profound implications for the bargaining power of both actors and for the resolutions of the conflicts.

Defense Burden-Sharing and Its Macroeconomic Implications

The U.S.-ROK alliance is one of the most successful Western alliances, which can be attributed in part to its patron-client nature with the United States as a benign patron and South Korea as a loyal client.[3] These vertical ties allowed South Korea to enjoy extensive security benefits from the United States. During the period 1950-1980, the United States provided South Korea with security assistance worth $5.6 billion. In addition, the United States extended a total of $2.3 billion to South Korea in the form of Foreign Military Sales (FMS) loans from 1971 to 1986. Even more critical was the presence of U.S. troops in South Korea, which served as the most effective deterrent against North Korean military provocation.[4] As the principal provider of military and economic assistance as well as an actual guardian, the United States cultivated a congenial and stable alliance with South Korea.

Table 13.1: ROK Support for the U.S. Forces in Korea (USFK)

(millions U.S.$, 1989)

Item	Content	Direct Assistance	Indirect Assistance
Real Estate	land and other properties	1,596	306
Manpower	Korean Augmentees to the United States Army (KATUSA), Korean Service Corps, and security personnel	203	4.1
Operational Maintenance Support	Joint U.S. Military Advisory Group, Korea (JUSMAG-K) combined budget for Combined Forces Command (CFC)	—	4.2
CDIP	Combined Defense Improvement Program	—	40
Logistics Support	magazine sites, storage areas, oil and service fees, etc.	286	48.4
Military Facilities	training camps, shooting ranges, air traffic control facilities	33	—
Tax Exemption	tariffs, toll charges, postage and communication fees, and other public utility charges	101	—
	Subtotal	2,219	403
			Grand Total 2,622

Source: Ministry of National Defense, Defense White Paper, 1990 *(Seoul: Ministry of National Defense, 1991), p. 164.*

Entering the early 1980s, however, the patron-client relationship began to change. Facing fiscal crisis at home and bilateral trade deficits with South Korea, the United States called for Seoul to increase defense burden sharing. South Korea accommodated Washington's demand by allocating six percent of gross national product to the defense sector, a level comparable to the United States share. As Table 13.1 illustrates, Seoul assumed substantial costs associated with the maintenance and operation of U.S. forces stationed in South Korea, including costs for land and facilities, force enhancement, and management of U.S. forces as well as the United States-ROK Combined Forces Command (CFC). Since the late 1980s, the United States' demands for defense burden sharing have become more specific. At the 1990 U.S.-ROK security consultative meeting (SCM), the United States proposed that South Korea cover the personnel cost of Korean workers employed by the United States and the construction costs for U.S. military facilities, in addition to traditional support areas (storage and management of U.S. wartime material stockpiles, maintenance of U.S. military equipment, and upgrades in the combined forces). In 1989, South Korea contributed a total of $2.62 billion towards defense cost sharing (Table 13.1). In 1990, the Korean government added $150 million more to the existing cost sharing arrangement. In the wake of the Gulf War, South Korea also shared U.S. defense costs by contributing money and materials as well as providing medical and air-sea transportation support, totaling $500 million.[5]

To ensure national survival amidst a precarious regional security environment, South Korea is compelled to strengthen its military power through expanded defense spending. Furthermore, in search of the lesser of several evils, Korea, whether divided or unified, might request an U.S. troop presence and security assurances.[6] To retain an acceptable level of U.S. forces, South Korea should then be prepared to assume a substantial portion of the costs associated with its presence. Likewise, a changing security environment is likely to deepen the burden of South Korea's military spending. The costs of each of these three options will be significant.

Can South Korea manage this increasing defense burden? Democratic consolidation at home and the advent of the post-Cold War environment abroad makes it difficult for the Korean government to push for additional defense spending. A strong national security infrastructure is no longer considered a political magic bullet. The Kim Young Sam government successfully placed the military under civilian control and reduced its political clout. The defense budget is no longer a sacred cow blessed with political insulation, but instead is now subject to intense bureaucratic politics and social and political pressures. Since the early 1980s, South Korea's defense budget showed a pattern of relative decline. The proportion of defense outlays in the government budget decreased from an average 33.5 percent during 1975-1984 to 28.7 percent in 1991 and 25.2 percent in 1993.[7] Because democratization and increased welfare spending created new fiscal demands, efforts to expand defense expenditures will invite considerable domestic opposition. It is ironic that the end of the Cold War and strategic realignment will bring South Korean political leaders not the anticipated peace dividend, but rather increased defense burden, macroeconomic constraints, and difficult policy choices.[8]

International Competition, Techno-nationalism, and Defense Industrial Conflicts

Another contentious issue involves the rise of U.S. defensive techno-nationalism and its impact on military-industrial cooperation. During the Cold War period, South Korea's force modernization and improvement was a vital American concern for both South Korea's self-defense and coalition warfare. To promote these goals, the United States played a critical role in facilitating South Korea's defense industrialization. From 1971 to 1986, the United States transferred 881 technical data packages, of which 128 items were utilized for production and improvement of defense chapters. South Korea also produced 23 major military hardwares under license and co-production agreements with the United States. In addition, the United States helped establish and upgrade research and manpower infrastructure by training South Korean scientists and engineers and providing various types of technical assistance.

Table 13.2: U.S. Techno-nationalism and the Structure of U.S.-ROK Defense Industrial Conflicts

Patterns of Conflict	Policy Cleavage and Structure of Conflict
3rd Country Arms Sales Regulation	U.S.: Imposition of quota, total ban, destination restrictions on Korea's exports of military hardware manufactured under U.S. technology for non-proliferation and domestic economic reasons. ROK: U.S. losing competitiveness; relaxation of regulations, joint production and marketing.
Restricting Transfer of Dual-use Technology	U.S.: Restriction of transfer of critical dual-use technology for security and economic reasons. ROK: Relaxation of restriction; proposing joint R&D, cost sharing, and bilateral cooperation.
Protection of Intellectual Property Rights	U.S.: Royalty imposition (eight percent); strict enforcement of Patent Secrecy Agreement (PSA); extensive application of the origin of U.S. defense technology. ROK: Royalty reduction or exemptio; compliance with PSA; limited application of the origin of U.S. defense technology.
Offset Production and Trade	U.S.: Seoul's offset terms are excessive; flexible application of the offset terms; offset as hindrance to defense industrial cooperation. ROK: Application of a uniform 30 percent rule; offset as an essential vehicle of U.S. techno-nationalism.

With extensive American support, the South Korean defense industry showed remarkable progress in a relatively short period. Satisfaction of domestic needs led to market saturation, even at low levels of production that were suboptimal because of few economies of scale. To overcome this, the Korean government opted for the promotion of military exports and defense industrial deepening based on cutting-edge technologies.

However, these efforts were constrained by American techno-nationalism in the form of supplier control policies. The United States began to tightly regulate South Korea's military exports and restrict the transfer of critical dual-use technology. Disputes over supplier control and recipient autonomy became more pronounced in the post-Cold War era.[9]

As Table 13.2 demonstrates, the most immediate dispute involves U.S. regulation of South Korea's arms exports to third countries.[10] A majority of Korean military hardwares were manufactured with American technical assistance. The U.S. Arms Export Control Act and the International Traffic in Arms Regulations require the Korean government to obtain prior written approval from the U.S. government to export to third countries defense chapters manufactured with American technical assistance. By taking advantage of these legal constructs, the United States imposed tough restrictions on the items and destinations of Korean arms exports. As of 1989, out of 42 Korean defense chapters requiring prior U.S. approval for third-country sale, four items were under a total ban regardless of destination, while quantitative restrictions were imposed on seven items. In addition, South Korea is not permitted to export any military hardware to countries that are involved in regional conflicts, classified as terrorist sanctuaries, or alleged to be violating human rights. The third-country arms sales regulations dealt a severe blow to Korean arms exports and defense contractors.

Seoul has tried hard to ease U.S. regulations through bilateral negotiations and transnational lobbying. These attempts were unsuccessful, however. Strong opposition from U.S. Congress and defense manufacturers coupled with legal and institutional barriers prevented South Korea from easing U.S. restrictions.

Although South Korea avoided placing the issue at the annual U.S.-ROK defense ministers' meeting since 1991, this does not imply the resolution of the conflict. Two potential frictions exist. One is the dispute over the origin of defense technology, and the other is Seoul's increasing reliance on the evasion strategy. The most effective way to avoid U.S. supplier control is to manufacture and export military hardwares of Korean origin. South Korea recently increased manufacturing of defense articles of Korean origin. However, they are usually modifications of U.S.-origin military hardwares. South Korea's exports of Korean-origin defense articles will trigger new frictions with the United States over the issue of intellectual property rights. The evasion option, namely exporting without U.S. approval, cannot be ruled out either. In the past, the South Korean government tightly monitored and restricted defense contractors' cheating behavior in fear of negative impacts on the U.S.-ROK alliance system. However, recent developments make the Korean government less able to monitor and regulate export activities of Korean defense contractors. Several factors explain the diminishing influence of the Korean government on defense contractors; sharp reduction of government support of the defense industry, exhaustion of domestic procurement, corporate survival, and precarious U.S.-ROK bilateral security ties.

Equally critical is a growing dispute over the transfer of advanced defense technology. South Korea's decision not to raise third-country arms sales at the annual U.S.-ROK security consultative meeting (SCM) was a calculated move to acquire cutting-edge, advanced technologies from the United States. The self-sufficiency in conventional weapons, the impressive performance of U.S. high-tech weapons in the Gulf War, and the anticipated spin-off effects on the commercial-industrial sector drove the South Korean government to move into development and manufacturing of advanced, high-tech weapons. However, South Korea's technological level is not mature enough to take its own independent initiative. Inflow of advanced technology from the United States is essential for the new take-off of South Korea's defense industry.[11]

In order to facilitate the transfer of critical technology, South Korea proposed a defense industrial cooperation scheme with the United States and was able to exchange a memorandum of understanding on bilateral defense industrial and technological cooperation in 1988. Despite the memorandum, bilateral cooperation in high-tech sectors remains minimal—the United States was reluctant to transfer critical technologies. South Korea's efforts to acquire laser beam, guidance system, submarine, and anti-submarine warfare technologies all failed. More recently, South Korea initiated the Korean Fighter Program (KFP), involving the importation and subsequent co-production of General Dynamics F-16s to modernize its air force. As part of this program, Samsung Aerospace Ltd., a prime contractor to the program, requested the transfer of avionics, engine hot section, and radar technologies. The United States again blocked the transfer.[12]

While U.S. refusals are a reflection of defensive techno-nationalism designed to minimize adverse boomerang effects on military security which might emanate from the transfer of critical dual-use technology,[13] effects on military security are a lesser concern for the United States than the fear of South Korea's commercial application of critical technologies and their impacts on U.S. competitiveness. South Korea plans to take advantage of the KFP and related technology-transfer to build a commercial aerospace industry for the twenty-first century, making American concerns relevant. The blurred demarcation of the dual-use technology and its implications for commercial competition is likely to tighten screening and regulation of technology exports. The self-oppositional posture of U.S. technology export policy will continue to undermine U.S.-ROK relations.

Related to this conflict of interests is friction about intellectual property rights. During the Cold War, free access to American intellectual properties was taken for granted, a natural side-payment of the U.S. alliance. This is no longer the case. As part of its strategic trade offensive, the United States pushed for protection of intellectual property rights. While South Korea accommodated

American demands in the commercial sector, these demands also extend to the defense industrial sector. The United States reinforced the imposition of a five percent royalty on domestic procurement, and an eight percent royalty on exports of military hardwares manufactured with American technical assistance.[14] The South Korean government and defense contractors requested the lowering of royalty rates and eventually their removal, but South Korea's declining military exports made the royalty payment a less salient issue.

However, a dispute over the Patent Secrecy Agreement (PSA) may become a major source of future bilateral tension. In the mid-1980s, South Korea expressed its interest in participating in research projects related to the Strategic Defense Initiative (SDI). The United States responded favorably, but a string was attached— South Korea must observe provisions of PSA which make it obligatory for the Korean government to keep technology acquired from the U.S secret, not only from enemy countries, but also to its own commercial sector. The United States' intention was to prevent the circumventive transfer of critical technology to enemy countries, as well as to block spinoff uses of the technology in South Korea's commercial industrial complex. American insistence on the PSA stirred strong opposition from South Korea. After a series of diplomatic deadlocks, the South Korean government finally signed the agreement in 1991. However, strict enforcement of the agreement has yet to be seen, leaving room for potential bilateral conflicts.[15]

The offset program has emerged as another trouble spot in U.S.-ROK defense industrial cooperation. Offset arrangements are designed to balance out the importing of new weapons or related technologies by compensating for all or part of the worth of the purchase through reciprocal exports or the coproduction of parts of the new weapons purchased. Offset programs are a source of the recipient's leverage because of its purchasing power, and serve as effective vehicles for limiting the negative impacts of foreign weapons acquisition as well as of coping with techno-nationalism. The South Korean government aggressively pursued this policy by applying a "30 percent" rule, which dictates that at least 30 percent of the purchase value must be compensated through offset arrangements.[16] American firms criticized this rule, requesting a more flexible management of offset terms. Friction over offset programs will continue, further straining U.S.-ROK defense industrial cooperation.

Growing defense industrial conflicts between Seoul and Washington reflect the shifting nature of the bilateral alliance system. In the post-Cold War era, the United States may not tolerate South Korea's free-riding for security reasons. The primacy of economic interests embodied in techno-nationalism may intensify U.S. supplier controls and restrictions. Meanwhile, South Korea will attempt to maximize its autonomy and independence as a recipient. Defense industrial links that served as a critical bond between the two countries are now turning into sources of friction fraying the bilateral alliance.

Economic Conflicts and Shifting Security Leverage

Some argue that South Korean economic success is partly an American creation. While American economic assistance was vital to reconstructing the Korean economy devastated by the Korean War, the transition to an export promotion strategy (which is regarded as the key determinant of the South Korean economic miracle) was also a result partly of American pressures and guidance. The United States provided capital and technology essential for South Korea's economic take-off, and perhaps the most important contribution was South Korea's unrestricted access to the American market. All these were side payments for South Korea's security alliance with the United States.[17]

However, South Korea's economic dynamism may become a liability to the American economy. As South Korea's export drive threatened United States economic interests, the congenial patron-client relationship gradually became strained. The American response to South Korean economic competition is aimed at disciplining its free-riding and spoiling behavior. Armed with the principle of strategic reciprocity, the United States initiated offensive trade policies against South Korea in 1983. Departing from previously defensive trade policy framed around import restrictions, the United States aggressively called for the correction of unfair trade practices and opening Korea's import markets for American goods and services. Korean access to the American market was predicated on its compliance with market opening and correction of adversarial trade practices. Apart from the offensive trade policy, the United States also graduated South Korea from beneficiary status of the Generalized System of Preference (GSP) and pushed for currency appreciation to balance its trade deficits with South Korea.[18]

Facing these pressures, the South Korean government initially utilized a linkage strategy using security ties as bargaining leverage. Seoul appealed for a more lenient trade policy from Washington by pointing to Korea's heavy defense burden: about six percent of its GNP was spent for military security, essential to the common defense of the East Asian theater. Demanding economic concessions for a heavy defense burden, however, produced backfire effects, resulting in a tougher U.S. position not only on trade issues, but also on security issues.

Since early 1991, bilateral frictions diminished as South Korea corrected its trade surpluses with the United States by complying with many American demands. Seoul's positive adjustment induced the United States to exempt South Korea from the target of Super 301 application. U.S. import restrictions on Korean manufactured goods also eased. However, there are still several pending issues, including the liberalization of agricultural import markets. The United States wants a reduction of high tariffs and quantitative restrictions on agro-fishery products and fuller market liberalization of rice, beef, and wine. Non-tariff barriers are another source of bilateral trade tension. Discriminating government procurement policies, shipbuilding subsidies, protectionist industrial standards, and precarious customs clearance caused U.S. critiques and grievances. As in Japan, these structural impediments also emerged as another trade conflict issue. The United States regards anti-import campaign and other various austerity programs as adversarial trade practices and demands their removal. Along with this, the American government is still pushing for further liberalization of financial and capital markets, exchange rates, and foreign direct investment.[19]

South Korea also is critical of U.S. protectionist policies. Ten Korean items, including color TVs, telephone exchange systems and sweaters, are under U.S. antidumping restriction. After 1986, both antidumping and countervailing duties were levied on South Korea's tableware. Textiles and steel are still under quantitative restrictions, and the American government banned importation of erasable-programmable read-only memory (EPROM) computer chips and plastic bags on the grounds of illegal business practices (Section 337). Recent anti-dumping accusations regarding South Korea's other semiconductor chips also became a source of Seoul's grievances against the United States.[20]

Some of these frictions may be resolved through GATT, but many will remain sources of bilateral trade disputes. The United States is likely to enjoy favorable outcomes in these disputes because of the asymmetry of economic power and Seoul's excessive dependence on the American market. In the past, South Korea could use its security alliance as bargaining leverage in resolving trade disputes with the United States. However, this is no longer the case. While explicit threats from North Korea and the emerging pattern of finite deterrence in the region increased South Korea's alliance dependence on the United States, Seoul's strategic value to Washington may diminish in the long term. In Snyder's terms, the new calculus of the alliance politics could aggravate South Korea's fear of "abandonment" by the United States, while forcing the United States to get away from the unnecessary risk of "entrapment" in the local conflict.[21] The asymmetry of strategic interests now allows the United States to exploit security leverage on economic issues more effectively.

The 1994 Framework Accord negotiations confirmed suspicions among South Korean policymakers that the United States now has this increased leverage. Although the negotiations were conducted in parallel with extensive consultations between South Korean and American government officials, there was still the impression that the North Koreans had achieved some success in gaining a role in the U.S.-South Korean alliance.

CONCLUSION: IMPLICATIONS AND OPTIONS FOR SOUTH KOREA

To South Korea, the demise of the Cold War is not the end of history. It is tantamount to opening Pandora's box. The emergence of the post-Cold War order leaves the North Korean threat intact, while fostering realignment of its alliance ties with the United States. Despite an explicit U.S. alliance commitment and historical bond, the dissolution of the bipolar logic weakened the complementarity of strategic interests between the two. As Kenneth Waltz argued, American disengagement and the subsequent rise of a multipolar regional order in the East Asian theater could revive the structure of finite deterrence and protracted regional instability.[22] To cope with the volatile regional security environment, South Korea needs U.S. troop presence and security assurances more than ever. The primacy of economic interests in the post-Cold War order makes the United States more impatient with free-riding behavior and more aggressive in seeking economic national interests. For both strategic and economic reasons, therefore, South Korea loses some of its political and diplomatic leverage in dealing with the United States. The newly emerging patterns of security-economic linkages will favor the United States, while undermining South Korea's bargaining position, as evidenced in the U.S-North Korean negotiations for the implementation of the Framework Accord. The U.S.-South Korean alliance system now faces severe pressures to undergo a major structural transformation.

South Korea has three options to deal with this transformation. First is an incremental tinkering or adjustment. This option involves efforts to maintain the existing U.S.-ROK alliance by complying with U.S. demands, assuming a larger defense burden, and making economic concessions. By increasing its loyalty to the United States, South Korea can manage short- and medium-term security dilemmas (North Korea, regional instabilities which might emerge from Japanese remilitarization, and Chinese military adventurism). In view of the external environment, this option seems feasible and desirable. However, domestic political dynamics may not permit such a move. Democratic consolidation and the revival of nationalist sentiment are likely to deter the loyalty option.

The second option is to diversify external ties and possibly exit from security and economic dependence on the United States. Since the launching of Nordpolitik in 1988, South Korea tried to expand its diplomatic, political, and economic spaces beyond the perimeter set by the United States. Increasing economic and technological cooperation with Russia is one example—Russia agreed to pay off loans to South Korea in the spring of 1995 with arms in lieu of hard currency. Some in South Korea even suggest moving towards Russia and China as sources of weapons and military technology acquisition. Russia showed keen interest in this regard, and since diplomatic normalization in August 1992, China is also emerging as an alternative. From the political point of view, the exit option may sound attractive. However, diversification into China and Russia might be a "retreat" path rather than a pioneering venture. Russia and China have little to offer in the short run, and South Korea is too dependent on the United States to sever or drastically reduce its existing security and economic ties with the United States.

The third option is constructive re-engagement. This option solidifies the existing bilateral alliance by forming a U.S.-South Korean condominium in East Asia.[23] According to this view, the post-Cold War order is supposed to enhance strategic consensus between Seoul and Washington precisely because neither the United States nor South Korea want the ascension of military and economic power by Japan, China, or Russia. In order to cope with precarious regional security and economic dynamics, the United States and South Korea are bound to cooperate more closely. Capitalizing on this alleged strategic consensus, the South Korean government recently proposed the formation of industrial and technological alliance with the United States.[24] The option is predicated on the creation of contrived threats and enemies. At the present moment, South Korea tacitly designates Japan as a common enemy. This idea can be very attractive in South Korea's domestic politics. Even some elements in the United States may support it as a way of challenging Japanese economic and technological dominance. Given the dynamics of international politics and domestic politics in the United States, however, this option seems neither feasible nor desirable. Despite rhetorical Japan bashing in the United States, Tokyo-Washington ties are much deeper and weightier than those between Seoul and Washington. In reality, U.S.-Japan bigemony is more feasible than U.S.-South Korean condominium, but difficulties within U.S.-Japan relations may change this status.

In view of the above, options for South Korea in the post-Cold War era are limited. South Korea is likely to alternate between the loyalty and exit options, making U.S.-South Korean relations erratic and strained. The issue of Korean reunification has exacerbated these tensions as the United States moves toward recognition of North Korea. However, it also provides cooperative opportunities such as the Korean Energy Development Organization, consultative diplomacy during negotiations, and implementation of the Framework Accord. The end of the Cold War left South Korea with uncertain promises and precarious milieu, in which choosing an optimal foreign policy becomes a difficult task.

NOTES

1. The United States still considers the Korean peninsula a potential flash point in Northeast Asia. The recent North Korean nuclear quagmire, negotiations, and agreement further strengthens this view. If the North Korean nuclear issue recedes, however, American attention to security and assurances are likely to diminish. See U.S. Department of Defense, *A Strategic Framework for the Asian Pacific Rim: Looking Toward the 21st Century* (April 1990); *Annual Report to the President and the Congress* (Washington,

DC:U.S. Government Printing Office, 1991); James A. Winnefeld, Jonathan D. Pollack, et.al., *A New Strategy and Fewer Forces: The Pacific Dimension* (Santa Monica: National Defense Research Institute, Rand, 1992).

2. For an earlier discussion of security-economic linkages between the U.S. and South Korea, see Chung-in Moon, "Between Supporting and Spoiling: Military Alliance and Economic Competition between the United States and South Korea," in Miles Kahler, ed., *Beyond the Cold War in the Pacific* (San Diego: University of California Institute of Global Conflict and Cooperation, 1991), pp. 23-40.

3. Wook-Hee Shin, *Security, Economic Growth, and the State: Dynamics of Patron-Client State Relations in Northeast Asia* (New Haven: Yale University, Unpublished Ph.D. Dissertation, 1992); Man Woo Lee, Ronald McLaurin, and Chung-in Moon, *Alliance under Tension: The Evolution of U.S.-South Korean Relations* (Boulder: Westview Press, 1988).

4. Moon, "Between Supporting and Spoiling," in Kahler, op. cit., p. 25.

5. Ministry of National Defense, *Defense White Paper, 1991-1992* (Seoul: Ministry of National Defense, 1991), pp. 165-166.

6. This represents a revisionist viewpoint in South Korea shared by conservative elements in the military circle. Douglas Paal, a National Security Council staff under the Bush administration, also suggests the continuing U.S. presence even after unification.

7. *Defense White Paper, 1993–94*, p. 181.

8. Chung-in Moon and Intaek Hyun, "Muddling through Security, Welfare, and Growth: The Political Economy of Defense Spending in South Korea," in Steve Chan and Alex Mintz, eds. *Security, Growth, and Welfare: the Political Economy of Defense Expenditure* (New York: Unwin & Hyman, 1992).

9. Kwang-il Baek, Ronald McLaurin, and Chung-in Moon (eds.), *Dilemma of Third World Defense Industries: Supplier Control or Recipient Autonomy* (Boulder: Westview Press, 1989); Moon, "Between Supporting and Spoiling," in Kahler.

10. Chung-in Moon and Kwang-il Baek, "Loyalty, Voice, or Exit: U.S. Third Country Arms Sales Regulation and ROK's Countervailing Strategies," *Journal of Northeast Asian Studies* 4:1 (1986).

11. On South Korea's weapons acquisition plan and technological needs, see Chung-in Moon, Mann-Kyu Kim et.al. *A Study of the Korean Defense Industry: Direction and Policy Options Toward the Year 2,000* (Inchon: Center for International Studies, Inha University, 1993), in Korean.

12. U.S.-Korea Forum on Science and Technology, *Proceedings of Inaugural Session on U.S.-ROK Science and Technology Cooperation* (Annandale, VA: JWK International, 1993), pp. 143-146.

13. Chung-in Moon and William Warner, "Beyond Defensive Technonationalism—Post-Cold War, International Competition, and U.S. Technology Export Control Policy," a paper presented at the annual convention of the International Studies association, Acapulco, Mexico, March 25-28, 1993.

14. At the 1988 SCM, the United States agreed to apply a flexible royalties policy through a case-by-case examination rather than a uniform rate. The U.S. concession resolved some of South Korea's grievances.

15. *Dongah Ilbo* (August 8, 1991).
16. Ministry of National Defense, *Guidelines for Offset Programs* (Seoul: Ministry of National Defense, 1984), in Korean; Moon and Kim et. al., *A Study of the Korean Defense Industry*, chapter 6.
17. Moon, "Between Supporting," in Kahler, pp. 24-27.
18. Chung-in Moon, "Irony of Interdependence," in Lee, McLaurin and Moon, *Alliance under Tension*, chapter 3.
19. For a comprehensive overview of recent developments in U.S.-South Korean trade relations, see Korea Economic Institute of America, *U.S.–Korea Economic Relations-Academic Studies Series Vol. 2* (Washington, DC: KEIA, 1992), Part IV, pp. 139-198.
20. *U.S.–Korea Economic Relations*, p. 167.
21. See Glenn H. Snyder, "The Security Dilemma in Alliance Politics," *World Politics* 36:4 (July 1984), pp. 461-495. For the time being, this logic may not be applied to Seoul-Washington relations. The North Korean nuclear quagmire has forged a new strategic consensus between the two, and has further strengthened their bilateral alliance tie. In the long run, however, the asymmetry of strategic interests between the two will become much more pronounced, and the delicate balancing between the fear of abandonment and the risk of entrapment will emerge as the primary agenda of bilateral alliance management.
22. Kenneth N. Waltz, *Theory of International Politics* (Reading, MA: Addison Wesley, 1979), chapter six.
23. Young-Koo Cha of the Korean Institute for Defense Analysis proposes the idea of a U.S.-South Korean security condominium.
24. Jin-Hyun Kim, former Minister of Science and Technology, suggested technological alliance with the United States in his recent speech, "Post-Cold War, International Competition, and Technological Cooperation: The Case of U.S.-South Korean Relations" at the Graduate School of International Relations and Pacific Studies, University of California at San Diego, April 27, 1993. Chulsu Kim, Minister of Trade, Industry, and Energy proposed an idea of industrial alliance with the United States in his speech at the Second U.S.-R.O.K. Bilateral Conference in Washington, DC, April 17, 1993. See his speech text, "Industrial Alliance between Korea and the United States."

About the Editors

Susan L. Shirk is director of the University of California's Institute on Global Conflict and Cooperation and holds joint appointments at the University of California, San Diego's Department of Political Science and its Graduate School of International Relations and Pacific Studies..

Christopher P. Twomey is a Ph. D. candidate at the Massachusetts Institute of Technology. From 1992-94, he was a staff policy researcher at the University of California's Institute on Global Conflict and Cooperation (IGCC).

About the Contributors

Tsuneo Akaha is a professor of international policy studies and director of the Center for East Asian Studies at the Monterey Institute of International Studies.

Desmond Ball, is a professor in the Strategic and Defense Studies Centre at the Australian National University, Canberra.

Michael Borrus is co-director of the Berkeley Roundtable on the International economy (BRIE) at the University of California, Berkeley.

Tai Ming Cheung is a Hong Kong-based consultant on Chinese affairs. He is a former correspondent for the *Far Eastern Economic Review*.

He Di is general manager of the Standard International Co., Ltd. in Beijing. He was a research fellow and assistant director of the Institute of American Studies at the Chinese Academy of Social Sciences in Beijing.

Jia Qingguo is a professor in the Department of International Politics at Peking University in Beijing. In 1991-92, he was a post-doctoral fellow at the University of California Institute on Global conflict and Cooperation (IGCC).

Eiichi Katahara is a professor in the Faculty of Law at Kobe Gakuin University, Japan. In 1991-92 he was a postdoctoral fellow at the University of California Institute on Global Conflict and Cooperation.

James Clay Moltz is director and senior researcher of the Center for Nonproliferation Studies at the Monterey Institute of International Studies. In

1991-92 he was a postdoctoral fellow at the University of California Institute on Global Conflict and Cooperation.

Chung-in Moon is a professor of political science at Yonsei University in Seoul and a former faculty member in the Department of Political Science, University of Kentucky.

K. S. Nathan is a professor of international relations in the International Studies Program, Faculty of Arts and Sciences, University of Malaya in Kuala Lumpur.

Kusuma Snitwongse is director of the Institute of Security and International Studies and a professor in the Department of International Relations at Chulalongkorn University, Bangkok, Thailand.

Wang Jisi is director of the Institute of American Studies at the Chinese Academy of Social Sciences in Beijing.

John Zysman is a professor of political science at the University of California, Berkeley, and co-director of the Berkeley Roundtable on the International Economy (BRIE) at the University of California, Berkeley.

About the University of California Institute on Global Conflict and Cooperation

The University of California Institute on Global Conflict and Cooperation (IGCC) was founded in 1983 as a multicampus research unit serving the entire University of California system. The institute's purpose is to study the causes of international conflict and the opportunities to resolve it through international cooperation. During IGCC's first five years, research focused largely on the issue of averting nuclear war through arms control and confidence-building measures between the superpowers. Since then the research program has diversified to encompass several broad areas of inquiry: regional relations, international environmental policy, international relations theory, and the domestic sources of foreign policy.

IGCC serves as a liaison between the academic and policy communities, injecting fresh ideas into the policy process, establishing the intellectual foundations for effective policymaking in the post-Cold War environment, and providing opportunities and incentives for UC faculty and students to become involved in international policy debates. Scholars, researchers, government officials, and journalists from the United States and abroad participate in all IGCC projects, and IGCC's publications—books, policy papers, and a semiannual newsletter—are widely distributed to individuals and institutions around the world.

In addition to projects undertaken by the central office at UC San Diego, IGCC supports research, instructional programs, and public education throughout the UC system. The institute receives financial support from the Regents of the University of California and the state of California, and has been awarded grants by such foundations as Ford, William and Flora Hewlett, John D. And Katherine T. MacArthur, Rockefeller, Sloan, W. Alton Jones, Ploughshares, the Carnegie Corporation, the Rockefeller Brothers Fund, the United States Institute of Peace, and The Pew Charitable Trusts.

Susan L. Shirk, a professor in UC San Diego's Graduate School of International Relations and Pacific Studies and in the Department of Political Science, was appointed director of IGCC in June 1992 after serving for a year as acting director. Former directors of the institute include John Gerard Ruggie (1989-91) and Herbert F. York (1983-89), who now serves as director emeritus.

Bibliography

PERIODICALS

Asahi Shimbun

Asian Military Review

Asiaweek

The Australian

Beijing Review

Bulletin of the Ministry of Foreign Trade and Economic Cooperation of the People's Republic of China, The

Central Daily News

Chengming (Hong Kong)

China Daily

China News Analysis

Daily Yomiuri

Dalnii Vostok Rossii Ekonomicheskii Ezhegodnik

Dongah Ilbo

Dongbeiya Yanjiu

The Economist

Far Eastern Economic Review (FEER), 1990-93

Foreign Broadcast Information Service (FBIS), 1986-92

FBIS, East Asia

FBIS, Soviet Union

Foreign Policy Bulletin

Free China Journal

Gongshang ribao (Industrial and Commercial Daily).

Guoji Jingmao Xiaoxi (International Economic and Trade Information) (PRC: Ministry of Foreign Economic Relations and Trade), 1990-93.

Hokkaido Shimbun

International Herald Tribune

Izvestiya

Japan Economic Journal

Komsomolskaya Pravda

Kyodo

Liaowang Overseas Edition (Hong Kong), 1989-92.

Los Angeles Times

Mainichi Shimbun

New Straits Times, 1991-94

New York Times

Nexus

Nezavisimaya Gazeta

Nihon Keizai Shimbun

Seafood Leader

Shijie ribao

SUPAR Report

Tai Gang Ao Qingkuang (Information on Taiwan, Hong Kong, and Macao), New China News Agency, 1988-93.

Taiwan Dongtai Zhoukan (Taiwan Information Weekly), Institute of Taiwan Studies: 1990-93.

TASS

Tikhookeanskiy zvezda (Vladivostok)

UN Monthly Bulletin of Statistics

Washington Post

Washington Times

Xinbao (Australian Chinese Daily)

Xinhua

Yomiuri Shimbun

BOOKS AND DISSERTATIONS

Ariff, Mohamed. *The Malaysian Economy: Pacific Connections* (Singapore: Oxford University Press, 1991).

Ariff, Mohamed. *The Pacific Economy: Growth and External Stability* (Sydney: Allen & Unwin, 1991).

Asia 1993 Yearbook (Hong Kong: Far Eastern Economic Review, 1993).

Asia 1994 Yearbook (Hong Kong: Far Eastern Economic Review, 1994).

Ball, Desmond, Richard L. Grant, and Jusuf Wanandi. *Security Cooperation in the Asia–Pacific Region* (Washington, DC: The Center for Strategic and International Studies, 1993).

Ball, Nicole. *Security and Economy in the Third World* (Princeton, NJ: Princeton University Press, 1988).

Barnett, Robert W. *Beyond War: Japan's Concept of Comprehensive National Security* (Washington, DC: Pergamon-Brassey's, 1984).

Baumol, William J., Richard R. Nelson, and Edward W. Wolff, eds. *International Convergence of Productivity, With Some Evidence From History* (New York: Oxford University Press, 1993).

Bergsten. C.F. and L.B. Krause, eds. *World Politics and International Economics* (Washington, DC: The Brookings Institution, 1975).

Bureau d'Information et Prevision Economique, *Europe in 1992* (Paris: BIPE, October 1987).

Carr, E. H. *The Twenty Years' Crisis, 1919–39* (New York: Harper Torchbooks, 1964).

Carter, Ashton, et al. *Beyond Spinoff: Military and Commercial Technologies in a Changing World* (Boston, MA: Harvard Business School Press, 1992).

Chan, Steve and Alex Mintz, eds. *Security, Growth, and Welfare: the Political Economy of Defense Expenditure* (New York: Unwin & Hyman, 1992).

Chang Chien-feng. *Tai-wan hai, Shen-chen ho* [Taiwan Sea and Shenzhen River] (Hong Kong: Baixin Publishing House, 1987).

Chen Guoshao, et al., eds. *Tai Gang Au Shouce* [Handbook on Taiwan, Hong Kong and Macao] (Beijing: Huayi Publishing House, 1990).

Chin Kim Wah. *Defense Spending in Southeast Asia* (Singapore: Institute of Southeast Asian Studies, 1987).

Chu Hai-yuan, et al. *Ta lu t'an ch'in chi fang wen ti ying* [The impact of visiting relatives and friends traveling to the mainland] (Taipei: Caituan Faren Zhang Rongfa Foundation and Guojia Zhengce Yenjiu Zhongxin, 1989).

Crawford, Sir John and Greg Seow, eds. *Pacific Economic Co-operation: Suggestions for Action* (Singapore: Heinemann Educational Books (Asia) Ltd., 1981).

Deutsch, Karl W., et al. *Political Community and the North Atlantic Area* (Princeton, NJ: Princeton University Press, 1957).

Doherty, Eileen M., ed. *Japanese Investment in Asia: Internal Production Strategies in a Rapidly Changing World* (Berkeley, CA: Asia Foundation and BRIE, 1995).

Drifte, Reinhard. *Japan's Rise to International Responsibilities* (London: The Athlone Press, 1990).

Encarnation, Dennis. *Rivals Beyond Trade: America versus Japan in Industrial Policy, 1925–75* (Tokyo: Charles E. Tuttle, 1982).

Ernst, Dieter and Mytelka, eds. *Catching Up, Keeping Up, and Getting Ahead: The Korean Model Under Pressure* (Paris: OECD forthcoming).

Eto, Shinkichi and Yoshinobu Yamamoto. *Sogo anpo to mirai no sentaku* [Comprehensive Security and Japan's Future Options] (Tokyo: Kodansha, 1990).

Frankel, Jeffrey and Miles Kahler, eds. *Regionalism and Rivalry: Japan and the United States in Pacific Asia* (Chicago: National Bureau of Economic Research, University of Chicago Press, 1993).

Garnaut, Ross. *Australia and the Northeast Asian Ascendancy* (Canberra: Australian Government Publishing Service, 1989).

Gordon, Bernard K. *Toward Disengagement in Asia: A Strategy for American Foreign Policy* (Englewood Cliffs, NJ: Prentice-Hall, Inc., 1969).

Graham, Edward and Paul Krugman. *Foreign Direct Investment in the United States* (Washington, DC: Institute for International Economics, 1989).

Haas, Ernst B. *Beyond the Nation State: Functionalism and International Organization* (Stanford, CA: Stanford University Press, 1964).

Hasegawa Tsuyoshi, Jonathan Haslam, and Andrew Kuchins, eds. *Russia and Japan: An Unresolved Dilemma between Distant Neighbors* (Berkeley, CA: University of California International and Area Studies, 1993).

Hermann, Charles F., Charles W. Kegley, Jr., and James N. Rosenau, eds. *New Directions in the Study of Foreign Policy* (Boston: Allen & Unwin, 1987).

Hirshmann, Albert. *National Power and the Structure of Foreign Trade* (Berkeley, CA: University of California Press, 1945).

Hopkins, John C. And Weixing Hu, eds. *Strategic Views from the Second Tier: The Nuclear Weapons Policies of France, Britain, and China* (New Brunswick, NJ: Transaction Publishers, 1995).

Igarashi, Takeshi. *Nihon no ODA to kokusaichitsujo* [Japan's ODA and International Order] (Tokyo: Kokusai mondai kenkyujo, 1990).

International Monetary Fund, *Direction of Trade Statistics Yearbook*, 1990-94.

Jang-Won Such and Jae-Bong Ro, *Asia–Pacific Economic Cooperation: The Way Ahead* (Seoul: Korea Institute for International Economic Policy, 1990).

Japan Defense Agency, *Defense of Japan*, 1992 (Tokyo: Japan Times, 1992).

Japan Foreign Ministry. *Diplomatic Bluebook 1991: Japan's Diplomatic Activities* (Tokyo: InfoPlus, 1992).

Jeshurun, Chandran, ed. *Arms and Defense in Southeast Asia* (Singapore: Institute of Southeast Asian Studies, 1989).

Kahler, Miles, ed. *Beyond the Cold War in the Pacific* (San Diego: Institute of Global Conflict and Cooperation, University of California, 1991).

Katahara, Eiichi. *The Politics of Japanese Defense Policy Making, 1975–89* (Brisbane: Griffith University, unpublished Ph.D. dissertation, 1990).

Keohane, Robert O. and Joseph S. Nye, Jr. *Transnational Relations and World Politics* (Cambridge, MA: Harvard University Press, 1972).

Keohane, Robert O. and Joseph S. Nye. *Power and Interdependence, World Politics in Transition* (Boston: Little, Brown and Company, 1977).

Keohane, Robert, ed. *Neorealism and its Critics* (New York: Columbia University Press, 1986).

Khoo Kheng-Hor, ed. and Hwang Chung-Mei, trans. *Sun Tzu's Art of War* (Petaling Jaya, Malaysia: Pelanduk Publications, 1992).

Kleinberg, Robert. *China's "Opening" to the Outside World: The Experiment with Foreign Capitalism* (Boulder, CO: Westview Press, 1990).

Knorr, Klaus and Frank Trager, eds. *Economic Issues and National Security*, (Kansas: University of Kansas Press, 1977).

Kojima Kiyoshi. *Japan and a New World Economic Order* (Boulder, CO: Westview Press, 1977).

Kojima Kiyoshi. *Japan and a Pacific Free Trade Area* (Berkeley, CA: University of California Press, 1971).

Koppel, Bruce M. and Robert M. Orr, Jr. *Japan's Foreign Aid: Power and Policy in a New Era* (Boulder, CO: Westview Press, 1990).

Kwang-il Baek, Ronald McLaurin, and Chung-in Moon, eds. *Dilemma of Third World Defense Industries: Supplier Control or Recipient Autonomy* (Boulder, CO: Westview Press, 1989).

Lafay, Gerard, Colette Herzog, Loukas Stemitsiotis, and Deniz Unal. *Commerce International: La Fin Des Avantages Acquis* [International Commerce: the End of Acquired Advantages] (Paris: Economica, 1989).

Li Songlin, ed. *Guomindang zai taiwan sishi nian* [Forty-years of KMT's rule in Taiwan] (Beijing: PLA Publishing House, 1990).

Li Ta. *Tai-wan yu san t'ung* [Taiwan and the "three exchanges"] (Hong Kong: Guangjiaojing Publishing Company, 1988).

Liao Kwang-sheng, ed. *Liangan jingji fazhan yu yatai quyu hudong* [Economic development in both sides of the Taiwan Strait and interactions in the Asia-Pacific region] (Hong Kong: Hong Kong Chinese University, 1991).

Lincoln, Edward J. *Japan's New Global Role* (Washington, DC: Brookings Institute, 1993).

Mahmood, Rohana and Thangam Ramnath, eds. *Confidence Building and Conflict Reduction in the Pacific* (Proceedings of the Sixth Asia-Pacific Roundtable (Kuala Lumpur: Institute for Strategic International Studies, 1993).

Man Woo Lee, Ronald McLaurin, and Chung-in Moon. *Alliance under Tension: The Evolution of U.S.-South Korean Relations* (Boulder, CO: Westview Press, 1988).

Montaperto, Ronald M., ed. *Cooperative Engagement and Economic Security in the Asia–Pacific Region* (Washington, DC: National Defense University Press, 1993).

Okita, Saburo. *Japan in the World Economy of the 1980s* (Tokyo: University of Tokyo Press, 1989).

Pyle, Kenneth B. *The Japanese Question: Power and Purpose in a New Era* (Washington, DC: The AEI Press, 1992).

Research Institute for Peace and Security, *Asian Security 1992–93* (London: Brassey's, 1992).

Richard Yang, ed. *China's Military: The PLA in 1992/93*, (Taipei: Chinese Council of Advanced Policy Studies, 1993).

Rosenau, James N. *Turbulence in World Politics: A Theory of Change and Continuity* (Princeton, NJ: Princeton University Press, 1990).

Roshia Kyokuto Deta Bukku [Russian Far East data book] (Tokyo: Roshia To'o Boekikai Roshia To'o Keizai Kenkyujo, 1993).

Ruigrok, Winifred and Rob van Tulder. *The Ideology of Interdependence* (Amsterdam: University of Amsterdam, unpublished Ph.D. dissertation, 1993).

Russett, Bruce and Harvey Starr. *World Politics: The Menu for Choice* (San Francisco: Freeman, 1989).

Samuels, Richard. *Rich Nation, Strong Army* (New York: Cornell University Press, 1994).

Sandholtz, Wayne, et al. *The Highest Stakes: The Economic Foundations of the Next Security System* (New York: Oxford University Press, 1992).

Segal, Gerald. *Rethinking the Pacific* (Oxford: Clarendon Press, 1990).

Shirk, Susan L. "Asia-Pacific Security: Balance of Power or Concert of Powers?" in *Regional Orders: Building Security in a New World*, David. A. Lake and Patrick Morgan, eds., (forthcoming c1996).

Shirk, Susan L., ed. *The Challenge of China and Japan: Politics and Development in East Asia* (New York: Praeger, 1985).

Shirk, Susan L. *How China Opened its Door: The Political Success of the PRC's Foreign Trade and Investment Reforms* (Washington, DC: Brookings, 1994).

Shirk, Susan L. *The Political Logic of Economic Reform in China* (Berkeley, CA: University of California Press, 1993).

Shirk, Susan L. and Michael K. Stankiewicz, eds. *The China Circle: Evolving Relations among Taiwan, the People's Republic of China, and Hong Kong–Macao* (forthcoming, c1996).

Soesastro, Hadi and Han Sungjoo, eds. *Pacific Economic Cooperation: The Next Phase* (Centre for Strategic and International Studies, Jakarta, October 1983).

Sogo anzen hosho senryaku [Comprehensive National Security] (Tokyo: Okurasho insatsukyoku, 1980).

Solomon, Richard K. and Masataka Kosaka, eds. *The Soviet Far East Military Buildup* (Dover, Massachusetts: Auburn House, 1986).

Sopiee, Noordin. *Economic Integration and Economic Cooperation in Pacific Asia* (Kuala Lumpur, Malaysia: Institute of Strategic and International Studies [ISIS], 1994).

Spero, Joan Edelman. *The Politics of International Economic Relations*, fourth edition (London: Routledge, 1993).

Tetlock, Philip, *Behavior, Society, and Nuclear War* (Oxford: Oxford University Press, 1989).

Thucydides. *History of the Peloponnesian War* (New York: Penguin Books, 1972).

Unger, Danny and Paul Blackburn, eds. *Japan's Emerging Global Role* (Boulder, CO: Lynne Rienner, 1993).

van Wolferen, Karel. *The Enigma of Japanese Power: People and Politics in a Stateless Nation* (London: Macmillan, 1989).

Waltz, Kenneth N. *Man, the State, and War* (New York: Columbia University Press, 1959).

Waltz, Kenneth N. *Theory of International Politics* (Reading, MA: Addison Wesley, 1979).

Whalley, John. *The Uruguay Round and Beyond* (Ann Arbor: The University of Michigan Press, 1989).

Winnefeld, James A., Jonathan D. Pollack, et al., *A New Strategy and Fewer Forces: The Pacific Dimension* (Santa Monica, CA: National Defense Research Institute, Rand, 1992).

Wook-Hee Shin. *Security, Economic Growth, and the State: Dynamics of Patron-Client State Relations in Northeast Asia* (New Haven, CT: Yale University, unpublished Ph.D. dissertation, 1992).

Xi Shuguang and Yang Ping, eds. *Kua Shiji Duihua* [A Dialogue Standing on the Century-dividing Point] (Chengdu: Sichuan Renmin Chubanshe, 1992).

Yi Guo Liang Zhi, ed. *One Country, Two Systems, Third Bureau of the United Front Work Department of the CCP Central Committee* (Beijing: Zhongguo Wenshi Publishing House, 1988).

Yuen Foon Khong, *Analogies at War: Korea, Munich, Dien Bien Phu, and the Vietnam Decisions of 1965* (Princeton, NJ: Princeton University Press, 1992).

Zhang Shanke, ed. *Taiwan wenti dashi ji* [Chronology of major events on the Taiwan question] (Beijing: Huawen Publishing House, 1988).

ARTICLES, REPORTS, AND SPEECHES

"Asia-Pacific in the 1980s: Toward Greater Symmetry in Economic Interdependence, A Report," (Jakarta: Centre for Strategic and International Studies, 1980).

"Australia: An Asia-Pacific Approach to Freer World Trade," *Australian Financial Review*, (25 May 1989), p. 14.

"Heiwa mondai kenkyukai hokokusho: kokusai kokka nippon to sogo anzen hosho seisaku" [Report by the Study Group on Peace Problems: Comprehensive National Security Policy for the International State Japan] (Tokyo: Okurasho insatsukyoku, 1985)

Abu Hassan, Omar. "Malaysian Foreign Policy in the 1990s." Address to the Malaysian International Affairs Forum (MIAF), on 3 May 1990. *Foreign Affairs Malaysia*, 23:2 (June 1990).

Agency France Press, "Navy Reportedly Completes Extensive Exercises," 3 June 1986.

Ai Wei. "The Development and Limitations of Taiwan-mainland Economic and Trade Relations," *Issues and Studies*, 27:5 (May 1991).

Allen, Kenneth W. "People's Republic of China People's Liberation Army Air Force," *Defense Intelligence Agency*, Washington, DC, 1991.

Babitskiy, Aleksandr. "A. Rutskoi ugovarivaet malayziytsev kupit' MiG-29," *Izvestiya*, 3 March 1993, p. 3.

Baker, James A. III. "America in Asia: Emerging Architecture for a Pacific Community," *Foreign Affairs*, 70:5 (Winter 1991-92).

Baker, James A. III. "A New Pacific Partnership: Framework for the Future," address to the Asia Society, New York, 26 June 1989, in *Department of State Bulletin*, 89:2149 (August 1989), p. 65.

Ball, Desmond. "Arms and Affluence: Military Acquisitions in the Asia-Pacific Region," *International Security*, 18:3 (Winter 1993/94).

Ball, Desmond. "The Council for Security Cooperation in the Asia Pacific," *Asia–Pacific Defense Reporter*, 20:6/7 (December 1993/January 1994).

Bao Kunming. "Jiejian Dongnanya Guojia de Jingyan Kaichuang Woguo Xibu Diqu Xiyin Zhijie Touzi de Xin Jumian" [Draw on the Experiences of the Southeast Asian Countries and Create a New Situation in Absorbing Direct Investment for Our Country's Western Regions], *Yatai Yanjiu*, no. 3 (June 1993).

Barnett, Robert W. "Japan's Concept of Comprehensive National Security in the Post-Cold War Era," seminar paper, (Tokyo: The Japan Institute of International Affairs, 27 November 1990).

Baum, Julian et al. "Ancient Fears," *Far Eastern Economic Review*, 3 December 1992, p. 9.

Baum, Julian. "Prepare to Surface," *Far Eastern Economic Review*, 4 February 1993, p. 10.

Baum, Julian. "The Hollow Centre," *Far Eastern Economic Review*, 7 January 1993, p. 14.

Baum, Julian. "The Mainland Dilemma," *Far Eastern Economic Review*, 18 October 1992, p. 29.

Beiyan, Wen. "Jiji Fazhan Guangdong Dui Yinni de Jingmao Guanxi" [Actively Develop Guangdong's Economic and Trade Relations with Indonesia], *Dongnanya Yanjiu*, no. 5 (October 1992).

Belykh, Ye. "Eto uzhe ne bednost', a nishscheta" [Not merely poverty, but destitution], *Krasnoye znamya*, 23 February 1993, p. 2.

Betts, Richard K., "Wealth, Power, and Instability: East Asia and the United States after the Cold War" in *International Security*, 18:3 (Winter 1993/94).

Borrus. "Reorganizing Asia: Japan's New Develoment Trajectory and the Regional Division of Labor" (BRIE Working Paper 53, March 1992).

Brooks, William L. and Robert M. Orr, Jr. "Japan's Foreign Economic Assistance," *Asian Survey* 25:3 (March 1985).

Business Week, "The Chinese Dealmakers of Southeast Asia," 11 November 1991, p. 61.

Buszyinski, Leszek. "ASEAN Security Dilemmas," *Survival* 34:4 (Winter 1992-93).

Buzan, Barry. "Economic Structure and International Security: The Limits of the Liberal Case," *International Organization*, 38:4 (Autumn 1984).

Cai Mengsun. "Threat Perceptions and Security Requirements in the Asian and Pacific Region," in UNIDIR, Conference of Research Institutes, pp. 2-3.

Calleo, David P. "Can the United States Afford the New World Order?," *SAIS Review* 12:2 (Summer/Fall 1992).

Canberra Times, "APEC Now 'Region's Top Forum,'" 30 November 1991, p. 14.

Chang Pao-Min. "China and Southeast Asia: The Problem of a Perceptual Gap," *Contemporary Southeast Asia*, vol. 9, no. 3, (December 1987).

Chen Jiaqi. "Haixia liangan canping de guoji shichang jingzheng fenxi [Analysis of competition for international market between the products from the two sides of the Taiwan Strait]," *Guoji Maoyi*, February 1992.

Chen Te-an. "Zhuguan Yixiang Daiti Bu Liao Keguan Xianshi: 'Zhongguo Weixie' Lunxi" [Subjective Fabrication Cannot Replace Objective Reality: A Comment on 'China Threat'] *Renmin Ribao* [People's Daily], 27 March 1993.

Chen Xiangming. "New Spatial Division of Labor and Commodity Chains in the Emerging Greater China Economic Region," in Patricia Roe, *Emerging Regions in the Pacific Basin*, (Austin, TX: ICCC Institute, 1994), pp. 127-154.

Chen Xuegen. "The Wind From the South," *Nexus*, no. 23 (Spring 1993).

Cheney, Dick. "Annual Report to the President and the Congress" (January 1993).

Cheng Jingbiao. "Asia-Pacific economic ties grow closer," *Beijing Review*, 36:6 (8-14 February 1993), p. 10.

Cheng Ye. "Riben Zhengzai Cong Jingji Daguo Zouxiang Zhengzhi Daguo" [Japan Is Moving from an Economic Power to a Political Power], *Waiguo Wenti Yanjiu* [Foreign Studies], no. 4, (December 1992).

Chiang Ping-kun. *Chung Yang Ji Pao*, 24 November 1993, p. 1.

Ching, Frank. "Scientific Meetings Being Held to Reduce Spratlys Tension," *Far Eastern Economic Review*, 27 May 1993, p. 30.

Chulsu Kim. Speech at the Second U.S.-ROK Bilateral Conference in Washington, DC, April 17, 1993. "Industrial Alliance between Korea and the United States."

Chung-in Moon and Kwang-il Baek. "Loyalty, Voice, or Exit: U.S. Third Country Arms Sales Regulation and ROK's Countervailing Strategies," *Journal of Northeast Asian Studies* 4:1 (1986).

Chung-in Moon, Mann-Kyu Kim, et.al. *A Study of the Korean Defense Industry: Direction and Policy Options Toward the Year 2,000* (Inchon: Center for International Studies, Inha University, 1993).

Clark, Gregory. "A Trade Bloc Divorced From Reality," *The Australian*, 1 November 1989, p. 11.

Coll, Alberto R. "Power, Principles, and Prospects for a Cooperative International Order," *The Washington Quarterly* 16:1 (Winter 1993).

Conference Papers, Monterey Institute of International Studies Center for East Asian Studies conference on "U.S.-Japan Cooperation in the Development of Siberia and the Russian Far East," 22-24 July 1993, Monterey, California.

Cronin, Patrick M. and Lt. Col. Noboru Yamaguchi. "Japan's Future Regional Security Role," *Strategic Review* 20:3 (Summer 1992).

Cronin, Richard P. "Changing Dynamics of Japan's Interaction with Southeast Asia," *Southeast Asian Affairs* 1991, (Singapore: Institute of Southeast Asian Studies, 1991).

Dalnii Vostok Rossii Ekonomicheskii Ezhegodnik 1992 (Khabarovsk: Economic Research Institute, 1992).

Davies, Derek. "The Pacific Community: Hands Across The Sea," *Far Eastern Economic Review*, 29 February 1980, pp. 34-35.

Defense White Paper (Washington, DC: U.S. Department of Defense, 1994).

Defts, Robert. "Accidental Tourist," *Far Eastern Economic Review*, 4 March 1993, p. 17.

Dewitt, David P. "Concepts of Security for the Asia-Pacific Region in the Post-Cold War Era: Common Security, Cooperative Security, and Comprehensive Security," delivered at the Seventh Asia-Pacific Roundtable, Kuala Lumpur, 6-9 June 1993.

Dobson, Wendy. "APEC: Redefining the Region?" Paper prepared for an international conference on Southeast Asia, "Challenges of the Twenty-first Century," Institute of Southeast Asian Studies, Singapore, 29 August-1 September 1993.

Drysdale, Peter. "Australia's Asia-Pacific Economic Diplomacy," *Current Affairs Bulletin*, 66:10 (March 1990).

Economic Report 1993/94 (Kuala Lumpur, Malaysia: Ministry of Finance, 1993).

Edwards, John. "U.S. Set to Join New Trading Group," *Sydney Morning Herald*, 18 March 1989, p. 3.

Elek, Andrew. "Asia Pacific Economic Co-operation (APEC)," *Southeast Asian Affairs*, (Singapore: Institute of Southeast Asian Studies, 1991).

Elek, Andrew. "The Challenge of Asian-Pacific Economic Cooperation," *The Pacific Review*, no. 4 (1991).

Elster, Helen. "Slow Start in the Pacific," *Far Eastern Economic Review*, 26 September 1980, pp. 90-91.

Erlanger, Steven. "What Russia Wants: Less Pain, a Strong Hand," *The New York Times*, "Week in Review," 18 April 1993, p. 5.

Evans, Gareth. "Security in the Asia Pacific Region," *International Defense Review*, 1992.

Fedotov, Vladimir. "Russia and the APR: Problems and Prospects," *International Affairs* (October 1992).

Fitifield, Russell H. "ASEAN and the Pacific Community," *Asia Pacific Community*, no. 11 (Winter 1981).

Friedberg, Aaron L. "Ripe for Rivalry: Prospects for Peace in a Multipolar Asia" in *International Security*, 18:3 (Winter 1993/94).

Fujian Statistical Yearbook, 1990, p. 298.

Fukusaku Kiichiro. *Economic Regionalization and Intra-Industry Trade: Pacific Asian Perspectives* (Paris: OECD Development Centre, 10 June 1992).

Galvin, General John (U.S. Army). Address at the University of California, Berkeley, 11 March 1993.

Garver, John W. "China's Push Through the South China Sea: The Interaction of Bureaucratic and National Interest," *The China Quarterly*, no. 132 (December 1992).

Gilbert Rozman. "Moscow's Japan-Watchers in the First Years of the Gorbachev Era," *Pacific Review*, no. 3 (1988).

Goldstein, Carl. "Strait Ahead," *Far Eastern Economic Review*, 5 March 1992, p. 54.

Gordon, David and Antony Scott. "Russia's Timber Rush," *The Amicus Journal* no. 14 (Fall 1992).

Grattan, Michelle and Carmel McGuley. "Hawke Pushes for Regional Economic Body," *The Age*, 1 February 1989, p. 5.

Gubernskie vedomosti [*Provincial Gazette*] (Yuzhno-Sakhalinsk), "Press-konferentsiya malogo soveta" ["Press conference of the lesser council"], 6 March 1993, p. 1.

Guerrieri, Paolo. "Technological and Trade Competition in High-Tech Products," BRIE Working Paper no. 54 (Berkeley, California: 1991).

Haas, Ernst B. "International Integration: The European and the Universal Process," *International Organization*, 15:3 (Summer 1961).

Hamilton, Lee H. "A Democrat Looks at Foreign Policy," *Foreign Affairs*, 71:3 (Summer 1992).

Han Jianguo and Xu Ningjiang. "Shandongsheng Tong Hanguo Kaizhan Guoji Maoyi Jingji Hezuo de Kaocha Yu Sikao" [Observations and Considerations of Developing Shandong Province's International Trade and Economic Cooperation with the ROK], *Yatai Jingji* [Asia-Pacific Economics], no. 5 (October 1992).

Harris, Geoffrey. "The Determinants of Defense Expenditure in the ASEAN Region," *Journal of Peace Research* 23 (1986).

Harris, Stuart. "Varieties of Pacific Economic Cooperation," *The Pacific Review*, no. 4 (1991).

Hasegawa, Tsuyoshi. "Resiliency of Soviet Legacies: Political Environment and Far Eastern Economic Development," prepared for the Monterey Institute of International Studies, Center for East Asian Studies' conference on "U.S.-Japan Cooperation in the Development of Siberia and the Russian Far East," 22-24 July 1993, Monterey, California.

He Shengda. "90 Niandai Zhongguo Xinan Yu Dongnanya d Jingji Hezuo" [Economic Cooperation Between China's Southwest Region and Southeast Asia in the 1990s], *Yunnan Shehui Kexue*, no. 5 (October 1992).

Hewitt, Daniel P. "What Determines Military Expenditure," *Finance and Development* (December 1991).

Higgot, Richard A., Andrew Fenton Cooper, and Jenelle Bonnor, "Asia-Pacific Economic Cooperation: An Evolving Case Study in Leadership and Cooperation Building," *International Journal*, 45:4 (Autumn 1990).

Holloway, David. "Military Security Implications of Imperial Disintegration—U.S.S.R," speech at the 17th Annual Berkeley-Stanford Conference on "The Disintegration of Multinational Communist States," University of California, Berkeley, 12 March 1993.

Huang Songzan. "Xinjiapo Huaren de Shengcun Daolu" [The Road of the Ethnic Chinese in Singapore], *Dongnanya Yanjiu*, no. 5 (October 1992).

Hughes, David. "Arms Experts Fear Nuclear Blackmail," *Aviation Week and Space Technology*, 4 January 1993, p. 59.

Hunter, Robert. "A Farewell to Arms, Not Influence," *Los Angeles Times*, 2 February 1990, p. B7.

Huntington, Samuel P. "America's Changing Strategic Interests," *Survival* 33 (January/February 1991).

Inoguchi Takashi. "Shaping and Sharing Pacific dynamism," *The Annals of the American Academy of Political and Social Science* 505 (September 1989).

ISIS Focus, no. 101 (Malaysia: The Institute of Strategic and International Studies, 1993).

ISIS Roundtable, Kuala Lumpur, 21-25 June 1992 (Kuala Lumpur, Malaysia: Institute of Strategic and International Studies, 1993).

Izvestiya, "Pavel Grachev: Armii cegodnya trudno, kak i vsemu narodu" [It's hard today for the Army, as for the whole people], 23 February 1993, pp. 1, 5.

James, William E. "Basic Direction and Areas for Cooperation: Structural Issues of the Asia-Pacific Economies." In Jang-Won Suh and Jae-Bong Ro, eds. *Asia–Pacific Economic Cooperation: The Way Ahead*, (Seoul: Korea Institute for International Economic Policy, 1990).

Japan Economic Journal, "The Rising Tide: Japan in Asia," special supplement, 1990.

Ji Guoxing, "The Diaoyudao (Senkaku) disputes and Prospects for Settlement," *The Korean Journal of Defense Analysis*, 6:2 (Winter, 1994).

Jia Qingguo. "Changing relations across the Taiwan Strait: Beijing's perceptions," *Asian Survey*, March 1992.

Jin-Hyun Kim. "Post-Cold War, International Competition, and Technological Cooperation: The Case of U.S.-South Korean Relations," speech at the Graduate School of International Relations and Pacific Studies, University of California at San Diego, April 27, 1993.

Johnson, Chalmers. "Inquiry into Bases of Japanese Power" in *Leviathan: The Japanese Journal of Political Science* 2 (Fall, 1992), pp. 145-164.

Johnson, Chalmers. "Japan in Search of a 'Normal' Role," IGCC policy paper no. 4 (La Jolla: University of California Institute on Global Conflict and Cooperation, July 1992).

Kagami Mitsuhiro. "Lessons from Trade and Investment in East Asia," Inter-American Development Bank and United Nations Economic Commission for Latin America and the Caribbean Working Papers on Trade in the Western Hemisphere, no. 53 (August 1993).

Kanter, Rosabeth Moss. "Foreign Policy Comes Out of Its Box," *Los Angeles Times*, 3 September 1992, p. B7.

Karp, Aaron. "Military Procurement and Regional Security in Southeast Asia," *Contemporary Southeast Asia*, no. 23 (March 1990).

Kawakami Takao. "21seiki ni muketa nihon no enjo seisaku" [Japan's aid policy towards the 21 century], *Gaiko Forum* 54 (March 1993).

Kiyofuku Chuma. "The Choice Is Clear: Diplomacy over Force," *Japan Quarterly* 38:2 (April/June 1991).

Klyuchnikov, B. "The Soviet Far East in the Pacific Century," *Far Eastern Affairs*, no. 4 (1988).

Kojima Kiyoshi, ed. *Pacific Trade and Development*, Center Paper no. 9 (Tokyo: The Japan Economic Research Center, February 1968).

Kojima Kiyoshi. "A Pacific Economic Community and Asian Developing Countries," *Hitotsubashi Journal of Economics*, 7:1, (June 1966).

Korea Economic Institute of America, "U.S.-Korea Economic Relations," *Academic Studies Series* 2 (Washington, DC: KEIA, 1992).

Krause, Lawrence B. "Trade Policy in the 1990s: Good-bye Bipolarity, Hello Regions," *World Today*, 46:5 (Royal Institute of International Affairs, May 1990).

Krauthammer, Charles. "The Unipolar Moment," *Foreign Affairs*, 70:1 (Winter, 1991).

Kuala Lumpur Concord On Open Regionalism, tenth PECC meeting, Kuala Lumpur, Malaysia, 22-24 March 1994.

Lampton, David M. and Alfred D. Wilhelm, Jr., co-rapporteurs. "United States and China Relations at a Crossroads" (The Atlantic Council and the National Committee on U.S.-China Relations, February 1993).

Leach, James A. "A Republican Looks at Foreign Policy," *Foreign Affairs*, 71:3 (Summer 1992).

Li Ning. "China Moves Closer to GATT," *Beijing Review*, 36:6 (8-14 February 1993), p. 13.

Lincoln, Edward J. "Japan in the 1990s: A New Kind of World Power," *The Brookings Review* (Spring 1992).

Lincoln, Kaye. "Signal Guns," *Far Eastern Economic Review*, 18 February 1993.

Low, Linda. "The East Asia Economic Grouping," *The Pacific Review*, no. 4 (1991).

Lu Zhongwei. "Northeast Asian Economic Cooperation in the Post-Cold War Era," IGCC policy paper no. 6 (La Jolla: University of California Institute on Global Conflict and Cooperation, October 1993).

Luo Bengu. "Lun Dongbeiya Jingji Hezuo Qu de Zouxiang Ji Hezuo Fangshi Yu Buzhou" [The Northeast Asia Economic Cooperation Region: Its Prospects, Pattern, and Process] *Dongbeiya Yanjiu*, no. 4 (August 1992).

Luttwak, Edward N. "The Shape of Things to Come," *Commentary* 87:6 (June 1990).

Ma Dangsheng Zhang Jianshu and Liang Zhenxing. "Analysis of the Present State of the National Defense Scientific and Technical Corps and an Exploration of Policies for its Development," *Zhongguo Keji Luntan* [Forum of Chinese Science and Technology], no. 5 (September 1989).

MacIntyre. "Arms and Defense Planning in Indonesia," a paper presented at the Workshop on "Arms and Defense Planning," (Singapore: Institute of Southeast Asian Studies, December 1991).

Mack, Andrew and Desmond Ball. "The Military Build-up in the Asia-Pacific Region: Scope, Causes and Implications for Security," Working Paper no. 264 (Canberra: Strategic and Defense Studies Centre, Australian National University, 1992).

Mahathir bin Mohamad. "Tak Kenal Maka Tak Cinta." In *Asia–Pacific in the 1980s: Towards Greater Symmetry in Economic Interdependence* (Jakarta: Centre for Strategic and International Studies, May 1980).

Mastanduno, Michael. "Strategies of Economic Containment: U.S. Trade Relations with the Soviet Union," *World Politics*, 37:4 (July 1985).

McMillan, John. "China's Nonconformist Reforms," IGCC policy paper no. 11 (La Jolla: University of California Institute on Global Conflict and Cooperation, December 1994).

Mearsheimer, John. "Back to the Future: Instability in Europe After the Cold War," *International Security*, 15:1 (Summer 1990).

Miller, Matt. "U.S. investor gets cold shoulder in Siberia," *San Diego Union-Tribune*, 3 April 1993, p. C1.

Minakir, P. "Ekonomika sovetskogo Dal'nego Vostoka: Vyzov krizisu," *Problemy Dal'nego Vostoka*, no. 5, 1991.

Ministry of National Defense. Defense White Paper, 1991-1992 (Seoul: Ministry of National Defense, 1991).

Ministry of National Defense. Guidelines for Offset Programs (Seoul: Ministry of National Defense, 1984).

Morse, Edward L. "The Transformation of Foreign Policies: Modernization, Interdependence, and Externalization," *World Politics*, 22:3 (April 1970), pp 373-392.

Morse, Edward L. "Transnational Economic Processes," *International Organization*, 25:3 (Summer 1971).

Nathan, K.S. "The Role and Significance of ASEAN in World Politics," *Foreign Relations Journal, 3:4* (December 1988).

Nathan, K.S. "Vision 2020 and Malaysian Foreign Policy: Part II: The New World Order," *Asian Defence Journal* (February 1992).

Nixon, Richard. "Clinton's Greatest Challenge," *The New York Times*, 5 March 1993, p. A15.

Nye, Joseph S. "Soft Power," *Foreign Policy* 80 (Fall 1990).

Nye, Joseph S. "Coping With Japan," *Foreign Policy* 89 (Winter 1992-93).

Ormonde, Tom. "APEC's Search for Achievement," *Sydney Morning Herald*, 11 November 1991, p. 16.

Ostrovskaya, Natal'ya. "Uzhe fevral', a my eshche zhivy! no ne vse" [It's already February, and we're still alive! But not all.], *Vostok Rossii*, 5:79 (February 1993).

Ostry, Sylvia. "Foreign Direct Investment in East Asia," prepared for a joint research project, Center for International Studies, University of Toronto, and the Berkeley Roundtable on the International Economy, 1992.

Pacific Economic Cooperation: Issues and Opportunities (Report of the Fourth Pacific Economic Cooperation Conference, Seoul, 29 April-1 May 1985) (Seoul: Korean Development Institute, 1985).

Papayoanou, Paul A. "Economic Interdependence and the Balance of Power: The Strategy of Commitment and Great Power Politics," unpublished dissertation, University of California, Los Angeles, 1992.

Parrenas, Julius Caesar. "China and Japan in ASEAN's Strategic Perceptions," *Contemporary Southeast Asia*, 12:3 (December 1990).

Peng Tianxiang. "Fazhan dalu yu xianggang he taiwan zhijian de sanbian jinmao hezuo (Develop the trilateral economic and trade cooperation between mainland, Taiwan and Hong Kong)," *Guoji Maoyi*, no. 10 (1992).

Pereira, Derwin and Martin Soong. "Apec Can 'Help Counter Major Economic Players'," *The Straits Times*, 2 September 1993, p. 12.

Pillai, M.G.G. "ASEAN Won't Be Rushed Into a Pacific Rim League," *The Canberra Times*, 28 July 1989, p. 9.

Popova, T. "Na protsent kazhdiy den' pastut tseny v Primor'e" [Prices rise a little every day in the Maritime Province], *Krasnoye znamya*, 2 April 1992, p. 3.

Potter, William C. "Nuclear Exports From the Former Soviet Union: What's New, What's True," *Arms Control Today*, 23:1 (January/February 1993).

Quinghai Provincial Radio. "Report on Deep-Water Naval Exercise," 1 June 1987.

Rix, Alan. "Japan's Comprehensive Security and Australia," *Australian Outlook* 41:2 (August 1987).

Rix, Alan. "Japan's Foreign Aid Policy: A Capacity For Leadership?" *Pacific Affairs* 62:4 (Winter 1989-90).

Roshia Kyokuto Gunmin Tenkan Misshon Hokokusho [Report of the military-civilian conversion mission to the Russian Far East] (Tokyo: Roshia To'o Boekikai Roshia To'o Keizai Kenkyukai, 1993).

Ross, Andrew L. "Growth, Debt and Military Spending in Southeast Asia" *Contemporary Southeast Asia 11* (1990).

Sargent, Sarah. "Canberra's Courtship of ASEAN Put to Test," *Australian Financial Review*, 3 November 1989, p. 17.

Satoh Yukio. "The Changing Currency of Power: Paper II." In *America's Role in the Changing World* Part I, Adelphi Paper 256 (London: International Institute for Strategic Studies, 1990-91).

Saw, David. "Defense Spending in Southeast Asia," *Military Technology*, (February 1992).

Saw, David. "Politics and Defense Modernization in Southeast Asia," *Military Technology* (April 1992).

Scalapino, Robert A. "The United States and Asia: Future Prospects," and Richard Holbrooke, "Japan and the United States: Ending the Unequal Partnership," *Foreign Affairs* 70:5 (Winter 1991-92).

Schott, Jeffrey. "Is the World Developing into Regional Trading Blocs?" (Washington, DC: Institute for International Economics, 1989).

Sestanovich, Stephan. "U.S. Power, Less Than Super," *The New York Times*, 23 March 1993, p. A15.

Shen Huasong. "Kaiming Qiquan Zhuyi Yu Shichang Yuanze Xiangjiehe" [The Combination of Enlightened Authoritarianism and Market Principles], *Shijie Jingji Yu Zhengzhi* [World Economics and Politics], no. 8 (August 1992) p. 34.

Shen Xu. "Fazhan Xinan Diqu Yu Zhongnan Bandao Jingmao Guanxi de Jidian Sikao" [A Few Suggestions About Developing Economic and Trade Relations Between the Southwest Region and the Indochinese Peninsula], *Yunnan Shehui Kexue* [Yunnan Social Sciences], no. 4 (August 1992).

Shirk, Susan L. and Christopher P. Twomey, eds. "Northeast Asia Cooperation Dialog II Conference Papers," IGCC policy paper no. 9 (La Jolla: University of California Institute on Global Conflict and Cooperation, August 1994).

Silk, Mitchell A. "Silent Partners," *The China Business Review*, September-October 1990, pp. 32-40.

Simon, Denis Fred. "The Orbital Mechanics of Korea's Technological Development: An Examination of the 'Gravitational' Pushes and Pulls," prepared for the conference "Redefining Korean Competitiveness in an Age of Globalization," Center for Korean Studies, University of California, Berkeley, 24 April 1993.

Sneider, Daniel. "Pacific Rim Nations Strengthen Economic Ties," *Christian Science Monitor*, 6 November 1989, pp. 10-11.

Sneider, Daniel. "Russian Armsmakers Take Care of Their Own," *The Christian Science Monitor*, 25 November 1992, p. 6.

Sneider, Daniel. "Tough Conversion for Russia's Armsmakers," *The Christian Science Monitor*, 27 November 1992, p. 6.

Snyder, Glenn H. "The Security Dilemma in Alliance Politics," *World Politics* 36:4 (July 1984).

South China Morning Post Weekly, "Overseas Chinese Set Region's Trends: Report" 30-31 January 1993, p. B-4.

Stefashin, V. "Varianty razvitiya voyenno-politicheskoy situatsii na Dal'nem Vostoke" [Scenarios for the development of the military-political situation in the Far East], (Moscow: Problemy Dal'nego Vostoka, 1992).

Stephens, Peter. "U.S. Proposal to Expand APEC," *The Age*, 1 November 1991, p. 8.

Stubbs, Richard. "Malaysian Defense Policy: Strategy versus Structure," *Contemporary Southeast Asia* 3 (June 1991).

Sun Zhenyu. "Zhongmei jingmao guanxi xianzhuang ji cunzai de wenti" [The status and problems of current Sino-U.S. economic and trade relations], *Guoji maoyi*, July 1991, p. 5.

Tadae Takubo. "Kenpo kaisei no odo," [The Royal Road to Constitutional Amendments] *Shokun* (March 1993) pp. 26-40.

Tai Ming Cheung. "Disarmament and Development in China," *Asian Survey*, July 1988.

Tai Ming Cheung. "Sukhois, Sams, Subs," *Far Eastern Economic Review*, 4 April 1993, p. 23.

Taiwan Yanjiu. "Haixia liangan guanxi dashiji" [Major Events in Cross-Strait Relations], no. 4 (1992), p. 83.

Tan Guolin and Su Wenjiang. "Zhong, Lao, Tai, Mian Pilin Diqu de Jingji Jishu Hezuo" [The Economic and Technological Cooperation in the Border Area of China, Laos, Thailand and Burma], *Yatai Yanjiu* [Asia-Pacific Studies], no. 3 (June 1993) pp. 68-72.

The New York Times, "Malnutrition Kills 4 Cadets; Russian Officers Suspended," 3 March 1993, p. A6.

Tong Zhiguang. "China Heading Toward a Trade Power," *Beijing Review*, 36:3 (18-31 January 1993), p. 10.

Tsuneo Akaha. "Japan's Comprehensive Security Policy: A New East Asian Environment," *Asian Survey* 31:4 (April 1991).

Tung, Ricky. "Mainland China in Taiwan's Economic Future," *Issues and Studies*, 26:5 (May 1990).

Twomey, Christopher P. and Michael Stankiewicz, eds. "The U.S. and Japan in Asia: Conference Papers," IGCC policy paper no. 10 (La Jolla: University of California Institute on Global Conflict and Cooperation, November 1994).

U.S. Department of Defense, *A Strategic Framework for the Asian Pacific Rim: Looking Toward the 21st Century* (April 1990); Annual Report to the President and the Congress (Washington, DC: U.S. Government Printing Office, 1991).

U.S.-Korea Forum on Science and Technology, Proceedings of Inaugural Session on U.S.-ROK Science and Technology Cooperation (Annandale, VA: JWK International, 1993).

United Nations Institute for Disarmament Research (UNIDIR), The, Conference of Research Institutes in Asia and the Pacific, Beijing, 23-25 March 1992 (New York: United Nations, 1992).

Waltz, Kenneth. "The Emerging Structure of International Politics," *International Security*, 18:2 (Fall 1993).

Wang Chongli. "Daxinan Kaifa de Duiwai Kaifang Shijiao" [The Opening Angle for Developing Great Southwest], *Yunnan Shehui Kexue*, no. 1 (January 1992).

Wang Zhile. "Zhongguo Canjia Yatai Quyu Hezuo de Mubiao Xuanze" [Setting Objectives in China's Participation in the Asian-Pacific Regional Cooperation], *Yatai Jingji* [Asia-Pacific Economics], no. 5 (October 1992).

Wei Tianqi. "Jinnian Miandian Jushi Zongshu" (A Survey of Burma's Situation in Recent Years), *Dongnanya Yanjiu*, no. 6 (December 1992).

Wen Song. "Zhongguo Yuanzhu Laowo de Xin Xuanze" [A New Choice in China's Assistance to Laos], *Dongnanya Yanjiu* [Southeast Asian Studies], no. 2 (April 1992).

Wen Yu. "Liangan xieshang daji fanzui" [The two sides of the Taiwan Strait consult on fighting crimes], *Haiwai Xueren* (Overseas Scholar), December 1991.

Wen Yu. "Zhonggong duitai lingdao tiaozheng zhenrong" [CCP leaders in charge of Taiwan affairs reshuffle], *Guangjiaojing Monthly*, November 1990, p. 9.

Woods, Lawrence T. "Non-governmental Organizations and Pacific Cooperation: Back to the Future?," *The Pacific Review*, 4:4 (1991).

World Bank. *The East Asian Miracle: Economic Growth and Public Policy* (New York: Oxford University Press, c1993).

Wu Naitao. "From Planned to Market Economy," *Beijing Review*, 35:2 (11-17 January 1993).

Wu Xingdu. "Taiwan dui dalu touzi de fenxi" [Analysis of Taiwan's investment on the mainland], *Guoji Maoyi*, May 1991.

Yang Jinsen. "Understand the Ocean, Exploit the Ocean," *Hongqi* [Red Flag], 1 April 1988.

Yi Yuanqiu and Wang Zhuanyou. "Establish Strong Border Defense Thinking," *Liberation Army Daily*, 6 October 1989.

Ying-jeou Ma. "The Republic of China's Policy Toward the Chinese Mainland," *Issues & Studies*, June 1992.

Yoichi Funabashi. "Japan and the New World Order," *Foreign Affairs* 70:5 (Winter 1991/92).

Yu Fengzhu. "Taishang fu dalu touzi jizhong xintai de sikao" [Psychological states of Taiwan businessmen who invest on the mainland], *Guoji Maoyi* 6 (1991).

Yung Chul Park and Won Am Park. "Changing Japanese Trade Patterns and the East Asian NICs," paper prepared for the National Bureau for Economic Research Conference, 19-20 October 1992.

Zadunayskiy, Roman. "Bezopasnost': Stanet li Rossiya vnov' morskoy derzhavoy?" [Security: Will Russia become a naval power again?], *Rossiyskiye Vesti*, 5 January 1993, p. 2.

Zagorsky, Alexei. "Russian Military Reform: Consequences for Asia-Pacific," unpublished paper, April 1993.

Zheng Renliang. "Guanyu Yinni Huaren Caituan Yinqi de Zhenglun" [Controversy Over the Ethnic Chinese Financial Groups in Indonesia], Dongnanya Yanjiu, no. 2 (April 1992).

Zhonghua Jingji Yanjiuyuan (Institute of Chinese Economic Studies), "Haixia liangan maoyi jinzhan zhi pinggu" [Estimate of the development of cross-strait trade], supplement, August 1989.

Zhou Peide. "Development and Modernization of Defense Industry in China," *Defense Journal*, May-June 1986.

Zhu Huiyi. "Despite the Difficulties Confronted by China's Nuclear Industry in Advancing Toward Peace, The Prospects are Broad," *China News Service*, 12 December 1988.

Index

Typographic Notes	
Body:	Galton 10/8
Display:	Galton/ Deroon 14/12
Tables:	Times 10/8